THE EVOLUTION OF
COLLEGE ENGLISH

PITTSBURGH SERIES IN
COMPOSITION, LITERACY,
AND CULTURE

David Bartholomae and
Jean Ferguson Carr, Editors

THE EVOLUTION OF COLLEGE ENGLISH

LITERACY STUDIES
FROM THE PURITANS
TO THE POSTMODERNS

Thomas P. Miller

UNIVERSITY OF PITTSBURGH PRESS

Published by the University of Pittsburgh Press, Pittsburgh, Pa., 15260

Copyright © 2010, University of Pittsburgh Press

Manufactured in the United States of America

Printed on acid-free paper

10 9 8 7 6 5 4 3 2 1

Library of Congress Cataloging-in-Publication Data

Miller, Thomas P.

The evolution of college English : literacy studies from the Puritans to the Postmoderns /
Thomas P. Miller.

    p. cm. — (Pittsburgh series in composition, literacy, and culture)

Includes bibliographical references and index.

ISBN 978-0-8229-6116-1 (pbk. : alk. paper)

1. English philology—Study and teaching. 2. English language—Rhetoric—Study and
teaching. I. Title.

PE65.M53 2010

428.0071'173—dc22   2010031723

CONTENTS

PREFACE

English departments are currently facing the biggest drop in tenure-track jobs since they were cut in half in the 1970s. Now, as then, English departments are struggling to come to terms with the economic, social, and technological changes that are redefining what we teach and how we study it. Since the birth of the personal computer in the 1970s, interactive technologies have pressed English departments to shift their standpoint from the individual reader to a more writerly stance on transactions in literacy. Since the 1970s, we have also seen a deepening erosion of the professional ethos that had traditionally served to defend enclaves of expertise from market forces. As a result of these and other trends, English departments in more broadly based institutions have expanded their field of study beyond a traditional conception of literature to include ESL, professional writing, and a range of studies that includes media, ethnic, and women's studies.

Looking back to the sources of these trends in the 1970s, we can see that English departments have been incapacitated by their failure to invest their intellectual energies in their institutional work. English departments have often ignored the needs of English teachers, including the legions of TAs and adjuncts who teach the comp courses that underwrite specialized studies in areas of English that have more professional status. Few professors work with English teachers, and few teach composition courses, even though they provide most of the student credit hours that English departments depend upon. As a result, most writing courses have been temped out, and some are being outsourced through dual enrollment programs that seem far removed from the evolution of college English, even though they will likely end up further eroding its base.

The disjunctures that structure our field become more apparent when we consider English studies as a sphere of literacy studies. Our field includes four separate areas of work: literature, English education, writing studies, and linguistics (which exists as a separate institutionalized discipline only in larger research universities). These four areas have historically evolved in tandem with broader developments in literacy and the literate. Many of us have worked across the boundaries between these areas. I began my graduate studies in literature, and then in 1977, I crossed over to join the first cohort of graduate students admitted to the doctoral program in rhetoric and composition at the University of Texas. In the late '70s such programs were being established across the country, mostly in public universities with large composition programs and sometimes by people with backgrounds in English education such as James Kinneavy and others of his generation.

In the last couple of decades, I have worked mostly in administrative positions. As a director of a writing program, then a graduate program, and now as an associate provost, I have been challenged to step back from the field to assess how we represent our work to broader audiences. Working with TAs, adjuncts, and faculty from other fields, I have often been pressed to consider how we understand our relations with our coworkers—particularly those who do not have the time to write books such as this. I have come to recognize that the sabbaticals and leaves that I have been granted to write this book have been underwritten by the labor of the TAs, lecturers, and adjuncts who teach most of the English courses in American colleges and universities. I have tried to keep that debt in mind as I wrote the chapters that follow.

Our obligations to each other have become more pressing as funding to do research in the humanities has been cut. This drop parallels the decline in jobs that we have seen in the last couple of years. In 2008 and 2009, the number of jobs listed in the MLA Job Information List dropped by almost fifty percent— the steepest drop since the collapse of jobs four decades ago. This drop was compounded by a decline in the proportion of tenure-track jobs, which decreased from 80 percent to 68 percent of postings. This drop in our professional labor market is but the clearest indicator of the declining fortunes of our field.

Our discipline's response to these historic changes has been limited and fragmented. Even some of our most broadly engaged professional organizations have remained strikingly indifferent to the profound economic changes that confront us. For example, the recent conference programs of the Conference on College Composition and Communication suggest that many professional leaders still assume that the discipline is continuing to operate under normal working conditions. Little or no attention has been paid at recent 4Cs conferences to the structural changes we are witnessing in American higher education. We need more concerted discussions of how college English professors can organize themselves to empower teachers to exercise collective agency, and those discussions need to be a focal point for our graduate programs, hiring procedures, and reward structures. We must come to terms with the disjunctures between our professional apparatus and our basic work if we are to sustain that work in the face of collapsing resources.

We do not do as well as we might in meeting this challenge because our discipline has historically followed the tendencies of other academic fields to concentrate on specialized modes of inquiry and devalue engagements with broader audiences. In our training, hiring, promotion, and research programs, we do not value writing for public audiences, collaborating with teachers, and building partnerships with public agencies, businesses, and schools. Such civic engagements have been overshadowed by academics' concentration on writing for specialized audiences. This concentration has incapacitated our discipline more than most because we have a more expansive institutional base than most academic disciplines. English is just about the only subject that is taught from grammar to graduate school, and what we teach is broadly involved with writing at work in public life, including the stories we tell ourselves about who we are and who we mean to be.

The disjuncture between high school and college English studies is one of the points of reference that needs to be included within our field of vision if we are to make use of the changes that confront us. We need to expand our field of vision to encompass the four corners of our field of work. Toward that end, I have focused my analysis on the historical junctures where transitions have emerged in how writing is taught, what literature is understood to represent, where language is inflected with changes in popular usage, and how educators relate what they teach to whom they teach.

My research on the conjunctions in the history of English education, writing studies, linguistics, and the teaching of literature has been supported by a fellowship from the National Endowment for the Humanities. I would not have received that fellowship if it were not for the support of Gerry Graff and Robert Scholes. I would also like to acknowledge the impact of the mentors whom I was lucky enough to work with at Texas, especially Maxine Hairston and Lester Faigley. They have shaped all that I do and how I understand it. More particularly, I need to thank Bruce Horner and John Brereton for their reviews of the manuscript; Susan Miller, John Warnock, and Ed White for their responses to chapters; and David Bartholomae and Jean Ferguson Carr for their editorial contributions. Dorine Jennette did a meticulous job editing the manuscript, and I am also indebted to several outstanding research assistants: Brian Jackson, Jillian Skeffington, Tammie Kennedy, and Sarah Harris.

Sarah was especially helpful in improving the readability of this manuscript. The limitations of this book are all my own.

Of all the debts that I have incurred while working on this book, the most significant is the time that I have taken away from my family. The Saturdays, evenings, and vacations that I stole away have mounted up to a debt that cannot really be repaid. To acknowledge that debt, I am dedicating this work to my wife, Kerstin, and our children, Marcus and Melina. Thanks also to Marcus for the drawing on the cover that embeds an image of scribal literacy in a picture of screen literacy to provide an ironic frame for this work of print literacy.

THE EVOLUTION OF
COLLEGE ENGLISH

Introduction

WORKING PAST THE PROFESSION

> Very much depends upon what we select from which to start and
> very much depends upon whether we select our point of departure
> in order to tell . . . what . . . *ought* to be or what *is*.
>
> John Dewey in 1954, *The Public and Its Problems*, 9.

MY HISTORY OF COLLEGE
English studies begins by looking past the rise of the profession in the last
century to explore how the teaching of English in American colleges has been
shaped by broader developments in literacy since the colonial period. Reflecting upon those developments can help us to come to terms with the changes in
literacy that are redefining what we teach and how we study it. Most English
departments have come to include a diverse array of critics, compositionists,
writers, applied linguists, and educators who sometimes seem to share little
more than a mailing address. If English is a discipline, what are its parameters
and priorities, and how does it encompass the varied subjects that are taught
in courses that run the gamut from first-year composition to graduate seminars
in literature and ESOL? The incoherence of the field is amply documented in
the bundle of courses that make up the traditional undergraduate major in
English. Rather than being guided by research on students' changing needs,
curricular requirements often reflect historical compromises and accommodations. As detailed in the national surveys that will be examined in later chapters, a traditional literature major generally includes a token course on language
and an advanced writing course, though many departments have responded to
the popularity of writing courses by adding a parallel major or track in creative
writing, and perhaps business or technical writing. Rarely do the transcripts
of English majors provide any cohesive sense of the range of concerns that are

I

addressed in departments that have expanded to include studies of world Englishes, online literacies, and the other areas of English studies that have grown up around a modern sense of literature. This incoherence is a product of our history, and I believe that a review of that history can help us make sense of what college English is, and perhaps what it ought to be as well.

English departments generally include a collocation of subject matters that can be grouped into four general areas: literature, language, English education, and writing. Each of these areas includes varied subspecialties. For example, writing is a disjointed area of study divided up by the developments in composition and creative writing that have tended to set them at odds. Because our concerns are so wide ranging, the historical developments of the four corners of our field have largely been examined in isolation from each other. The best-known account of our discipline is Gerald Graff's recently rereleased history of "the profession of literature," *Professing Literature: An Institutional History*. As Graff acknowledges in the preface to the new edition (2007), the reduction of English studies to literary studies has tended to marginalize the teaching of writing, language, and English education. For their part, histories of rhetoric and composition have tended to concentrate on the development of composition courses, and have paid little attention to the efforts of teachers of fiction and poetry to distinguish themselves from journalists and other teachers of writing. Few histories of English have attended to the development of grammar, philology, or linguistics within English studies, in part because linguistics is presumed to have its own disciplinary history (even though departments of linguistics are generally confined to research universities). The institutional history of English education has also not been studied, though that is changing as historians have begun to reexamine how English education became peripheral to English studies.

Each of these areas has a history that predates the establishment of English departments, and those histories are integral to the institutional development of the teaching of English in American colleges. I integrate those areas' histories into that institutional development by characterizing English studies not as literary studies but as literacy studies. I realize that using the term *literacy studies* in this way is problematic. With the "New Literacy Studies," literacy studies (like cultural studies) has become an interdisciplinary, even postdisciplinary movement. Literacy studies cannot really be claimed by any particular discipline—and if it could, professors of education could make a better claim than professors of English.[1] Nonetheless, defining English studies as literacy studies provides a frame of reference that connects the teaching of English to broader trends in literacy and the literate. Attending to those trends can help us see our discipline's concentration on a modern sense of literature as one chapter in a history that extends back to previous eras when literature was defined in religious, oratorical, and belletristic terms. Each of those historical formations has included different modes of reading, writing, and teaching with their own distinctive epistemologies, technologies, and political economies. In each case, literature was upheld as the paragon of literacy that was defined by genres and modes of expression that were taken to represent the literate in highly valued ways.

Literature, literacy, and the literate define each other within a shifting field of cultural production whose structure can be framed by drawing on the theories of Pierre Bourdieu. As Bourdieu discusses in *The Field of Cultural Production*, a field of literary or artistic production differs from a field of study that has obvious use value (such as the teaching of basic reading and writing) because an aesthetic field has to distinguish not only its objects of discourse but also the values that legitimize the distinctions it draws around those objects (164). The "symbolic capital" of any artistic field has economic and political value, but that value accrues only through long-term investments that enable an individual to assume the prestige vested in the aesthetic object (7). Through experience and instruction, practitioners in a field develop "a feel for the game," often tacitly, as they acquire a sense for what makes a story or stance interesting or useful (17). In the process, practitioners come to distinguish themselves from amateurs and others who put their objects of study to different uses (*Practical Reason* 102). A discipline's generic expectations form the competencies and capacities that constitute its field of cultural production (*Field* 176). In this sense, the *discipline* of college English studies is broader and more mutable than the *profession* of college English as we generally understand it. Our profession is but one institutional formation with its own distinctive conceptions of literature and literacy that are integrally involved with how literacy is acquired and evaluated—which are in turn shaped by broader developments in educational access, changing technologies of literacy, and the modes of self-representation that are valued by the literate classes in a particular period.

This framework can help us to look past some of the assumptions that have limited our perspective on our field of work. Even our best histories have tended to view our past from the standpoint of research universities. Research universities tend to be central to our professional sense of self because they are where most of us acquired the professional credentials to do what we do. However, when we center "our" history on research universities, we tend to overlook much of our field of work, and many of our coworkers. If we consider changes in literacy as a framework for disciplinary developments, then we would expect to see those developments emerge not at the centers but at the boundaries of the field—in more accessible institutions where literacy changes as privileged forms are put to new uses by less assimilated populations. Yet much of our thinking about disciplinary developments still tacitly presumes that theory is disseminated from research institutions down to practitioners on the ground. Hence, histories of ideas within disciplines have tended to center on leading thinkers as the sources of change. This stance is understandable because "our" histories are generally written by those of us who have been granted time to do research, and those of us who occupy positions that provide time to do research would like to think that what we write shapes what we do. How that actually works remains an open question. Commentaries on the discipline generally ignore how its changing assumptions are shaped by development in its social engagements, institutional practices, and critical capacities.

If we define our field of study by the work we do, we may be able to acknowledge that changes in the discipline are less akin to the history of ideas than to changes in languages and literacies. Languages and literacies change in broadly based, socially negotiated ways—through use, particularly in spaces and institutions where received modes of expression are inflected by new users. To understand disciplinary changes at work, we need to hold our theories accountable to the transactions of teachers and students at work in class, where literate forms change in tandem with the uses that are made of them. In broadly based institutions, literate conventions are explained to those who have not acquired them as part of their natural upbringing. In the process, conventions may come to seem less "natural" as they are questioned and explained in ways that may or may not make sense of the experience of others. In such spaces, which Mary Louise Pratt has taught us to see as "contact zones," the discipline has evolved at an elemental level as it has been pressed to come to terms with the experiences of those who make their way through our gateway courses. In such spaces, college English has been inflected by the idioms and aspirations of those working through it. Canonical texts have been reinterpreted through shifting registers of experience in a process that Pratt has termed "transculturation."[2]

Attending to those points and processes can help us come to terms with the expansive institutional base of college English studies. English is the most widely taught subject in American schools and colleges. Our field extends from teaching people how to articulate their aspirations to interpreting the classics of the literate culture and preparing the literate to write for popular and specialized audiences. The profession has discounted these expansive engagements in ways it has come to regret as more than "service" courses have been temped out to paraprofessionals. Most college English classes are now taught by "temporary" faculty and teaching assistants. This development has pressed the profession to take account of its broader responsibilities. According to the Association of Departments of English (ADE) Ad Hoc Committee on Staffing in 1999, "The institutionalization of a multitiered faculty that is sharply divided in its levels of compensation and security of employment" threatens "the capacity of the academic profession to renew itself and pass on to the future the ideal of the scholar-teacher—the faculty member who, while pursuing new knowledge, takes active responsibility for the institution, the department, and all parts of the curriculum" (4).

This capacity can be strengthened by investing more of our intellectual energies into our expansive power base. One way to think about that need is to think about English studies as literacy studies. English is taught from grammar to graduate school, but English professors rarely attend to their expansive educational base because academics have historically claimed professional standing not as educators but as disciplinary specialists. College English studies have been particularly debilitated by academics' tendency to distance their professional purposes from their service duties. English departments have had to discount broadly influential areas of their work to disarticulate their specialized expertise from their expansive engagements with general and teacher education. The hierarchies that have structured the profession have systematically ignored writing, teaching, and teacher preparation—a curiously dysfunctional structure given the fact that these are precisely what are involved in the "capacity of the academic profession to renew itself and pass on" its distinctive forms of expertise. Our disciplinary expertise is centrally concerned with studying and teaching literacy, insofar as many undergraduates and most graduate students in English will teach for a living—though you would hardly know that from most of the programs of study that prepare them for that work.

Literacy studies provides an integrative framework that founds work with literature, language, writing, and teaching on an equal footing by providing a bottom-up perspective that focuses on the expansive power base of our discipline. Literacy studies synthesizes histories of the teaching of literature, language studies, English education, and writing in American colleges. A broadly based historical perspective on college English studies is needed to provide a more coherent sense of what English departments are about, and for. As I and others have noted, English departments have become bastions of the culture of the book as they have assumed a position with respect to the literate culture that parallels that which classics departments came to with the transition from classical to modern cultural studies a century ago. Teaching close reading can be a radical undertaking in a culture beset by attention deficit disorder, but we need to develop more expansive and integrative accounts of what English departments do. Such accounts may be able to foster a shared sense of purpose that is responsive to the technological and social changes that have redefined what it means to be literate. English departments are not as stable as they were when the classics of literature were viewed as central to the education of every literate person. Rhetoric and composition programs may well follow the centrifugal trajectories that took speech, drama, and journalism out of university English departments as they came to define themselves by a modern sense of literature. English departments are losing their hold on professors working with projects ranging from ethnic to media studies. The centrifugal forces that are pulling college English apart are paralleled by the centripetal pressures that are converging on its institutional base. Both sets of forces are coming from social and institutional changes that can best be addressed by developing coalitions with other teachers of English. Such coalitions have proven effective at other historical junctures when literacy studies have been pressed to adapt to broader changes in literacy and the literate. Reviewing what English studies have been about can help us assess what they are about to become.

Histories of the Four Corners of the Field

Historic transitions in English studies arise at critical junctures when developments in literacy studies, literacy, and the literate converge. A pragmatic stance is attentive to the possibilities for change that emerge at junctures where expanding disciplinary trends connect with social and technological shifts in literacy. Those shifts sometimes converge with institutional changes, especially those that shape educational access to the literate classes. These socio-institutional developments have been touched upon by some of the most useful research on the historical development of studies of literature, writing, language, and English education. This research has contributed to the pragmatic stance that the profession has adopted in recent decades as institutional resources have declined and the profession has been pressed to account for itself in more practical terms. Those declines have pressed the profession to attend to the debilitating disjunction between its traditional research mission and its basic institutional duties. In response, our histories and professional commentaries have begun to pay more attention to institutional processes such as professionalization and articulation. Stanley Fish was one of the most visible representatives of the pragmatic turn that was adopted in response to first the collapse of jobs and majors in the 1970s and then the "culture wars" in the 1980s. This pragmatic stance has become increasingly important as the numbers of professional positions in the field have continued to decline. This pragmatic stance provides a focal point for converging trends in several of the best-known histories of the teaching of literature, language, English education, and writing.

The pragmatic turn of the 1980s shaped the institutional focus of our most noted disciplinary history: Gerald Graff's *Professing Literature: An Institutional History.* Graff surveys how professional practices have been shaped by the debates among shifting alliances of humanists, philologists, teachers, and critics, with each generation failing to make practical use of its generative oppositions. Successive generations were accused of "elevating esoteric, technocratic jargon over humanistic values, coming between literature itself and the student, [and] turning literature into an elitist pastime for specialists" (4). Graff offered incisive assessments of the pragmatics of institutional change, including the tendency of departments to accommodate change by adding isolated courses in areas such as feminist theory. Graff called for professors to make use of their differences by "teaching the conflicts" among schools of criticism. Graff claimed that teaching the conflicts would help departments develop cohesive programs of study without marginalizing differences. On this and other points, Graff set out practical strategies for intervening in institutional change. Graff's own engagement with the pragmatics of professionalism have expanded in ways that parallel developments in the careers of other noted commentators such as Robert Scholes, Stanley Fish, and Richard Lanham. After gaining recognition in the 1970s with works on literary theory, Graff and these other critics turned in the 1980s to position disciplinary debates in institutional contexts, and then they expanded their focus still farther afield to explain the discipline to broader audiences, as in Graff's *Clueless in Academe: How Schooling Obscures the Life of the Mind* and the textbooks he has published to provide students with heuristics for reading academic conventions. In the writings of such commentators, one can see how our discipline's focus has shifted from traditional objects of study to the institutional practices of the field, and then to articulating the work of the field to broader audiences.

One of the most insightful examples of the pragmatic turn in literary studies in the 1980s was Evan Watkins's *Work Time: English Departments and the Circulation of Cultural Value* (1989). *Work Time* has some of the limitations of other accounts that equate English studies with literary studies, but in other respects, the work has a considerable range and depth of vision. Watkins examines English departments as "a site of cultural production" that is positioned within economies in which the values of literary studies circulate as evaluations of students' literate abilities (8). With a theoretical sophistication that is quite instructive, Watkins acknowledged that the professed values of literature occupy a "marginal position in the circulation of ideologies," as compared to television, film, and advertising. However, English departments have a "relatively crucial position in the social circulation of people" through education (25). Watkins called upon the discipline to attend to the circulation of its work through the lives of those who work through it, particularly those spaces where the critical responses of students can exercise practical agency. Watkins attended to the pragmatic conditions and consequences of what gets done in English departments. He recognized that students often see a critical analysis of a literary work as an "empty" promise because they do not have free time to reflect upon the politics of signification in the ways that professors do. Unfortunately, Watkins did not consider that many teachers of English are also denied the time to reflect upon what they do by the institutional economies at work in English departments. Watkins strategically presumed upon the fact that virtually all college students are required to take composition courses to argue that literary studies has a "crucial" position in the circulation of literacy. This presumption has been critiqued by Richard Miller in "Fault Lines in the Contact Zone." *Work Time* calculatedly explained the pragmatics of literary studies without acknowledging their dependence on composition, which in the eighties had grown from a peripheral service area with only 4 percent of job listings in MLA postings to become the single largest area of professional hiring. In 1987, there were twice as many MLA postings for rhetoric, composition, and technical writing (30.3 percent) as for all periods of British literature (15.1 percent) (Huber, Pinney, and Laurence). By 1989, graduate programs in rhetoric and composition had been added to one-third of doctoral institutions, with public universities three times more likely to have added such programs (Huber, "A Report on the 1986 Survey of English Doctoral Programs in Writing and Literature"). Those programs are one of the clearest examples of how shifts in our institutional base have bubbled up to force changes in professional structures, rather than trickled down from elite institutions. In fact elite research universities have programmatically ignored the expansion of graduate studies to include studies of rhetoric and composition, and have confined the teaching of writing to service units, sometimes led by a token faculty member with professional expertise in rhetoric and composition.

The pragmatic turn in the 1980s deepened as the exclusion of writing teachers from the "profession of literature" began to be reassessed. Where Graff saw the profession arising out of a moribund classicism and outmoded belletrism in nineteenth-century colleges, Susan Miller and other historians of composition and rhetoric blamed the profession itself for reducing rhetoric to ancillary courses in stylistic formalities that were divorced from the broader concerns of classical rhetoric. In *Rescuing the Subject* in 1989 and then two years later in *Textual Carnivals*, Miller argued for recentering disciplinary studies on acts of student writing in order to redress the presumed opposition of subjects and objects of literacy. As Miller discussed, the moments in which writers develop their intellectual capacities through collaborative mediations are central to realizing the critical potentials of literacy studies. In his 1994 article criticizing those who have failed to attend to the pragmatics of pedagogy, Richard Miller concludes that the history of our discipline needs to be rewritten from the standpoint of how student writing has been "solicited, read, and responded to" (175).[3]

This pragmatic standpoint was set out in David Russell's history of writing across the curriculum in 1991. As Russell discussed, disciplines are rhetorically composed through the writings that make up the field—beginning with student examinations and theses, proceeding through the publications that yield promotions, and culminating with the research that composes the field's body of knowledge. Like Graff, Russell offered topoi that have proven their explanatory power in how they have been used to explain institutional forces at work. Russell's concept of "the rhetoric of transparent disciplinarity" helps to explain why academics have paid so little attention to their work with teaching and writing. The process of composing disciplinary expertise tends to be conceived as simply a matter of writing up research, because acknowledging that expertise is rhetorically negotiated raises critical questions about whose purposes that knowledge serves. Russell's history shows how disciplines reduce their learning capacities by treating writing as a basic skill to be mastered elsewhere. "Content" faculty become detached from the pragmatics of what they do if they fail to attend to the rhetorical forms and collaborative processes that shape their work. Because our discipline has such an expansive involvement with writing and teaching, it has been especially incapacitated by failing to attend more fully to these forms and processes. Part of what has been missed is the historical contribution of women to our work. Teaching was the first area of the public sphere that opened up to women. The "feminization" of teaching shaped the development of English education, and English departments' reactions to it. Teacher education has been the primary conduit for women, workers, and people of color who looked to education as a means to social advancement, and professors at vital junctures in the development of our discipline have looked down upon teaching in part because they saw it as women's work.

A similar reaction against popular needs and aspirations has shaped the history of writing instruction, most obviously the distancing of creative writing from journalism and other areas of writing studies. Writing for the public has generally been discounted because academics define their standing by their specialized expertise rather than by their ability to communicate that expertise to others, but the interactive technologies that are transforming literacy are giving renewed significance to the discipline's engagement with writing at work in public life. Redressing the disjuncture between creative and other writing courses can foster vital intradisciplinary alliances, as Mayers discussed in (Re)Writing Craft: Composition, Creative Writing, and the Future of English. In the only book-length history of creative writing classes, D. G. Myers has examined how they emerged out of advanced composition courses in the Progressive era (see also Adams, A History of Professional Writing Instruction in American Colleges). According to Myers, creative writing was welcomed as a means to engage with "the literary act, not the literary record" by humanists such as Norman Foerster, who founded the noted program at Iowa to prepare writers to promote the humanities to the public (31). Courses in creative writing and journalism set out historical alternatives to the modes of authorship that academic critics used to set themselves above journalistic critics. Such hierarchies need to be reevaluated. The discipline's historical concern for writing for public audiences is one of its most powerful capacities, and the Progressive era provides one of the most telling examples of the political potentials of journalism and journalism majors. The Progressive tradition in creative writing has generally been ignored because it treated the creative experience as part of everyday life, and did not give literature the special standing that the profession was building for itself, as reflected in works such as Dewey's *Art as Experience* and *Experience and Education*.

Little attention has been given to the pragmatic alternatives that were available to college English at the origins of the profession, and even less has been given to the public engagements of the third corner of the field, language studies. The civic potentials of language studies have been insightfully explored in Andresen's *Linguistics in America, 1769–1924*. Andresen looks past the origins of the profession to locate the historical sources of the discipline in republican efforts to codify the national language, its literature and teaching. Language conventions were only one domain that reformers organized into an area of expertise as the sphere of educated discourse expanded beyond the republic of letters in which the literate had represented the public. Noah Webster and his contemporaries formalized linguistic and literary conventions in order to provide standards that upheld the authority of the literate. Unlike their better-known European contemporaries, antebellum linguists were more pedagogical and less intent on making language into a science. As Andresen details, this "conventionalist" conception of language was engaged with language use and learning in ways that were lost when linguistics (and literature) became conceived as autonomous disciplines divorced from their educational sources and applications. Andresen centers the history of linguistics on sociolinguistics and the other applied studies that have taken on renewed importance with the rise of ESOL programs within English studies. Andresen's analyses are aptly complemented by histories of attitudes toward literacy and literature, such as those of Cmiel, Zboray, and especially Lawrence Levine. These histories will provide the context for my analysis of how a modern sense of literature became instituted as a subject of study in reaction to the cheapening of literacy by the spread of the periodical press and common schools in the antebellum period.

Historical studies of literature, linguistics, and composition take on broader significance when they are brought to bear on the least professionally visible and most broadly influential corner of the field, English education. The history of English education has been examined by Arthur N. Applebee's *Tradition and Reform in the Teaching of English: A History*. In the decades since Applebee's history was published in 1974, we have come to think differently about the institutional and ideological dynamics of education, though we sometimes still tacitly perpetuate the sort of assumptions that Applebee worked from. For example, Applebee's chapter on "The Birth of a Subject" begins with the commonplace that before it "could emerge as a major school study, English, and in particular English literature, had to develop a methodology rigorous enough to win academic respect" (21). Such assumptions locate historical agency in researchers and leave teachers as consumers of knowledge composed elsewhere. English teachers have sometimes been generations ahead of English professors in elite institutions, as Lucille Schultz has examined in her account of how nineteenth-century teachers developed process-oriented models to teach writing while professors perpetuated the formalism of "current-traditional" rhetoric. A more richly conceptualized view of pedagogy is provided by the works of Salvatori and Carr, Carr, and Schultz. Such archival research is vital if we are to expand our understanding of how knowledge is socially constructed and institutionally negotiated, particularly in the traditions of women, laborers, and minorities who have historically been denied access to the educational centers of the elite culture.

In English education, as in other strategic areas, the development of the discipline has been interlaced with the anxieties and aspirations of teachers and writers, of women and working people, and of those who work with them in less prestigious areas and departments. Those anxieties and aspirations converge on introductory courses. From the start, the profession has looked down upon such menial matters and set higher purposes for itself. Unfortunately, the profession's worst fears have limited some of the discipline's best hopes for articulating its practical benefits in ways that might have strengthened the positions of practitioners in the field. To expand our historical frame of reference beyond the politics of the profession, we need to look not up to trends in elite institutions but down to elemental changes at work in classrooms. We need to question many of our historical assumptions, including the self-serving tendency of researchers to center "our" history on advances in research. Many useful insights into our work have been provided by Graff and others who have drawn upon studies of the sociology of professionalism, such as Bledstein's noted *The Culture of Professionalism: The Middle Class and the Development of Higher Education in America.* I will draw upon such sources as I examine what has now become the most pressing trend in our field: deprofessionalization. We need to acknowledge that we have contributed to this trend through our own historical failure to integrate our institutional duties into the professional apparatus of our discipline, including the graduate programs that prepare practitioners and the publication venues that we use to articulate our intellectual work. This failure has been compounded by how English departments have devalued their public engagements in ways that follow academics' general tendency to discount writing for popular audiences, applied research, and collaborations with schools and other public agencies.

Bledstein and other researchers on the sociology of professionalism have helped us to become more attentive to how universities have served to instill professionalism as the unifying ideology of the middle classes. English studies have been instrumental in instilling that ideology, as becomes more broadly apparent when we attend to the educational experiences of "traditionally underrepresented" populations. Colleges for workers, women, and minorities have been examined by Susan Kates and other historians, such as Karyn Hollis. Kates has expanded our historical alternatives by looking past the rise of the profession to explore how teachers and students from various backgrounds have made use of the discipline in ways that enabled them to exercise rhetorical agency in their own lives. As one can see in the historical work of representative figures such as Mary Louise Pratt, Anne Ruggles Gere, Victor Villanueva, and Jackie Royster, perspectives on literacy studies have expanded as women and scholars of color have moved into leadership positions. Consequently, the discipline has begun to come to terms with the fact that its least respected work has traditionally been done by women, often in writing and general education courses.

Much of that work is concerned with articulating the discipline to broader audiences, often in gateway courses and sometimes in outreach programs offered in collaboration with high schools. Articulation is central to the concerns of both rhetoric and composition. Rhetoric has long been concerned with the art of persuasively articulating oneself to public audiences, while compositionists are often involved in the articulation programs through which college requirements are disseminated and credits are transferred. As a director of a writing program, I helped oversee articulation agreements and participated in articulation conferences with teachers and community college representatives. These networks are part the articulation apparatus of broadly based English departments. The professional apparatus of English departments includes the same elements as other academic disciplines—graduate programs that initiate students into the discipline, journals and conferences that advance the discussions that define the discipline, the undergraduate programs of study that disseminate the discipline's distinctive modes of inquiry, and collaborations with practitioners who do related work outside the academy. English is more broadly based than most academic disciplines because work with literacy is an elemental part of teaching students how to articulate themselves as they move from grammar to graduate school. English courses have traditionally been involved with writing at work in public life, including journalistic and literary genres that range across personal, professional, and political domains of experience.

Articulation theory provides a frame of reference for assessing how literacy and literacy studies have developed in tandem with transitions in what has been considered literary and who has been considered literate.[4] The conjunctions between literacy, literacy studies, the literate and literary take on historic significance at pivotal points where technologies and economies of literacy contribute to transitions in broader class formations. "Articulation" is concerned, according to Stuart Hall, with the transmission of prevailing ideologies and social practices through the conjunctions between established institutions and broader social movements. Those conjunctions provide coherence to historical formations by circulating cohesive accounts of shared needs and purposes:

> A theory of articulation is both a way of understanding how ideological elements come, under certain conditions, to cohere together within a discourse, and a way of asking how they do or do not become articulated at specific conjunctures, to certain political subjects. (Hall 53)

The conjunctions between literacy and literacy studies turn critical when the relations between learning and the learned, between literacy and the literate, become redefined in ways that reconfigure not just subjects of study, but also the subject positions that students are taught to assume. Those pivotal junctures will be examined in later chapters. Before surveying those historical transitions, I will outline a framework for what Stuart Hall has termed a "conjunctural history" of college English studies as literacy studies.

Literacy, Literacy Studies, the Literate and Literary

Ethnography provides a way of thinking about literacy that has been vital to the "New Literacy Studies" and to broader trends in literary, cultural, and linguistic studies (see, for example, Street's "What's 'New' in New Literacy Studies?" and Atkinson's *The Ethnographic Imagination*). More anthropological models of literacy have become common as we have moved away from the sense of literature and literacy that was invested in the experience of books as individual artifacts. As Street and others have discussed, literacy and literature ceased to be seen as autonomous objects of study as conceptions of literacy shifted with broader changes in literacy. In the 1970s, literature and literacy became understood as socio-institutional constructions as people began to recognize that "the function of literature and the role of English teachers cannot be understood except within the context of a given society and politics" (Ohmann, *English* 303). *Literature* became more of an anthropological category, which was imbedded in the pragmatics of how people read, write, and teach the forms that constitute what is taken to be *literary* in a particular period, as Terry Eagleton discussed in his influential account of the theoretical trends that contributed to reassessments of the pragmatics of reading and writing in the 1980s (24). Over the last three centuries, the most valued forms of literacy have evolved from religious literature through an oratorical concern for style and delivery to a modern sense of literature as nonfactual works of the imagination. Literature has changed as access to education expanded and the educated came to play new roles in an increasingly diversified public sphere. While literature and the literate have always defined each other, the modern conjunction of literacy and schooling only became established when public education became state mandated. Out of that conjunction emerged a modern sense of literature.

In the antebellum period and at other junctures in the history of literacy and literacy studies, the literate have distinguished themselves by being able to distinguish the virtues of literature. A century ago, English education and literary criticism became academic subjects of study, and the opposition of the latter to the former came to structure our profession. A noted college textbook on methods for teaching English was Percival Chubb's *The Teaching of English in the Elementary and Secondary School*. Chubb also published articles for teachers such as the "Blight of Bookishness," which blamed "the tyrant print" for closing "our ears to the music of words and minstrelsy" (15). Chubb's idea that it is voice that distinguishes the power of literature was a throwback to the elocutionary tradition. However, oral modes of interpretation were still a recognized disciplinary methodology at the formation of the profession of literature. A prominent proponent of oral interpretation was Chubb's contemporary Hiram Corson at Cornell, who taught literature entirely through dramatic readings (see Payne, *English in American Universities* 60–65). With Corson as an authority, Chubb argued that "the book lies between us and the essentials of literary beauty." According to Chubb, "literature is to be read with the ear, as a great conductor reads a musical score," for only in well-orchestrated gestures can the "emotional appeal of literature" return us "to our senses!" ("Blight" 19, 22). Disparaging the "fashionable worship of Ph.D.-ities," Chubb exhorted teachers to look back to "the fairy princess, Song," in order to save their students from the "uniform vulgarity of the culture of the slums" (18). Chubb was just the sort of passionate pedagogue who embarrassed those who were establishing literature as a professional specialization. Chubb was an anachronistic figure. He was part of an older tradition in which the literate distinguished themselves by delivering an impassioned reading. In elocutions, as in essays, students deliver a reading to demonstrate that they have internalized the "feel for the game." At different points in our history, the literate have distinguished that "feel" for literature with acts of sacred devotion to the Word, with elocutionary performances, and with essays tracing out the nuances of a poem.

Students' writings document how modes of reading and reasoning have shifted at historical junctures in the development of learning and the learned. English exercises were included in American colleges from the founding of Harvard in 1636 to prepare preachers to teach the Word. While English was included in classroom exercises, students displayed their learning in Latin disputations before the assembled college, and at graduation before the learned community. Colonial communities were as closed as the "circle of learning" embodied in the deductive syllogisms composed by students. Colonial colleges and communities were scribal information economies in which books were rare and writing served primarily as an aid to memory. Between the populist evangelism of the 1740s and the American Revolution, scholastic disputations were replaced by forensic debates in English as the ability to write persuasively gained currency with the spread of the periodical press. As elsewhere in the British provinces, the transition from ancient to modern cultural studies turned on the introduction of courses in rhetoric and belles letters.[5] That transition was shaped by the emergence of the essay as a vehicle of popular instruction. Belletristic essays helped to mediate polite tastes through the spread of the periodical press, as I discussed in my history of English studies in the British cultural provinces. In antebellum America, the essays of popular lecturers such as Emerson circulated through lyceum networks and then were reprinted in magazines and the first anthologies of American literature. These anthologies provided students with models for their own compositions, for *literature* was still understood to be something that students might not only read but also write.

As I will discuss in the first chapter, the scribal literacies of the first century of college English studies document the schematics of literate technologies and economies in their starkest forms. Scribal literacy was acquired through apprenticeships with masters, who composed compendia from a book or a predecessor's notes and then passed that distillation down to students, who recited what they had been read. Writing was recorded speech and was acquired and put to use orally. "Books" of commonplaces served as an aid to memory, because a literate person was understood to be a "walking library" or *obambulans bibliotheca* (Meriwether 76). Students' efforts to reduce all that was known to what could be remembered are documented in the writings of students. Through the intricate intimacies of learning systems of thought by heart, the schematics of learning became overlaid on the workings of the mind, with the science of *technologicae* charged with charting the relations of mental faculties to all the arts and sciences. The primary technology of literate inquiry was the deductive syllogism, with a deductive "system or synopsis" serving as the archetype for graduate theses. Some students stayed on after being ceremoniously granted "the privilege of reading in public" at graduation, but when graduate tutors at Harvard first tried to gain recognition as part of the teaching staff in the early eighteenth century, the administration recommended they be viewed as servants, not faculty.[6] While graduate students are still treated as apprentices in labor negotiations, the deductive field of scribal literacy broke up with social diversification and the spread of print. The expansion of literacy and literacy studies is apparent in the disappearance within decades of the syllogistic modes of reasoning that had for centuries distinguished the learned by their ability to reason deductively from ancient traditions to individual experiences.

In the second chapter, I will connect with some of the developments that I explored more fully in my history of English studies in Britain. In America, as in Britain, especially Scotland, the shift from a deductive to an inductive epistemology as the paradigm for literate inquiry was fundamental to the "new learning," and what was popularly known at the time as "experimental religion." The transition in students' writings from syllogistic disputations to forensic debates documents the historic shift in epistemologies, technologies, and social relations that gave rise to the first college courses in English literature, rhetoric, and composition. The introduction of modern cultural studies contributed to a fundamental reformation of the trivium by what Hume characterized as "the science of human nature," as I discussed in *The Formation of College English*. The transition from Aristotelian logic and Ciceronian rhetoric to empirical reasoning and an unadorned style occurred almost simultaneously in American, Scottish, and Irish colleges and English Dissenting academies, as W. S. Howell has most fully detailed. These shifts in the three disciplines at the center of the liberal arts mark the historic transition from classical to modern cultural studies. From the center of the learned culture, the breakdown of the classical tradition was looked down upon as a literacy crisis quite comparable to that which is bringing an end to modern literary studies. While the schematics of scribal literacy provide the clearest example of shifts in literate technologies, the "new learning" provides a complex but well defined model for reflecting on how literacy studies as a field of cultural production was transformed by the emergence of modern psychologies and political economics.

The continuities and discontinuities between educational reforms in pre-Revolutionary America and post-Union Scotland are most pointedly apparent in the courses in rhetoric and moral philosophy that became the culminating studies in the Revolutionary curriculum as it began to accommodate increasing numbers of lawyers and others not intent on becoming ministers. The college at Philadelphia that Benjamin Franklin helped establish in 1755 included the first professorship of English in America.[7] At the newly founded colleges in Philadelphia and Princeton, Scottish college graduates taught courses in rhetoric, composition, and criticism in conjunction with moral philosophy courses that combined civic humanist and natural law doctrines with the epistemology of Newton and Locke, along with some practical advice on such legal and ethical matters as drawing up contracts. The rhetoric and moral philosophy courses of John Witherspoon at Princeton are notable because he was a classmate of Hugh Blair, a teacher of James Madison, and a signatory of the Declaration of Independence. The College of Philadelphia had a similar significance, and a different sort as well. It included a Young Ladies Academy that offered the first rhetoric courses for women. Priscilla Mason used the opportunity of her graduation oration in 1793 (and its publication) to condemn "despotic" men for denying women access to public forums where they might use their developing skills to speak for the public good (qtd. in Connors 40–41; see also Kerber, *Federalists* 221–22). Women were at the time testing the limits of "republican motherhood" (Eldred and Mortensen).

The College at Philadelphia was the sort of hybrid institution that became common in prosperous midwestern towns in the antebellum period. As I will discuss in the third chapter, more colleges were founded in the first half of the nineteenth century than in any other period in American history. Most were liberal arts colleges with denominational affiliations. Such colleges commonly served as all-purpose institutions that offered secondary instruction along with a seminary, women's academy, and teacher's institute (which were sometimes all but one and the same).[8] With the spread of common schools and the emergence of the first mass media (the penny press), the public sphere expanded and became more diversified. Books ceased to be objects of devotion and became a popular pastime, creating a "revolution in reading" (see Davidson). The establishment of a national reading public and state-mandated schooling provided unprecedented numbers of positions for journalists, lecturers, and teachers, enabling women, minorities, and working people to earn an independent living by working with their minds instead of their hands. One of the first surveys of American literature, Duyckinck and Duyckinck's *Cyclopedia of American Literature*, observed in 1866 that "it is only of late that a class of authors by profession has begun to spring up" (v).[9] Looking back upon that development a half century later, Payne's *American Literary Criticism* concluded that "not until early in the nineteenth century did literature in America become what we commonly understand by the term—a product in which artistic considerations prevail over all others" (4). Teaching and writing for the periodical press were integrally involved with literary criticism until the latter established itself as an academic specialization that was divorced from such popular concerns.

Payne published the first survey of college English departments, *English in American Universities*, which I will discuss in chapter four on the Progressive era. I will examine how the profession was configured in the two professional organizations that were established in this period. In the Modern Language Association, professors organized themselves as researchers, while professors made common cause with teachers in the National Council of Teachers of English. From its start in 1883, the MLA largely excluded literary journalists and practicing critics, for its members were more likely to have academic affiliations than comparable disciplinary associations such as those formed by historians and social scientists (Veysey 70). Within two decades, the MLA consolidated its standing by narrowing its purposes to advancing research. MLA ceased publishing the articles on pedagogy that had comprised most of the first issues of *PMLA*, and it closed down its pedagogy section, which had conducted national studies of working conditions and institutional trends in areas such as composition (Graff 121). Fred Newton Scott and others with an interest in such broader issues formed NCTE to organize coalitions with teachers. NCTE was an avowedly Progressive organization that drew most of its college members from public institutions in the Midwest, while the leadership of the MLA came largely from elite institutions in the East (Graff 34–35). NCTE was specifically set up to provide a representative assembly where teachers could consider collective action against oppressive workloads and assessment priorities. NCTE is the largest association of English teachers in the world, but as a teachers' organization, it has not had the sort of professional standing that MLA has had among research faculty, who control the graduate programs that produce the faculty who set the priorities for departments in diverse institutions. The origins and development of these two associations provide contrasting sets of possibilities for organizing our field of work.

As I will discuss in chapter five on recent developments in our field, the historical points where teachers and professors have worked together often mark generative junctures where basic changes have emerged in the teaching of English. One of those collaborations was the Dartmouth Conference in 1966 that is often seen as a formative source for modern composition studies (Harris, "After Dartmouth"). That conference opened with one of the leading rhetoricians of the period, Albert Kitzhaber, giving a plenary entitled "What Is English?" Kitzhaber reviewed the answers provided by a decade of unequalled federal funding, which had enabled professors and teachers to create regional curriculum centers. From those efforts, Kitzhaber concluded that English studies should build in an integrated and cumulative manner through studies of language, literature, and composition. While Kitzhaber drew on some of the most broadly based research ever conducted on the teaching of English, his approach did not prove to be compelling to the British and American teachers and professors who gathered for three weeks at Dartmouth. His question got lost in the discussion when James Britton responded by shifting the focus from what English should be to what students should be doing. As Zebroski discussed in his response to Harris's insightful analysis of how Dartmouth set out a model for the scholarship of teaching, the historical impact of the Dartmouth Conference arose from how it shifted disciplinary deliberations to focus on learning and writing processes. As evident in the influential collaborations at Dartmouth, that focus has gained historic power when professors and teachers have been pressed to work together by broad changes in literacy that raise basic questions about what English studies are to be and do.

In the decade following Dartmouth, the profession saw a dramatic drop in its fortunes. In the 1970s, our profession experienced a historic collapse in BAs, PhDs, and tenure-track jobs, which were all cut in half within the decade. As discussed in chapter five, majors in English were overshadowed by the rising popularity of more practical programs of study, including some that had previously been housed in English departments, most notably communications. Research universities continued to prosper, but disciplines became increasingly stratified, along with the rest of the higher educational system.[10] The "profession of literature" suffered along with other established professions as the services of professionals began to be evaluated in market terms.[11] As Brint discusses in *In an Age of Experts*, professions came to be seen as merely commercial enterprises, while professionals themselves began articulating their distinctive standing as simply a matter of expertise. Less emphasis was given to the traditional idea that professions provide a public service that would be compromised if not protected from market forces. This shift away from "social trustee professionalism" was part of a historic "splintering of the professional stratum along functional, organizational, and market lines." While some professions continued to distinguish themselves by articulating "work as a calling," those with more direct use value tended to identify themselves as simply experts (Brint 5–7). This same splintering of professional functions emerged within our own field in the divisive conflicts between critics and compositionists in the 1980s. As becomes evident at such critical junctures, the history of our profession turns out to be part of the broader history of professionalism, in large part because English has traditionally played a fundamental role in credentialing professionals.

The history of college English is also integrally involved with the history of literacy, as we are being pressed to acknowledge by changes in literacy that have traditionally been ignored by the profession. While the profession has not considered research on the public standing of literature to be part of its concerns, surveys of American reading habits have been undertaken by the

National Endowment for the Arts. Drawing upon census surveys conducted in 1982, 1992, and 2002, *Reading at Risk* reported historic declines over the last three decades in the reading of books and works of "literature" (including popular genres as well as poetry and drama). This definition of *literature* excludes nonfiction in a way that may detract from the validity of the study, but which is consistent with how literature has traditionally been defined in English departments. In 1982, 56.9 percent of respondents reported they had read a work of literature in the last year that had not been assigned in school, while in 2002 that number dropped by 18 percent to 46.7 percent. The steepest decline was in the age group who sits in our classrooms: 59.8 percent of 18–24-year-olds reportedly did "literary reading" in 1982, but only 42.8 percent said that they had done such reading in 2002. Women were 25 percent more likely than men to report that they had read literature in the last year. While the reading of literature seems to have dramatically declined, the writing of literature was actually found to have significant standing: 7 percent of the respondents in 2002 reported that they did creative writing, and 13 percent said that they had taken a creative writing course. That would add up to some 27 million Americans. Nine percent of the respondents reported having used the Internet to read and research literature.

Like *A Nation at Risk* twenty years earlier, *Reading at Risk* was meant to energize the literate by underlining deepening threats to their values. Unlike scholarly organizations such as the MLA, which have long bewailed declines in learning and literacy, the NEA took public action to intervene in a locally situated and nationally orchestrated way. The NEA launched "The Big Read," a national initiative that enlisted more than five hundred communities in organizing reading groups to focus on a selected literary work. This initiative was seen to have contributed to the turnaround in "literary reading" that was reported in *Reading on the Rise: A New Chapter in American Literacy* in 2009: while the respondents who stated that they had read a poem, novel, play, or story in the last year dropped by 14 percent between 1992 and 2002, between 2002 and 2008, that number rose 7 percent (with 54 percent reporting they had done literary reading in 1992, 46.7 percent in 2002, and 50.2 percent in 2008) (4). Even with that upturn, the 2008 results were still almost 15 percent lower than the percentage of respondents who reported they read literature in 1982 (59.8 percent). The increase may also have been due to changes in the survey items, for the 2008 study gave more attention to reading online, with 15 percent of the respondents reporting that they read literature online. These trends highlight developments that need to be considered if we are to make productive use of the historic changes that confront English departments. Literary reading has clearly declined in dramatic ways in recent decades. If we are to intervene in that decline, we are going to have to develop much more broadly engaged coalitions with librarians, teachers, and reading and writing groups in our local communities, and toward that end, we are going to have to adopt a more pragmatic engagement with the potentials of interactive technologies. Those technologies are fundamental to the historical shift from reading to writing that we can witness every day in virtually any public place, including the virtual public places that we increasingly inhabit.

These reports and the other surveys that I will cite in later chapters provide benchmarks for reflecting upon how the standing of English departments has been undercut by changes in literacy that the profession has tended to discount. The debilitating impact of this tendency has been compounded by the profession's failure to invest its intellectual capital in its institutional work. This failure is epitomized by the equation of English studies with *literary studies*, in the modern sense of that term. English departments in elite universities have been insulated from broader changes in literacy and education, and such departments have also been isolated from the partnerships that might enable the discipline to respond to those changes. Broadly based departments of English include a rich array of applied linguists, English education specialists, compositionists, journalists, creative writers, and scholars involved with ethnic, media, and gender studies. We need a vision of the discipline that includes the expansive possibilities of these areas of study. Literacy studies provides a model that encompasses research and teaching in all four corners of our field: literature, language, English education, and writing. The basic distinction between teachers and researchers is fundamentally disorienting because we are all teachers. The real question is whether our programs of study will attend to that fact. As I have tried to set out in this introduction, insofar as the profession has not taken this basic reality into account, it has incapacitated the discipline by misrepresenting what practitioners do. Looking at our history from the bottom up can help us think through our disciplinary capacities in more productive ways. Given our deepening labor problems and the expanding changes in literacy that confront us, we need to reassess our historical alternatives in order to develop a more productive engagement with our rich institutional base. We have an expansive power base, and we need to invest more of our collective intellectual energies in exploring how to harness the power of what we do.

1

Learning and the
Learned in Colonial
New England

By the power of eloquence, ould truth receivs new habit . . . The
same verity is again and again perhaps set before the same guests,
but drest and disht up after a new manner, and every manner
season'd so well that the intellectuall parts may . . . [provide] fresh
nourishing virtue.

Michael Wigglesworth in 1650, "Prayse of Eloquence," 9.

We are now in circumstances similar to those which produced the
greatest orators of ancient days . . . Our governments are popular.
The arts and sciences are fast advancing among us, and our present
difficult situation urges us to every effort for our political safety.
These considerations should lead us to cultivate this noble art,
and cannot fail to produce men who, pleading our great American
cause, shall consume all before them, with the ardent blaze of
Demosthenes, or the wide spreading flame of a Tully.

Thomas Ennals in 1775, "On Ancient Eloquence," 3.

THESE STUDENT ORATIONS ON
the virtues of rhetoric highlight several of the converging textual, epistemological, and political changes that shaped the first century of English studies
in American colleges. Wigglesworth's oration seems rather quaint, and not just
because he wrote before English was standardized by print. His notebooks show
that he learned to define eloquence as the art of dressing up "ould truth" in a
new style from reading Peter Ramus. Such assumptions were consistent with
the duties that seventeenth-century college graduates assumed as preachers of
virtue in isolated communities. Wigglesworth's oration has a timeless quality

that ironically makes it feel quite dated, while Ennals spoke directly to the politics of his time. Before a commencement audience that included the Continental congressmen assembled in Philadelphia, Ennals invoked the civic virtues of rhetoric in order to strengthen the public authority of the liberally educated in an era of revolutionary change. The religious and political divisions of the latter half of the eighteenth century helped created a need for graduates who were prepared to speak and write for diverse audiences. Colleges responded by introducing forensic debates to prepare students to speak to contemporary issues.

From the founding of Harvard until the establishment of a half dozen colleges a century later, the colonial curriculum maintained the emphasis on deductive reasoning in an ancient language that had long prevailed in Britain and Europe. The rhetorical dynamics of literacy and literacy studies changed as the colonies gave rise to a reading public that drew upon republican doctrines to constitute a national identity. The literate were challenged to persuade audiences that for the first time had choices to make regarding which church to attend and what to read. In response to these challenges, rhetoric came to replace logic as the paragon of literate inquiry in the college curriculum, and the prevailing conception of literature shifted from a religious to an oratorical framework. The transition from religious to oratorical literature was part of the response to the expansion of literacy and the diversification of the literate, most notably the rising numbers of graduates who went into secular careers. The increasing access to books and magazines broke down the confines of the scribal curriculum, which had compensated for the lack of books by relying on classroom recitations and declamations. These oral modes of instruction and the deductive mindset of scholasticism were consistent with the didactic sermons that college graduates would preach to their isolated congregations of fellow believers, while the changes in literacy and literacy studies in the middle of the eighteenth century were part of the response to the debates over individual religious and political rights that began with the Great Awakening of populist evangelism in the 1740s.

The earliest description that we have of the scope and purpose of the American college curriculum is provided by *New England's First Fruits*, which was published in London in 1643 to enlist support for the new college: "After God had carried us safe to *New England*, . . . One of the next things we longed for, and looked after was to advance *Learning* and perpetuate it to Posterity; dreading to leave an illiterate Ministery to the Churches, when our present

Ministers shall lie in the Dust" (6). To prepare the literate to preach and teach the Word, Harvard students participated in monthly "declamations in *Latine* and *Greeke*, and Disputations Logicall and Philosophicall" to display their mastery of the "tongues and Arts" before a "publique" audience of "Magistrates, Ministers, and other Schollars" (7). "Magistrates" and other laymen sat on the boards that incorporated colleges, as was common in Scotland but not England. Harvard is in fact the oldest American corporation operating under its original charter.[1]

Colonial colleges lacked the endowments of an Oxford or a Cambridge, and had to rely on public grants and donations. This dependence made American colleges more responsive to broader changes in education and literacy than the more insulated English universities. New Englanders looked to public education to perpetuate their values amidst the perceived barbarism of the frontier, as Bernard Bailyn has discussed. Mandatory public education was instituted with the first Massachusetts School Law of 1647. Up to the middle of the eighteenth century, most students became clergymen in communities where they were often the only college graduates.

The scribal literacy of the New England colonies was not expansive but introspective. In the classroom as in society more generally, information was largely transmitted through face-to-face conversations that cemented social hierarchies. Most people only read a few devotional texts, which were learned by heart. Graduates were taught how to speak to such communities through a regime of recitations and disputations that required students to reduce the few available books to compendia that could be memorized and recited. These scribal methods of instruction enacted a deductive mode of learning that upheld the syllogism as the paradigm for human reasoning and moral judgment, with individuals taught to deduce their individual duties from traditional precepts. Religious uniformity broke up with the popular debates of the revolutionary period. Those debates built the circulation of the newspapers and magazines that came to provide alternative sources of information. Social diversification and the expansion of print literacy contributed to the emergence of what was known as the "new learning," which looked to science for a methodology that was often less experimental than experiential. After serving for centuries as the epitome of learned inquiry, syllogistic disputations in Latin were replaced by forensic disputations in English in the decades between the Great Awakening and the American Revolution. These disputations were identified with a more inductive model of reasoning from experience. The departure from the deductive mindset of scholasticism provides an epistemological benchmark for assessing how literacy studies changed with the breakdown of the scribal information economies that characterized colonial communities, and the curriculum that prepared graduates to speak to them.

College English studies emerged from the growth of the periodical press and the diversification of viewpoints that it helped to legitimate. As at other junctures in the history of the teaching of English, literacy and the literate evolved in tandem with literacy studies. That evolution was rooted in the covenanting tradition that clergymen invoked to claim the authority to speak for the public. The covenanting tradition lost its unifying authority as increasing numbers of people grew up outside the church. This development is documented in Kenneth Lockridge's ethnographic study of Dedham, Massachusetts, which provides a case study in how social diversification led to a more rhetorical stance on literacy. [2] This diversification helped to prompt a parallel transition in the curriculum. Literacy was traditionally acquired in the virtual absence of books by having individuals inscribe all that was deemed to be worth remembering in orderly hierarchies that could be dictated and recited. Like the rural communities that students graduated into, the scribal curriculum was a self-contained space, a narrow space encompassed by the "circle of learning" that included all that could be memorized by a well-versed student (Johnson, *Elementa Philosophia* viii). In the third section, I will discuss how this well-enclosed field of cultural production was broken up by the debates over individual rights that began to spread through the popular press during the Great Awakening. In the fourth section of this chapter, I will examine how the growth of the periodical press contributed to the introduction of English courses in the decades between the Great Awakening and the American Revolution. I will conclude this chapter by relating these epistemological and social changes in literacy and literacy studies to a formative development in the political economy of American higher education—the distinction of private colleges from other institutions of public education. That demarcation would become fundamental to the American higher education market, and to the elaboration of related distinctions within American civil society, most notably the ideology of professionalism.

The Corporation on the Hill

The polity of New England communities was shaped by the covenanting tradition. New Englanders were well versed in the idea that they had formed a pact with God that bestowed certain rights and duties upon them. This idea was a common theme in sermons and religious works, and it was woven into the contractual relations of pastors and other elected officials with the members of the elect who had voted for them. In the covenanting tradition, such social contracts were not understood to be a compact between autonomous individuals so much as an enactment of the hierarchical nature of the providential order. The social contract set out a model for how the literate understood their relations to the public. Upon disembarking at Massachusetts Bay, Governor John Winthrop preached a lay sermon to his Puritan followers that deduced their duties as citizens in the "city upon the hill" from the assumption that "God Almighty in His most holy and wise providence hath so disposed of the condition of mankind as in all times some must be rich, some poor; some high and eminent in power and dignity, others mean and in subjection" (Miller, *American Puritans* 79). As a model for the political relations of the literate and the public, the social contract was less concerned with individual rights than with the obligations that individuals were to deduce from received hierarchies. This aspect of the social compact is important to underline because we tend to assume that natural rights doctrines served to justify individual equality, while such doctrines would traditionally have been identified with hierarchies founded on the subordination of those who were seen as naturally inferior.

In principle and in practice, the covenanting tradition limited the polity to those who shared a faith in God's covenant with the saved. In many communities, church membership was limited to those who had demonstrated their personal salvation with a conversion narrative that recounted the introspections that led to their accepting Christ's saving grace. If an individual delivered a rendition of the religious experience that was consistent with the experience of the members of the church, members voted to accept the person and the membership roll was signed. Such membership was required of all voters in Massachusetts. Congregationalist churches were largely autonomous and ordained their own ministers, whose authority rested on their contract with their congregants. While Congregationalism created considerable communal independence, such autonomy was not extended to individuals, and especially not to individuals who challenged the community's guiding sense of itself.[3] Nonconformists such as the Quakers were ostracized, tortured, and even executed as a matter of principle. The irony at the center of America's idealized democratic traditions is that Puritans were Dissenters who could not tolerate dissent. As Patricia Roberts-Miller has discussed, the "paradoxical" democracy of Puritan New England is the American archetype for a deliberative public that could only make sense of its differences by excluding them as unreasonable and therefore intolerable.

The public sphere of the local assembly was understood to be a closed space where reasonable people could speak from shared assumptions to advance common needs. In such forums, according to Roberts-Miller, "only the righteous have rights" (78). True believers do not engage in debates with the unorthodox because the truth is not open to question. Clergy did not generally try to persuade those doomed to be damned but spoke as a prophetic "voice in the wilderness" against the corruptions of outsiders (63). The religious literature of the time provided a template for interpreting the smallest details of daily life as signs of Providence. Puritan literature had "a palimpsest quality" that documents the rich interpretive frameworks of the literate mentality of the time (Roberts-Miller 123). A citizen was envisioned to be a freeholder who possessed land, but in much of New England, land was granted not to individuals but to groups that incorporated as towns. A congregation would be formed, and it would become the nucleus for the corporation. The fabled New England town meetings were often held in the local church and presided over by its members.

Social diversification soon began to fragment these closed communities. A detailed sense of this process is provided by Lockridge's history of a single colonial town, Dedham, founded ten miles southwest of Boston in 1636 on a two hundred square mile grant given to about thirty middle-class families. The founders signed a contract that provided for internal mediation of conflicts. The "contrary minded" were to be excluded, in part by restricting the sale of land to outsiders. Land was distributed disproportionately according to tacitly accepted differences in "rank and quality" (5, 8). Several members were chosen to begin the process of collaborative soul searching to constitute the church, and 70 percent of the community became members. Rather than dividing up the land into autonomous farms, a closely knit town was established, and fewer than three thousand acres were divvied up in the first twenty years. Into the eighteenth century the town remained an isolated middle-class farm community. Dedham functioned as "a self-governing corporation of the saved" (24). However, by the second quarter of the eighteenth century, four separate towns had been set up. Land reserves were exhausted, and population growth intensified the pressures on increasingly contested social hierarchies. Instead of acceding to the decisions of the elected "Select Men," town meetings became a forum for factions maneuvering to establish their own churches and schools. When community deliberations failed, such groups turned to the courts (Lockridge 135). Faced with such developments, the educated began to take new interest in mastering the art of public debate.

Education was challenged to compensate for the increasing numbers of people who were growing up unversed in religious literature. As early as 1670, most people in Dedham were no longer members of the church. Because only members could have their children baptized, just 40 percent of children were being baptized. Many who were baptized failed to come before the congregation to bare their souls with a conversion narrative. Pressed to accommodate increasing numbers of individuals who were not orthodox believers, towns such as Dedham could no longer function as "closed corporate communities" that dealt with diversity by excluding nonbelievers (Lockridge 81). The breakdown of religious conformity increased colonials' concern for the educational upbringing of the rising generation. This concern was well founded, for research suggests that while white immigrants were more literate than the communities they had left behind, literacy tended to decline among the children and grandchildren of immigrants as a result of migration to less settled areas (see Kaestle and Grubb). While Massachusetts law traditionally required larger towns to establish grammar schools, laws were tightened and more rigorously enforced in the last decades of the century. Small-town schools were generally presided over by the local clergyman or his assistant, who taught students to recite religious platitudes along with the rudiments of literacy. Students might then move on to a textbook such the *New England Primer*, which was known as "the little Bible of New England" (Meriwether 19). However, even grammar schools required few books, because students generally drew up their own grammars and lexicons from recitations.

Such were the ideological and institutional contexts within which scribal literacy functioned. New England was the most intensely literate area of the colonies. In seventeenth-century New England, about 60 percent of adult, white males were literate (50 percent higher than England's literacy rate of 40 percent). While American women were about half as likely to be literate as men, such high literacy levels for men and women were only equaled in areas such as Scotland, Sweden, and Switzerland, which shared the Puritans' commitment to literate devotion. Literacy was closely tied to religion, as is evident in the fact the literacy rates of white women depended less on the wealth and education of their parents than on whether they were active church members

(Graff, *Legacies* 163–65). However, even in New England, literacy remained largely scribal until the Great Awakening in the 1740s. Most New England households included only a few books, such as a Bible, an almanac, and a work of popular religious literature like *Pilgrim's Progress*. Most people read but a few sacred texts and wrote an occasional letter, deed, or contract, with sermons the most influential form of public discourse. In such communities, literacy tended to perpetuate a pietistic reverence for received beliefs. Print functioned as "a technology of the self" that worked in a deductive manner to impress the authority of the divine Word on the individual psyche through the process of learning by heart (Warner 19–20).

This scribal information economy was an "economy of scarcity" that followed "a hierarchical diffusion pattern," according to Brown's *Knowledge Is Power: The Diffusion of Information in Early America* (280). Information was transmitted through face-to-face conversations that reinforced the conversants' respect for their respective ranks. Signs of deference became part of the transaction, strengthening communal hierarchies by reinforcing the authority of those who could presume to know better because they circulated more widely within the community and beyond it. In many communities, the minister was the only one with a college degree or library, and he often corresponded with his former classmates and joined with them as a town representative in regional associations. Such networks strengthened the cultural authority of the literate by making their learning rhetorically influential in daily life and political relations.

Into the middle of the eighteenth century, most college graduates exercised public authority from the pulpit, preaching didactic sermons that deduced individuals' obligations from biblical truths. The purpose was not to persuade the unconverted, but to teach the faithful, because Puritans assumed that people either were or were not elected for salvation. Learned sermons aimed at the converted remained the norm up to the Great Awakening of popular evangelism that prompted ministers such as Jonathan Edwards to attempt to persuade broader audiences that they were "sinners in the hands of an angry God." Individuals had long been taught to look inward to seek signs that they had received grace and been selected to the elect, which would be visible to others in the good done by them and to them. Of course any individual was free not to sign a covenant with God—free to be excluded and damned. The very idea that one could achieve grace by seeking it was a heresy—*Arminianism*, which according to Hofstadter was "a curse word as full of resonance as the word *communism* has become to modern Americans" (*America* 227). Individuals monitored their thoughts and interactions, searching for signs of grace, and looking to religious literature to help them deduce whether their experiences were marked by such signs. Sacred literature was studied by most people for introspective devotions, but in the hands of ministers, books were generally used to lead public devotions to the Word.[4]

The Great Awakening of popular evangelism had its broadest impact on the unchurched and uneducated. These groups increased as the population expanded to frontier communities that lacked preachers to teach them. Traveling evangelists destabilized communal hierarchies by encouraging the alienated to leave the congregations of uninspiring clerics. The traditionally uncontested authority of the literate was further undermined when evangelists began to found their own colleges. Like new churches, these colleges gave people the power to choose among competing institutions. Some evangelicals became ambivalent about this power as the changes they set out began to undermine the authority of clerics by fostering popular religious divisions. These divisions undercut the ability of churches to represent themselves as public institutions. As in Dedham, the unchurched became more organized and politically active. This trend was advanced in Massachusetts and other colonies by the reduction of property requirements on voting. In the third quarter of the century, the percentage of adult white males who could vote in a town such as Dedham rose from 40 to 70 percent (see also Katherine Brown). This expansion of the electorate challenged the educated to learn how to speak persuasively to audiences that might not share their assumptions. Higher education had been charged with preparing the literate to represent the public, but as modes of representation became more contested, rhetoric came to replace logic at the pinnacle of literacy studies.

The "Circle of Learning" within the Curriculum

The colonial curriculum was a scribal information economy much like those that students would enter upon graduation. Information was acquired and perpetuated orally through a daily regime of dictations, recitations, declamations, and disputations. Students had limited access to books. Learning by rote transmitted knowledge in a tacit and unreflective manner. When a text is "learned by heart," time and energy are invested in memorizing key phrases, patterns, and rhythms. Little attention tends to be paid to exploring the applications or implications of the ideas. This emphasis on rote mastery was consistent with a deductive mindset that assumed that one reasoned from traditional assumptions to individual applications.

This epistemology was shaped by the need to schematize all areas of study in categorical terms so that they could be remembered. "The whole circle of learning" was charted by Samuel Johnson in his notebooks so that he could memorize all he needed to know (see Johnson, *Elementa* viii; also Fiering). Following the division of learning into the "tongues and arts" in *New England's First Fruits* in 1643, commencement theses at Harvard were divided into philosophical and philological theses, with the former including ethics, physics, and metaphysics, and the latter listing theses under grammar, logic, and rhetoric. In 1653 this basic dichotomy was dropped, metaphysics was replaced by mathematics, and a new category was added: *technologicae,* which was charged with mapping out disciplines upon the faculties of the mind as a microcosm of the providential order. This assumption that the workings of the mind followed the natural laws that governed the knowable world was the center point of the circle of knowledge inscribed by the curriculum. From that point, students drew axes out to other categorical propositions from which they were to deduce theses in all areas of study. Students demonstrated their mastery of these schematics by disputing theses in Latin in a syllogistic manner to show that they had acquired learned languages and scholastic commonplaces that had remained largely "unchanged from the days of Abelard" (Morison, *Harvard College in the Seventeenth Century* 1:143).

For almost a century from the setting out of the original three-year program of study in *New England's First Fruits,* the curriculum retained its basic emphasis on ancient languages and modes of reasoning. All three years included studies in ancient languages and divinity. The first year also included logic and physics, and the second year began the studies of ethics and politics, with the third year devoted to arithmetic, geometry, and astronomy. Throughout their studies, students were tested through a regular program of disputations and declamations. Disputations made syllogistic reasoning the paradigm for all learned inquiry, but they eventually evolved into modern modes of examination through the inclusion of a moderator who concluded by questioning the disputants. These examinations would eclipse the ritualized disputation itself (see Walsh 313). Since these disputations and declamations were traditionally conducted in Latin, they supported the interdisciplinary standing of learned languages. As noted in the laws of Harvard in 1646, students were officially forbidden to speak in "their mother Tongue except that in pub-lick exercises of Oratory or such like, they be called to make them in English" (Hofstadter and Smith 9). Such requirements were repeated in college laws until 1734 at Harvard and until 1774 at Yale. However, even before they lapsed, it is notable that Harvard diverged from British universities in having formal provisions for public exercises in English.

In assessing the colonial curriculum and its successors, we need to acknowl-edge that official representations of programs of study may not represent what was actually taught. Even before the requirement for speaking Latin was omit-ted from the college laws, it may not have been followed in the classroom, or even on official occasions. College laws also required that to gain admission students had to demonstrate that they could use Latin extemporaneously and translate selections from Greek. Cicero, the Bible, and occasionally Virgil are cited in such requirements through the middle of the eighteenth century. En-trance exams would have been quite demanding if students were actually ex-pected to translate and explicate unfamiliar Greek and Latin passages. However, students were allowed to enter without any Greek if they came from areas with-out grammar schools (which included most of colonial America at the time). Some laws go beyond citing a handful of texts to specify the parts that would be examined, perhaps so students could recite them by rote (see, for example, Hofstadter and Smith 117). In contrast with official requirements, private ac-counts suggest that students were often admitted with a rote knowledge of the core texts, with many students never learning to use Latin extemporaneously—as all students were officially required to do.[5] Students' notebooks suggest that Latin was less commonly used in classrooms from the beginning of the eigh-teenth century.

Within the narrow range of subjects set out in formal curricula, students read intensively and not extensively, in part because they had few books to read. Generally only juniors, seniors, masters, and faculty could borrow books from the library. Books were fragile and precious, and it was generally as-sumed that students could be told what they needed to learn. Colonial college libraries were quite limited, particularly on more modern materials, until more frequent book shipments began to arrive in the eighteenth century. Pivotal texts such as Bacon's *Advancement of Learning* and Locke's *Essay Concerning Human Understanding* could be found in college libraries, but that does not mean that a student could find them there. Bacon's treatise was in the library bequeathed by John Harvard in 1638, and Locke's *Essay* was sent to Yale in 1714, and to

Harvard by 1725. However, Locke was read mostly in an abridgement in the popular *Young Students Library*. When Samuel Johnson discovered a copy of the *Advancement of Learning* after graduating from Harvard in 1714, he thought he had found "perhaps the only copy in the country" and sweepingly concluded that "nobody knew its value." Johnson observed that there were no "books of learning to be had in those times under a 100 or 150 years old such as the first settlers of the country brought" (*Samuel Johnson* 1:7). The fact that a highly literate graduate such as Johnson thought that Bacon was his discovery alone provides a telling example of what students actually read and discussed at Harvard.

As a tutor at Yale in 1717, Johnson excitedly introduced the works of Bacon and Locke to his students. Colleges relied on recent graduates such as Johnson as tutors because there were few if any professors other than the president. Much like a graduate assistantship today, a tutorship was generally held for a short time—two and a half years on average in the latter half of the seventeenth century at Harvard, rising a century later to nine years at Harvard and three at Yale (Herbst, *Crisis* 17; Moore 41). When tutors attempted to gain seats as teaching faculty on the Harvard Corporation in the first quarter of the eighteenth century, the administration responded that they should be grouped with the servants and not the faculty (see Hofstadter and Smith 21–27).

Before discovering the new learning, Johnson had learned in the traditional way, by compiling "synopses" of "scholastic systems" into encyclopedic tables (*Samuel Johnson* 1:6). Such student compositions document the scribal modes of learning of the time. A popular textbook such as Legrand's *Entire Body of Philosophy* was valued for how neatly it summarized all that needed to be known about logic, theology, physics, metaphysics, ethics, and aesthetics. Instructors and students distilled such surveys down still further to compose compendia, as in William Brattle's "Compendium of Logick according to the Modern Phylosophers, Extracted from Legrand and others theire Systems," which circulated at Harvard for almost a century after he was tutor and fellow from 1685 to 1717. The transmission of the text may well be more notable than the outmoded ideas that it contained. Several students' notes in English remain from Brattle's lectures in the first decade of the eighteenth century. As printed textbooks became more common, the lectures were published in 1750 —over thirty years after he had quit teaching and his derivative ideas had long been superseded. The tacitly perpetuated power of these ancient doctrines is evident in how a Latin manuscript version of Brattle's lectures was passed down from one generation to the next until at least 1791, including one set of notes bearing the comment that "This compend of Logic by the Rev'd Wm. Brattle of Cambridge was <u>long</u> recited in Harvard." That sharply underlined word suggests that at least one student recognized that the text had continued to be used long after it had outlasted its usefulness.

As Brattle's "Compendium of Logick" documents, the scribal form of our first college textbooks was as important as the ideas they contained. Such painstakingly copied compendia served as a substitute for the books themselves. Within the scribal world of a colonial college, such compendia were often not transcribed from a book but from a lecturer's rendering, which was then recited by students and their successors, often for several generations, and sometimes repeatedly by the same student in the same year to ensure that the text was memorized. These textbooks were reduced to commonplaces to be repeated in declamations and disputations. Students were often required to submit their commonplace books as well as their declamations, orations, and disputations to have their compositions corrected by tutors. Originality was obviously not what teachers looked for. Commonplace books were meant to be faithful summaries of the arguments of readings, sermons, and other students' declamations. Into the eighteenth century, such commonplace themes were read before the assembled college in the chapel as part of the program of evening exercises because it was assumed that the preservation and transmission of learning entailed reciting known truths that had been reduced to a regular system. In these ways, students came to understand learning as a process of dutifully inscribing, internalizing, and performing received truths rendered into orderly hierarchies.

At commencement, students demonstrated their ability to deduce individual obligations from traditional assumptions in learned languages, and then they were ceremoniously initiated into the literate community gathered for the occasion. As translated by Cotton Mather, the pronouncement at commencement was "I admit you to the first degree in Arts, that is to say, to the privilege of responding in debate, according to the custom of the English Universities; and I deliver to you this book, with the privilege of reading in public, in such profession as you shall select, as soon as you are summoned to that duty" (Hofstadter and Smith 18). After being ceremoniously given a book to symbolize their right to read to the public, graduates were "summoned" by a congregation. Or, if they stayed on to tutor, they could earn a master's degree by revising one of their compendia into a polished system, which served as the scribal predecessors to modern graduate theses. Drawing up a "system or synopsis" was first noted as a requirement of MA candidates in *New England's First Fruits*. The Harvard laws of 1734 stated that candidates had to draw up "A Common Place, or Synopsis of any of the Arts and Sciences and be ready to defend this Thesis." As in the classroom, this research was not traditionally intended to generate new knowledge.

From the founding of Harvard through the middle of the eighteenth century, syllogistic disputations remained the principal mode of learning throughout the program of studies, which culminated with weekly disputations in the final year. The respondent in a disputation composed a response to a question set by the instructor, carefully clarifying the terms and narrowing the scope of reference and then setting out his thesis in a syllogism, usually a categorical one. One or more opponents then responded by attacking the definition of terms or the forms of reasoning, and the respondent then defended his theses with further syllogisms and critiques of his opponent's reasoning. The instructor served as moderator and concluded the disputation by correcting errors, asking questions, and providing the definitive answer. Such ritualized modes of inquiry enshrined the idea that a literate person was *aut logicus aut nullus*, "either logician or nothing." Logic functioned as "the *organon* of the soul" to provide a model for learning and the learned (Hall, "On the History" 148). According to Bartholomew Keckerman's popular guide, syllogistic disputations required a "sacred and theological spirit" to conduct the search for the truth with deference to rules that were "political and ethical" as well as logical (translated in Meriwether 238). According to Fiering, scholastic casuists had established that the conscience reasoned deductively, from major premises supplied by natural reason to individual obligations. Yet in the first decades of the eighteenth century, the syllogism ceased to serve as the model of logical reasoning and moral judgment. In 1726 Cotton Mather advised ministers that "the most valuable thing in Logic, and the very Termination of it, is the Doctrine of Syllogisms." Because he had come to value the new learning, he added that "it is notorious," however, that "all Syllogizing is only to confirm you in a Truth which you are already the owner of" (qtd. in Ota 26). Mather's predecessors would not have disagreed, but they would have seen such an assessment as a confirmation and not a repudiation of the values of syllogistic reasoning.

Within a scribal curriculum dominated by the logic of syllogistic disputations in a dead language, rhetoric was reduced to an easily memorized list of schemes and tropes that could be used to embellish commonplaces. Invention and even arrangement had been allotted to logic by Ramus, and Ramistic works on rhetoric remained predominant into the first quarter of the eighteenth century, according to the most detailed commentator on rhetorical studies in the colonial period, Warren Guthrie. According to Guthrie, the two most commonly cited stylistic rhetorics were William Dugard's *Rhetorices Elementa*, a catechism of less than fifty pages on delivery and figures of style and thought, and Thomas Farnaby's *Index Rhetoricus*, a fuller and more classically oriented but still predominantly figurist rhetoric. Both were cited as the texts in rhetoric at Harvard as late as the laws of 1723. Most accounts of seventeenth- and early eighteenth-century rhetorical study in America agree with Guthrie's characterization of it as a "period of rhetorical decadence" ("Colonial" 48). The first thesis at Harvard to treat rhetoric as the art of civic discourse rather than stylistic embellishment was in 1717, the same year that a thesis criticizing syllogistic reasoning was delivered (see Perrin 53; Guthrie, *Development of Rhetorical Theory* 31; and Potter, *Debating* 19–21).

The Ramistic compartmentalization of the curriculum enabled Calvinists to be classicists without having to confront the contradiction between their studies in the humanities and their belief in humanity's fallen nature. A practical art like rhetoric could readily be appropriated for Calvinist purposes, but rhetoric's identification with the civic concerns of moral philosophy presented a competing set of values. Such contradictions could be contained by confining the ancients to social duties and upholding the Bible as the authority on humanity's higher obligations. In the last two decades of the seventeenth century, scholastic texts were replaced by works that set out the more optimistic view of natural reason associated with Newton and Descartes. According to Fiering, the convergence of "evangelical pietism and scientific naturalism" made it increasingly difficult to maintain that all moral judgments could be deduced from biblical truths (*Moral Philosophy* 17). Calvinist introspections on one's state of grace began to connect with writings on "experimental religion" as providential naturalism became more Newtonian. These generative contradictions came to the fore in the study of moral philosophy. The rise of moral philosophy in the curriculum was pivotal to the transition from deductions from established beliefs to inductive inquiries that looked to experience as a source of knowledge. Moral philosophy had long been taught in the second or third year after the foundational first-year course in logic, but moral philosophy came to challenge divinity as the concluding emphasis of the college curriculum in the latter half of the eighteenth century.

At Harvard, the development of the new learning into a new pedagogy can be dated from the arrival in 1686 of Charles Morton, who had emigrated to escape prosecution for running the influential Dissenting academy where

Daniel Defoe was educated (see Miller, *Formation*). As professor and vice president, Morton was instrumental in introducing new modes of learning at Harvard, and he links that development with the reforms in the Dissenting academies that supported the teaching of English. Continuing the innovations that had made his academy a center of reform, Morton introduced a Newtonian approach to natural and moral philosophy by instituting a course of "experimental" studies of the physical and moral sciences much like those being instituted by Scots and Dissenters. As in his own academy, Morton taught entirely in English in the assumption that learning should be accessible to those of "either sex," even those who had not acquired "the Command of Learned Languages" (qtd. in Fiering 208). Morton was concerned with developing more accessible modes of inquiry, and he helped to advance the transition from a deductive to an inductive frame of reference that was more attentive to the inventive capacities of individual experiences, not just in the sciences but in moral and political affairs as well. To help students make sense of the new learning, he reduced his ideas to rhyming couplets in broadly accessible lectures that remained popular until superseded by Francis Hutcheson's moral philosophy.

Like Hutcheson, Morton swept away the scholastic jargon that enshrouded Aristotelian ethics to revitalize its civic emphasis on purposeful action. He treated the Aristotelian conception of "prudence" as a model of "Practical Understanding" concerned with assessing the practical means and ethical ends of purposeful action. The students' notes from Morton's classes are not detailed enough to assess how fully he developed this philosophy. He refers to generative concerns such as the laws of nature and nations, and he commented on how prices are set by supply and demand in terms that suggest he took a nascent interest in the movement of economics away from classical doctrines of domestic economy toward the science of political economy that emerged from Adam Smith's lectures on moral philosophy at Glasgow University in the middle of the century (Williams, *Commonplace Book*). The limited extant evidence suggests that Morton taught students to look to the ancients not with scholastic veneration but for their practical relevance to contemporary political, economic, and moral issues, which he apparently discussed in largely nontheological terms.

As long as moral philosophy was deduced to be more or less synonymous with natural religion, it did not threaten the curricular primacy of theology, but broader challenges arose when human nature began to be studied "experimentally" to reason inductively from individual experiences. As a student at Harvard in the first decade of the eighteenth century, Samuel Johnson was advised not to read Descartes, Boyle, Locke, and Newton "because the new philosophy" would "corrupt the pure religion of the country" (*Career* 1:6). While the corrupting secularism of classical humanists had been carefully compartmentalized within the Ramistic curriculum, Johnson's sense of the "circle of learning" was ruptured by modes of inquiry that challenged the primacy of received beliefs in the creation of knowledge (*Elementa* viii). In contrast, the new learning treated the individual as a source of knowledge, in part because differences in experience had to be accounted for in new ways as a result of social diversification. The new learning did not really evolve into a new pedagogy until students gained enough access to books to be able to survey a range of experiences. The individual reader with access to varied accounts of experience provided a standpoint that unsettled how literate people understood the logic of their experience. Ironically, the midcentury expansion of the periodical press was fueled in part by the fervent orality of the Great Awakening. The impassioned oratory of evangelists helped build an audience for periodicals because readers wanted to keep up with the news of figures such as the leading evangelist of the time, George Whitefield, who was also known as *Whitfield* because even the spelling of names had not yet been completely standardized by print.

The Great Awakening, When "The word was sharper than a two-edged sword"

In addition to providing newsworthy controversies, the Great Awakening contributed to the growth of the press by invigorating the style of print with the idioms of the popular vernacular. In this and other ways, the Great Awakening raised basic questions about how the literate represented the public. The populist revivalism of the Great Awakening is best known through sensationalist sermons such as Edwards's "Sinners in the Hands of an Angry God." The impact of such powerful rhetoric is recounted in Whitefield's journal:

> The word was sharper than a two-edged sword. The bitter cries and groans were enough to pierce the hardest heart. Some of the people were as pale as death, others were wringing their hands, others lying on the ground, others sinking into the arms of their friends, and most lifting up their eyes to heaven and crying to God for mercy. (qtd. in Cheyney 19–20)

Whitefield and his supporters traveled throughout the colonies in the 1730s and 1740s preaching the need to be reborn in the spirit and attacking "letter-learned" but unregenerate clergy (Tennent, *Danger* 474). Critics of the established clergy founded Princeton, Dartmouth, Rutgers, and Brown. To attract students, emerging colleges often distanced themselves from sectarian divisions and deemphasized theology by confining it to students' private studies. Divisive religious debates helped to build a receptive audience for the rhetoric of the American Revolution, which according to Howard Miller was seen to be "the secular fulfillment" of the renewal of the covenant in the Great Awakening (xviii). In these ways, published debates over religious differences expanded the sphere of public deliberations by making print an important force in shaping popular opinion, while at the same time undermining religious control of public education by moving sectarian differences toward the private sphere.

The Great Awakening made it difficult for clerics to maintain conformity within their congregations. Itinerant preachers, some of whom were not formally educated, toured the colonies preaching to hundreds and even thousands in tent revivals that condemned local clerics if they failed to offer support. People were sometimes encouraged to leave established congregations and found their own churches, which in some cases were led by lay preachers who were not college graduates. The idea that an uneducated itinerant could be qualified to preach the Word if he, or even she, had experienced personal regeneration undermined the educational authority of the literate, while the threat of expulsion lost its force when factions absented themselves to form their own institutions. The numbers of those growing up outside the church rose dramatically as the population increased some 600 percent between 1700 and 1760 (from 250,000 to 1,170,000). Even in New England, only about 1 in 7 were church members, and only about half that number in the middle colonies.

Such groups were persuasively addressed by George Whitefield, who became one of the most famous orators of the eighteenth century. A marginally literate farmer painstakingly recorded in his journal how he had traveled for miles along roads so packed with seekers that the dust looked like "fog rising." After hearing Whitefield preach in an open field on the damnation that awaited the unsaved, the farmer experienced a "heart wound" that "lasted almost two years" (Sloan, *Documentary History* 70–71). Whitefield spoke for an *experimental* knowledge of Jesus Christ and concluded that the intense reactions of his audiences demonstrated the power of such knowledge.[6] His sermons became legendary, not for their ideas but for their delivery. Even a skeptic such as Franklin found that he was not immune to "the extraordinary Influence of his Oratory." Franklin was surprised to see people so moved by being harangued as "*half Beasts and half Devils*," and then he found his own frugality overcome as he emptied his pockets into the collection plate (*Autobiography* 87–88). Franklin circled the audience, computed the area, and calculated that Whitefield could be heard by twenty-five thousand people.

Many better-educated "Old Light" clerics were put off by the populist rhetoric of "New Light" evangelicals. Their responses offer insights into the dynamic relations between orality and literacy during the decade when English was established as an object of formal study in higher education. Samuel Johnson observed that revival meetings "looked like a very hell upon earth; some sighing, some groaning, some screeching and wringing their hands, the minister all the while, like a fiend, tormenting them till they would come to Christ." Johnson was so repulsed by how evangelists "broke through all order and rule" that he joined those who retreated into the Anglican Church "as their only ark of safety" (*Career* 1:28). Johnson felt that the "congregational form of church government" was too open to the populist fervor created by the "extempore" style of evangelists. Johnson reacted by retreating into the "preconceived, well-composed forms" of Anglican worship as a check on oratorical excess. Johnson believed that the disturbing tendencies of rhetorical "invention" could only be constrained by having individuals recite assigned texts, as students had for centuries in the classroom (*Career* 1:11–12). Other established clerics also condemned the "*extemporaneous*" style of illiterate "enthusiasts" (Chauncy 9–12).

A direct challenge to the representative authority of literate clerics was raised by Gilbert Tennent's *The Dangers of an Unconverted Ministry*. In an often repeated phrase, Tennent criticized "letter-learned" "Pharisee-Teachers" as uninspired and thus uninspiring (474). He encouraged audiences to leave such preachers and called for new colleges to produce more eloquent ones. Tennent was praised and attacked in newspapers and pamphlets across the colonies. New Light itinerants were quick to exploit the idea that "the common people claim as good a right to judge and act for themselves in matters of religion as civil rulers or the learned clergy" (qtd. in Henretta 136). Old Light clerics defended their positions in works such as John Hancock's *The Danger of an Unqualified Ministry* and Charles Chauncy's *Enthusiasm Described and Caution'd Against* (1742). Chauncy advised readers to conclude that preachers were "enthusiasts" if they spoke in impassioned style from personal experience rather than the Bible, or if they challenged public officials or let women preach (492). Few terms had the condemnatory power of "enthusiasm" among educated audiences, because it meant that one was speaking not with learned authority but from "the delusions of a vain imagination" (Chauncy, *Enthusiasm* 500).

For their part, evangelists were less concerned with preserving conventions than with reaching out to the less educated, including slaves and Native Americans. Following in the Calvinist tradition of literate devotion, evangelical New Lights such as Samuel Davies set up reading and corresponding societies that could serve as alternatives for communities that lacked a preacher, or felt they had little to learn from the one they had (see "Reading Revivals," rptd. Sloan 222–26). These groups were forerunners to the corresponding committees who would help to unify the colonies in the cause of independence, and also to the correspondence societies that Dissenters helped working people set up in Britain (see Miller, *Formation*). Unlike many New Lights, Davies did not found an academy, but he treated his church as a school, seeking out books for those who could not afford them and writing religious poetry in an evocative style aimed at the less literate. Such efforts broadened the base of print literacy at the same time that published debates over individual rights and public authorities were beginning to make the press an important factor in popular politics.

While they were not themselves college graduates, Davies and Tennent were instrumental in founding Princeton and the other colleges that evolved out of the sixty-five Presbyterian academies that were established in the last three-quarters of the eighteenth century. Many were started by Scots or Scots-Irish immigrants, and most had strong ties with reformers in the English Dissenting academies and Scottish universities. The most influential of the Presbyterian academies was the "Log College" where Gilbert Tennent had himself been educated by his father, William Tennent, a Scots-Irish immigrant who had graduated from Edinburgh University in 1695. New Lights were far more active in setting up such academies than their opponents, with the leading exception being the academy set up by Francis Alison, who had emigrated from Scotland after graduating from Edinburgh in 1732. According to a letter by a graduate eulogizing Alison in the *Pennsylvania Journal* on April 19, 1780, Alison's academy emphasized English and had students write "themes," letters, and "abridgements of a paper from the Spectators or Guardians (the best standards of our language)" (rptd. in Sloan, *Documentary* 176). In 1738, the Old Lights attempted to exploit the fact that evangelists such as Tennent and Davies lacked degrees by requiring them of all ministers. The New Lights responded by setting up their own synod at New York and then founding their own college at Princeton in 1746.[7]

Traditionalists responded by tightening their control of established colleges and restricting "private" teaching and preaching. When Whitefield described Harvard and Yale as centers of "Darkness" in 1744, he was attacked by Harvard Professor of Divinity Edward Wigglesworth (rptd. Hofstadter and Smith 64). Wigglesworth charged Whitefield with seeking to discourage "publick spirited Persons from becoming *Benefactors*" to colleges (rptd. Hoftstadter and Smith 72, 67). Under President Clap, the Yale college laws of 1745 specifically forbade attendance at "Public or Private" services that were not "appointed by Public Authority or Approved by the President" (Hofstadter and Smith 55). Under this proscription, two evangelical students were expelled for attending "a private separate Meeting in a private House" to hear a "Lay-Exhorter"— not while at college but while at home with their families (rptd. Hofstadter and Smith 77). President Clap maintained that even a majority of a congregation had no "right" to separate from "the publick Place appointed by the General Assembly and the Parish" (77, 79). Clap's reactionary attempt to maintain the public authority of clerics was clearly a reaction both to the social divisions that are documented by Lockridge's study of Dedham, and to the resultant tendency of emerging colleges to treat sectarian divisions as a private matter.

As with traditional edicts on the use of Latin in the classroom, Clap's reactionary proscriptions document the expansion of the sort of change that they were meant to contain. The boundaries of private and public spheres were clearly shifting. These shifts are evident in Wigglesworth's response to Whitefield's charge that Harvard faculty were failing "to examine the Hearts of their Pupils." Wigglesworth rejected the idea that professors should examine individual's private beliefs, which he treated as a personal matter (rptd. in Hofstadter and Smith 69–70). Wigglesworth distanced his role as a teacher from that of preachers. While preachers and teachers had publicly examined the personal feelings of those seeking to join the church as members and preachers, Wigglesworth found it publicly expedient to disavow such intrusive examinations of individual beliefs as an invasion of privacy. Protections of private religious opinions were publicized in the laws of the colleges that became Dartmouth, Princeton, Brown, Rutgers, and Columbia. While Dartmouth was associated with Congregationalists, Princeton with Presbyterians, Rhode Island with Baptists, and Columbia with Anglicans, all were careful when constituting boards and establishing curricula to distance themselves from sectarian differences in order to identify their mission as serving the general public.

These positions provide practical political benchmarks for relating literacy and literacy studies to changing conceptions of the public and public education. Related changes are also evident in the forms of public discourse that were gaining popularity. Debates in the periodical press over the Great Awakening gave rise to hybrid genres that combined the evangelical appeals of popular eloquence with traditional features of academic discourse and emerging elements of print literacy. For example, one of the many periodicals that emerged in the decade of the Great Awakening was the *American Magazine and Historical Chronicle*, which began its first issue in 1743 with a "Dissertation on the State of Religion in North America." This "dissertation" praised Whitefield's moving "Elocution" but then concluded with an early attempt at a balanced journalistic stance: "*weak enthusiastick hot-headed Men*, according to some, *the Work of God and the Cause of Christ*, according to others" (3–4). The first issue of the magazine placed statements from various factions alongside accounts of the graduation theses that had been delivered at a Harvard commencement (printed in English as well as Latin to reach less literate readers). Popular debates and learned pronouncements were being mixed up in the periodical press with tales of foreign travels, cures for diseases, and such "Poetical Essays" as a "Riddle for Ladies" and "The Gentleman Lover." The periodical press made political debates, personal refinement, and learned inquiry accessible to the reading public—a public no longer confined to a local community or dependent on its traditional spokesmen for information.

In magazine commentaries on the populist rhetoric of the evangelicals, one can see how conceptions of public and private were being mediated in new ways. For example, in the first magazine in America, the *American Magazine; or a Monthly View of the Political State of the British Colonies*, a letter to the editor was published in 1741 on the issue of whether private individuals have the right to question public authorities:

> What is the Publick, but the collective Body of private Men, as every private Man is a Member of the Publick? And as the Whole ought to be concerned for the Preservation of every private Individual, it is the Duty of every Individual to be concern'd for the Whole, in which himself is included. (1741: 112)

While the citizen is still a gendered construct, all "Men" are assumed to have rights to speak in public, and the "Publick" is assumed to be as accessible as the periodical press is taken to be. The author's arguments are supported with long excerpts from an anonymous article from the *London Journal* and an un-named Commonwealthman commentator on the English Revolution. These authors are unnamed, as is the author, for it is assumed that one's standing in literate debates is determined by the virtues of one's argument and not by one's standing in the community. Interestingly, the letter is cast in the form of a response to a disputed question: "Whether private Persons have a Right to inquire into the Nature of Government, and in the Conduct of Governors?" Imitating the genre of a forensic debate, the author directly addresses his opponents as if they were facing each other in an academic forum (109). In the print version of this traditional oral form, correspondents who served as representative citizens model the virtues of reasoned debate for those with less access to higher education.

The adoption of the genre of an academic disputation is notable because the genre was about to be transformed by the epistemological and institutional changes that can be identified with the rise of the periodical press. As I will discuss in the next section, the transition from syllogistic to forensic disputations turned on an expanding engagement in the popular debates that supported the introduction of formal English studies. The Great Awakening challenged the authority of clerics by suggesting that anyone, even an uneducated outsider, was qualified to speak if he, or even she, had personally experienced regeneration. Authoritarian clerics such as Clap fought a rearguard action to maintain the public authority of educated clerics by forming local associations against itinerant evangelicals' encroachments—the "County Watchdogs" as they were known in Clap's case (see Tucker). However, the social contract between clerics and congregations was becoming understood in less sacred and more secular terms. As communities became more fluid and diversified, they came to view their ministers as contractual employees and began to fire them much more frequently (see Henretta 210). With the reinterpretation of the social contract in economic terms, even the leading descendant of the great New England divines, Jonathan Edwards, could be dismissed by his congregation for trying to reintroduce the custom of having people bare their souls in public to become members. By the middle of the eighteenth century, conflicts over such traditional assumptions had been fueled by social diversification in ways that shattered the "Christian corporatism" that had characterized such communities as Dedham (Lockridge 172). According to Bailyn, increased mobility and intensifying economic pressures converged to weaken the patriarchal structure of the extended family and strengthen the role of education as a means to maintain shared values (*Education* 24–25). These trends shaped the field of cultural production in which English was constituted as an object of formal study.

The Introduction of Formal English Studies

While the Great Awakening helped expand access to print literacy by building an audience for the periodical press, the greatest impact of the evangelical New Lights, according to Harvey Graff, was "to renew the power of speech," "freeing it from conventions and returning public speaking to everyday rhetoric" (*Legacies* 253). The deductive form and didactic purposes of New England pulpit oratory had been consistent with the emphasis on syllogistic reasoning in the curriculum, but from the 1740s on, graduates faced increasingly diverse audiences. After serving as the model for learned discourse for centuries, syllogistic disputations began to be replaced by forensic debates in the middle of the eighteenth century. Syllogistic disputations disappeared from most college curricula and commencement exercises before the last decades of the century. While syllogistic reasoning had reinforced the traditional emphasis on Latin and logic, forensic debates provided students with opportunities to speak to the popular controversies of the time. The Harvard Laws of 1723 required students to dispute twice weekly in their first three years and once weekly in their final year. As with other requirements, these statutes may not be accurate records of what actually went on, for contemporary accounts note that students were not composing disputations. In the 1720s President Wadsworth frequently complained in his diary that he had to fine students for failing to conduct disputations, and in 1732 he noted that only two disputations had been held all year. According to Potter, this resistance prompted colleges to deemphasize syllogistic disputations (*Debating* 25). At midcentury several colleges began to reduce requirements of syllogistic disputations and introduce forensic debates in both classroom and graduation exercises. Forensics became a common requirement in most college laws, while syllogistic disputations disappeared from the college laws at King's in 1763, from Princeton in 1764, from William and Mary in 1782, and from Rhode Island in 1783. By the last quarter of the century, syllogistic disputations had become little more than perfunctory exercises at most commencements. They disappeared altogether from such programs at King's in 1770, at Princeton in 1774, at Philadelphia in 1775, at Yale in 1788, at Harvard in 1792, and at Dartmouth in 1798 (Potter, *Debating* 27–29).

While syllogistic disputations treated received beliefs as categorical assumptions, forensic debates provided students with opportunities to speak in less academic registers that included ethical and pathetic as well as logical appeals. Forensic speeches were typically two to three pages and almost always in English, and they were not confined to Scholastic commonplaces or even academic themes. While syllogistic disputations had been seen as the epitome of learned discourse, forensic disputations were identified with popular argumentation, as in the Yale Laws of 1766, which praised forensics for being "better adapted to the common Use and Practice of Mankind, in the Conduct of Publick Affairs" (Clap, *Annals* 82). Isaac Watts was widely read to teach forensics, which he modeled on the "Sorts of Disputations in publick Assemblies or Courts of Justice, . . . especially in civil matters" (*Improvement* 173). Watts was concerned with popular argumentation because he wanted to teach students to speak against the restrictions imposed on Dissenters such as himself (Miller, *Formation*). This concern for popular politics was shared by many colonial students in the decades between the Great Awakening and the Revolution, as documented by the orations they composed to celebrate their graduation into public life. The issue of American independence was debated at the first commencement at Rhode Island in 1769, and by the time war broke out, public commencements were popularizing a litany of republican themes drawn from civic humanist and natural rights traditions, including the social contract, natural rights, civic duties, and the corruption of public virtue by private luxuries.[8]

The transition from syllogistic disputations to more broadly applicable forms of debate infused rhetoric with new significance. The first commencement thesis on rhetoric at Harvard to stress public debate was in 1718, and from 1720 theses on rhetoric began to reclaim the attention to invention and arrangement that had been lost under Ramus (Ota 117). From the second quarter of the century, civic humanist works such as Cicero's *De Oratore* and Quintilian's *Institutes* began to be more widely cited in accounts of studies and library loan records. The classical emphasis on public oratory also gained currency with the popularity of neo-Ciceronian works such as Lamy's *The Art of Speaking* and especially John Ward's *System of Oratory*.[9] In a Ciceronian fashion, Ward and Lamy examined all five arts of rhetoric and subordinated style to purpose as the controlling element in composition. Americans were also influenced by the sources that established English composition, rhetoric, and literature in Scottish and Dissenting curricula. Henry Home's *Elements of Criti-*

cism was shipped to Harvard when it was published in 1762, and at Princeton in 1768 John Witherspoon instituted an approach to rhetoric and belles lettres that was less belletristic and more civic than Blair's (see my "Blair, Witherspoon, and the Rhetoric of Civic Humanism").

As syllogistic disputations were being replaced by forensic debates, logic and ancient languages were being reduced to introductory subjects in the first year, with very few texts in Latin adopted in other areas of the curriculum after the middle of the century, as detailed in Dexter's *Documentary History of Yale*. Syllogistic reasoning had been a mainstay of the curriculum when logic was studied throughout the curriculum, but President Stiles of Yale reported that when he visited Harvard, logic was only being taught for less than an hour every other week in the final term of the first year (Ota 73). The era when logic "triumphed over the arts" had ended according to Clarke's *Letters to a Student in the University of Cambridge*, and "syllogisms seem now to be passing into oblivion" (80, 85). Syllogistic disputations had provided students with opportunities to display a formulaic mastery of Latin, but studies of classical languages were also receding. Traditional proscriptions against using English were not kept on the books after 1734 even at Harvard, and emerging colleges generally adopted English as the language of instruction. The broad-based decline of classical languages is evident in Teaford's examination of the collapse of the grammar school tradition in Massachusetts. Beginning in 1647 Massachusetts had required all towns of over one hundred families to fund a grammar school, and up to 1718 fines had been raised to keep them higher than the costs of a school. After the middle of century, the government ignored the rising numbers of towns that failed to fund grammar schools, and Teaford's detailed research shows that such failures were not due to poverty, isolation, or a lack of teachers but to a change in attitudes to classical education (297–98). Such changes led to public calls to repeal the law because "so many Latin grammar schools" prevented students from attaining "such a degree of English learning as is necessary to retain the freedom of the state" (qtd. in Teaford 35). Teaford contrasts the declining support for classical languages with the rising numbers of "writing schools," which taught many of the same subjects to the same aged students, but with a practical emphasis on learning to write (7–14).

Inside the academy, interest in English studies increased along with the trends that I have noted: a transition from syllogistic to forensic disputations, a resurgence of a civic perspective on rhetoric, the intensifying political debates of the time, and the declining emphasis on Latin and logic. To improve their writing and speaking skills, students began forming literary clubs, with one of the first being the "Telltale" or "Spy Club" established at Harvard in 1721. Like many of the societies that were being founded throughout the British provinces, the Telltale was modeled on the Spectator Club. The essays of the *Spectator* were imitated, and the students' essays were bound together and circulated as "Criticisms on the Conversation and Behaviour of Scholars to promote right Reasoning & good Manners." Student essays addressed the virtues of "well regulated" conversation and polite refinement and criticized classroom disputations as "Packs of Profound Nonsense" ("Telltale"; see Lane). Student interest in the belletristic essays of the *Spectator* and related works on taste such as *The Gentleman Instructed* is evident in commonplace books such as those of Jonathan Belcher from 1727 and John Winthrop's from 1728. Literary societies provided students with opportunities to discuss such interests and receive criticisms from their peers on their compositions at the same time that forensic disputations and orations were increasing the attention to English in the classroom. As I will discuss in the next two chapters, student literary societies were instrumental in shaping the first century of the development of college English studies.

Because colonial colleges tended to be governed by lay administrators and depended on the support of their local communities, popular attitudes to literacy had a greater influence than in richly endowed universities such as Oxford and Cambridge. This responsiveness to social change helps explain why formal instruction in English was introduced in the British cultural provinces a century earlier than at the centers of English education. Such studies were being introduced at the same time that professorships dedicated to teaching English composition and rhetoric were being founded in Irish, Scottish, and English Dissenting institutions of higher education. In 1754 a Harvard Board of Overseers committee was set up to "project some method to promote oratory." The following year the committee recommended to the corporation that the president lecture on oratory to all students and that the program of declamations at the Overseers' semiannual visitations be replaced with dialogues in English and Latin and disputations "in the forensic manner, without being confined to syllogisms" (qtd. Josiah Quincy 2: 124, 127). And the year after that, the Overseers praised the English exercises they had observed on their visitation and recommended that they be continued to encourage "Eloquence and oratorical attainment." In 1766 the Overseers recommended that a special tutor be established to teach all students "Elocution, Composition in English, Rhetoric, and other parts of the Belles Lettres" (Quincy 2:135).[10]

A public donor gave funds for a professorship in rhetoric in 1771, but Harvard did not actually establish the professorship until thirty-three years later when a descendant of the donor tried to sue to recover the funds. The Boylston Professor of Rhetoric and Oratory was founded in 1804 and first staffed by Senator John Quincy Adams in 1806. However, the corporation made the teaching of English part of the responsibilities of the Professor of Oriental Languages in 1786. To make up for the declining interest in Syriac, Chaldiaic, Samaritan, and Hebrew, the professor was required to teach a freshmen English grammar course and a sophomore composition course with weekly assignments, and also to respond to the biweekly compositions submitted by upper-class students. This reform would not be the last time that composition would be assigned to professors whose classes had failed to attract students with more contemporary interests.

While at Harvard public representatives took the initiative, at Yale it was the students themselves who pushed for the teaching of English. President Clap introduced weekly forensic disputations in the 1750s, but he was forced to resign in 1766 after the students left the college in mass to protest his authoritarianism. Instruction in English apparently began on an informal basis the very next year (Brooks Kelley 78–80). A dozen students took it upon themselves to buy their tutor a copy of Ward's *Lectures on Oratory* and get him to preside over weekly meetings in which they critiqued each others' compositions (Ota 91). Students also began to complain more strongly about the stifling emphasis on dead languages and Scholastic metaphysics. The most notable critic was John Trumbull, who graduated in 1767, became a tutor, and anonymously published *The Progress of Dulness* ridiculing colleges for maintaining an outmoded curriculum that excluded contemporary life and letters (see Kingsley 1:98). In 1776 a group of seniors went to the corporation to request permission to have one of the tutors, Timothy Dwight, teach them a course in "Rhetorick, History, and the Belles Lettres," which the corporation agreed to as long as students got a note from their parents (see Clark). A recent Yale historian has haughtily responded to this historic transition by noting that the curriculum had "contained what the Western world had long felt an educated man should know. And the criticism tended to be of the strain that has produced cries for more 'practical' or 'relevant' college courses throughout American history" (Kelley 82–83). This stance would come to distinguish the neoclassical perspective of elite institutions such as Yale and Harvard from the more broadly based approach to literacy studies that would be adopted by more accessible institutions of public education.

Then as now, more broadly based colleges could not afford to dismiss changing perceptions of what "an educated man should know" because they did not have alumni and other donors among the traditional elite and had to attract broader classes of students to survive. As a result, several newly established colleges made the transition from syllogistic to forensic disputations before Harvard or Yale. Also, English was formally taught in several of these colleges before Yale or Harvard. The first professorship of English in America was founded at the establishment of the College of Philadelphia in 1755. As I will discuss in the next chapter, much of the time of this professorship was dedicated to teaching basic writing and reading in the English school and women's academy that were associated with the College. Overworked and underpaid, like many writing teachers today, none of the professors of English at Philadelphia published their lectures, and few records of their classes remain. The second professorship to include the teaching of English was founded at King's College when it was reorganized as Columbia College in 1784, but before that, the first president of King's, Samuel Johnson, had taught a freshman rhetoric course in English. Johnson established English as the language of instruction and required regular forensic disputations and English compositions. The first college text on the teaching of English came out of the course in "Composition and Criticism" that John Witherspoon taught at Princeton, where he served as president after immigrating in 1768. These developments will be examined in more detail when I look beyond the first New England colleges in the next chapter.

Conclusion: From Public Seminaries to Private Corporations

From their first incorporation with boards that included lay representatives, colonial colleges were understood to be public seminaries charged with perpetuating "Learning and Godlinesse" (*First Fruits* 6). Into the eighteenth century, the learned preached the Word in towns where they were often the only college graduates. They were prepared for such duties by a curriculum that was as closed as the communities they would lead. Students demonstrated their mastery of ancient languages and deductive reasoning in syllogistic disputations that served as a model for the didactic sermons that they would preach to the converted. While New England was more literate than England, most households included but a couple of sacred texts used for private devotion. Books generally held authority in daily life only in the hands of a clergyman, and that authority was reinforced by his position in the community and his contacts beyond it. In such communities, as in the classroom, individuals learned not from books but from people, with what was learned inseparable from who it was learned from. Knowledge was transmitted through a hierarchical diffusion pattern much as it was in colleges through oral recitations and scribal compendia. In this scribal information economy, learning was a process of reasoning deductively from established beliefs to individual obligations, and the learned controlled a public sphere that was centered in the services over which they presided, with membership decided by individuals' ability to account for their personal experiences in ways that fit received assumptions about how it felt to be one of the elect.

As colonial society expanded and diversified in the late seventeenth century, religious uniformity could not be maintained, even with compromises that expanded church membership to those who would not review their individual religious experiences in public. In the 1730s and 40s, the expanding numbers of the unchurched prompted a Great Awakening of populist evangelism. Itinerant preachers challenged the public authority of the educated by propagating doctrines of individual rights and establishing institutions that gave individuals choices in how they worshipped and how they learned. Evangelists helped expand access to literacy by establishing schools and colleges, fostering debates that expanded the reading public, and encouraging individuals to see themselves as having the authority to interpret sacred texts. The number of colleges tripled within a quarter century, and new colleges had to promote a nonsectarian sense of their public mission to attract funds and students. Intense public criticism arose when Anglicans established a college in New York that would be open to all, but headed by an Anglican. The leading critic, William Livingston, argued in newspaper articles and pamphlets that "a public academy is, or ought to be a mere civil institution, and cannot with any tolerable propriety be monopolized by any religious sect" (*Independent Reflector* March 29, 1753; rptd. in Hofstadter and Smith 1:101). These debates promoted the doctrines of freedom of opinion and expression that had been espoused during the Great Awakening, leaving Anglican presidents such as Johnson to defend their position by arguing that divisive religious doctrines would be treated as private matters within colleges (Hofstadter and Smith 110).

In response to shifts in the boundaries between private and public life, President Clap attempted to position Yale as a private religious corporation that should be kept free of state governance. Students responded to his authoritarian encroachments on their individual rights by appealing to the government to intervene. Clap defended his authority by publishing *The Religious Constitution of Colleges* (1754) and later pamphlets that rewrote the history of Yale to date its founding from a donation of books by ten clergy. He changed the date of that donation from his earlier manuscript histories so that it preceded the government's chartering of the college in 1701 (Tucker, *Puritan* 35–36). Drawing on the protections for individual and property rights in English Common Law, Clap argued that while anyone had a right to establish a college, students who chose to come to an established college were obliged to accept its doctrines. As the "Property" of its founders, Yale was set out as a private domain free from public authority (rptd. Hofstadter and Smith 115). Clap advanced the lines of argument that would be followed to overturn the appropriation of the colleges by republican legislatures after the Revolution.[11] As Clap had set out, elite educational institutions followed religion in moving into the private domain in reaction to the increasing heterogeneity of the public. While Clap held that the religious heterodoxy of the colony made the college an authority unto itself (115), his critics responded that there was "*no sense*, in calling the College a Society of Ministers" because it had been vested with "*civil*" and not "*ministerial*" authority (rptd. Hofstadter and Smith 127–28).

The pamphlet war that Clap participated in over whether Yale was a private corporation or a public institution first set out the position that elite colleges would come to assume in the American public sphere. This position was established as a point of law with the famous Dartmouth Supreme Court case in 1819, which overturned the imposition of state control by the republican governor and legislature of New Hampshire as an usurpation of "corporate privileges" (rptd. Crane 67). The judgment overruled republican efforts to control what the governor had characterized as "literary establishments." The Supreme Court looked instead to the logic of a market economy to make sense of the increasing diversification of the public sphere. In a marked departure from established conceptions of colleges as public seminaries, elite institutions were able to secure a privileged position as private enterprises that should be kept free of state control (rptd. Crane 65). Invoking free market economics to demarcate private corporations dedicated to "acquisitions to literature," Chief Justice Marshall's decision positioned the state in a regulative relationship to the higher education market that is distinctly American, quite different as it is from the integrated state educational systems in most other countries (rptd. Crane 74).[12] The differing positions and purposes of private and public colleges have generally been ignored by disciplinary specialists, but that distinction would come to structure literacy studies as a field of cultural production within higher education. As I will explore in successive chapters, studies of literature and the teaching of composition serve distinct purposes in differing classes of institutions, and the elaboration of those distinctions is integral to the expansion and stratification of the literate public. Attending to such structural developments is vital to understanding how literacy studies have been and are being shaped by broader changes in literacy and the literate, including access to higher education, especially to those colleges traditionally reserved for the upper classes.

2

Republican Rhetoric

AMERICA remain'd, during a long Period, in the thickest Darkness of *Ignorance* and *Barbarism*, till Christianity, at the Introduction of the *Europeans*, enlightened her *Hemisphere* . . . At length, several Gentlemen residing in and near the Province of *New Jersey*, . . . having observ'd the vast Increase of those Colonies, with the Rudeness, and Ignorance of their Inhabitants, for want of the necessary means of Improvement, first projected the Scheme of a Collegiate *Education* in that Province.

Tennent and Davies in 1752, *A General Account of the Rise and State of the College Lately Established in the Province of New Jersey*, 92.

Among the Foreigners, who were as numerous as the English, many Distinctions were forming upon their different Customs, Languages and Extractions, which, by creating separate Interests, might in the Issue prove fatal to the Government. They wisely judg'd, therefore, that Nothing cou'd so much contribute to make such a Mixture of People coalesce and unite in one common Interest, as the common Education of all the Youth at the same public Schools under the Eye of the civil Authority.

William Smith in 1753, *A General Idea of the College of Mirania*, 10.

Thus instructed, youth will come out of this school fitted for learning any business, calling, or profession, except such wherein languages are required; and though unacquainted with any ancient or foreign tongue, they will be masters of their own, which is of more immediate and general use, and withal will have attained many other valuable accomplishments . . . [that] may qualify them to pass through and execute the several offices of civil life with advantage and reputation to themselves and country.

Franklin in 1779, *Sketch of an English School*, 7:252

THESE PASSAGES SET OUT
the purposes that would shape the teaching of English in the colleges that were founded at Princeton by Tennent and Davies and at Philadelphia by

Smith and Franklin. As New Light Presbyterians, Tennent and Davies assumed that a college would advance "enlightened" religion. As an unplaced minister and uneducated printer, Smith and Franklin justified education in more secular terms. Even though Smith had himself recently arrived from Scotland, he appealed to anxieties about "Foreigners" by arguing that education would instill a common culture. Smith published his vision of the "College of Mirania" in an unsuccessful effort to secure a job in the new college in New York, but Franklin was so impressed that he persuaded Smith to become the first provost of the College of Philadelphia at its founding in 1755. The College of Philadelphia offered, according to Rudolph, "the first systematic course in America not deriving from the medieval tradition nor intended to serve a religious purpose" (32).[1] Franklin's contribution to these reforms is especially notable because he became the model for the sort of enterprising individual who capitalized on the potentials of the periodical press. Printers such as Franklin were coming to rival ministers as arbiters of public opinion, according to Bailyn (*Education* 93). The expansion of print shaped the origins of college English studies, and from their origins they have been shaped by broader efforts to instill traditional values in the rising generation.

The first professorship dedicated to the teaching of English was established at the College of Philadelphia in 1755, and the first textbook on rhetoric and belles lettres by an American professor was published from the course that John Witherspoon began teaching in 1768 at the College of New Jersey in Princeton. To attract students and contributors, such colleges also introduced courses in experimental science, commerce, government, and studies such as surveying that were useful to students not interested in becoming clergymen. The new colleges in Philadelphia and New York set out to appeal to what Longaker has characterized as the "emergent and established bourgeoisie," while the college in Princeton was oriented to the "commercial interests" of middle-class farmers (139, 178). These class interests were intertwined with religious affiliations. While the College of New Jersey had ties with New Light Presbyterians, it received no regular church or state funding. While King's College was built on land granted by the Anglican Church, Anglicans were a minority in New York, and the college had to distance itself from religious divisions to position itself as a public institution. Like those in New York and Princeton, the college in Philadelphia mediated the religious diversity of the middle colonies by treating sectarian doctrines as private matters best left to students and their parents. Of the three colleges, the College, Academy, and

Charitable School of Philadelphia was the most secular, and the most broadly based. It included charity schools for boys and girls, a "mechanics" academy, and in 1787 a Young Ladies Academy opened to offer the first secondary English courses for women.

The colleges that were founded in the middle of the eighteenth century were responsive to the rising numbers of students who were not interested in following the career path of previous college graduates. Only 41 percent of the graduates of Yale continued to enter the clergy from 1745 to 1771, and Yale was a staunch defender of orthodoxy (Moore 45). According to President Ezra Stiles, it was "the only American College in the Hands of Ecclesiastics" (*Literary Diary*; rptd. Hofstadter and Smith 166). At the College of Philadelphia, even before the Revolution, fewer graduates joined the ministry than the law (Walsh 247). Emerging colleges educated different sorts of students than Harvard or Yale. Ninety percent of King's College students were first-generation college students (Humphrey 191, 225–26). Fewer than 10 percent of the graduates of King's became ministers before the Revolution, with twice that going into law, and four times as many entering trade and manufacturing. Almost half of Princeton students were entering the clergy at midcentury, but from the time Witherspoon became president in 1768 until his death in 1794, only a quarter did so (McLachlan, *Princetonians: 1748–1768* xxi–ii; Maclean 357, 402–03; Collins 2:222).[2] As Brown discusses in *Knowledge Is Power*, clergymen were losing their "virtual monopoly on public address" as other voices came to be "respected as authoritative" (102). Lawyers tended to adopt a popular oratorical style that combined neoclassical resonances with the "evangelical style that George Whitefield had popularized throughout the colonies during their youth" (Brown 101). Composition courses and the transition from syllogistic to forensic disputations helped lawyers form such a style, and according to one lawyer of the time, courses in moral philosophy provided an "excellent foundation to begin the study of law upon" (qtd. in Humphrey 167).

Courses in rhetoric and moral philosophy played pivotal roles in the curriculum in each of the colleges at Philadelphia, New York, and Princeton. Moral philosophy courses enabled emerging colleges to rise above sectarian divisions and focus on "forming a Succession of sober, virtuous, industrious Citizens and checking the Course of growing Luxury" (Smith, *Mirania* 9). The civic virtues of sobriety and industry were imbedded in a republican ideology that drew upon Scottish moral philosophers such as Francis Hutcheson and

David Fordyce. Such sources had a formative impact on the generation of Jefferson, Madison, and Hamilton, each of whom took courses in rhetoric and moral philosophy that were taught from Scottish texts by Scottish college graduates. These sources shaped the Declaration of Independence and the U.S. Constitution, as discussed in Garry Wills's *Inventing America* and *Explaining America*. These efforts to articulate and institute a unified American identity were but the most noted examples of the representative forms of self-governance that were established in the oratorical literature of this period. The next chapter will examine antebellum efforts to create a national literature and educational system, while this chapter focuses on how the periodical press expanded the reading public into a national audience for deliberations on self-improvement and self-governance. Readers who had limited access to education were introduced to literate usage and taste by the grammars, rhetorics, elocutionary manuals, and literary anthologies that appeared in increasing numbers at the end of the eighteenth century. Such texts provided aspiring readers with models of polite self-restraint that helped to strengthen the representative institutions of the new republic.

In this chapter, we will look past New England to the half dozen colleges that were founded in the middle colonies in the latter half of the eighteenth century. As discussed in the last chapter, Latin ceased to be the means of instruction in the first half of the eighteenth century as literacy studies shifted from a deductive framework to develop a more expansive engagement with changes in literacy and the literate. Literature shifted from a religious to an oratorical register as magazines and newspapers began to break up the scribal information economy and involve readers of more varied backgrounds in debates over political self-governance. Related curricular trends gave rise to the first professorships dedicated to teaching English, and those courses contributed to the collaborative learning opportunities that students created in their own literary and debating societies. These literary societies were but one example of how the diversification of civil society reshaped the field of cultural production within which the first professors of English were established. The political standpoint of these courses was shaped by closely related courses in moral philosophy. My discussion of these courses will follow through on the lines of analysis I introduced in the last chapter. These courses included the surveys of ethics, politics, and economics that shaped the oratorical literature of the Revolutionary period. These courses appealed to students not intent on joining the clergy, especially the rising numbers who would go into the law.

While the teaching of English was shaped by efforts to preserve traditional values in a frontier environment, those efforts expanded to meet the need to assimilate the rising numbers of non-English immigrants. That educational challenge was compounded by the fact that the population of the American colonies more than doubled every twenty-five years throughout the eighteenth century. As a result of rising rates of immigration, over half of the population south of New England was not of English descent by the Revolution.[3] The largest white immigrant group was the Scots-Irish, who had a hyphenated identity because they had migrated not once but twice. Scots and Scots-Irish immigrants tended to be poor, but between 65 and 75 percent were literate, according to Lockridge (*Literacy in Colonial New England* 82). Scots had strong cultural ties with their former proprietary colony in New Jersey, and even stronger economic ties to Maryland and Virginia through the tobacco trade with Glasgow. In the middle colonies, the public was represented as "generally of the middling sort," according to the *Pennsylvania Journal* of 1756, which characterized Pennsylvania as comprised mostly of "industrious farmers, artificers or men in trade; they enjoy and are fond of freedom, and the *meanest among them* thinks he has a right to civility from the greatest" (qtd. in Hofstadter 131). According to Henretta, "a political system based on compromise and accommodation gradually (and grudgingly) emerged in this area during the course of the eighteenth century, giving institutional legitimacy and an encompassing constitutional form to its cultural diversity" (115).

Educational institutions were shaped by these accommodations. In 1763 funds were raised for the new colleges at Philadelphia and New York by arguing that "so mixed a multitude" would be a problem if "left destitute of the necessary means of instruction, differing in language and manners[,] unenlightened by religion, uncemented by a common education, strangers to the humane arts, and to the just use of rational liberty" (qtd. in Herbst, *Crisis* 63). This "common education" would be provided by colleges that promised that "public teaching" would exclude "sectarian differences of opinion" in order to leave students to study religion "in a personal" way (rptd. Hofstadter and Smith 136). In this way, as Blair noted in his *Account of the College*, emerging colleges set themselves up as public bastions of "liberty and free enquiry" that respected students' rights to "private judgment" (rptd. Hofstadter and Smith 28). On these and other points, the colleges that were founded in the middle colonies were shaped by the social diversity of the region. Franklin and Smith both stressed that colleges would help assimilate the "vast numbers of Foreigners [who] are yearly imported among us, totally ignorant of our Laws, Customs and Language." Franklin proposed an academy to prepare the better sort to lead, and the "poorer Sort" to teach (rptd. Montgomery 120). Religious differences in Philadelphia had already prompted the creation of a system of free elementary schools. The College of Philadelphia would also be steadfastly nondenominational, with students left to attend whatever churches their families chose (*Minutes of the Trustees of the College* 1:134).

The College of Philadelphia was created by a group of merchants, doctors, and lawyers led by Franklin. Franklin wanted to establish an English school, but he found that the "learned languages" had to be included to get funds from "persons of wealth and learning" (*Observations* 87). When instruction began in 1751, Franklin promoted his utilitarian model of English studies by publishing his *Idea of an English School.* The structure of the school shows that he had been forced to compromise on his model of "English education" by the trustees, at least nine of whom were educated in English universities (Turner 108). The English teacher was to teach twice the students for half the pay of the Latin teacher, who would head the whole school (*Minutes of the Trustees of the College* 1:4–5). Both wings of the school were to stress English and history, geography, rhetoric, and science, but the Latin school became the preparatory division of the college upon its chartering in 1755. The subordinate status of the English school is important because its head was "Professor of English Tongue and Oratory" and has been recognized as "our first college professor of English" (Parker 7).

Franklin's model of an "English education" gave unprecedented emphasis to oratorical literature and composition as part of a broad program of study in "liberal Arts and Science," including modern languages, history, and "Natural and Mechanick Philosophy" (*Minutes of the Trustees of the College* 1:1). According to Franklin's "Proposals," students would learn "the *clear* and the *concise*" style by "Writing Letters to each other, making Abstracts of what they read; or writing Stories lately read, in their own Expressions. All to be revised and corrected by the Tutor, who should give his Reasons, explain the Tone and Import of Words, & C." Franklin redefined the "classicks" of the literate culture to include political and literary essayists—"*Tillotson, Addison, Pope, Algernon, Sidney, Cato's* Letters" (497). The only subject given emphasis comparable to that placed on oratorical literature was history, which would be taught to demonstrate "the wonderful Effects of ORATORY." History courses were to teach how "the Pen and the Press" had made the impact of "Modern Political Oratory" "more extensive" and "more lasting" (498). In addition to tracing out the progress of literacy, historical studies would also examine the "Rise of Manufactures, Progress of Trade," and the development of "*Commerce,*" while natural history would document the practical values of trade and agriculture (500). This pragmatic educational philosophy became a strong strain in American education and continued through Horace Mann's efforts to establish a public school system, and through those efforts to the pragmatism of John Dewey. Franklin's synthesis of the mechanical and liberal arts was a product of his own career as a self-educated printer who gained note by writing practical self-instruction works. For generations of educators, and the self-educated, Franklin came to personify "the republican man of letters, the citizen of print" (Warner 77).

Franklin thought he had found someone to implement his vision of the "classicks" of English literature when he persuaded Smith to come teach at Philadelphia in 1754, but Franklin came to regret his choice as soon as the college was chartered. Smith and Franklin adopted opposing political stances, with Smith siding with the Penn family proprietors and Franklin a leading figure in the elected assembly, which often identified itself as "the friends of the people" (qtd. in Griffin xii). Governor John Penn served as president of the trustees of the college, and the Penns rewarded Smith and the college for supporting them. When Smith criticized the assembly in his *American Magazine*, he was for a short time sent to prison, where his students dutifully continued to attend his lectures (*Minutes of the Trustees of the College* 1:91). Franklin several times took to print to attack Smith and other "Latinists" among the trustees for failing to implement his vision of a modern program of study that would provide a practical alternative to the classical curriculum. The conflict between Franklin and the trustees has been examined in Longaker's *Rhetoric and the Republic,* which identifies Franklin's pragmatism with the interests of aspiring merchants, while the trustees were responsive to the more established classes' interest in learning as a mark of gentility (141). These conflicting class affiliations have shaped English studies from the establishment of the first professorship of English at the College of Philadelphia, which was chartered to teach "all the liberal Arts and Sciences, the ancient Languages, and *English* Tongue" (*Charters* 12).

The three-year curriculum that Smith implemented was shaped by the reforms that had been implemented at Smith's alma mater, Marischal College, Aberdeen. According to Smith's "Account of the College, Academy, and Charitable School," lectures on "Classical and Rhetoric Studies" were included in all three years of study, along with English translations, orations, and compositions that included one of the fullest programs of public exercises of any colonial college. First-year students were also lectured on mathematics, metaphysics, and logic. Belletristic essays from journals such as the *Spectator* were recommended "for the improvement of style and knowledge of life" (1:58–59). The second year continued lectures on rhetoric, logic, and mathematics, as well as navigation and surveying. Lectures on natural and moral philosophy were begun in the second year and continued through the last year, and these studies provided the subject material for a writing-across-the-curriculum course. Required texts included works on moral philosophy by Fordyce and Hutcheson, and the *Preceptor* edition of William Duncan's *Elements of Logic*. In courses on rhetoric, students read the *Preceptor* along with Cicero, Demosthenes, and Quintilian.[4] The influence of the reforms at Aberdeen are evident in the experimental approach to natural philosophy. Smith adopted the works of William Duncan and other proponents of what Howell has characterized as the "new logic," and he expanded moral philosophy along Scottish lines to discuss natural rights, modern history, and contemporary theories of politics and economics.

Perhaps the most innovative aspect of the College of Philadelphia is that it was intended to be a comprehensive institution that served not only the well-to-do but also working people and women. Then as now, the study that spanned those varied purposes and populations was English. The first professorship of English in America was created in 1755 as a "Professor of the English Tongue and of Oratory." It was held by Ebenezer Kinnersley. Kinnersley was supposed to supervise the English school, teach a weekly class on oratory, and oversee all the college exercises in oratory and composition. While no lectures from Kinnersley's English courses remain, notes from his experimental lectures on electricity have been preserved. Kinnersley had an international reputation as a researcher on electricity. Kant called him the "modern Prometheus," and Smith claimed his work had been plagiarized by Franklin (qtd. in Montgomery 80, 401). While Smith maintained that no "institution in the world can boast a better education in *oratory*," Kinnersley did not actually receive adequate support to teach basic writing and reading in the English school, or to work with all the college's students on their compositions (*Gentlemen's Magazine*, February 1, 1757).[5] Kinnersley's ill health led to a reliance on tutors, with the most notable being James Wilson, who had emigrated from Scotland in 1765.[6] William Riley Parker has cited Wilson as offering the first college lectures on English literature in America.

Kinnersley's courses seemed to have served the sort of service function of modern composition courses, while Smith's "Classical and Rhetoric Studies" was integrally involved with his courses in natural and moral philosophy.[7] Students took Smith's rhetoric class in their second year before they began the "Composition" studies, which continued through the third and final year of the curriculum. Smith devoted the first half of his rhetoric course to surveying classical theories of invention, arrangement, delivery, and style, and in the latter half he summarized Longinus's *On the Sublime*. Smith assumed that the ancients provided the best models for English composition, but Smith's lecture notes suggest that he largely taught the classics in translation. Smith's approach to the closely related studies of moral and natural philosophy was more innovative.[8] Like the Newtonians he had studied with at Aberdeen, Smith praised the virtues of inductive reasoning from experimental inquiries. However, he did not confine instruction to speculating about the natural order in the manner of traditional courses in physics. His notes recount how students broke up into groups to work with the college's experimental apparatus (40). Such hands-on experience was exceptionally rare even in colleges that publicized their commitment to scientific studies by advertising their purchases of experimental equipment. Such equipment too often remained museum pieces to be displayed, untouched by students in the classroom. Experimental studies of science were fundamental to the reforms implemented at the College of Philadelphia, particularly the establishment of the first American medical school in 1765.

Curricular reforms and class affiliations much like those at Philadelphia led to the establishment of the second professorship of rhetoric in America in 1784 at King's College (which later became Columbia University). When King's College opened in 1754, it instituted the same practical service courses and neoclassical conception of literature as the College of Philadelphia, and for the same basic reason: emerging colleges depended on public support to survive, and many students had little more than a rudimentary background in Latin. In New York as in Philadelphia, fewer students came from clerical backgrounds. As in Smith's course, an oratorical conception of literature helped to bridge the transition to a new sense of the classics. The first president of King's, Samuel Johnson, also published newspaper articles and pamphlets that promoted the college by stressing its emphasis on elocution and composition and promising courses on such practical subjects as navigation and surveying (though such courses were not actually offered). While Johnson was a conservative classicist who believed that all clergymen should master Hebrew, he found that many students did not even know Latin. To meet their needs, he drew up anthologies of the classics to teach Latin declensions along with lessons on morality and style (see Humphrey 162).[9] In less traditional institutions, Latin was already losing its centrality in general education by the end of the eighteenth century. No pretence was made at King's to require students to speak Latin, for English was used as the language of instruction, as at Philadelphia and other emerging colleges. At New York as elsewhere, learned languages lost their cross-curricular emphasis and became little more than a foreign language requirement, and learned reasoning ceased to be confined to the form of syllogistic disputations. Only one such disputation was offered at commencements before 1762, and only one was included after 1765 (Humphrey 165; Roach 9–10). These changes shifted literacy studies from a classical to a modern footing, much as Smith had begun to do by teaching classical literature in translation in his "Classical Studies and Rhetoric" course.

Johnson himself taught rhetoric, elocution, and composition courses that surveyed classical theories of invention, arrangement, and delivery, while emphasizing the basics of English grammar and style (see Potter, *Debating* 34). This neoclassical approach was guided by the sort of educational vision that is elaborated in Johnson's *Elementa Philosophica* (1752), which was one of the first philosophy textbooks written in America. *Elementa* documents how Johnson attempted to maintain an enclosed system of knowledge by drawing on the idealism of Bishop Berkeley to chart varied fields of study by the providential order of the human mind. Like the rest of Johnson's teaching, *Elementa* is a transitional source that had clear continuities with the scribal compendia that had traditionally been used to reduce all learning to a memorizable system. Johnson divides all knowledge into philosophy and philology, with the latter set out as the primary concern of students until age fifteen or sixteen (which was about the average age of a college student in the middle of his studies). After studies of ancient and modern languages, students moved on to philosophy, with the final year devoted to moral philosophy, including pneumatics, ethics, politics, economics, and natural theology.[10] Johnson left King's

College when it was taken over by the republican state legislature after the Revolution. At the new University of Columbia, a professorship in rhetoric was established in 1784 to teach a senior course that was advertised as including the "Rise and progress of Language—Universal Grammar, Rise and progress of the Written Character—Criticism," with students required to submit essays to be corrected and then inspected by the administrators of the college (rptd. Roach 20).

A departure from classicism was also made in the literature and composition class that was taught at Princeton by John Witherspoon. Witherspoon began teaching his course in "Composition and Criticism" when he emigrated from Scotland to become president of the college in Princeton in 1768. Since the college did not receive even the limited government funding provided to the colleges in New York and Philadelphia, Witherspoon and his predecessors depended upon donations and student fees. In one appeal for support, *Address to the Inhabitants of Jamaica, and Other West India Islands, in Behalf of the College of New Jersey* (1772), Witherspoon stressed that English composition and elocution were taught throughout a program of studies that culminated with courses in history, natural and moral philosophy, and "Composition and Criticism." As at other colleges, students began their studies by translating Cicero and concluded them with orations modeled on his. However, students' reports suggest that Latin was moving to become something akin to a foreign language requirement (see Guder 163–66). According to Witherspoon's own account, the first year was devoted to "Latin and Greek, with the Roman and Grecian antiquities, and Rhetoric." The second year also included language studies, along with geography, mathematics, and "the first principles of Philosophy." In the third, "languages are not wholly omitted," but time was devoted largely to mathematics and natural philosophy. The last year continued the studies of moral and natural philosophy, history, and a program of public "orations of their own composition, to which all persons of any note in the neighbourhood are invited" (Witherspoon, *Selected Writings* 109).

While the college at Princeton had been founded by the evangelical wing of the Presbyterian Church, Witherspoon went so far as to *advertise* that he did not know the churches his students attended (112). Setting out some of the same arguments that his student James Madison would use to defend the Constitution as a representative institution, Witherspoon argued that the College of New Jersey was a public college that was "altogether independent" of factional interests because it represented "a public so diffusive that it cannot produce particular dependence." As a result, the college was "as far removed, as the state of human nature will admit, from . . . mean servility in the hope of Court favour" (111). To appeal to a "diffusive" reading public that reached to the West Indies, Witherspoon identified Princeton as a republican bastion against "ministerial" control. Princeton was upheld as a representative institution that balanced competing interests to promote "the spirit of liberty and independence." From this position, schools and colleges could claim to represent not "those in power" but the public itself (111). As with the other representative systems of self-governance, schools and colleges taught the literate to see themselves as sharing a common oratorical literature that was responsive to their practical needs and social aspirations. Republican values were fundamental to the claims of colleges to be representative institutions. Those values were taught in moral philosophy courses that provided an eclectic survey of liberal doctrines of individual freedom along with the basics of how to draw up a contract and strike an honest deal. Before turning to those courses and the political transformations they contributed to, I want to examine how the literate were taught to represent themselves as spokesmen for the public.

Oratorical Literature and the New Learning

To understand how an oratorical stance on literature came to be seen as representing the literate in a way that religious literature no longer did, we need to understand that moral and natural philosophy courses were based on a sense of the *experimental* method that was more *experiential* than *scientific*—in the modern sense of the term. This point is evident in Witherspoon's observation that "experimental knowledge is the best sort in every branch, but it is necessary in divinity because religion is what cannot be truly understood unless it is felt" (*Selected Writings* 296). "Experimental" lectures using scientific equipment were pioneered by Smith, Johnson, and other promoters of the inductive logic of Watts (see Brubacher and Rudy 85–86). Such lectures were only the most obvious example of the pedagogical innovations that followed upon the "new learning." Adopting what was known as the "comparative method," professors such as Witherspoon surveyed differing perspectives on issues in order to help guide students' independent reading. This mode of learning seems so natural to us that it is easy to forget that it only became possible when students had enough access to books that they could conduct independent programs of reading. The comparative method of instruction was first developed in the Dissenting academies to prepare students to speak against the restrictions imposed on "nonconformists" (see Miller, *Formation* 87). Such methods also began to be adopted in the colonies as books became more available. The comparative method treated received beliefs as topics for debate rather than premises for syllogisms. With the transition from syllogistic to forensic disputations, learning ceased to be a process of reasoning deductively from indisputable premises, and reading became a more open-ended process of inquiry that generalized from the individual experience to broader claims that were too uncertain to be reduced to categorical syllogisms.

Lectures that surveyed sources for further reading were still a notable innovation in the latter half of the eighteenth century. Many less effective teachers perpetuated the dictation-recitation method through the nineteenth century. As already noted, half of Smith's rhetoric course at Philadelphia was devoted to dictating a compendium of Longinus's *On the Sublime* because colonial bookstores did not have sufficient numbers of even such canonical texts as Quintilian's *Institutes* to require students to buy a copy, even if they could have afforded to do so (see Roach 4–5). Students at Philadelphia and elsewhere were still routinely required to reduce published texts to compendia for their own use, with many such abridgements still extant. However, such scribal practices were beginning to be questioned. At Princeton in 1754, Tennent and Davies advertised that the college would not follow the custom of dictating "prolix Discourses" that burdened students' memories but would instead use the "*Socratic* Way of free Dialogue between Teacher and Pupil, or between the Students themselves" (rptd. Hofstadter and Smith 93–94). In such comments, one can see how the new learning was evolving into a new pedagogy concerned with experiential processes of inquiry, and not just rote mastery. However, this historic evolution was not so much an application of new theories of knowledge as it was an accommodation to changes in literacy. As students began to read and own more books, memorizing and reciting passages must have come to seem like a waste of time, at least to those who could look past learned traditions to observe how students were learning (Blair, *Account* 29).

These emerging changes in learning and literacy shaped the origins of perhaps the most distinctly American course in the college curriculum—the composition courses that would replace remedial Latin courses as the gateway for broader classes of students seeking access to higher education. While it is often assumed that composition courses were not institutionalized until a century later, the course in "Composition and Criticism" that Witherspoon began teaching in 1768 addressed many of the formal concerns that would come to define the teaching of composition. With an eye to the page rather than the podium, Witherspoon discussed thesis sentences, outlining, topic sentences, paragraph unity, punctuation, spelling, and other formal matters that only became issues when the focus shifted from speaking to writing, and print began to standardize literate usage. The formation of English as an object of formal study was an integral part of the mid-eighteenth-century effort to reduce English to a logical system governed by laws that were as regular as print (see Miller, *Formation* 38–43). Witherspoon referred to popular attempts to regularize spelling, and he noted several other matters that became the bugbears of composition courses, but which were not seen as problems until print made people more attentive to irregularities in usage.[11] He provided a long list of commonly confused words to help students use language in the methodically univocal way that only became imaginable as literate usage began to be standardized by print with the popularization of grammars and dictionaries (242, 245n–46n). As with other modern proponents of clarity, Witherspoon systematically set about simplifying English prose, though he found it "exceedingly difficult to bring young persons especially to a taste for the simple way of writing" (270).

While Witherspoon addressed the conventions that would come to characterize composition courses, he also revitalized the civic orientation of classical rhetoric. Witherspoon did not subordinate composition to criticism or romanticize creative genius in the ways that his classmate Hugh Blair did (see Miller, "Blair, Witherspoon"; also Longaker 177–206). Witherspoon was concerned with teaching students how to write and speak to contemporary situations (the pulpit, bar, or senate) and purposes (information, demonstration, persuasion, or entertainment). Though he surveyed the arts of invention, arrangement, style, and delivery, he assumed that invention was best left to "the spontaneous production of capacity and experience" (280). While such assumptions were characteristic of what Howell has identified as the "new" rhetoric, Witherspoon did not accept the view that the heated oratory of the ancients had lost its significance in an era of refined tastes and well-managed politics (see Blair 1:42–43). He maintained that "oratory has its chief power in promiscuous assemblies, and there it reigned of old, and reigns still by its visible effect" (258). Witherspoon was critical of the tendency of "persons of finer taste" to look down on those with less refinement (297). Witherspoon was less concerned with teaching taste than with preparing students to become "members of the provincial assemblies" (304). For Witherspoon, rhetoric was a political art integrally involved with the republican ideology that he taught in the course on moral philosophy along with his course on "Composition and Criticism" (205).

We have only fragmentary remains of students' classroom experiences because far more attention has been paid to what teachers taught than to how students learned. The fullest accounts come from the societies that students founded to teach themselves how to write and speak to issues that were important to them (see Potter, "The Literary Society"). A typical society held weekly meetings to share compositions, debate current issues, and practice public speaking. Members' elocution and compositions were then critiqued, sometimes by elected peer editors. The best compositions were then copied into minute books, and some groups even required compositions to be submitted for peer editing before being delivered in class to ensure that they maintained the society's literary reputation. These literary and debating societies were far more academically oriented than the fraternities that replaced them in the middle of the nineteenth century, though the oldest surviving one was in fact the first Greek letter organization—the Phi Beta Kappa Society founded at William and Mary in 1776.

Some of the reforms that shaped early English courses were first instituted by students in their societies (see Potter, *Debating* 77–80). Student societies made the transition from syllogistic to forensic disputations earlier than the formal curriculum. English literature was studied in student societies before it was formally taught, and the essay was adopted as a model of taste and style before it became institutionalized as the genre for teaching composition. The archetype of these societies was the literary society immortalized in the *Spectator*. The essays from such journals were commonly read in meetings, and some societies even circulated collections of essays that imitated the belletristic style and stance of the *Spectator*. Such groups as the Brothers in Unity at Harvard went so far as to produce handwritten collections of essays numbered in successive issues that were circulated among the student body. Student literary societies were vital to the development of students' independent programs of reading. The libraries of some societies were larger than those of colleges themselves in areas that were popular with students such as modern literature and letters. Literary societies provided collaborative venues for students to talk through the implications of what they were learning. Dramatic performances as well as debates were organized by such societies as the Hasty Pudding Club, which developed out of a debating society in 1795.

To demonstrate the oratorical skills that they had learned, graduates at commencement delivered orations, debated public issues, and read their compositions. Commencement exercises typically lasted all day, sometimes with musical "interludes" between orations, disputations, and dialogues that might last as long as an hour each. The publication of commencement programs, newspaper accounts, and award-winning compositions helped spread republican doctrines to audiences who had limited access to formal education. This publicity helped to strengthen the standing of colleges as representative institutions. For example the commencement program at Philadelphia in 1761 included a litany of republican orations on the social contract, the right to rebel to preserve the common good, and the benefits of a mixed constitution. Similarly, at the commencement at Princeton in 1770, orations, disputes, and dissertations argued for natural equality, the natural right to rebel against unjust governments, the civic virtues of the nonimportation agreements, and the right to individual opinion (see Walsh 225, 158–59; also Longaker 189). Commencement disputations and orations on abolition, independence, and religious freedom are widely available in Potter and Thomas's *The Colonial Idiom*. These compositions document how print transformed a major community event into a forum for popular political debate. Like the pamphlet literature of the time, commencement pieces had an oratorical form that represented readers as auditors at a public assembly, creating a sort of representative publicity that made reading a deliberative process that worked to instill respect for the self-restraint and balanced style in a manner that characterized the oratorical literature of the time.

Fundamental to the changing dynamics of print literacy was the evolving conception of readers as independent agents who had choices to make for themselves. An oratorical stance on literature was attuned to the experience of readers who did not share an intense devotion to a handful of sacred texts. This stance is powerfully apparent in one of the most rhetorically influential sentences in the political literature of the eighteenth century:

> We the People of the United States, in Order to form a more perfect Union, establish Justice, ensure domestic Tranquility, provide for the common defence, promote the general Welfare, and secure the Blessings of Liberty to ourselves and our Posterity, do ordain and establish this Constitution for the United States of America.

Generations of students have joined together to recite this passage, perpetuating one of the last elocutionary exercises still common in American classrooms. In the process of reverently reciting the Preamble to the United States Constitution, students experience an oratorical sense of literature that is founded upon the persuasive dynamics of *"E Pluribus Unum"*—"Out of many, one." Such recitations are rituals of self-fashioning that work to instill the balanced style and self-restrained sentiments of the American Constitution. The Constitution is a powerful example of how the literate were represented in the political literature of the time. The American Constitution was written down in a single authoritative text, while the British Constitution was an amalgamation of texts drawn from medieval traditions and common law. As Bailyn discussed, a *constitution* was traditionally understood not "as we would have it, a written document," but "as the constituted—that is, existing—arrangement of governmental institutions, laws, and customs" (*Ideological Origins* 68). This new, more literal and literate sense of the constitution of representative forms of self-government was shaped by the republican ideology that was taught in moral philosophy courses, and by the modes of self-fashioning that were popularized by the periodical press.

Moral Philosophy and the Politics of Republican Education

Insofar as the ideology of the American Revolution was formally taught, it was taught in courses on moral philosophy. According to Bailyn, the "ideological origins of the American Revolution" included classical republicanism, "Enlightenment rationalism," English common law, and the covenant theology of the Puritans (*Ideological Origins of the American Revolution* 23–33). These sources were synthesized within the interpretive traditions transmitted by such Scottish moral philosophers as Francis Hutcheson and such Dissenters as Philip Doddridge, Isaac Watts, Joseph Priestley, and Richard Price (*Ideological Origins of the American Revolution* 40). From these sources came the "commonplaces of the liberal thought of the time": "natural rights, the contractual basis of society and government, [and] the uniqueness of England's liberty preserving 'mixed' constitution" (*Ideological Origins of the American Revolution* 45). According to Bailyn, "the more sensitive observers were to ideological issues —the more practiced in theoretical discourse—the more likely they were to find irrefutable evidence" that there was a British conspiracy against American rights (*Ideological Origins of the American Revolution* 120). From such lines of analysis, revolutionary rhetoricians argued that the Church of England was conspiring to establish an American bishop to suppress religious freedoms. Taxes were being raised and trade restricted to line the pockets of corrupt ministers, who had already reduced the judiciary to dependency and imposed a standing army to cower the American public into servility. This conspiracy was set out for the public by influential rhetoricians such as Jefferson, Hamilton, Burr, Madison, and Richard Henry Lee, each of whom drew upon the theories he had studied in moral philosophy courses taught by Scottish immigrants from Scottish textbooks.

Scottish moral philosophers were among the first professors in Britain to lecture in English on modern history, politics, and culture (see Miller, *Formation*). One of the first university courses on English literature, composition, and rhetoric was taught by Adam Smith while he was professor of moral philosophy at Glasgow from 1752 to 1764. In 1776 the birth of consumer society was heralded by the publication of Smith's *An Inquiry into the Nature and Causes of the Wealth of Nations*, which was instrumental in persuading the literate to try to keep civil society free from politics to allow the natural laws of the market to govern human relations. Smith's own moral philosophy professor, Francis Hutcheson, had drawn on civic humanism and the natural law tradition to combine Addisonian doctrines of "sympathy or fellow feeling" with "Newtonian" methods intended to establish political laws as natural as the "principle of gravitation" (Hutcheson, *Short Introduction* 21; Smith, *An Inquiry* 198). Hutcheson was the most influential Scottish moral philosopher in colonial America.[12] Hutcheson assumed that society was founded on the "consent of the body of the people," and thus "the general happiness is the supreme end of all political union" (*Short Introduction* 287; *System* 2:226). While such doctrines are often identified with Locke, Garry Wills has argued that Locke was less known as a political theorist than as "the Newton of the mind—the man who revealed the workings of knowledge, the proper mode of education, and the reasonableness of belief" (*Inventing* 171). Unlike Locke, Hutcheson set out two arguments of critical importance at the time: enslaving a people violates natural law, and colonies have a right to seek independence when their interests are not being served by union. At a greater distance from Hobbes and closer to the optimism of the Enlightenment, Hutcheson set out a liberal viewpoint that valued commerce and refinement, with traditional virtues founded on a moral sense that was governed by natural laws promoting the common good.

Hutcheson's *Short Introduction to Moral Philosophy* was taught by Francis Alison at the College of Philadelphia. Alison had graduated from Edinburgh in 1732, and he corresponded with Hutcheson. In students' notes from Alison's "Practical Philosophy" course from 1760, one can see how students composed compendia of Hutcheson's discussions of the three parts of moral philosophy: ethics, "the Law of Nature," and "Politicks and Oeconomicks." From the "Constitution" of human nature, Alison's course turned to the natural laws governing political relations and economic transactions. The course concluded by stressing the need to balance political powers in a mixed constitution. Alison follows Hutcheson in maintaining a civic conception of society that did not reduce politics to the libertarian essentials of protecting personal rights and private property. Hutcheson did not assume that the social compact was formed as a means to escape a violent state of nature that threatened property, as Hobbes and Locke had maintained, but because people need others to develop their benevolent nature. Hutcheson argued for "inalienable" rights to life, liberty, opinion, and labor, but not to property, because property may be taken in the interest of the common good. This departure from Locke is one of the most distinctive aspects of the Declaration of Independence, and Wills argues quite convincingly that Jefferson's source is Hutcheson. [13] Unfortunately, Jefferson was less persuaded by Hutcheson's idea that "nature makes none Masters or Slaves" (Jones, "Practical Philosophy"). A collection of Hutcheson's arguments against slavery was in fact the first of his writings to be published in America.

Hutcheson's civic philosophy was also taught by John Witherspoon at Princeton. Witherspoon's course provided a comparative survey of the sources of American Revolutionary thought, including the civic humanism of Cicero and Aristotle, natural law authorities such as Grotius and Pufendorf, the Whig canon that included Locke, and Scottish moral philosophers such as Fordyce, Ferguson, Kames, Hume, Reid, Smith, and Hutcheson. Following Hutcheson, Witherspoon surveyed a broad domain that included ethics, politics, and jurisprudence, moving from natural law to natural rights and economic relations in the ways that Hutcheson had laid out. Witherspoon also maintained that there is no moral justification for slavery, that commerce improves sociability, and that property rights are subordinate to "common utility," rather than being an inalienable right and the principal motive for the social contract (227, 181). Like Hutcheson, Witherspoon also assumed that "self-interest" and the public good were balanced by a moral sense. From that principle followed many of the doctrines that his student James Madison would draw upon to help compose and defend the Constitution. For Witherspoon, and Madison, the inevitable exercise of self-interest could only be controlled if the constitution of powers is "so balanced that when every one draws to his own interest or inclination, there may be an over poise upon the whole" (203).[14] The virtues of a balanced constitution were a commonplace of republicanism, and Witherspoon and Alison helped teach those maxims to the generation who would constitute the representative systems of self-governance that would define the American national identity.[15] According to Witherspoon, it was a matter of common sense that "men are originally and by nature equal, and consequently free," with all duly constituted authority resting on consent (191).

Witherspoon has been characterized by Pocock as "the one authentically radical Scottish voice" of this era, but he has also been criticized for introducing a common-sense philosophy that treated received beliefs as the dictates of a natural faculty (276; see Martin and May). Witherspoon in fact only made a few passing references to the common-sense philosophy of James Beattie and Thomas Reid to support his general assumption that "the dictates of common sense . . . are the foundations of all reasoning, and without them, to reason is a word without meaning" (173). To save the Newtonian synthesis of natural religion and natural philosophy, Witherspoon had to refute Hume's criticisms of "the certainty of our belief upon cause and effect, upon personal identity and the idea of power" (Witherspoon 172). Common-sense philosophy legitimized the cultural values of the literate by founding established conventions on a natural sense. Appeals to the good sense of the common person also had less conservative potentials. That potential is pointedly apparent in Thomas Paine's *Common Sense*, which sold a half a million copies within a few months of its publication in 1776. The title of the work was reportedly suggested to Paine by Benjamin Rush, who had persuaded Witherspoon to come to Princeton and was one of the most devoted American students of Scottish culture. Paine's *Common Sense* prepared readers to understand the doctrines of the Declaration of Independence.[16] According to Wills, Jefferson's sense of "self-evident truths" came from the Newtonianism of the common-sense school (*Inventing America* 183). Jefferson was broadly influenced by Thomas Reid's "egalitarian epistemology, his humble empiricism, and his communitarian morality," as is evident in Jefferson's famous comment that his purpose in composing the Declaration was "to place before mankind the common sense of the subject in terms so plain and firm as to command their assent"

(Wills, *Inventing America* 184, 191). Jefferson often defended the good sense of the common person, as in the famous letter where he stated that if a "moral case" was stated to "a ploughman and a professor," "the former will decide it as well and often better than the latter, because he has not been led astray by artificial rules" (qtd. in Wills, *Inventing America* 184).

The principles of common-sense philosophy had both conservative and liberal implications, but what is most important here is how those principles shaped college graduates' sense of their relations to a reading public that was in the process of developing a shared national identity. Common-sense philosophy maintained the consistency of science and religion by drawing upon the inductive logic of the new science to account for the vagaries of individual experience in a time of revolutionary change. While the more introspective orientation of Scottish moral philosophy worked to preserve traditional values by founding them on the logic of human experience, the more sociological impetus of moral philosophy helped to make it into a seedbed for the social sciences. Common-sense doctrines were particularly instrumental in helping to constitute an American cultural identity that combined a pragmatic bent with an assimilationist impetus that was powerfully hegemonic. I discuss the hegemonic workings of common sense more fully in *The Formation of College English* (206–8). Drawing upon Gramsci's philosophy of intellection as a sociological process, I argued that Scottish moral philosophy was quite attentive to the grounds upon which intellectuals articulate their relations to the historical groups that they purport to represent. As Gramsci has discussed, "it was natural that 'common sense' should have been exalted, . . . when there was a reaction against the principle of authority represented by Aristotle and the Bible. It was discovered indeed that in 'common sense' there was a certain measure of 'experimentalism' and direct observation of reality, though empirical and limited" (348). In this respect, it was "natural" for common sense to be invoked against both outmoded beliefs and radical challenges to traditional hierarchies at a juncture when the literate were refashioning their shared sense of themselves.

The Reading Public That Became the Republic

Literacy studies shifted from a logical to a rhetorical footing with the transition from Latin to English as the language of instruction in higher education. That transition turned on the republican standpoint set out in moral philosophy courses. The public sphere was being transformed by print to create a national audience. According to Habermas, a "structural transformation" of the public sphere occurred in the early eighteenth century in Britain, a trend that I have identified with the Great Awakening, which fueled the growth of the periodical press and the debates over the Revolution that established the ideological framework for the reading public that became the republic. As commerce expanded, "news letters" and then newspapers appeared to circulate information of distant markets and political developments. In Britain, parliament began to rely on the press to publicize its position when opposition parties created journals to appeal to public opinion. The periodical press expanded in the first decades of the eighteenth century from debates on politics and news on commerce to the creation of a middle-class reading public whose conventions and aspirations became subjects of popular discussion in journals of taste and manners such as the *Spectator*. According to Habermas, these developments entailed a structural transformation that expanded civil society beyond the realm of private commerce and domestic relations to create a print sphere that represented "the people" in new ways. In the colonies, this transformation was legitimized by the republican values taught in moral philosophy courses. Courses in rhetoric and composition were instrumental in formalizing the roles, relations, and purposes that print was opening up to the reading public.

As in Britain, the periodical press was instrumental in expanding and consolidating the reading public. British newspapers first appeared in the middle of the seventeenth century as governmentally approved organs of publicity. Because it had not secured such approval, the first American newspaper, Boston's *Publick Occurrences Both Forreign and Domestick*, appeared in just one issue in 1690. The second, third, and fifth American newspapers also appeared in Boston, which had five newspapers and twenty thousand inhabitants by 1735.[17] When the Stamp Tax was imposed thirty years later in an attempt to tax the circulation of information, newspapers were being published in every colony except Vermont. Newspapers were first published in commercial centers, generally by printers, and often by printers who were postmasters. Cheap access to the mail gained importance as newspapers began to circulate more widely, with networks of printers exchanging information and writings through the mails. The four to six pages of these early papers were filled with a hodgepodge of speeches, proclamations, ship arrivals, and more international than local news, which continued to circulate mostly through conversation. A page or two of advertisements were also essential to make a profit. The circulation of news depended on the patronage of merchants. According to Brown, "not only were they the chief patrons of newspapers, as advertisers and subscribers, but their strategic role in their communities' information system meant that they, even more than clergymen, lawyers, or magistrates, defined what was newsworthy" (*Knowledge Is Power* 115). In the colonies, as in Britain, newspapers were both a vehicle of commerce and a commodity, and they provided a media for publicizing politics and commerce that gained importance with the expansion of what Adam Smith termed "commercial society."

Up to the middle of the century, the colonial press followed trends set in the capital, with reports on commerce and politics expanding to include essays on the tastes and manners of civil society. Essays from the *Spectator* and the *London Magazine* had often been imitated, or simply reprinted, in newspapers such as Franklin's *Pennsylvania Gazette*. Franklin had hoped to publish the first American magazine, but his competitor, William Bradford, hired away his editor. In 1741 Bradford published the *American Magazine; or a Monthly View of the Political State of the British Colonies*, followed several days later by Franklin's *General Magazine and Historical Chronicle, for All the British Plantations in America.*[18] A *magazine* provided a storehouse of poetry, essays, political debates, and extracts from books and periodicals. Subscribers were promised that "every Reader that can afford One Shilling a Month, may in a few Years be furnish'd with a Sett of Books, from whence Tradesmen, Husbandmen and even Wives and Children may gather much Learning as well as much Entertainment" (*American Magazine and Historical Chronicle*, iii). *Magazine* was also a term used for pocket libraries such as *The Young Man's Magazine: Containing the Substance of Moral Philosophy and Divinity, Selected from the Works of the Most Eminent for Wisdom, Learning and Virtue, Among the Ancients and Moderns* and *The Young Misses Magazine: Containing Dialogues between a Governess and Several Young Ladies her Scholars*. By popularizing literate tastes and aspirations to broader classes of readers, the literature of self-improvement helped to legitimize college English studies until they came to rely on the institution of public school systems in the early national period.

Broader audiences learned to respect the increasingly secular authority of the literate by reading magazines that taught readers republican values and the proprieties of English taste and usage. The first issue of Bradford's *American Magazine; or a Monthly View of the Political State of the British Colonies* included reports of political debates intermingled with lessons on the social contract, the English Constitution, and classical exemplars. This republican framework enabled writers to set out lines of argument that "return immediately into *Maryland* from *Sparta*" (35). Bradford's short-lived effort was followed in 1743 by the *American Magazine and Historical Chronicle*. Readers of "all Ranks, and of different Sentiments in Religion, Politicks, &c." were invited to subscribe to the journal, which included poetry, accounts of foreign customs, biographies, belletristic essays, parliamentary debates, reports of experiments, and commentaries on social issues such as the status of women (i). Readers were introduced to a republic of letters centered in capitals such as London and Paris, but which also included accounts of provincial centers such as Edinburgh and its university. Essays presented Newtonian perspectives on the balance of self-interest and benevolence in human nature and a well-constituted state. Essays on rhetoric and belles lettres taught readers to defer to classical authorities, British models, and elocutionary principles.

An account of how those with less education taught themselves to imitate literate taste and usage is provided by the most famous work of self-improvement in the history of American literature, Franklin's *Autobiography*. Franklin recounts how he formed a group that operated in the same manner as student literary societies. Like those societies, Franklin's Junto Club was modeled on the club described in the essays of the *Spectator*. Franklin's group included uneducated printers, a shoemaker, a scrivener, a surveyor, a joiner, and a clerk (*Autobiography* 48). After parsing the sentences and sentiments of the *Spectator*, meetings turned to critiquing individuals' compositions and practicing the arts of conversation. Franklin's literacy narrative documents how belletristic essays and literary societies spread cosmopolitan tastes among provincials with little access to formal education. Franklin relates how he studiously eliminated unreserved assertions such as "'certainly' and 'undoubtedly'" from his speech and writing in order to develop a less self-assertive style (11). Franklin's literacy narrative provided a model for self-instruction much like those provided by the religious literature that previous generations had studied to form their own conversion narratives. Franklin advised readers to imitate the deferential style of "modest and sensible men, who do not love disputation." Franklin internalized that style as many other provincials did, by painstakingly imitating the syntax of the *Spectator* and then closing the book to see if he could express his ideas in its style. The "Spectator" of the *Spectator* essays was a nameless narrator who observed and commented upon characters such as Roger de Coverly, a cosmopolitan gentleman who served as a model of the eccentricities of the gentry. For readers interested in self-improvement, the "Spectator" carefully observed how feelings played out in the gestures of others in order to assess their characters, while carefully monitoring his own expressions to avoid disturbing polite company with heated controversies. The "Spectator" was a representative spokesman for the values of self-governance, but the belletristic concern for polite decorum did not play out as well in Revolutionary America as it did in post-Union Scotland. While impartiality was less of a virtue in a time of war, Americans also learned to respect the well-balanced constitution of the man of letters as a representation for the virtues of self-restraint.

Essays composed for the press and the classroom document how cosmopolitan tastes circulated through the British cultural provinces to shape the assumptions upon which college English courses were founded. A particularly relevant example is the account of a Scottish literary society modeled upon the Spectator Club that was reprinted in the *American Magazine and Historical Chronicle* from the *London Magazine* (529–30). Such essays provided models for provincials to form their own societies, as Franklin and many students in many colleges did. The reprinting of anonymous articles from cosmopolitan journals provided models for authors to speak as representative figures rather than as individuals. This distinction is strikingly apparent in the circulation of another essay, "An Essay on Taste," which appeared in the *American Magazine and Historical Chronicle* in 1744. The essay recounted the polite commonplace that "the Design of Schools, the Use of Universities, the Benefit of Conversation, should all centre" on inculcating taste because it "comprehends the whole Circle of Civility and Good Manners and regulates Life and Conduct" (468). What is notable about this commonplace theme is that this exact same essay had also been submitted by David Clerk in 1740 in the first university course to stress English composition and literature—John Stevenson's class at Edinburgh (Miller, *Formation*). One of the first collections of college papers still extant thus includes an essay that seems to have been plagiarized. Clerk likely lifted the essay from a London journal, and the *American Magazine and Historical Chronicle* later took the piece from the same source without acknowledgement—a common practice before modern concepts of individual authorship were instituted. As evident in both these essays, colonials looked to Scotland as a province that was industriously improving itself by imitating the tastes and manners of the capital. The best example of how provincial ambitions were mediated through cosmopolitan tastes may well be the formation of college English itself. The formative paradigm of "rhetoric and belles letters" paired an ancient discipline with a Scottish appropriation of a French term to teach English to Americans.[19]

In the periodical press, as in the classroom, belletristic essays provided readers with modes of expression that were more broadly representative than those that had characterized the scribal curriculum. Students were given the opportunity to contribute essays of taste to another American magazine, the *American Magazine and Monthly Chronicle*, edited by William Smith from 1757 to 1758. The journal set out to provide opportunities for "our young Students to become literary adventurers" under the "Safety" of their professors' editorial supervision.[20] Writers and readers corresponded in essays that adopted the form of letters—a common stylistic contrivance before the essay became established as a genre unto itself. Essays were cast in the form of correspondence from the "Planter" (who spoke for the landed interest), the "Prattler" (who was characterized as a ladies' man), the "Hermit" (who played the part of the ascetic muse), and the "Antigallican" (who spoke against the corruption of civic virtues by French refinements). These correspondents enabled the journal to hold a mirror up to readers' experiences, as the religious literature of the previous century had until essay journals such as the *Tatler*, *Idler*, and *Spectator* came to provide more broadly representative characterizations of literate experience. Narrators positioned themselves as observers of popular manners and printed letters from characteristic readers. Before *correspondents* became a synonym for *news reporters*, "correspondents" submitted letters to the editor that modeled the modes of expression and response of representative readers by quite literally writing them into the text.

Such journals helped to establish the genre of the essay as it would come to play out in English classes. Such essays spoke from personal experiences in a conversational style that could be savored by anyone with taste—and could thereby serve to distinguish those who had taste from those who did not. By characterizing his correspondents as representative figures, an editor such as Smith could speak from readers' experiences in his own terms. This ventriloquist act parallels the roles played by teachers in their editing of students' essays. Smith's didactic spokesman was the Prattler. As a representative for "persons of leisure," the Prattler held up "the *Glass to folly*, wherein she may contemplate her own visage, and perceive what it would otherwise be difficult to persuade her of" (*American Magazine and Monthly Chronicle* 1757, 76). Readers stepped into the mirror by joining in the ironical reflections on the characters the Prattler described. Because the Prattler assumed it would be immodest to describe himself, he enlisted "Dick Dimple" to do so. Dimple characterized the Prattler as "little better than a fool," but the butt of the joke ended up being Dimple himself, as readers came to realize that he resented having his self-indulgent vanities criticized by the Prattler. Such transparent comedies of manners lacked the nuanced ironies of their cosmopolitan sources. Some of the essays dropped such pretenses altogether and adopted a straightforwardly didactic stance intended to "inlarge the understanding, refine the manners, and mend the heart," and thereby to "reluminate the dying virtue of our country" (*American Magazine and Monthly Chronicle* 1758, 169).

In comparison with the sophisticated cultural politics played out in London periodicals, colonial writers tended to be amateur literati who had to earn their way with other skills—sometimes their skills at putting letters into print. As Botein discusses, American printers remained "men of letters" for almost a century after printing had been reduced to a "mechanic's trade" in London. From the Restoration, British booksellers had begun to take control of the publishing process by buying copyrights from authors and hiring printers ("Printers" 14–15). Because most books were imported, American printers tended to rely more on periodical literature, which was often written by themselves and others in their communities. In the decades between the Great Awakening and the Revolution, colonial writers and readers developed a more reciprocal relationship than the commercialized modes of authorship that first emerged in the capital.

The representative politics of the American reading public shaped the constitution of the republic. Against the traditional assumption that all Britons had a "virtual representation" in Parliament, colonials adopted a "medieval" conception of representation that maintained that an elected official had to have a reciprocal relationship with his community to speak for its interests (Bailyn, *Ideological Origins* 163–66). Colonials conceived of political representation in ways that were based on their experience in closely knit communities. The critical transformation of the public sphere came when state attempts to regulate private enterprise led to public debates over taxes, capital, and consumption. This intervention "became 'critical' also in the sense that it provoked the critical judgment of a public making use of its reason" (Habermas 24). In the colonies, the trigger was the Stamp Act, which explicitly targeted the juncture where commerce converged with the circulation of information, including the documents critical to the legal profession. The government was attempting to regulate not just commerce and consumption but all paper used for public purposes, including legal documents as well as books and newspapers. When colonial assemblies were disbanded for publishing critical pamphlets, the press became crucial to publicize nonimportation agreements, coordinate actions, and provide credibility for ad hoc assemblies as representatives of the public. The periodical press began to reach a national audience as the postal service became more efficient, helping to raise the number of periodicals from twenty-three to forty-four between 1764 and 1775.

Revolutionary rhetoricians often used the anonymity of print to represent themselves as members of the community, as John Dickinson did in his famous "Letters from a Farmer in Pennsylvania" to the *Pennsylvania Chronicle* (1767–68). This mode of representation was adopted in the most widely read piece of political literature from the era. Paine used the fact that *Common Sense* was anonymously published to position his persona above "every thing which is personal among ourselves" as "individuals" (24). Paine has been characterized as "the first anglophone theorist of democratic revolution in a capitalist society" (Pocock, "Empire" 307), but he presented himself simply as an anonymous "AUTHOR." From that stance, he invited his reader to assume "the true character of a man, and generously enlarge his views beyond the present day" to view "the cause of America" as "the cause of all mankind," an issue "not local, but universal," concerned as it is with "the natural rights of all Mankind" (36, 23). As a representative "AUTHOR," Paine composed a national audience where no nation existed by situating himself and his readers in the world of print, an expansive domain where "common sense" was removed from received beliefs and situated in the correspondence of enlightened readers and writers.

Conclusion: The Formation of English and the Transformation of Civil Society

The first professorship of English in America was established in the most broadly based colonial college—a hybrid institution that combined academies for women and "mechanicks" with a college intended to provide an "English education" to prepare students for "any business, calling, or profession" (*The Complete Works* 7:252). As a self-educated man of print, Franklin saw how cheap books had spread learning to the "common people," and he perceived that the new learning made learned languages "absolutely unnecessary" for "acquiring knowledge" (*Works* 10:113). While Franklin was not entirely successful in breaking from classicism, he provides a historical alternative for thinking about English studies as a practical discipline concerned with preparing students for public life. Such concerns were instrumental in shaping the first college English courses. Composition, rhetoric, and the oratorical literature of the time were set out as a program of study that was closely related with studies of modern history, politics, and science to create a curriculum that was responsive to the needs of a broader educated public. While there were tensions between the commercial aspirations of students and the classical backgrounds of Smith and the trustees at Philadelphia, at Princeton Witherspoon drew upon rhetoric's civic vision to develop a more synthetic philosophy of liberal education. In one of his appeals for public support, Witherspoon advised parents who had risen "to opulence" "through their own activity and diligence" to ensure that their children received "a liberal Education" to instill a taste for moderate self-improvement (103). To appeal to such audiences, Witherspoon drew on republican virtues to teach "virtuous industry and active public spirit" (146). Whether inflected by republican sentiments or pragmatic aspirations, English studies emerged from the expansion of education to include those whom Longaker has characterized as "the emergent and the established bourgeoisie" (139).

The mercantile and manufacturing classes found much to value in the republican synthesis of public duties and private rights that was transmitted through courses in moral philosophy and rhetoric in emerging colleges such as those at Princeton, New York, and Philadelphia. Moral philosophy courses provided students with a civic philosophy that legitimized commerce, private rights, and public debate, while courses in rhetoric and belles lettres taught students how to represent themselves as models of self-restraint and the public good. These courses contributed to the expansion and consolidation of the reading public by formalizing the conventions of English and the natural laws of a laissez-faire political economy that provided a model for the reading public as a domain for the free exchange of ideas between autonomous individuals. The expansion of the educated public by print and the standardization of educated taste and usage shaped the methods and mission of English studies. Students had traditionally read more intensively than extensively. All that needed to be known had been reduced to compendia that could be memorized and declaimed, with logic defined as the art of deducing individual obligations from unquestionable premises, and rhetoric the art of embellishing such received truths. The transition to forensic disputations and the introduction of the comparative method of instruction treated received beliefs as topics for debate. Such topics were examined against the diverse views accessible through print, and then debated in an informal manner that was broadly applicable to public life. The new learning was introspective as well as expansive. Students were taught to look inward to observe the natural workings of their faculties. This process of introjection modeled human psychology according to the natural laws that balanced self-interest and the common good within the general economy.

The teaching of moral philosophy and English assumed greater importance in New York, Philadelphia, and Princeton than in New England because the diversity of the middle colonies created a need to instill a unifying cultural ideology. This need has shaped the teaching of English ever since it was introduced into comparatively broad-based colleges in the eighteenth-century British provinces. William Smith was the most explicit about the purposes of teaching English to Americans. While he was himself an immigrant, he fostered public anxieties about "foreigners," particularly Germans, who comprised an estimated one-third of the population of Pennsylvania. In pamphlets such as *A Brief View of the Conduct of Pennsylvania*, he called for English-only laws to enable only English speakers to vote. He also maintained that legal transactions should be written only in English, and non-English publications should be outlawed. As with later promoters of English-only provisions, Smith also looked to the public schools to ensure that immigrants learned to obey the rules of taste and usage. Smith and Franklin were both active in the Society for Promoting English among the Germans, which raised funds for schools and clerics to teach immigrants the English way of life. Smith opposed efforts to attract German students to Princeton because he did not want to see the New Lights' anti-establishmentarian evangelism spread among immigrants (Turner 316). To promote the College of Philadelphia as a bastion of English values, he appealed to the Society for the Propagation of the Gospel in Foreign Parts for support, arguing that "Education, besides being necessary to support the Spirit of liberty & Commerce, is the only means for incorporating these foreigners with ourselves" (rptd. Smith, *Life* 1:29–38).

In response to the popular perception that Smith did not support democratic values, his students presented their notebooks to the trustees in 1756 to show that his moral philosophy course in "Ethics, Government, and

Commerce" only taught the doctrines of "Grotius, Puffendorf, Locke, and Hutcheson; writers whose sentiments are equally opposite to those wild notions of Liberty, that are inconsistent with all government, and to those pernicious Schemes of Government which are destructive of true Liberty" (*Minutes of the Trustees of the College* 1:70–71). This republican ideology addressed itself to the area that was central to the eighteenth-century transformation of the public sphere: the zone of contact between government and commerce that became a critical site for public debate when politics and commerce were publicized by the periodical press. The republican virtues of a balanced constitution legitimized the politicization of the reading public as a domain of deliberative debate over the public good. Print mediated the emergence of possessive individualism by constituting a discursive domain that in principle was open to all—all who could buy books and had been taught to respect them. Those who possessed literacy and had internalized its logic were free to participate in public debate, and the transformation of the reading public into a forum for such debate consolidated the virtues of a balanced constitution that treated citizens as autonomous individual property holders.

3

When Colleges Were
Literary Institutions

> The two most prolific branches of literature in America are
> journalism and educational works . . . Newspapers and school-
> books are, therefore, the characteristic form of literature in the
> United States . . . There is, however, still another phase of our
> literary condition equally significant; and that is the popularity
> of what may be termed domestic reading—a species of books
> intended for the family, and designed to teach science, religion,
> morality, the love of nature, and other desirable acquisitions.
>
> Henry T. Tuckerman in 1867,
> "Sketch of American Literature," rptd. Backus 357.

IN HIS OFTEN-REPRINTED
survey of American literature, Tuckerman set out a premodern conception of
literature that included the religious writings of the seventeenth century, the
oratory of the Revolutionary era, and the magazine literature of the antebellum
period. *Literature* and *eloquence* were closely associated terms in the antebellum
period. Graff identified this broad conception of literature with an "oratorical
culture" that "pervaded the college and linked the classical courses with the
courses in English rhetoric and elocution, with the literary and debating societies, and with the literary culture outside" (35). These relationships shaped the
founding of the first professorships of English, as I discussed in the last chapter. In this chapter I will follow through to examine the antebellum cultural
networks expanded from magazines and literary societies to include lyceum
lecture circuits, teacher institutes, and the proliferating numbers of colleges and
academies. These networks expanded as access to schooling began to increase
dramatically with the spread of common schools. To staff those schools, academies and teacher institutes were established, and these institutions provided

women, working people, and African Americans with opportunities to earn an independent living by teaching, writing, and lecturing in various community forums. These networks provide a vital frame of reference for assessing the development of college English studies as a field of cultural production that is shaped by broader social movements. Early nineteenth-century abolitionist, suffragist, labor, and religious movements provide a rich historical context for assessing how literacy, literacy studies, and the literate evolve in tandem as groups gain access to the means of expression needed to represent their collective experience and claim their individual rights (see Calhoun).

To expand our historical perspective on English studies, I will review a transitional conception of professionalism: *civic professionalism* as defined by Thomas Bender. From his studies of the social history of the sciences, Bender concludes that "the great story of nineteenth-century science is the shift from community-based amateur science to . . . professional disciplines" (*Intellect* 21). Bender acknowledges that "community-based" academics were less scholarly than university researchers, but he values their efforts to sustain forms of civic involvement that provide an alternative to the specialized frames of reference that emerged as academics established disciplines as autonomous fields of expertise. The history of our profession is integral to the broader history of professionalism. Like many other disciplines, the teaching of English at the college level was professionalized by abstracting its higher purposes from its basic services. Those services are much broader than most disciplines, insofar as the teaching of writing, reading, language, and literature is caught up in broader social movements. The antebellum period provides a key period in which to consider how the discipline might revitalize its expansive engagements, not just with teaching but also with writing for the popular press and collaborating with various community and professional groups. Assessing the development of antebellum academics as community-based intellectuals has special relevance for areas such as women's studies and community literacy that are closely involved with external constituencies. Increasing numbers of English professors are coming to value such collaborations, in part because English departments are being pressed to rearticulate the values of their services as support for research is narrowed to invest in disciplines that generate external revenues. Given this situation, a survey of our discipline's broader sources of support may be helpful.

From the perspective of the research university, the antebellum period has been viewed as an era of decline in higher education, even though the rate of college founding was the highest in our history. The number of colleges rose from 9 after the Revolution to almost 250 at the start of the Civil War, with the sharpest increases in less-developed provincial areas.[1] Many colleges served ill-prepared students who attended for short periods in order to teach or preach, with between 20 and 40 percent of some colleges' graduates going into teaching on a long-term basis. According to Burke's research, antebellum colleges beyond the eastern seaboard educated more diverse student populations than the research universities that emerged at the end of the century because religious associations provided scholarship funding that was unsurpassed until after World War II. Up to the end of the era when they were described as "literary institutions," most colleges were hybrid institutions that compensated for the lack of formal education in their areas by including a preparatory department, a women's academy or coeducational provisions, and a seminary, law, or medical school. Most were underfunded attempts to meet the needs of isolated towns and territories. Few students had a classical background. To attract and keep them, colleges experimented with "English" curricula—especially if their students planned to teach, as many women and poorer students did. These curricula were shaped by the broad conception of *literature* set out by Tuckerman in this chapter's epigraph.

These formative educational developments in college English studies were shaped by the diversification and stratification of literacy. Penny papers and dime-store novels transformed reading from an act of private devotion into a daily source of entertainment and information. As print became part of daily life, women and people of color became not just objects but agents of literacy. A literate but not learned culture circulated in libraries, schools, academies, and lyceum networks, with sixty lyceums founded in Ohio alone between 1831 and 1845. A literary figure such as Emerson delivered his essays as lyceum lectures before publishing them in a magazine, from which they were compiled into "readers" to be performed in classrooms as models of literary taste. Circulating through such networks, *literature* was understood to include a broad range of genres—"Poetry and Fictitious Prose, Historical, Epistolary and Essay writing" (Newman, *Practical System* 65). The distinction between the literary and popular cultures was not yet clearly drawn. According to Levine, the polite and the popular were not fully demarcated until the latter half of the century, when the arts became "sacralized." A belletristic conception of *literature* laid the groundwork for the development of a modern sense of *literature* by helping to distinguish between reading for pleasure and for self-improvement.

This distinction helped to underwrite efforts to establish a national literature as well as the broader republican project of instituting representative self-governance. Such institutions extended from the state house to the school house. The spread of state-mandated education helped build the audience for the first mass medium—the penny paper. The growth of literacy and schooling undermined the traditional confines of higher education. In the colonial period colleges such as Yale had reacted to the expansion of the literate public by positioning themselves as private corporations, and in the antebellum period elite colleges sought to preserve their standing by raising costs and standards. More accessible colleges reformed their curricula to appeal to students with broader career aspirations. After resisting such reforms, Harvard adapted to the diversification of literate expertise by instituting more specialized programs of study. These trends fed into the institution of gradated educational systems, as is documented in English studies by the proliferation of varied genres of textbooks, most notably the evolution of "readers" into anthologies of literature (see Carr, Carr, and Schultz 81–146). These texts document how English studies adapted to the expansion of education by shifting from a republican to a professional framework for studies of writing, language, literature, and teaching. Composition courses became common, linguistic studies moved away from the pedagogical project of formalizing the national language, and literary studies shifted from an oratorical to a belletristic orientation. The foundations of the discipline were laid upon the establishment of teaching as a "classless profession" well suited to the nurturing capacities of women, traditionally set out by the ideology of "republican motherhood" (see Mattingly and Robbins). That self-effacing ideology worked to contain the aspirations of women and others who looked to teaching as a means to advancement. Those students and their aspirations have shaped college English studies from their origins until the present day, and their experiences provide us with a broader field of vision from which to assess what our field has been, and could be.

The Diversification and Consolidation of Literate Expertise

The inability of classically oriented republicans to come to terms with the populist politics of the new republic is dramatically apparent in how John Quincy Adams lectured on the virtues of classical oratory as professor of rhetoric and oratory at Harvard while he was a U.S. senator in 1806, and then as a matter of principle refused to deliver campaign speeches to get reelected as president in 1828, contributing to his defeat by the populist Andrew Jackson. Adams felt it was beneath him to speak as one of the crowd. In his diary, he noted with disdain that "the principal leaders of the political parties are traveling about the country from State to State, and holding forth, like Methodist preachers, hour after hour, to assembled multitudes, under the broad canopy of heaven" (qtd. in Brown 277). Colleges traditionally identified themselves as oratorical institutions that taught the educated to speak for the public. As the authority of the educated became contested, colleges were drawn into the broader project of teaching the public to defer to reasonable authorities. To constitute representative systems of self-governance, republicans founded asylums, hospitals, prisons, schools, and colleges. As part of this effort, the literature and language of the nation became constituted and taught as a rule-governed system. The formalities of literacy took on increased significance with the "revolution in reading" that was created by the penny press and common school at the turn of the nineteenth century (see Davidson; Kaestle et al. 53). As more people began to buy more books, more attention had to be paid to teaching the literate how to distinguish themselves by how and what they read. These developments had an impact on all four corners of the field: language studies gained currency from efforts to teach the public to obey the rules of good usage; a belletristic stance on literature was adopted to distinguish popular fictions from works of taste; rhetoric expanded to include the composition of varied print genres; and education was transformed by the modern convergence of schooling and literacy, which still tended to be acquired in informal and intermittent ways but was becoming more institutionalized.

A useful point of departure for assessing how education was shaped by the transition from a republican to a professional sense of the literate's relations to the public is provided by the career of Benjamin Rush. Like many reformers of the Revolutionary generation, he looked to education to unify the nation. Like Jefferson, Rush sought to create a state system of education to instill the unifying virtues of industry and economy in the general public. Rush assumed that citizens are "public property" and should be educated as "republican machines" (*Essays* 14). He published several proposals for state-funded schools for "laboring" citizens, with the most capable rising through gradated classes to attend state colleges and a national university. This educational system would transform outmoded hierarchies into a meritocracy in which individuals would rise in a well-ordered manner according to their individual abilities. Rush's educational philosophy advanced the pedagogical innovations that followed from the new learning. Reasoning from an experiential model of education, Rush argued that students learn by doing. Mind-numbing recitations were to be replaced by exercises in observing, experimenting, and writing, and subjects would be sequenced by the stages of child development. This educational philosophy was part of a broader effort to translate republican modes of authority into representative systems of professional expertise (see Meranze). While Rush helped establish at least three colleges, he also proposed to create prisons, asylums, and hospitals in an effort to establish orderly systems of expertise to govern various areas of public life. Rush's *Essays, Literary, Moral, and Philosophical* (1798) argued for placing immigrants, indigents, and indigenous peoples under the supervision of preachers, teachers, doctors, criminologists, and other experts. While republicans had largely relied upon eloquence to exercise public authority, Rush set about constituting systems of expertise that would bring the increasingly diversified public sphere under the control of experts. These efforts shifted the public standing of the educated from a republican to a professional footing.

Linguists' efforts to reduce public usage to a rule-governed system were part of this historical transition. The most broadly influential attempt was Noah Webster's pronouncing dictionary. The dictionary was packaged as the first part of the *Grammatical Institute of the English Language*, or simply "The Blue-Blacked Speller." According to Webster, at its peak it was selling two hundred thousand copies a year (Webster, *Letters* 292). The second and third parts of the *Grammatical Institute* were a grammar and a reader. While neither was as popular as Webster's speller, his grammar went through over twenty-five editions between 1784 and end of the century. Like other republican advocates of making English into a rule-governed system, Webster felt illiterate usage undermined reasonable authority, for example by confusing *liberty* with *licentiousness*. Designed to teach the public to respect the rules, his textbooks constituted authoritative standards for speaking and writing.[2] According to the advertisement he wrote for the revision of his speller in 1788, "a *federal language*" would be created if all Americans were to study "the same book, that all may speak alike" (*Letters* 80). Webster's *American Dictionary* would be instrumental in standardizing usage, but only after his death in 1841, when most of his spelling reforms were expunged by the Merriam brothers. The Merriams bought the copyright and had the dictionary revised by Webster's son-in-law, Chauncey Goodrich, who had become the first professor of rhetoric and oratory at Yale in 1817. As a result of the Merriams' national marketing, *Webster's* became an everyday term for dictionaries as they became commonly consulted authorities for daily usage in ways dictionaries had not been when they circulated among the learned in editions of a few thousand copies.

To set standards for literature, Webster founded his own *American Magazine* in 1787 "to gratify every class of readers," ranging from clerics through "laborers" to "fair readers." Webster reached out to those readers in essays such as "A Letter to a Young Gentleman Commencing His Education." This essay was a member of a hybrid genre that imitated a parent's letter to a college student to invite readers to join in moralizing on the virtues of self-discipline, and thereby identify themselves as members of the educated public, even if they had not been formally educated. Such self-improvement literature helped readers who were not well bred appear well read.[3] Toward that end, Webster's *American Magazine* carefully distinguished literary modes of close reading from the more popular reading habits that became commonly available with the spread of cheap print:

> The readers of books may be comprehended in two classes—those who read chiefly for amusement, and those who read for instruction. The first, and far the most numerous class, give their money and their time for private gratification; the second employ both for the acquisition of knowledge which they expect to apply to some useful purpose. The first gain subjects of conversation and social entertainment; the second acquire the means of public usefulness and of private elevation of character. The readers of the first class are so numerous, and the thirst for novelty so insatiable, that the country must be deluged with tales and fiction; and if you suffer yourself to be hurried along with the current of popular reading, not only your *time*, but your *mind* will be dissipated; your native faculties, instead of growing into masculine vigor, will languish into imbecility. (*Collection* 300)

Novels are identified with a "dissipated" and "insatiable" taste for private amusements that debilitate manly virtues. Such commonplace sentiments document how the anxieties and aspirations of the literate were mediated through a genre that adopted the conventions of personal correspondence to allow readers to moralize along with a literate father, while being tutored along with his son.

Such magazines were instrumental in constituting a national reading public. Magazine writers such as Webster set out to appeal not to learned patrons but to the "merchants, grocers and shopkeepers" who bought and sold their work (*Letters* 124). Such classes of readers increased dramatically from 1815 to 1850, as the country grew from seventeen to thirty states and from eight to twenty-three million. While only twelve magazines existed in 1780, forty were being published in 1810, one hundred in 1825, and almost six hundred in 1850, including the *North American Review*, the *Saturday Evening Post*, *Scientific American*, *Godey's Lady Book*, and a host of magazines for specialized audiences ranging from the *Yale Review* to the *Ohio Farmer*. During this time, laborers and people of color began to turn to the press to publicize their experience. In 1827 *Freedom's Journal* was cofounded by the first African American college graduate, John B. Ruswurm (Bowdoin College, 1826). That same year the first labor paper also appeared, the *Journeyman Mechanics Advocate*. Periodicals became nationally marketable as haphazard networks of itinerant peddlers and stage coaches were replaced by railroad and postal systems that enabled shopkeepers to order publications (and return them if they didn't sell). According to Zboray, print was "one of the first industries in which firms were required to move hundreds of thousands of units of diverse, highly complex goods to thousands of consumers, few of whom actually *needed* any of the particular items" (17). To promote a taste for consumption, the first multicity advertising agency appeared in 1849. Such agencies helped to support the first mass paper, the *New York Sun*, which had appeared in 1833, the year of Jackson's second inauguration. A more literate alternative was provided by Horace Greeley's *New York Tribune*, which included a weekly edition with two hundred thousand subscribers. With such papers, the American press began to produce more newspapers per capita than any other country—three million more than Britain (Hall, "Uses" 44; Emery 150).

Literature also began circulating on a massive scale through popular anthologies of fables, speeches, and poems such as the *McGuffey Eclectic Readers*, which sold a reputed 122,000,000 copies within a century of their first publication in 1836. Such texts made schools and colleges into national markets before they became state systems: forty-one American grammars appeared in the second decade of the century, eighty-four in the third; the expanding market accommodated another sixty-three in the 1840s, and yet another sixty-six in the 1850s (Lyman 80). As Carr, Carr, and Schultz have detailed, textbooks were instrumental in making schools "more inclusive, stratified, and systematic" (4). Gradated schooling expanded and consolidated the culture of literacy, with the number of academies and other secondary schools more than doubling from 1840 to 1860—from 3200 to 6700 (Burke 37). The stratification of the educational market was part of the development of a more centralized print economy.

The "golden age of local publishing" ended around 1840 as press runs increased with better capitalization (Hall, "Uses" 40). The manufacture of books began to be dominated by companies like Harper's that had the steam presses and railroad distribution networks to market to the nation's schools. Print became dominated by large corporations who marketed textbooks and self-improvement literature, including conduct manuals, elocutionary readers, letter-writing handbooks, and educational novels.

The proliferation of print increased the need to teach the literate to read with discernment. Five times more books were published in the 1830s and 1840s than had appeared in the previous sixty years (Kaestle et al. 54). According to Cmiel, "the diffusion of basic linguistic skills condemned all coherent efforts to exclude people of 'middling culture' from public debate" (15). If they could not be excluded, at least they could be taught to behave. As the reading public expanded beyond the realm of devotional literature to include dime-store novels and cheap magazine fiction, the didactic purposes of literature gained broader importance as a means to preach the virtues of personal restraint and social refinement. This ethos has been characterized as "an emerging civil religion—the American version of Victorianism" (Hall, "Uses" 44). Belletristic literature helped to distinguish the modes of dress and expression that enabled readers to identify themselves with literate tastes (see Zboray). Literary forms were comparatively open to interpretation and appropriation because, as Davidson has discussed, popular fictions were not yet scripted by generic proscriptions. By modern measures, literary genres were not yet clearly distinguished. As Jane Tompkins has discussed, "the aesthetic and the didactic, the serious and the sentimental were not opposed but overlapping designations" (*Sensational* 17). As reading became common, aspiring readers had to be taught to show more discerning tastes. A didactic concern for taste and style came to distinguish belletristic from oratorical conceptions of literature. As I discussed in *The Formation of College English*, abundance prompted the refinement of consumption as a means to distinction, as elaborated in the literature of self-improvement (see *Formation* 35–37). Unlike in Britain, however, the educated classes could not assume that displays of refinement would evoke deference, because Americans were often indifferent, and even openly hostile, to aristocratic pretensions.

Cmiel's *Democratic Eloquence* examines how modes of public address were inflected with popular idioms as republicans vied for support with popular speakers in penny papers, tent revivals, stump speeches, and lyceum lectures (see also Antczak; Clark and Halloran; and Eldred and Mortensen). Speakers and writers, ranging from Horace Greeley and Henry Ward Beecher to Abraham Lincoln, adopted a plain style that shifted from folk wisdom and dialect humor to euphemistic prudery and "high falutin'" language, sometimes to show deference but often to mock refinement (Cmiel 63–66). From his years as a popular lecturer, Emerson noted that "every one has felt how superior in force is the language of the street to that of the academy" ("Eloquence" 8:124). Such perceptions undermined the authority of the neoclassical style that the educated had used to speak for the public. An orator took on a different sort of representative authority when speaking in the "language of the street." This conversational style opened up possibilities for women and others who did not fit the classical image of the "good man speaking well," but who could speak from the heartfelt experience of a common person.

The blurred boundaries of the expanding literate culture prompted a "literacy campaign . . . that permeated virtually every dimension of American culture" (Stevens 99). That campaign had several fronts. Massachusetts established a state board of education, with Horace Mann as its secretary, in 1837. The first compulsory school attendance law was passed there in 1852. At the same time, efforts were also made to limit the spread of literacy to enslaved African Americans. After the Nat Turner Rebellion of 1831, several southern states made it a crime to teach slaves or even freed African Americans. Despite such restrictions, increasing numbers of African Americans were able to gain access to literacy, print, and literary societies (see Bacon and McClish; Royster). Yet another literacy campaign was fought by those who attempted to strengthen the boundaries between the merely literate and the truly learned. Traditional intellectuals at Yale and elsewhere responded to the expanding access to education by insisting upon ancient languages as a prerequisite for access to the learned culture. Such reactions were largely a rearguard attempt to defend a receding literary tradition. Only elite institutions could presume students had a Latin grammar school education. More diverse programs of study were offered by more accessible types of secondary schools—academies and the gradated high schools that began to emerge at midcentury. Many high schools stressed English studies before colleges did. The popularization of literature and the expansion and stratification of public education established the institutional foundation and the ideological justification for the growth of college English studies.

Schooling the Public in "Republican Institutions of Self-Government"

According to John Dewey, Horace Mann is "the patron saint of progressive education," because he promoted schools "as republican institutions of self-government" (*Later Works* 2:181). Dewey aptly characterized the transitional role of Mann's generation of reformers, who preached the republican virtues of public education in order to justify their efforts to establish the institutional apparatus of professionally administered school systems. Mann and his collaborators established state mandates, governing boards, teachers' institutes, and professional associations. Infused with an evangelical faith that a prosperous republic depended upon a productive citizenry, Mann and his contemporaries established the professional justifications and institutional apparatus of well-administered schooling. Characterizing teaching as a "classless profession" made poor working conditions into opportunities for self-sacrifice (see Mattingly). Such selfless devotion was seen to be well suited to women, as Robbins has discussed in *Managing Literacy, Mothering America*. The entrance of large numbers of women into education was justified by invoking the virtues of "republican motherhood," which is yet another example of how republican doctrines were used to constitute professionally administered systems of representative "self-government" (see Kerber, "Daughters of Columbia").

While the conjunction of schooling and literacy is second nature to us today, literacy was traditionally acquired as part of one's upbringing in families, churches, and ungraded schools that often had a domestic feel and a religious purpose. The status of teaching was still shaped by the tradition of dame schools and the involvement of preachers as teachers, but those traditions receded as teaching became subjected to professional administration. Efforts were made to professionalize teaching, but then as now, teaching was low-status work for college graduates. While normal schools began to be established in the 1830s, teachers' institutes and lyceum lectures were the principal vehicles for training teachers, especially primary school teachers, who were mostly women.

The institution that was perhaps most central to these informal educational networks was the lyceum. Within two decades of the emergence of the first lyceum in 1826, over four thousand towns had become integrated into lyceum networks that included festive entertainments along with literary lecturers, who toured the provinces to supplement their income, often from writing and teaching. Overlapping associative networks were used by suffragists and abolitionists. These networks worked in tandem with the periodical literature of the time to expand the literate culture. Emerson was one of the best-known lecturers in lyceums, which he characterized as "the new pulpit" after he quit preaching and began touring the country to lecture (qtd. in Kuklick 81). Three-quarters of Emerson's essays were first delivered as lectures, according to Zboray. Lyceums and mutual education groups enabled teachers to publicize their learning and network with touring scholars and writers. Mutual education groups such as literary societies were often aligned with the teachers' institutes that were helping to give teaching a semblance of professionalism. In the weeks between terms, a teachers' institute functioned as a virtual "revival agency" to keep up teachers' zeal for their mission (Mattingly 61). Isolated female teachers looked to such opportunities to validate their experience by connecting with others who shared in their work, much as academic conferences and summer seminars would become vital to the professional development of later generations of teachers. Lyceums and philosophical societies also provided opportunities for scientists to gain public recognition by giving experimental demonstrations. According to Reingold's meta-analysis of previous research studies, about 25 percent of all college faculty were involved in such activities in the antebellum period (61, 57). This statistic belies the traditional depiction of antebellum faculty as half-educated antiquarians who were not involved in research.

These informal cultural networks played a vital role in providing women with access to more advanced education, first in academies and then in normal schools. Some of the first women's academies to offer more advanced instruction were Emma Willard's Troy Seminary (1821), Catherine Beecher's Hartford Seminary (1828), and Mary Lyon's Mount Holyoke Seminary (1837).[4] While some four hundred women's academies were founded between 1790 and 1830, many other academies were "promiscuous" institutions that taught both girls and boys, often with scholarships to prepare teachers and preachers. A few of the thousands of academies that were operating at midcentury evolved into colleges, but most became high schools (Sizer 40). Unfortunately, the consolidation of state-administered schools marginalized many of the academies that had opened up access to higher education. Private teacher academies were founded in Vermont in 1823 and in Massachusetts in 1827, and in 1834 state funding was given to teacher academies in New York; these private institutions were condemned by Mann and other professional administrators intent on developing integrated state systems (Reese 34; also Borchers and Wagner 282–83).

The first state normal school was founded in Massachusetts in 1838. Like academies, normal schools were "people's colleges" (Herbst, *And Sadly Teach* 81). Many students did not really plan to become teachers, but turned to normal schools because they were accessible to working people and women. Many could only afford to attend for short periods. In fact often only about a third of the students from one term stayed on for the next, though some did stay on for more advanced studies in rhetoric, literature, history, and natural and moral philosophy (see Beadie). These institutions opened up access for broader classes of students and made it possible for large numbers of women to get into education: in Massachusetts, over half of teachers were women in the 1830s, rising to two-thirds in the 1850s, and three-quarters in the 1860s. By that point, a majority of teachers across the country were women (Ogren 12). As a result of their expanded involvement in education, the literacy rates of women rose to equal those of men for the first time in history. These increases in women's education and literacy were fundamental to their involvement in the abolitionist and suffragist movements (see Schwager).

The feminization of teaching was integral to the professionalization of school administration in the latter half of the century, when evangelical reformers such as Horace Mann and Henry Barnard were succeeded by a generation of professionally credentialed administrators (see Mattingly, who describes them in detail). Schools became integrated systems that instituted a gradated model of human development, with norms for each age, discipline, and class. High schools became leading institutions, sometimes by identifying teachers as "professors" and generally by hiring fewer women, who were paid as little as a third of men's salaries (Reese 120–30). Henry Barnard was a major promoter of high schools, both as editor of the *American Journal of Education* and then as the head of the first federal bureau of education. Centralized school systems also offered increasing numbers of professional administrative positions. As a result, better-educated educators ceased moving into the private sector to become independent entrepreneurs with their own schools. Credentialed educators began to invest their expertise in state institutions sanctioned by professional journals and organizations. As schooling expanded, literacy rose, and the two became integrally related (see Harvey Graff). In the census of 1840, 96.01 percent of adult white males identified themselves as literate, and for the first time most white children under ten were in school.[5] Schooling worked to instill the virtues of the print culture, and printers and publishers reciprocated by promoting the benefits of public education. As Stevens discusses, local newspapers often played vital roles in efforts to create and expand school systems, not simply because more students meant more readers, but also because alliances of schools and newspapers strengthened their respective standings as representative institutions (114–15).

Common schools established the institutional foundations for college English studies by disseminating "a watered-down version" of the literary culture through elocutionary manuals and readers that instilled an oratorical sense of reading that treated reading with feeling as a performance in sensibility (Kaestle et al. 59–62). As already noted, the best known were the *McGuffey Eclectic Readers*, with students moving from the *First Reader* through the *Fifth Reader* in a sequence of instruction that included a Hamlet soliloquy alongside a "Dissertation on Roast Pig."[6] To teach advanced reading skills, the *Fifth Reader* began with thirty pages discussing inflections, accents, and "poetic pauses." In such elocutionary treatments, reading became "a rhetorical exercise" concerned with conveying "to the hearer, fully and clearly the ideas and feelings of the writer" (McGuffey 21). Such anthologies taught students to invest literature with personal feeling by performing a reading that demonstrated appropriate sensibility. To instill tasteful self-restraint, elocutionary manuals included notation systems to script appropriate modes of self-expression (see Miller, *Formation* 139–41). The elaboration of textbook genres is one of the best examples of the reciprocal relations between the expansion of public schooling and the diversification and stratification of literate society.

Reports from such schools suggest that many teachers had too little training, too few books, and too many unprepared students to do more than rely on class recitations. The stifling effects of the traditional reliance on rote mastery are perhaps nowhere more apparent than in the use of grammars to teach reading and writing through the memorization of elaborate systems of rules. Lindley Murray's *Grammar* was a standard source in colleges and academies. After it was published in England in 1795, the text passed through more than forty American editions in just over a decade, and it was reprinted more than six hundred times throughout the English-speaking world from Canada to Calcutta. Along with Webster and a host of others, Murray codified the proscriptions that would become the bane of English professors and teachers, including the logical absurdity that two negatives equal a positive and the elaborate distinction between *shall* and *will*.[7] Whenever prevailing conventions are formalized into elaborate codes to be recited by rote, students are taught to concentrate on the mastery of mind-numbing minutiae and are thereby distracted from learning how to speak and write with power. This conservative approach to systems of expertise worked to restrict access to the powerful potentials that were opened up by cheap print literacy.

While elaborate codifications of polite proprieties served as a barrier to the educational advancement of the less literate, such studies helped to spread a liberal understanding of the educated culture among better classes of students by replacing a tacit deference to genteel conventions with a linguistic methodology for systematically categorizing different classes of usage and users. For those who made it through the rudiments of literacy, "verbal criticism" was taught from the canons of usage that had been formulated by George Campbell: the language of the educated (like the educated themselves) was that which was deemed to be *national, reputable,* and *current,* as opposed to those conventions confined to the provinces, the illiterate, and the antiquarian. Campbell's *Philosophy of Rhetoric* combined moralistic pieties with an empirical methodology that formalized the grammatical, rhetorical, and logical conventions of literacy according to the "science of human nature" (see Miller, *Formation* 216–22). The widespread adoption of his methods for assessing usage helped to move linguistic studies away from speculations about original languages and universal grammars toward more systematic descriptions of linguistic conventions. This movement was facilitated by the practical appeal of the methods of scientism, which represented logical inquiry not as a deduction from received beliefs but as a generalization from observations of the individual experience. This methodology legitimized the aspirations of the middle classes by disrupting the tacit transmission of traditional deferences and instilling a middle-class faith in the progress of reason.

Of course it is difficult to assess how teachers actually taught these texts, and harder still to know what students made of them. Creative teachers did adopt more dialogical forms of pedagogy, in some cases turning to the lyceum as a model (see Borchers and Wagner 286–89). From extensive analyses of "first books" of composition, Schultz argues that more interactive pedagogies first emerged not in colleges but in common schools, as more progressive teachers recognized how useless most grammars were and began to have students learn to write by writing. While belletristic assumptions prevailed in colleges, Schultz argues that experiential pedagogies contributed to a "democratization of writing" that began "composition instruction, as we understand it today" (4). Rather than reciting half-understood rules, students wrote from observations of familiar objects and experiences, using textbooks such as Elizabeth Mayo's

Lessons on Common Things, which was edited by John Frost.[8] Frost studied with Channing at Harvard and served as a "professor of belles lettres" at Philadelphia Central School before devoting himself to publishing more than three hundred textbooks. "Object" textbooks treated learning as something more than memorizing rules. Instead of a stifling emphasis on errors, teachers were advised to have students free-write in journals, use peer response groups, and gather writings in portfolios. Drawing upon institutional records, teachers' publications, and students' compositions, Schultz identifies such textbooks with a broad-based "reform tradition" that is best known for its implementation in innovative schools such as Bronson Alcott's Temple School (founded in 1834), which stressed introspection, observation, and collaboration, as described in Elizabeth Palmer Peabody's *Record of a School* (Schultz 36, 49; see also Warren). Experiential pedagogies were also advocated by some normal schools later in the century (see Borchers and Wagner).

These pedagogical innovations were responsive to the experiences of the increasing numbers of women, working people, and African Americans who began to look to education as a means to earn an independent living. The careers of the best known followed a pattern that moved from teaching to writing and touring on the lecture circuit. Such was the case with Margaret Fuller, who taught composition, literature, and rhetoric in a secondary school for men and women before becoming a community educator associated with Emerson and the transcendentalists. Fuller wrote one of the most noted feminist works of the era, *Woman in the Nineteenth Century,* as well as essays for periodicals ranging from Greeley's *New York Tribune* to the transcendentalists' *Dial* magazine. She also conducted literary societies informed by a feminist pedagogy that helped women overcome their limited access to education by engaging in critical discussions of their own social conditions (see Kolodny; Warren).[9] As Rouse discusses, Fuller appropriated republican doctrines to advance feminist purposes. Figures such as Fuller call for more research on how the entrance of women into teaching drew upon contested ideologies such as republican motherhood to advance collectivist responses to the rising professionalism of male administrators (see MacDonald). These community-based intellectuals provide an alternative point of reference for assessing how republican doctrines were translated into professionalized modes of expertise. Unlike professional administrators and other "experts," teachers, writers, and lecturers such as Fuller had a civic engagement with the communities that they represented. Women, minorities, and workers generally relied less on professional expertise than on generalist vehicles of representation such as magazine literature, because such groups had limited access to the educational credentialing needed to gain professional standing.

Defining teaching as women's work helped to justify elite colleges' efforts to distance themselves from the rest of public education. "Liberal arts purists," according to Borrowman, refused to get involved with preparing teachers, and their refusal helped to make teacher preparation a marginal concern of higher education. For their part, educationalists such Mann resisted the tendency of normal schools to expand into liberal arts institutions as they attempted to move up in the higher educational market. Mann and other reformers saw the liberal arts as a distraction from teaching the rudiments to instill character in teachers, as in students (Borrowman 45). Teacher "training" thus failed to develop the intellectual and institutional engagements that might have helped teachers to improve their professional status, and thereby professionalize the institutional base of our field of cultural production. These trends can be traced back to how the liberal arts were set in opposition to professionalization, most obviously in the back-to-basics campaign launched by classicists at Yale, but also more generally in efforts such as Mann's, which sought to professionalize schooling. More accessible institutions had the power to serve as broadly representative institutions, and that power differs from the influence exercised by more exclusive colleges. The power to provide access works somewhat differently from the power to deny access, insofar as the former is expansive, while the latter is essentially conservative. Emerging colleges, academies, and normal schools gained influence by distributing education within their communities, while elite colleges preserved their standing by limiting access to upper-class groups who would better represent their alma maters. This distinction in the political economy of higher education tends to be overlooked, because broadly based institutions have historically sought to improve their standing by emulating more exclusive colleges, and as a result, such institutions have tended to undercut their own powerbases.

The Political Economy of the Liberal Arts

One of the most influential historians of American education, Richard Hofstadter, has characterized the antebellum era as "the great retrogression" that resulted from the dispersal of enlightened innovations into too many poorly funded institutions with ill-prepared students, unscholarly faculty, regressive curricula, and sectarian administrators more concerned with piety than progress. Hofstadter maintained that financial support for higher education was too broadly disbursed, as evident in the fact that as many as three-quarters of antebellum colleges were unable to attract the support needed to survive. This failure is commonly cited to substantiate the view that colleges offered an antiquarian curriculum that was out of step with the needs of the time. Drawing on these conclusions, histories of college English tend to dismiss antebellum colleges and begin in earnest with the emergence of specialized scholarship in research universities.[10] Unfortunately, these conclusions are in some respects wrong and in others misdirected. Detailed research on the varied institutions of the period demonstrates that students came from diverse social backgrounds, and that the rate of successful college founding was higher than in any other era in American history.[11] These facts challenge us to expand our history to include the developments in literacy and education that I have discussed. The diversification and stratification of literacy and education set out the institutional and ideological space for the rise of the "profession of literature," as Graff has termed it, but a reassessment of the antebellum period underlines how this disciplinary specialization worked to undercut the vital engagements of literacy studies with broader developments in literacy.

According to Burke, antebellum colleges tended to be "multi-level, multi-purpose institutions that compensated for the absence of a democratic and efficient primary and secondary education system in the rural and less economically affluent areas of the country" (5). Most colleges were local institutions of twenty to eighty students with a handful of faculty members and tutors, making specialized instruction all but impossible. As Burke discusses, competition among New England colleges intensified as the number of colleges in the region increased faster than the population, resulting in the saturation of traditional markets for college graduates. Such factors need to be carefully assessed if we are to understand the socioeconomic forces at work in the reforms that shaped the political economy of the liberal arts in the early national period. The criticisms of antebellum colleges by reformers such as President Francis Wayland of Brown University have often been taken as accurate assessments of the antiquarianism of colleges. However, such accounts do not explain why more vocational institutions in New England also suffered declines in enrollment in the second quarter of the nineteenth century, or why more traditionalist colleges did not experience comparatively deeper declines.

Rather than assuming that there was a pent-up demand for professional expertise, we need to examine the political economy of the liberal arts against the professionalization of broader sectors of society. According to Burke, antebellum colleges provided "social mobility" unsurpassed until after World War II (96). Poorer students tended to be older, having worked, generally as teachers, to pay for college, which cost about one-third of a "skilled manual laborer's income" in 1800, rising to about 60 percent of such an income in 1860—a proportion that is equal to the costs of many colleges today (Burke 50). The percentage of white males in college barely surpassed 1 percent before the Civil War, with no more than 4 percent in all of higher education at the end of the century (including normal and technical schools). In both periods, those percentages roughly parallel the percentage of the population entering the professions: 1.58 percent in 1860 and 4.5 percent in 1900 (including ministers, physicians, and lawyers, as well as editors and professors). This fact suggests that enrollments were correlated with the professionalization of middle-class work. Before costs increased and denominational support systems declined in the middle of the century, "pauper scholars" were common in even the most elite college in America, though Harvard systematically reduced access in the second quarter of the century by increasing costs to twice that of other New England colleges. Admission requirements were also raised to levels accessible only to students from the preparatory schools it helped finance and staff.[12] While historians have generally assumed that state-controlled institutions opened up access to education, the most prestigious tended to be unresponsive to lower-class students interested in teaching.

Into the 1820s, a student could be admitted to even elite institutions with as little as a year of classical languages (Story 77). Classical languages dominated the first year of the curriculum, but such studies were often rudimentary. It is hard to assess how much classical literature was actually taught in translation.[13] In the second quarter of the century, elite institutions began to raise admissions and levels of study. Grading became more common, and efforts were made to refuse graduation to students who failed to meet grade requirements. This concern for standards seems to have been a response to the diversification of the student population (Smallwood 77, 92–95). According to Allmendinger, "the invasion of the poor shattered the order, and uniformity, if not the content, of the classical curriculum" (67). Instead of trying to perpetuate traditional standards of learning, more broadly accessible colleges responded to their students' lack of preparation by shifting modes of instruction. Alternative curricula emphasizing English and science were instituted in the 1820s at Union, Dartmouth, and Amherst colleges and at Rensselaer Polytechnic Institute. Institutions such as Butler University (founded 1845) that opened up access to women and minorities often replaced the study of the ancients with "a critical and thorough study of the English language," in part because their students had not studied in grammar schools (qtd. in Weidner 252).

As more broadly accessible institutions began to shift literacy studies from a classical to a modern footing, Yale reacted by attempting to strengthen Latin requirements. After political leaders at commencement and in the legislature called for deemphasizing ancient languages, the lay members of the Yale Corporation formed a committee to consider eliminating "the study of dead languages" (*Reports on the Course of Instruction* 3). That proposal was soundly rejected by the faculty committee headed by President Day. According to the Yale Report of 1828, "the present state of literature" required an emphasis on the ancients in order to sustain the fundamental distinction between "liberal" and "professional" education (*Reports* 32). At this same time Oxford and Cambridge were defending classicism against the expansion of the curriculum at such institutions as the University of London (see Miller, *Formation*). The Yale Report upheld classical languages and mathematics as the best means to discipline students and limit the encroachment of the "*mercantile, mechanical, or agricultural*" arts (16–17).[14] The Report disdainfully dismisses the "commercial high schools, *gymnasia, lycea*, agricultural seminaries," and academies that were opening up higher education to the public. A classically grounded liberal arts education was seen to be necessary to limit access; otherwise, the value of a college degree would be undercut, just as a "merchant who deals in a single class of commodities" would have to reduce prices to compete with lower-class products (*Reports* 26).

This attempt to use classical literature to stratify the educational market was part of a general effort to buttress the neoclassical authority of more conservative elements in the literate classes.[15] A less reactionary response to the populist politics of the era involved translating republican values into professionalized systems of control. That approach was eventually adopted at Harvard, but it took two generations to overcome the resistance of the faculty. An attempt to diversify the curriculum was first made by Harvard President George Ticknor. Ticknor was Smith Professor of the French and Spanish Languages and Literature and professor of belles lettres at Harvard from 1817 to 1835. Ticknor corresponded with Jefferson about their parallel efforts to implement the "elective system." Ticknor drew on his own experience as part of the first American generation to study in Germany, and supported his proposals by citing such Scottish reformers as George Jardine. Ticknor wanted to organize faculty members into departments in order to encourage them to publish. Students would be grouped by ability levels, with some allowed to bypass classical language studies, though all would be required to take regular exams in lecture courses based on professors' research. Reforms of general education would make Harvard into "a thorough and well-disciplined high school" to prepare students for more advanced "professional studies" (rptd. Hofstadter and Smith 1:271–73, 265–66). Ticknor sought to open up access to prosperous managers of "manufacturing establishments" and spread "liberal education" to "all classes of the community" in order to undercut the support for the colleges that continued to "spring up" (rptd. Crane 79–82). These arguments did not apparently convince the faculty, for the proposed reforms were only implemented in his own course in Literary History and in his own department of Grammar, Rhetorick and Oratory. Ticknor finally resigned after fifteen years of unsuccessfully promoting his plans.

Another noted failure that highlights how diversification and stratification were starting to reshape the political economy of higher education is Thomas Jefferson's unsuccessful effort to establish a comprehensive educational system in Virginia. Almost forty years after his first proposal, Jefferson succeeded in establishing the University of Virginia in 1824 upon the same principles that Ticknor attempted to implement at Harvard. Several other state universities had already been founded in the South—in Georgia in 1785, North Carolina in 1794, Tennessee in 1794, and South Carolina in 1801. Drawing on the same republican assumptions as Rush, Jefferson sought to establish a state educational system that culminated in a research university. This gradated system was to provide three years of free schooling that would function to sort "the learned" from "the laboring." The most promising would rise into the "learned professions" along with "the wealthy" by completing programs of study that culminated with the "General" and "Professional Schools" of the state university (rptd Crane 39).[16] Like Rush, Jefferson envisioned an educational system that functioned as a meritocracy that would channel students into professional hierarchies by sorting out the most capable from the lower orders to rise through classes with the wealthy. In Jefferson's proposals, as in other reforms, the liberal arts became equated with a general education intended to prepare students for more professional studies. This emerging hierarchy was what the back-to-basics campaign at Yale was attempting to resist by using classical languages to preserve the exclusiveness of liberal arts institutions, while Jefferson and Ticknor attempted to capitalize on the power of expanding access to broader audiences, and thereby channel their aspirations into the educated culture.

The sort of reforms that were attempted at Harvard and in Virginia were more fully implemented at Brown University, though the results were also uneven. Brown is an interesting case in point because it was founded upon an oratorical conception of literature, and its president, Francis Wayland, was a leading political economist. The college took its name from a donor who gave five thousand dollars to set up a professorship of "Oratory and Belles Letters." While teaching the rising generation to speak with eloquence appealed to public benefactors in the Revolutionary era, Wayland recognized that the public appeal of higher education was changing with the proliferation of literate expertise. He calculatedly set out to increase Brown's market share by making college studies more attractive to the middle-class students who were attending academies. In his report to the Corporation of Brown University in 1850 and in other frequently cited reform proposals such as *Thoughts on the Present Collegiate System*, Wayland embraced the socioeconomic trends that were condemned by the Yale Report. Wayland concluded that colleges were outmoded and undermarketed. Colleges should become "popular" institutions that prepared students for the "business" of life. Rather than English universities that only served the "aristocracy," he looked to Scottish sources, as Rush, Franklin, and Jefferson had before him (rptd. Crane 145). Wayland called on colleges to meet "the demand for general education" by offering "scientific and literary instruction to every class of person," especially those in "the productive professions" (rptd. Crane 143). Any student who could pay had a "right" to a college education, according to Wayland. To raise revenues to pay professional salaries, colleges should develop varied programs offered at convenient times on flexible schedules. If the classics could not compete, "then let them give place to something better" suited to the needs of "merchants, manufacturers, and every class of citizens" (rptd. Crane 146, 114).

Reasoning from an analysis similar to the Yale Report, Wayland sought to position Brown quite differently in the market for professional expertise. He agreed that tuition, like the cost of any product, is determined by prevailing prices and the costs of production. However, he maintained that the way to raise revenues was to expand product lines, not to preserve an elite market niche, as the Yale Report had tried to do. To accomplish this purpose, Wayland created the most noted innovations of the first half of the nineteenth century. He hired star scholars and established flexible programs in science, engineering, and agriculture. He created extension courses that were predecessors to night school and distance-education programs. All departments, including English Language and Rhetoric, had to develop majors and general education courses. While these innovations foreshadow later trends, Wayland's reforms failed to attract the promised enrollments, and the students who did enroll failed to meet faculty expectations (see Burke 69). In fact, enrollments increased less at Brown in the decade after Wayland instituted his noted reforms than at Yale in the decade after the Yale Report. Such facts suggest that there was not a pent-up demand for professional expertise, as has been assumed by criticisms of antebellum colleges. Rather than responding to demand, higher education would become instrumental in organizing markets for professional expertise as public education and the public sphere became more fully elaborated in the ways that Ticknor, Jefferson, and Wayland had attempted.

At Harvard in 1841, President John Quincy established a model that mediated between the Yale and Brown responses to emerging trends in the political economy of higher education. Quincy upheld the liberal arts as suited to the traditional elite and expanded general education to meet the needs of students with broader professional ambitions. He estimated that classical languages took up one-third of a program of studies comprised of "Mathematics, the Ancient Languages, History, Natural History, Chemistry, the Modern Languages, Philosophy, Physics, Theology, English Themes, Declamations, Forensics" ("Remarks" 24). Quincy maintained that the classics had been appropriate for those traditionally served by higher education—the small but "learned" class who valued the ancient languages as "the only vital element of a liberal education." However, a traditional literary education was less suited to the "larger, less generally learned, but intelligent, influential, popular, and wealthy" classes who did not value "classical literature" but wanted to have the "distinction" of a "liberal education" (12). Banking on the identification of literary studies with the upper classes, Quincy implemented specialized programs of study to prepare graduates to take charge of various domains of experience in the ways that Rush had imagined a half century before. In 1840 the curriculum was reformed to reduce classical language requirements to the first year, with students able to substitute other historical, scientific, and linguistic studies thereafter. As one of "the most important parts of a liberal education,"

English was required in each year of the curriculum, with a proposed course on the "History of English Literature" called for to "give completeness to this department" (2). In these reforms, one can see how English was coming to replace the classics as learning and the learned expanded along with the diversification and consolidation of the public sphere.

Antebellum English professors presided over an extensive general education program of declamations, debates, and orations. At Brown, as elsewhere, rhetoric had traditionally been a part of the first two years of instruction, though exercises in oratory and composition also took up much of students' time in their last two years of study. The curriculum culminated with the moral philosophy courses that were beginning to give rise to such social sciences as political economy in this era. Under Wayland, college catalogs characterized rhetoric as "the most important branch of a University education," with descriptions of English studies that are far more detailed than any other subject. The "oratorical culture" of student societies, literary journals, compositions, and public orations has been discussed in Graff's account of how professionalized literary studies developed out of "the collapse of the communal literary culture and corresponding estrangement of literature from its earlier function in polite society, where it had been an essential instrument of socialization" (20). Literary societies compensated for the limitations of the curriculum by providing students with opportunities to debate and write about political and cultural issues.[17] Student societies shaped the origins of modern literary studies in colleges, as is evident in the fact that poetry and fiction were by far the most commonly checked-out books from the student society library at Princeton that McLachlan studied, totaling almost a third of all students' reading (477). As McLachlan discusses, when students' collaborative work in literary societies is taken into account, the antebellum educational experience comes to appear "intellectually solid, rigorous, broad in scope, and surprisingly well tailored to the character and interests of the individual student" (485).

That claim takes on broader significance when one considers the diverse students served by more accessible colleges. Many of those colleges were affiliated with religious denominations, but that does not mean that they were necessarily sectarian institutions. One of the colleges founded by the evangelicals of the Second Great Awakening was established at Oberlin in 1833. Oberlin Collegiate Institute was founded by the Presbyterian "colonists" who established a town in Oberlin, Ohio. Like many antebellum colleges, and republican predecessors such as the College of Philadelphia, Oberlin was a hybrid institution. It was founded to support "the education of ministers and pious school teachers—secondarily the elevation of female character, and thirdly the education of the *common people* with the higher classes, in such a manner as suits the nature of Republican institutions" (qtd. in Fairchild 35). The institution included a preparatory department and a theological seminary, French and music schools, a teachers' academy and a commercial academy, and college tracks for women and men, with the latter distinguished from the former by the inclusion of classical languages and oratorical exercises. The college was set up on a plan "sufficiently grand . . . to be called a University" (Fairchild 5). Oberlin offered extensive work-study programs for men and women students, who came from diverse backgrounds and areas, in part because the institution was widely known for its fervent abolitionism. African Americans were first admitted when several arrived with a cohort of abolitionist students who had left a seminary that had tried to proscribe antislavery activism, and then a couple of faculty members agreed to join the college only if access for African Americans was established as a formal policy (Fairchild 20–22). An African American parent visiting the college in 1840 noted that of the four hundred students, fifteen were African American, including three women (see "Negro Higher Education").

Oberlin tried to maintain traditional conceptions of a separate sphere for women by proscribing public speaking activities until women students could no longer be silenced (Fletcher 1:290). Connors has argued that the presence of women in rhetoric classes brought an end to the disputations and oratorical displays that had functioned as ritualized forms of combat to instill the martial spirit of republicanism. According to Connors, when small colleges such as Oberlin found it impossible to sustain a program of study in rhetoric and oratory distinct from the "Ladies' Course" in literature and composition, the former was combined with the latter. The Ladies' Course at Oberlin was renamed the Literary Course in 1875 (Connors 51; see also Mountford). The Oberlin custom of having the rhetoric professor read award-winning essays by women students at commencement has also been discussed in disciplinary histories (Connors 54–57; see also Weidner). Women gained the right to read their own essays at graduation in 1859, and after decades of agitating to be able to deliver orations along with their male classmates, in 1870 a suffragist student, Harriet Keeler, stunned the audience by delivering her essay as if it were an oration, without reading from the page. By 1885, all such oratorical displays were gone from graduation ceremonies except a single valedictory address.

These developments document how reading, writing, and speaking became inflected by new registers of expression and experience in ways that constituted the institutional practices that made English literature into an object of formal study, not so much as a response to theories advanced in elite institutions, but as a response to pressures working upward from the diversification of literacy and the literate. Those pressures have historically converged on the general education courses through which diverse students enter higher education, and from which college English studies developed as a scholarly discipline.

The Transition from Rhetoric through Composition to Literature

As education and literacy expanded to classes of students with less access to public forums, rhetoric and belles lettres courses evolved into introductory composition courses and surveys of British and American literature. Transitional texts such as Blair's *Lectures on Rhetoric and Belles Lettres* provided a complete course of English study that began with the history of language, reviewed classical concepts of rhetoric, and offered advice on composition before concluding with a survey of genres more diverse than those included in a modern sense of literature. As various areas of expertise became consolidated into representative systems of self-governance in the ways that Rush had envisioned and the curriculum was beginning to encompass, literary and literacy studies became elaborated and consolidated in the textbook genres that are examined in Carr, Carr, and Schultz's *Archives of Instruction: Nineteenth-Century Rhetorics, Readers, and Composition Books in the United States*, including anthologies of literature. The teaching of literature by professors of rhetoric gave rise to the first professorships of literature. While linguistic and literary studies did not establish a specialized "research base" until the next century, one of the most noted of the first professors of literature had gained enough standing by 1876 that he was able to use an outside offer from a research university to free himself from teaching composition. Francis Child had disdained the duty of commenting on compositions ever since he became the fourth Boylston Professor of Rhetoric and Oratory in 1851. Upon taking the position, he reshaped his senior course from Rhetoric and Criticism to English Language and Literature to relate it to the research he had undertaken on Chaucer in his graduate studies in Germany (Paine 86). Such developments mark out the priorities and boundaries that would come to define the profession.

A good way to benchmark these emerging trends is to consider how they affected what students wrote. A couple of benchmarks I have examined are the writings of John Fitch at Yale (graduate of 1803) and John Brackett at Brown (graduate of 1857).[18] Fitch's work in a literary society complemented his studies of rhetoric and oratorical literature, which extended to taking detailed notes on sermons and the court cases that he attended to begin to learn the law. Fitch wrote essays on the press, state-required schooling, immigration, emancipation, and the dispossession of Native Americans. A half century later, Brackett's writings have a distinctly less oratorical and more belletristic feel. At Brown, as at most colleges at midcentury, writing across the curriculum requirements still shaped students' whole program of study, but the cross-curricular requirements were losing their sense of purpose.[19] Brackett's essays adopt a belletristic style that is quite different from the oratorical stance that Fitch had set out in the compositions he delivered before the assembled college. While Fitch spoke to public issues in a self-consciously rhetorical manner, Brackett wrote about such topics as the "Development of Milton's Genius" in a style that lacks the same clarity of audience and purpose.

Fitch and Brackett adopted different standpoints in their writings because the subject positions set out for students shifted in the first half of the nineteenth century as English studies moved away from the oratorical perspective that had been set out by the noted professorships at Harvard and Yale. The Boylston Professorship of Rhetoric and Oratory that was founded at Harvard in 1805 has been discussed by Reid, Douglas, and Paine. The provisions for the professorship were taken almost verbatim from Ward's neoclassical *Lectures on Oratory*. Public lectures on oratory were to be delivered to seniors and resident graduates, while freshmen were to be taught classical rhetoric. Sophomores and juniors were to be taught modern rhetoric, elocution, and composition, and professors were also supposed to correct students' compositions, though when Adams took the chair, he insisted that work be assigned to a teaching assistant. The professorship was held from 1817 to 1839 by Chauncey Goodrich, whose *Select British Eloquence* established the canons of rhetorical criticism that remained influential in studies of speech into the next century.[20] In addition to his public lectures to seniors, Goodrich taught a first-year composition course. Notes from Goodrich's "First Lessons in English Composition" show that he worked closely with students' writing. At his retirement in 1839, the professorship was renamed the professor of rhetoric and English literature.

This transition turned upon the belletristic conception of literature popularized by Blair's *Lectures on Rhetoric and Belles Lettres*. Blair's *Lectures* remained the most widely adopted college text into the 1840s, when it was surpassed by those of George Campbell and Richard Whately (see Carr, Carr, and Schultz 33–49). American publishers produced sixty-six full editions and seventy-four abridgments of Blair's *Lectures*. Blair's doctrines were reduced to a methodical system for the expanding textbook market in abridgements that distilled lectures down to formulaic precepts on taste and style with questions and answers for students to recite. As a predecessor to the discussion questions still included in readers for composition classes, this question-and-answer format translated traditional recitation methods of instruction into technically sophisticated textbooks with complex layouts and typefaces. The precepts of Blair, Campbell, and Whately were even more broadly disbursed by other popular textbook authors such as Samuel Newman, Henry Day, and a host of imitators.[21] The scope of these texts is evident in their most popular English competitor—Jamieson's *Grammar of Rhetoric and Polite Literature: Comprehending the Principles of Language and Style, The Elements of Taste and Criticism; with Rules for the Study of Composition and Eloquence Illustrated by Appropriate Examples, Selected Chiefly from the British Classics* (1826). Neatly packaged in a handy format, these encyclopedias of the literate culture promised to purify students' taste, improve their writing, and introduce them to a modern sense of the "classics."

As Sharon Crowley has discussed, while these textbooks were highly "derivative . . . , the first generation of nineteenth-century American rhetoric textbooks represented serious attempts to adapt the principles of British discourse theory into a form suitable for young or inexperienced writers" (*Methodical* 57). Crowley's focus on the uses of rhetoric to teach composition is well taken. According to the content analysis of eighty-six rhetoric and composition textbooks reported in Nietz, almost a quarter of the textbooks published before 1830 gave little or no attention to composition, while books published after that date devoted up to 50 percent of their pages to the topic. At the same time, oratory declined in emphasis, with over a third of textbooks after 1830 ignoring it completely. Taste was similarly deemphasized. Taste was not discussed in over two-thirds of textbooks after 1830 (Nietz 24). These changes mark the historical shift from rhetoric and belles lettres to the approach to composition that developed out of attempts to help increasing numbers of less-prepared students write without overwhelming faculty, many of whom were growing tired of the traditional regime of orations, declamations, and themes. These attitudes contributed to the decline of rhetoric, and to the subordination of composition instruction to a modern conception of literature.

At the same time that rhetoric was being reduced to the mechanics of composition, upper-level courses were shifting to a more modern conception of literature. The last professor to lecture on rhetoric to Harvard seniors was Edward Channing. Channing saw oratory as an art whose time had passed. He shifted college English studies to focus on "the written book, the novel, the history, the fable, and the acted play" (33). Channing was repelled by the popular orators who prompted his student Emerson to marvel over how the "overpowering personality" of a speaker could take "sovereign possession of the audience" (Emerson, "Eloquence" 8:79, 65; see also Warren 24–25, 48).[22] Such orators had been put under "restraints" in modern society, according to Channing:

> A modern debate is not a contest between a few leading men for a triumph over each other and an ignorant multitude; the orator himself is but one of the multitude, deliberating with them upon common interests, which are well understood and valued by all. (17)

By identifying debaters as representatives of the "multitude" (rather than as orators vying for control over it), this passage conveys sentiments that Wallace Douglas and Susan Miller have characterized as "truly radical" and "startling[ly] . . . democratic" (Douglas 116; Susan Miller, *Textual* 62).[23] Channing was responding to the democratization of reading that had blurred the distinction between "our popular or literary speech" (243). Faced with the appearance of the first mass medium, Channing taught students to resist the sensationalism of the penny press, as Paine has discussed (75–76). To teach students "the restraint of taste," Channing delivered lectures on the virtues of "Habits of Reading," on how to form "Literary Tribunals," and on the "Forms of Criticism" that would maintain self-composure.

As a former editor of the leading literary magazine of the time, the *North American Review*, Channing had a sense of his field of study that was quite different from that of a neoclassical republican such as Adams. That difference is apparent in an oration on "Literary Independence" that Channing delivered in 1818 before the first Greek letter student society, Phi Beta Kappa. This oration is the most direct point of contact between the teachings of Channing and the expanding literary class represented by Channing's student Ralph

Waldo Emerson. Channing discussed "The American Scholar" in terms that resonate with Emerson's essays (3). Channing advised students to rise above provincialism and create a national literature. With an oratorical flourish, Channing concluded by repeating the call to "cultivate domestic literature" six times to exhort his audience to inculcate the critical habits of mind needed to rise above "local distinctions" and "meet on one ground" in the field of literary studies (4). This call to "cultivate domestic literature" celebrated the expansion of literary studies beyond the neoclassical public sphere to include broader classes of readers and writers. Oratorical studies had prepared the literate to preach virtue and argue the law in a public sphere where a *private citizen* was an oxymoron, while modern literary studies enabled students with more diverse aspirations to acquire a shared cultural base for their professional aspirations. In basic respects, literary studies functioned as a representative institution of self-governance comparable to those that Rush had envisioned. The modes of representation by which the literate were to shape the literature of the time are addressed in Channing's concluding course lecture on "Permanent Literary Fame," which discusses how critics serve as representatives for the "fair-minded common reader" by setting out the "laws of the mind" that give authority to "canons of criticism" (285–89).

Channing provided a prominent justification for the sorts of courses that were becoming common in the more broadly based institutions of the day.[24] One of the more rigorous was the survey of literature course that Francis March taught in an academy from 1845 to 1854, and then at Lafayette College from 1855 on. Forty years later March was enlisted to describe his course in Payne's *English in American Universities by Professors in the English Departments of Twenty Representative Institutions.* March's popular *Method of Philological Study of the English Language* (1865) was often hailed by later critics as a pioneering contribution to the professional literature. In the first issue of *PMLA* in 1884, Theodore Hunt cited Lafayette College as the first to "fully recognize" English studies, and embarrassingly added that the fullest programs of study tended to be in "the smaller and weaker colleges of the South and West" (119). After introductory philological studies of Anglo-Saxon, March's textbook includes units on Chaucer, Shakespeare, Milton, Bunyan, and Spenser. March's pedagogy assumed that students would have broad access to literary works and critical commentaries. Writing assignments focused on biographies, plot synopses, and historical backgrounds. March called upon "Professors of Rhetoric" to give over some assignments to writing for "reviews and magazines" (iii–vi). Much of the textbook is comprised of sections that include several lines from a literary work along with a list of questions for discussions of the minutia of style and historical sources. March focused on the "study of the language as it is found in masterpieces of literature, the immediate aim being the interpretation of these masterpieces, the rethinking of the thoughts of master minds, and storing the memory with their minds" ("Teaching" 76). With such texts, literary and literacy studies shifted away from preparing students to speak for the public, and began to concentrate more on instilling responsiveness to representative masterpieces.

At such historic transitions, one can see how shifts in the field of study have set out distinctive modes of authorship and readership that have differentiated the truly literate from less critical readers and more popular writers. Some of the most widely adopted surveys of literature were derived from Shaw's *Outlines of English Literature*, a compendium originally drawn up by a Cambridge graduate to teach Russian nobles English tastes. This remarkably transcultural text became the source for generations of popular American textbooks.[25] These texts followed upon the technological innovations in the composition market to advertise a "modern text-book form" complete with varied typefaces and tables (Backus 400). In addition to providing students with overviews of Anglo-American history, these textbooks traced out genealogies of "master minds" with critical commentaries. Literary studies still included philosophy and history as well as poetry, novels, dramas, and essays. As in March's textbook, studies of Anglo-Saxon provided philological rigor to the project of using English literature to teach Americans the values of the "Anglo-Saxon race." That hyphenated identity was formed by a history of conquest and assimilation that demonstrated, according to Backus, the "inevitable law" that "guides the North American Indians to the certain fate that must come from their contact with the same Anglo-Saxon race." The supremacy of that race was represented in "the lives and the works of the great men who have contributed to the riches of our literature." Studies of such masterworks helped aspiring students to eradicate dialectical differences and identify themselves with an "Anglo-Saxon" heritage that might not be theirs by birth but could become theirs with study (Backus 7, 5).

One can see how such surveys of literature departed from belletristic concerns for style and taste in Henry Reed's *Lectures on English Literature*, which was published posthumously in 1855. In his introduction, Reed's brother justified publishing the unrevised lectures from Reed's course at the University of

Pennsylvania by characterizing them "as popular lectures, or rather essays at lectures" (xv). Reed repudiated the "shallow criticism" of Blair and Kames because he felt that a rigorous discipline could not be founded upon "that vapid, half-naturalized term 'belles-lettres.'" *Belletristic* was already being repudiated for having treated literature as "an easy, indolent cultivation, a sort of passive, patrician pleasure, instead of demanding dutiful and studious and strenuous energy" (34–35). Invoking De Quincy's influential distinction between the literatures of *knowledge* and *power*, Reed demarcated writings that merely conveyed information from those concerned with moving audiences. Literary critics were to sort through the "multitude of books" addressed to particular sects, professions, and parties to concentrate on close readings of those that spoke for "universal humanity" (53, 30). In our "liberal communion with books," our "womanly thought and feeling" will "mingle naturally with men's judgments" to establish "literature as a means of culture of character, manly and womanly" (45). Such assessments facilitated a broadly based historical transition in literacy studies that adapted republican virtues to the expansion of civil society, including public roles for women as teachers of self-refinement.

Textbooks such as Reed's surveyed centuries of literature in a way that is commonplace today, though they represented a distinct innovation at the time. While the doctrines of taste and sympathy that Blair popularized provided a moral justification for literary study, he had examined literary genres from a rhetorical stance concerned with teaching students how to compose them, while Reed surveyed varied literary genres and concluded by confining his discussion of writing to the most domestic of genres—letters. Reading and writing became distinct domains of experience as literature became organized historically to help students appreciate that "the true enjoyment of books is when there is a cooperating power in the reader's mind—an active sympathy with the book" (Reed 48). In such passages, one can see how the expansion and consolidation of literacy and schooling gave rise to a modern sense of literature in which the literate invested their creative efforts in reading texts responsively, without presuming that they might themselves compose works of literature. Such distinctions emerged with the transition from *belles lettres* to *literature*, in the modern sense of the term, as can be seen in Wozniak's study of thirty-six eastern college curricula. In the 1850s, courses in rhetoric and composition were offered through departments that included *literature* in their title in one-third of the sample, with another third including the term *belles lettres* as part of the name of the department. A decade later, *literature* had become a distinguishing term in one-half of the sample, while *belles lettres* appeared in less than a quarter. This transition was integral to the changes in literacy and schooling that followed upon expansions in educational access, and to the shift from intensive to expansive habits of reading that blurred the distinctions between leisurely and critical forms of literacy—distinctions that a modern sense of literature focused on sorting out.

The conception of literature as something to be consumed but not composed was consistent with the expansion of the reading public, and with the conceptions of consumer society propounded by professors of rhetoric and moral philosophy such as Adam Smith (see Miller, *Formation*). The expansion of print blurred the boundaries of the learned culture, as in Britain, but a belletristic stance was harder to establish in Revolutionary American than in post-Union Scotland. Witherspoon and his contemporaries adopted a more oratorical and less belletristic stance to address the political controversies of the time, and literary hierarchies proved to be more difficult to institute in America, because Britain had an established class hierarchy and a cultural capital that provided cosmopolitan standards by which middle-class provincials could distinguish themselves. The American republic of letters did not have a courtly literature or a metropolitan center. As larger towns grew into cities, they came to be seen not as cosmopolitan centers but as blights on the landscape—as underworlds run by crooks and overrun with immigrants.[26] The small town ethos of middle-class culture created considerable challenges for efforts to demarcate provincial and polite tastes in music, art, theater, and literature (see Levine). To those versed in a more cosmopolitan sense of literature, previous efforts to establish a distinctly *American* literature were merely a sign of provincialism. As James Russell Lowell wrote in a review of Longfellow's *Kavanagh* in 1849, "mere nationality is no more nor less than so much provincialism . . . Literature survives, not because of its nationality, but in spite of it" (9–10). Such cosmopolitan men of letters repudiated their predecessors' calls to "produce a national literature, as if it were some school exercise in composition to be handed in by a certain day" (11).[27]

Lowell repudiated the didactic stance assumed by belletristic conceptions that looked to popular writers such as Longfellow as models to imitate and not just study.[28] That standpoint was maintained by writers like Tuckerman, whose "A Sketch of American Literature" was published in 1852 in Shaw's *Outlines of English Literature*. Tuckerman's revised "Sketch" was included in several of the popular revisions of Shaw's text, including *A New History of*

English and American Literature with Henry T. Tuckerman's *Sketch of American Literature*. Backus surveys British literature from the Normans to nineteenth-century novelists (along with references to a companion anthology). Tuckerman stated that "the two most prolific branches of literature in America are journalism and educational works . . . Newspapers and schoolbooks are, therefore, the characteristic form of literature in the United States" (rptd. Backus 357). Tuckerman perpetuates a premodern conception of literature that includes didactic literature, and also rhetoric, insofar as "oratory is eminently the literature of republics" (rptd. Backus 358). The "germ of American literature" was, according to Tuckerman, the antebellum "reviews, lectures, and essays," which he characterized as "that delightful species of literature which is neither criticism nor fiction—neither oratory nor history—but partakes somewhat of all these, and owes its claim to a felicitous blending of fact and fancy, of sentiment and thought—the belles lettres of writing of our country" (375, 377). This belletristic conception of literature as something for students to write and not just read was repudiated as academics came to assume a cosmopolitan disdain for the literature of self-improvement and the informal cultural networks in which that literature circulated.

Conclusion: Literature and Literacy in the Extracurriculum

The paragon of literacy shifted from an oratorical through a belletristic to an aesthetic frame of reference as literacy studies were restructured to accommodate the diversification of the public sphere by the expansion of print literacy in the first half of the nineteenth century. As in earlier periods, literacy and literacy studies evolved with developments in the literate, and the modes by which they were represented in the literature of the time. In the seventeenth century, literacy was shaped by scribal modes of learning that followed a deductive epistemology and culminated with religious literature to prepare graduates to preach received beliefs in isolated communities. Colonial society became more diversified in the eighteenth century, especially in the middle colonies where English courses were first introduced into emerging colleges. Those courses attended to syntactic formalities and oratorical modalities that became more of a concern as literacy became defined by print and the public authority of the literate became more contested. After the political debates over independence and the constitution of the republic, an oratorical conception of literature persisted as republican reformers worked to institute representative forms of self-governance in varied spheres of civil society. Efforts were made to establish a national language and literature as education expanded to include women and others who were able to earn an independent living by teaching, lecturing in lyceum networks, and writing for belletristic magazines. The literature of self-improvement helped to instill standards of taste and usage that had become blurred as the literate culture expanded beyond learned languages and expensive folios. That blurring of boundaries gave rise to a literacy campaign with several fronts. At an elemental level, it included state-mandated schooling systems, and on a higher plain, a back-to-basics campaign was launched to limit access to liberal education to those who had mastered learned languages. Even as the Yale Report attempted to defend that position, its base was shifting as English came to replace Latin as the means to gain access to higher education, and through it the professions.

College English is today so fully elaborated as an academic discipline that the antebellum period appears to us to be part of the prehistory of the profession, as Gerald Graff has discussed. Looking back from a broader perspective on literary and literacy studies, we may be able to acknowledge that the "profession of literature" is but a chapter in the history of college English teaching. From that perspective, we can come to acknowledge that the conceptions of literature that divorce it from its applications are what have made it the consummate school subject. While every discipline constitutes its objects of study through the methods used to study them, the methods of literary study tend to be even more didactic than the methods of most disciplines because literary criticism produces readings that serve to teach people how to read. Literature was not constituted as a course of study unto itself until education developed into a gradated system that could undergird the differentiation of disciplines. The basic structure of that system began to emerge in the middle of the nineteenth century. Grade schools had largely replaced grammar schools by the Civil War, and in the subsequent decade a quarter million students in thirty-six states were attending six thousand academies. Most were coeducational, and many were already evolving into gradated high schools (Cohen, *Education in the United States* 2:xv–xvi). Those academies overlapped into the normal schools that provided lower-class colleges for lower-class students, who were channeled back into primary schools to expand the base of the educational system. That system propagated the "ideology of literacy" that instilled a faith in schooling as a means to progress through refinement (see Soltow and Stevens). Teaching that faith to the less educated was seen to be women's work, for over 60 percent of teachers were women (Cohen, *Education in the United States* 3:1316–17).

While the modern equation of literacy with schooling came into focus in the antebellum period, the belletristic literature of the time also circulated beyond classrooms through what has been characterized as the "extracurriculum." The cultural networks and periodical literature that I have surveyed have been identified by Applebee as among the historical sources of modern English studies, and Gerald Graff has also looked to the "cluster of literary societies, debating clubs, student literary publications, and public lectures and lyceums" as a forerunner to the academic apparatus of the profession (Graff, *Professing* 44). These "agencies of intellect" have been put forward to challenge the confines of our profession by Anne Ruggles Gere. The associative networks and self-instruction literature of the antebellum period take on renewed relevance with the interactive literacies and networks that have gained currency as the "culture of the book" has come to occupy a position comparable to that which classical literature assumed a century ago. Literature takes on different representative functions when positioned in the associative networks formed by lyceums, libraries, and periodicals, which were more accessible to women, workers, and people of color than institutions of higher education, as has also been detailed by McHenry and Heath and others cited in this chapter. The "rise of literature as a college subject with its own departments and programs coincided with the collapse of the communal literary culture and the corresponding estrangement of literature from its earlier function in polite society" (Graff, *Professing* 20). Now that many of those departments are themselves threatened with collapse by the assignment of the majority of English courses to temporary and part-time instructors, it seems prudent to reassess our historical alternatives.

The profession of college English teaching has been shaped by oppositions that emerged a century ago, most notably the historical opposition of liberal and professional education. This opposition worked to undercut the professionalism of teaching. That opposition begins to shape the political economy of higher education not just in the reactionary stance set out by the Yale Report, but also in the positions staked out by reformers such as Francis Wayland and John Quincy, who sought to accommodate those who did not value "classical literature" but wanted to have the "distinction" of a "liberal education" (Quincy 12). Such accommodations would end up reducing liberal education to general education. The classics had served to prepare students for the learned professions, but *liberal* and *professional* studies were set in opposition to each other as professors of classical literature and languages came to adopt a studied impracticality to distance themselves from those who looked to education to gain practical advancement, including the rising numbers of working-class and women students looking to teaching as a means to social advancement. With the transition to a modern sense of the classics of literature, that position hardened into the "literary antiprofessionalism" of modern literary studies, as Stanley Fish has discussed ("Profession" 353).

The opposition of liberal and professional education became established as a principle of stratification in higher education with the institution of land grant colleges. While land had been granted to new states to establish academies and colleges as early as 1804, the Morrill Act of 1862 provided the resources needed to transform normal schools into state university systems. The purpose of the Act was "to promote the liberal and practical education of the industrial classes in the several pursuits and professions of life" (qtd. Lucas, *American Higher Education* 148). According to Lucas, it was not easy to convince farmers and miners of the values of higher education.[29] Then as now, it was assumed that the best way to articulate those values to the less educated is with practical appeals to utilitarian needs. This assumption positioned and positions the liberal arts on a higher plain divorced from the menial concerns of working people. Such assumptions set up literature as an appropriate study for the most literate, and consign working people to vocational tracks that deaden their imaginative capacities with relentlessly methodical instruction. These class politics may serve the needs of those who work in elite institutions, but defining literature by its impracticality undercuts the teaching of literature and literacy by denying their pragmatic uses and political power. An alternative to the disabling dualism of professional and liberal education is provided by the community-based intellectuals who set out a practically engaged conception of literature that was responsive to the experience of those with less formal education, as I will discuss further when I turn to other alternative perspectives on literature and learning in the Progressive era.

4

How the Teaching of
Literacy Gave Rise
to the Profession of
Literature

> [Universities should not allow themselves to be drawn into] such
> enterprises as professional training, undergraduate instruction,
> supervision and guidance of the secondary school system,
> edification of the unlearned by "university extension" and
> similar excursions into the field of public amusement, training
> of secondary school teachers, encouragement of amateurs by
> "correspondence," etc. . . . The work of teaching properly belongs in
> the university only because and in so far as it incites and facilitates
> the university man's work of inquiry.
>
> Thorstein Veblen in 1918, *The Higher Learning in America: A*
> *Memorandum on the Conduct of Universities by Business Men*, 17.

THORSTEIN VEBLEN'S *THE*
Higher Learning in America is as pointed as his better-known account of "conspicuous consumption" in his *Theory of the Leisure Class* in 1899 (396). Veblen complained that universities were being "given over to the pragmatic, utilitarian disciplines" (34). The "disinterestedness" of traditional intellectuals would be undermined if universities did not establish a critical distance from the rest of public education. While schools were intended to prepare students for "civil life," universities should remain aloof from teaching anything practical, for teaching itself "properly belongs in the university only . . . in so far as it incites and facilitates the university man's work of inquiry" (17). Veblen upheld the "scientist and scholar" as belonging to a different class from teachers. "Schoolmasters and utilitarians" served as a popular enemy that enabled scholars and

critics to make common cause with scientists, and even social scientists such as Veblen (though social scientists were often identified with the utilitarians by humanists who resented encroachments on their cultural authority).[1] Veblen's condemnations of commercialization, bureaucracy, and vocationalism set out an academic's enemies list that has remained remarkably constant for almost a century. Through the last century, this vision has shaped traditional academics' shared sense of mission, while all around them universities were developing into engines of economic development that enabled aspiring middle-class professionals to rise above the provincialism of their local communities and be credentialed as experts. By dismissing the technical and applied disciplines that were coming to dominate universities, traditional academics could ignore the fact that they were in fact educators who faced some of the same challenges as their coworkers in the schools.

Those challenges increased considerably as the educational system expanded. The imposition of written entrance exams and required first-year composition courses was a response to a series of changes that transformed literacy studies and teaching. These changes are set out in the noted Harvard *Report of the Committee on Composition and Rhetoric* in 1897: as a result of rising enrollments,

> classes increased in size nearly fourfold, so as to become wholly unmanageable for oral recitation, and the elective system was greatly enlarged; step by step, the oral method of instruction was then abandoned, and a system of lectures, with periodical written examinations, took its place, so that at last the whole college work was practically done in writing. The need of facility in written expression was, of course, correspondingly increased. (Brereton 112)

As evident in this passage from the last of the four Harvard reports, writing skills became a problem with the diversification of learning and the learned. Broader classes of students gained access as the numbers of high school students doubled each decade.[2] The increases broke up the confines of the curriculum and fueled specialization in public education and throughout the public sphere. The rising enrollments and diversification of disciplines overwhelmed oral modes of instruction, and recitations were replaced by lectures and exams that changed how knowledge was acquired and assessed. Writing became "an implement essential" to all educated work in the classroom, as elsewhere.[3] Entrance exams were instituted to require students to write essays on eight literary works. As such exams spread across the country, they served to justify the spread of first-year composition courses, and the departments built upon them.

As exams in vernacular literacy became the gateway to college, English assumed the role that Latin had played in upholding the learned culture. Given the forces at work, that role was cast in a rather surprising fashion. Then as now, most English courses were in composition, and reformers called for the teaching of writing, not literature, to alleviate the literacy crisis publicized by the Harvard reports. Another possible disciplinary configuration was provided by philology. Philology was an appealing candidate because it combined the promise of the sciences with the prestige of classical languages. Defining the discipline as a "historical scientific study" was seen by some to be a way to force out amateurs and dissuade "utilitarians" from reducing the discipline to a service mission (H. C. G. Brandt 61). However, the rigor of philology's linguistic methods was difficult to sustain in the courses that proliferated as English became the most popular major at Harvard and many other colleges at the beginning of the twentieth century (Cohen, *Education in the United States* 2745–48). A more teachable subject emerged from the surveys of literature that had been introduced before the Civil War. According to Graff, "the profession of literature" issued from the late nineteenth-century "union of Arnoldian humanism and scientific research," though "the teaching of literature could never have achieved its central status" without the "enterprise" of composition (*Professing* 3, 2). Those involved with that "enterprise" have taken issue with accounts of how the teaching of writing became subordinated to the profession of literature (see Friend). In the last chapter, I examined the transition from oratorical to aesthetic conceptions of literature that emerged from the expansion and diversification of literacy and the literate. In this chapter, I will examine how English studies were shaped by the professionalization of literacy and literacy studies.

Like many other fields of work, the teaching of English in college became structured by the historical tendency of professions to download onerous responsibilities onto paraprofessionals such as nurses, paralegals, and adjuncts. General education was assigned to junior faculty and teaching assistants to reduce workloads for an elite class of research faculty. In English departments, as in other professional organizations, the process of downloading time-consuming service work onto paraprofessionals was complicated by the need to control the methods for producing and reproducing the profession's distinctive forms of expertise. The reproductive systems of professions are often controlled in a tacit manner to avoid raising questions about the ways professions work. By denying that they taught for a living, professors could treat teaching as an informal process that required no professional expertise—unlike research, which was upheld as the guiding purpose of the profession. There actually was very little funding for research outside agriculture until midcentury, and even then research in the humanities largely depended upon resources that were freed up by teaching general education on a mass scale. English departments were able to tacitly ignore their reliance on general education as long as they were able to presume that the research enterprise was a single undifferentiated mission. This "tacit component" of professional expertise is, according to Wilensky, fundamental to its "tenacious conservativism" (149). This conservative tendency is evident in how English departments have divorced their professional purposes from their basic institutional functions in ways that have reduced introductory courses to mechanics, thereby undercutting the standing of teaching, and marginalizing the more expansive potentials of the discipline's power base.

At the beginning of the twentieth century, academics in English and other fields that encompassed domains of public discourse consolidated their professional standing by distinguishing their expertise from the services of less credentialed practitioners.[4] High school teachers were still sometimes called *professors*, but that changed as academics distanced themselves from practitioners: social scientists from social workers, linguists from grammarians, and academic critics from literary journalists.[5] In teaching, as in other applied areas, practitioners were more likely to be women, members of the working class, or people of color. Such professional distinctions are difficult to draw, according to Wilensky, when "the lay public cannot recognize the need for special competence in an area where everyone is 'expert'" (145). The discipline's concentration on literature as its distinctive area of expertise thus presented distinctive challenges. Literature was understood to be the province of any well-read person. In response to the popularity of literature, many founders of the profession set themselves up as scholars rather than critics. *Teacher* seems not to have been a viable option for aspiring academics. There are more and less obvious reasons for that. In the antebellum period, teaching had replaced preaching as the principal conduit for those from the lower classes looking to move up through education. Normal schools were largely responsible for the diversification that is often cited as proof that the research university expanded access to underrepresented groups. Thirty percent of students were in normal schools in 1900, as compared to only four percent in 1860, according to Burke. While normal schools were "almost exclusively female institutions," their character changed as they moved up in the college market to become teachers' colleges and then universities (Mattingly 150; see also Harmon 88). This movement decreased attention to teaching and teachers, not simply because research had more prestige, but because the prestige of any college is determined by the standing of its graduates, and teaching offered status only to those who had none.

While such attitudes positioned teaching as beneath the concerns of academics, the rising importance of writing would seem to have made it an attractive study for those seeking to secure their professional status in universities. Writing was central to the service mission of English departments, but other aspects of professionalization also worked against writing studies. According to Susan Miller, writing was becoming not "just a way of preserving thinking for speech," but "a way of thinking" (*Rescuing the Subject* 64). Distinctive modes of thinking were embodied in the methods used by disciplines to compose their characteristic forms of expertise. Making disciplinary genres compelling was a highly rhetorical process that had the potential to raise questions about ethics and ethos, about appeals to emotions and values, and about what was deemed reasonable. Rhetoric had long provided categories for examining these processes, but just as fields of expertise were becoming demarcated in complexly rhetorical ways, the study of rhetoric became relegated to marginal courses with no professional standing.[6] While professionals depended upon their rhetorical mastery of expert conventions, the tacit quality of professionalization worked to make the rhetorical dynamics of disciplinary conventions transparent. As David Russell has discussed, the rhetorical challenges involved in composing disciplinary conventions come to the fore with practical force in the classroom. Teaching and writing are part of the intimate workings of reproducing a discipline, and one of the operating assumptions of such systems is that it is unprofessional to discuss reproduction in public. This assumption helps to explain why, in an era when most graduate students were becoming not scientists or critics but educators, work with education was systematically ignored in ways that were particularly debilitating for college English because of its expansive base and strategic role in regulating access to higher education.

Writing and teaching are fundamental to how any academic discipline articulates its distinctive expertise, but they are doubly important within English studies. Like other academics, English professors write and teach, but they also teach writing. This work is central to the expansive articulation apparatus of college English studies.[7] Concerned with acquiring and exercising literacy at all levels of education, English studies are vital to assessment and teacher training. Into the twentieth century, English departments were also broadly involved in preparing people to write for the popular press and speak to public audiences. Like most disciplines, at the beginning of the twentieth century English studies began to elaborate its professional apparatus by establishing graduate programs and professional journals. However, the professional structure of English studies worked to undercut the broader engagements of the discipline. Journalists and other teachers of public address left departments of English as those departments came to specialize in literary studies. These departures limited the discipline's ability to articulate its values to the public. Writing for public audiences would be further incapacitated by the disabling dualism of technical and creative writing. The former became concerned with writing for work, while the latter came to exclude journalistic writing, and both were marginalized by the professional hierarchies that dismissed writing for general audiences. These divisions were compounded by the devaluation of English professors' expansive work in general education. These restrictions undercut the learning capacities and political influence of the rising profession. Practitioners were discouraged from seeing themselves as teachers and writers who are involved in local communities and institutions in the ways antebellum academics were. To reassess the broader potentials of the work that got left out of the profession's sense of its mission, I want to consider how our discipline was organized in ways that failed to value its work. Our discipline has suffered more than most from the failure of professors to help professionalize teaching, and the Progressive era provides us with a powerful case in point for reflecting upon how broader social movements can be advanced by building coalitions with other educators.

To explore the broader historical capacities of our field of work, I will bring together histories of teacher education, literature, linguistics, and writing courses—including composition, journalism, and creative and technical writing courses. I will begin with collaborations between professors and teachers on entrance exams, which provided a historic opportunity for the discipline to articulate its values to the public. The articulation apparatus of the discipline also included entrance requirements. The failure of English departments to attend to that work compounded the tendency of assessment measures to reduce the functions of literacy to mere formalities. Such formalist tendencies shaped the teaching of literature as well as assessment-driven courses in com-position. Other junctures where the profession articulated the values of its work are noted in a survey of twenty English departments in 1894. The concentra-tion of undergraduate studies on a modern conception of literature was al-ready working to exclude journalism, speech, and linguistics. The potential of a broader conception of literacy studies becomes evident when we look past the centers of the profession to the colleges that offered access to women, workers, and people of color, in large part because of the demand for teachers and writers. The possibilities posed by this development are evident in the Pro-gressive movement, which had a broad impact on high school English courses and general education, and almost no impact above them.[8] The challenges of teaching the less literate to read with refinement contributed to the rise of the New Criticism, but New Critics opposed themselves to the vulgarity of the popular culture and Progressive "educationalists." That opposition strength-ened some of the disabling hierarchies that came to structure the profession.

Articulating the Cost of Admissions

Most historians agree that admissions exams were used to demonstrate the deficiencies that composition requirements were instituted to fix, and that those requirements provided the institutional base upon which English de-partments were built. As a result of its association with entrance exams, com-position has often been consigned to a gatekeeper role. Identifying composition with this function has helped subordinate the teaching of composition to the "higher" purposes of literary studies, even though they have depended upon it, not just institutionally but ideologically. From a critical distance, English professors can ostracize the instrumental role of composition without having to reflect upon how their own positions have been shaped by work with stu-dents seeking professional advancement. Students who failed an entrance exam were often placed into a special writing class to teach them to acknowl-edge their limitations.[9] Such examinations and courses articulated the values of literature and literacy to populations who would never be admitted to elite colleges, as becomes evident when one considers the broader impact of en-trance exams on high school curricula. Efforts to raise college standards in the Progressive era tended to focus on entrance exams as part of an effort to down-load writing instruction on schools. Such efforts are doomed to fail because writing in college is integral to learning in college, and the only way to presume that college writing can be taught in high school is to reduce writing to a set of basic skills. Similarly, the use of literature in college entrance exams tended to routinize literary studies in some of the same ways that instituting composition as an assessment-driven discipline did.

English literature was constituted as an object of formal study in the admissions exams at Harvard that provide the best-known benchmarks for considering how colleges articulated what was required from those who sought to join the educated classes. Harvard stated its plans to assess the speech of entering students in its catalog for 1865–66, and then in 1870 Harvard shifted to testing not speech, but literacy, with examinations on the "critical" and linguistic elements in designated works by Shakespeare and Milton. In the catalog for 1872–73, the criteria were spelled out to emphasize mechanics, and the next year compositions were set on a longer list of literary works—three Shakespearean plays, the *Vicar of Wakefield, Ivanhoe,* and the *Lay of the Last Minstrel.* Literature was initially articulated not so much as a subject to be examined, but as a means to examine whether students had the "the style of a straightforward gentleman," as Harvard professor Le Baron Briggs explained it (rptd. Brereton 61). In "The Harvard Admission Examination in English," Briggs complained that naive students always felt the crude "necessity of infusing morality" into literary works. Briggs haughtily noted that the moralistic tone of one student's essay marked him out for severe "lashing," because "if there is one thing that Harvard College will not tolerate, it is 'gush,'—'gush' in general, and moral or oratorical 'gush' in particular" (rptd. Brereton 69). Examinations of students' character focused on stylistic proprieties until the 1890s, when a battery of tests included an exam on "literary form" and another on general topics drawn from a longer list of literary texts (Brereton 33–37). Because Harvard and other colleges canonized different works of literature, such reading lists presented problems for teachers preparing students for colleges. This problem brought teachers and professors together to deliberate upon what students should be reading and how they should be writing. In 1893 these discussions led to the most influential articulation effort in American history, the Committee of Ten. Under the leadership of President Eliot of Harvard, the committee was set up by the National Educational Association with nine disciplinary subcommittees charged with looking past admission exams to map out high school curricula. The subcommittees worked from the dubious premise that all students should study in the same way as those going on to college, even though fewer than 10 percent did. The ten members of the English subcommittee included seven professors, most notably its secretary, the Harvard Shakespearean George Kittredge. The subcommittee set out a curriculum that devoted 60 percent of coursework to literature, 30 percent to composition, and 10 percent to rhetoric and grammar.[10] Teachers were advised not to lecture on histories of literature but to stress close readings of "Masterpieces" (*Report of the Committee on Secondary Studies* 90). The committee argued that students should write about literary works rather than commonplace themes from daily life (94–95). The canonical texts and methods set out by the Committee of Ten, according to Graff, "not only gave definition to college English as a literary enterprise, but compelled the secondary schools to conform to that definition" (*Professing Literature* 99).

Examinations of literature tended to strip it down to formal elements that were easier to master and measure, much as writing has often been reduced to mechanics in assessment-driven composition courses. The committee might have confronted the formalist tendencies of assessment if the participants had attended to teachers' complaints that requiring lists of texts whose only connection was that they were deemed to be literary made literature ahistorical and virtually unteachable. Articles by teachers in journals such as *Educational Review* and magazines such as *Harper's Monthly Magazine* provide a sense of the forums that were open to teachers and professors of English. Professors with popular reputations, such as Brander Matthews, still wrote for magazines, and teachers' contributions to such publications show that some had the expertise to join in deliberations upon the "best methods of teaching English literature" (Pancoast 133; see also Matthews). As discussed in such articles, the lists of unrelated masterpieces set out by entrance requirements almost compelled "the disconnected reading of books" by imposing a formalist approach that divorced texts from the contexts that enabled a student to understand their historical and contemporary implications (Pancoast 136–37). This isolation of texts from their interpretive contexts was compounded by requiring such classics as Arnold's *On Translating Homer* that seemed irrelevant to students (see James Russell). Such criticisms eventually dislodged reading lists from entrance exams, and thereby eliminated what could have been a historic opportunity for teachers and professors to create cohesive and coherent programs of study. If they had been supported by the profession, such collaborations might have yielded disciplinary alternatives to the skills-based aptitude exams that would be marketed by testing experts and private corporations. By distancing itself from such articulations, the profession "lost considerable power to transform its professional values into public policy" (Trachsel 178).

Such developments were not inevitable. More sustained collaborations might have arisen out of the articulation programs that were established before 1900 in forty-two institutions, mostly land-grant institutions in the Midwest and West (Lucas, *American Higher Education* 154). In these accreditation programs, faculty became involved in certifying schools after reviewing curricula, observing classes, and even negotiating workloads with school boards. In other national educational systems, such as Germany's, these school-college partnerships offered professors strategic opportunities to shape public education (see Hays). English professors in California and elsewhere published teacher manuals such as Gayley and Bradley's *Suggestions to Teachers of English in the Secondary Schools* that articulated the methods and values of the discipline to broader audiences. The spread of such efforts led to the creation of the North Central Association in 1895. Disciplinary faculty such as Fred Newton Scott helped organize the agency and spoke for its "organic" collaborations as a less hierarchical alternative to the reading lists that Scott felt had been dictated in a "feudal" manner by private colleges in the East (qtd. in Stewart and Stewart 48).[11] Scott repeatedly called upon professors to work with teachers. Unfortunately, rapid rises in enrollments put intense pressure on articulation, and research universities generally failed to value such service duties, even in departments of education.[12] "Content" faculty were freed to divorce their sense of purpose from their broader educational duties. Articulation became the responsibility of professors of education, who were pressed by their peripheral positions and expansive obligations to be as practical as possible, which in practice meant concentrating on "methods" courses that were often as isolated from "content" disciplines as mechanics-driven composition courses tended to be.[13]

The dismissal of teacher preparation consolidated the structure of disciplines as national organizations with marginal obligations to local institutions. The collaborations with teachers that continued often used the Committee of Ten report as a point of departure. According to a foreign observer in 1895, the report had "for America the importance of an official pedagogy, scientifically progressive and professional" (rptd. in Cohen, *Education in the United States* 970). *Progressive, professional,* and *scientific* were complexly related terms that shaped the institutional and ideological grounds upon which English departments were built. The definition of high schools by their preparatory function provoked opposition from Progressive coalitions of administrators and professors of education, who maintained that the Committee of Ten's failure to attend to students' experiences led to its elitist conclusions. These divisive conflicts among disciplinary specialists and professional educators had even broader impacts than the exams themselves, according to Krug and to Angus and Mirel. A leading scientific spokesman for the professional educators was the psychologist G. Stanley Hall, a founding figure in research on childhood development who had a formative influence on his student John Dewey. According to Hall (1905), the Committee of Ten was "almost an unmitigated curse to high schools" because it had ignored differences in individual development (rptd. in Cohen, *Education in the United States*). Building on his work with the Committee of Ten, Eliot in 1900 helped establish the College Entrance Examination Board.[14] If the discipline had become more broadly involved in addressing teachers' and professors' shared needs to articulate the values of what they taught, these collaborations could have had a more positive impact on the public education system. What emerged instead was an educational corporation that capitalized on this public need. While tests of basic skills discounted the practical values of literacy studies, such examinations also limited the social functions of literary studies by shrouding them in formalist presuppositions.[15]

At its founding in 1883, the Modern Language Association did include discussions of teaching, though one of the common aims was to shift skills instruction onto schools.[16] Most of the articles in the first volume of *PMLA* were actually on pedagogy. Some contributors did not have PhDs, and others held professorships that bridged diverging areas of study, such as "Rhetoric and the English Language." These articles examined how to disarticulate the discipline's research agenda from its broad educational duties. Such articles as Hunt's "The Place of English in the College Curriculum" set out the discipline as "an intellectual study for serious workers" and not just a "desultory" pastime for "leisure hours." According to Hunt, "in this day of specialties," the discipline needed to develop rigorous "philosophic and critical methods." Such methods would force out practitioners with only "a general society knowledge of the literature," and "efficient" teachers could then be tasked with teaching composition (40–47). These articles generally opposed literary studies to the methods of both science and rhetoric (see Easton, Garnett). According to James Morgan Hart's "The College Course in English Literature, How It May Be Improved," philology was worthy of research, and rhetoric might be useful in composition (which was deemed to be a precollegiate study). However, "the proper object of literary study is to train us to read, to grasp an author's personality in all its bearings. And the less rhetoric here, the better" (35). Unsullied by rhetoric, literature was set out as an ennobling study of masterworks of the imagination. By instilling the tastes of the "aristocracy" in the "bourgeoisie," such histories of "the cultured classes" would help the educated appreciate the virtues of well-ordered subordination (Hart 91; Shumway 36).

PMLA ceased publishing on pedagogical topics around 1903, when the MLA closed down its Pedagogical Section. Under the leadership of Scott, this section had surveyed members regarding what should be included in graduate studies in rhetoric, how writing should be taught, and what purposes were to be served by such teaching (rptd. Brereton 186–233). The "unusual if not alarming energy" that was noted in the Pedagogical Section just before it was closed down suggests that some members were energized by questioning disciplinary assumptions, while others were alarmed by such questions (rptd. in Brereton 187). As one noted, the "business" of composition was not really part of "veritable authorship," which "is something far higher, something of an altogether different order. I am unable to define it, but I know it when it comes across my path" (rptd. in Brereton 231). Because such "higher" truths could not be openly stated in practical terms, they were better left to the imagination. The Pedagogical Section was closed down as the MLA revised its stated purpose from "the study of the Modern Languages" to the "the study of the Modern Languages and their Literatures through the publication of the results of investigations," and then in 1916 to simply "research" (see Douglas, "Accidental Institution"). The movement of MLA away from discussions of the institutional work of the discipline left a wide range of concerns unaddressed.

These problems led to the organization of the National Council of Teachers of English in 1911 (with Scott as president). The NCTE was organized to address two related problems: the unprofessional workloads imposed on basic literacy courses and the dominance of secondary curricula by the literary works set by entrance requirements. Workloads were the first item of business at the first conference and in the first issue of the organization's *English Journal*, but NCTE really began with the English Round Table set up by the National Education Association to "protest" the impositions of the College Entrance Examination Board (Hosic 102). From his work as chairman of the NEA Round Table, James Hosic published *English Problems* in 1912, and the report was excerpted in *English Journal* that same year. Hosic and his collaborators were concerned that college entrance exams restricted the broader purposes of high schools, especially since the tests concentrated on a narrow set of skills and texts that were imposed on teachers who taught a wide range of students. Criticisms of entrance requirements and debates over how to address the overwhelming workloads of teachers of writing were a mainstay of the first NCTE conventions, with much of the guiding terminology drawn from the Progressive educational movement of the time. Teachers were struggling to negotiate institutional pressures to concentrate on utilitarian applications and expressed concerns that instruction was moving away from "culture and toward mere vocation" (College and High School Section 55). By supporting these important discussions, the NCTE was serving the purpose set out by its founders to provide a "Progressive" forum where teachers could develop their "class-consciousness" by deliberating upon their shared methods and needs, especially workloads ("National Council of Teachers of English Proceedings" 38).

These deliberations provide a case study in the challenges involved in organizing the profession to address the shared needs of teachers and professors of English. Scott had helped launch a national study of working conditions in 1909 through the midwestern division of the MLA after the Pedagogical Section was closed down. The first issue of *English Journal* began with a report on the study undertaken by Edwin Hopkins and his committee, entitled "Can Good Composition Teaching Be Done under Present Conditions?" The answer was a resounding "no." The committee provided statistics that demonstrate that the poor working conditions faced by most college and high school English teachers have been fundamental to the profession since its founding. Hopkins's *Report of the Committee on the Labor and Cost of the Teaching of English* was based on surveys of a thousand college and high school teachers in thirty-three states. English teachers were found to teach more students for less pay than those in other disciplines. College composition teachers typically had more than a hundred students, resulting in continuous turnovers that left the least experienced with the most demanding courses (Hopkins, *Labor and Cost*). The 1920s saw the onset of "mass higher education" according to David Levine (39). Confronted with too many students with too many needs, Hopkins and his NCTE collaborators tried to establish English as a "laboratory" subject founded on scientific research about student learning that could be enlisted to persuade schools to reduce teachers' workloads ("Can Good Composition" 3). It is impossible to know what could have been achieved if the discipline had devoted more of its institutional and intellectual resources to these collaborations.

Scott criticized efforts to make an "exact science" of teaching in "Efficiency for Efficiency's Sake," which was his presidential address to the North Central Association of Colleges and Secondary Schools in 1914 (49), but in his presidential address to the NCTE in 1912, he set out two questions that mirrored the concerns of the prevailing professional hierarchy: "The first is, How shall the efficiency of our teaching of composition be tested or evaluated? The second is, How can we arouse and maintain in our students a genuine interest in the English classics?" ("Our Problems" 2). By identifying literature as a higher calling and writing as a basic skill to be tested, the profession made part of its work a mystery and the rest merely methodical. From a cynical perspective, one could argue that the rising status of the profession is evident in how it succeeded in placing its more laborious duties beneath its consideration. By such a measure, the closing of the Pedagogical Section of the MLA was an important step in its rise to become a scholarly organization. From a more pragmatic perspective, we can observe that a discipline loses the capacity to learn from and intervene in the work that it ignores. The learning capacities of the discipline have been most critically overloaded in those areas where the heaviest demands are placed upon it: at the borders of the field where it articulates its values to those learning its uses. It is precisely in such areas where the pressures to be methodically efficient are strongest, as evident in assessment-driven composition courses. The formalist tendencies of assessment restricted the purposes of the discipline, along with access to it. By reducing the cost of admissions to basic skills, the discipline discounted its general education offerings and denied itself the chance to learn from them in ways that could have been more equitable, and empowering.

Mapping Out the Field of Work

Students generally major in engineering to become engineers, and most music majors hope to become musicians, but English departments have been hesitant to specify what they make of students ever since English majors were disarticulated from general education offerings. Even to ask what an English major prepares students to do is to raise doubts about whether one understands what English studies are about. Professional anxieties about the functions of English studies are evident in the first survey of English majors, which was published in *English in American Universities by Professors in the English Departments of Twenty Representative Institutions* in 1895. In the previous year the Chicago periodical the *Dial* had published descriptions of curricula from around the country, and they were then gathered into a volume by the magazine's editor, William Morton Payne. Payne was one of the journalist critics who worked in the field until it became demarcated as an academic discipline. Payne also surveyed the field in a companion anthology, *American Literary Criticism*, in 1904. *English in American Universities* is, according to Gerald Graff, "the single best source" on "the ideological divisions" that structured the discipline, which were handled with an "unexpectedly high degree of sophistication" (*Professing* 101). The discipline was assuming a literary orientation that was becoming disarticulated from philological studies, most commonly in historical surveys oriented to teaching "literature as literature, with true aesthetic discernment of its spiritual quality" (Payne 124). Some departments were already confining writing instruction to first-year courses, and others had raised admissions standards to download such duties onto schools. The varied stances set out by the departments that Payne surveyed document the range of possibilities that confronted the discipline—and the forms and forces that were coming to contain them.

In his introduction to the collection, Payne reviews how the reading public had become interested in college English studies as a result of the Committee of Ten and Harvard reports on composition and rhetoric that gave "the reform movement its strongest impulse" (12). That "movement" had advanced to the point where "the teaching of English" was becoming equated with "the teaching of English literature." Matthew Arnold was the lead figure in that equation, and J. S. Mill was factored in to divide literary studies from utilitarian concerns (8). Such calculations set composition off as a service function and treated rhetoric as an anachronism. Language studies were also viewed as a distraction from the "kindling of the soul" that makes "literature a personal message to the individual" (9). These assessments shaped curricula in varied ways, as can be seen in the descriptions, which range from three to eleven pages. Respondents also provided details on staffing, course offerings, and institutional constraints and purposes. The sample includes "venerable Eastern institutions," "small colleges" (including a women's college, Wellesley, with the only woman respondent in the sample), and the "state-supported institutions of the New West." State universities were perceived by Payne to be the most innovative precisely because they had to work with "cruder material" (22–23). For their part, contributors from more broadly based departments often apologized for the limitations of their efforts to imitate more prestigious universities, and blamed their limitations on the provincialism of their students. Just as Le Baron Briggs complained about naive students' tendency to moralize over literature, several respondents attributed their curricular shortcomings to their having to spend time correcting students' language and character, particularly their crude tendencies to read literary texts as morality plays.

As such responses suggest, English professors were intent on articulating a less didactic and more professional sense of purpose, with efforts to professionalize the discipline working in tandem with students' efforts to professionalize themselves. Philological and literary studies competed for priority in graduate and undergraduate curricula in ways that set out diverging trajectories for the discipline. Like many of his contributors, Payne opposed the "intrusion of science upon a domain set apart for other, if not higher, purposes" (20). According to Payne, the methods of linguistics had become well established, but "aesthetic criticism" was still in a state of comparative "anarchy." Nonetheless, neither "the science of linguistics nor the art of rhetoric" could any longer "masquerade as the study of literature." Both were thought to be better off in separate departments, as was being instituted in departments ranging from Columbia to Stanford (26–27). According to Graff, "humanistic moralists" were at the time joining forces with "aesthetic formalists" to set out the agenda for studying literature as literature, with "much of the program of the latter-day New Criticism" already "formulated by the mid nineties" (*Professing* 123).

As Graff and others have discussed, the methods of the New Criticism were shaped by trends in general education, including the assessment pressures that worked to concentrate literacy instruction on autonomous literary works (see also Applebee, *Literature* 55–65). As several contributors stressed, "the study of literature means the study of literature, not of biography, not of literary history, . . . or anything except the works themselves, viewed as their creators wrote them, viewed as art, as transcripts of humanity" (96). A half dozen contributors took pride in noting that they taught texts, not textbooks. This approach had become possible with the cheap reprint series of the time, and it had become necessary to instill discernment in students who lacked a shared history. The concentration on literary criticism was also justified by the assumption that professors should lecture from their research rather than having students recite commonplaces. Most of the curricula surveyed in Payne are organized historically.[17] While some professors still spoke of moral senti-ments, others repudiated preaching the "beauties of the poet's utterance" as a distraction from having students "systematically approach the work as a work of art, find out the laws of its existence as such, . . . the meaning it has, and the significance of that meaning" (Payne 96).

The need to establish an autonomous discipline distinct from the work of education helps to explain why some of the most broadly appealing areas of literary study were given so little attention in curricula. One might expect an emerging field to use popular interests to attract more practitioners, but few contributors to *English in American Universities* considered students' interests or needs in setting out programs of study. In fact students were often required to begin with the least accessible and most difficult area of study—medieval philology. At the transition from rhetorical to literary studies in the antebellum period, such studies had been enlisted to make English as rigorous as ancient languages by such figures as Francis March at Lafayette College. In his con-tribution to *English in American Universities*, March took pride in how his de-partment had become internationally recognized for its philological emphasis, even though he acknowledged that few students had much use for it (Payne 81). Emphasizing such inaccessible topics in gateway courses served purposes more complex than simply limiting access or shoring up credibility. As with college entrance requirements, beginning with rigorously methodological ele-ments helped ensure that students learned to distinguish the concerns of the discipline from the interests that attracted students to it. After a semester trac-ing the etymological sources of a work of literature, students would have tacitly understood that whether they enjoyed a book was irrelevant to how they were to read it.

While Payne praised the Committee of Ten for recommending that teach-ers have students concentrate on close reading, he deferred to the "instructor's individuality" to answer practical questions about how to teach students to read (16). Pedagogy is so routinely ignored in the descriptions of curricula in *English in American Universities* that any mention at all is noteworthy. Even when a contributor discusses intended outcomes, as Martin Sampson did in describing the curriculum at the University of Indiana, the prevailing assess-ment seems to be that "each instructor teaches as he pleases," or as Barrett Wendell of Harvard noted, "each teacher's best method is his own" (Payne 95, 48). Sampson ironically notes that some professors filled "the student full of biography and literary history," while others merely taught "literary parsing" or "the moral purposes of the poet or novelist; anything, in short, except placing the student face to face with the work itself, and acting as his spectacles when his eyesight was blurred" (Payne 95). As long as such differences were not subjected to critical inquiry, professors such as Sampson could remain tacitly assured that "our ultimate object is the same." Pedagogy was discussed by one of the contributors who published on teaching, John Genung of Amherst. Genung set out "workshop" methods that treated students' writing as literature in the making, as I will discuss in the next section (Payne 112). Pedagogical methods were also addressed by the contributor from the University of Chicago, which offered a course on the teaching of composition that included rhetorical theory and history; a course in the "theory of literary teaching" was offered at Nebraska, where complaints were raised that students had neither "literary traditions or taste or training, or interest in pure literature" (126).

Of the twenty institutions included in *English in American Universities*, only Harvard, Amherst, and Michigan had composition programs with any standing, and even at Amherst, Genung had to acknowledge that first-year composition was taught by "incompetent and inexperienced teachers" (Payne 111). At Michigan and other institutions with a separate composition program that reported enrollments in detail, fewer faculty and more instructors taught more students than in other areas of English studies, where the loads were as low as six or eight classroom hours per week. The contributor from one of the institutions with the lowest teaching loads detailed how those loads had been achieved. Melville Anderson from the newly established Leland Stanford University discussed how admissions standards had been raised to reduce the "inundation of Freshman themes" that had threatened to sweep away "all the literary courses" (Payne 52). An exchange between the contributors from Stanford and Berkeley over who had instituted higher admissions requirements provides a telling example of how such issues defined the standing of departments, and through them their institutions.[18] Universities such as the University of California, which adopted the certification system, also wanted to raise their standing, but by working with rather than away from public schools. Another example is provided by the University of Nebraska, which worked with fifty-five certified schools to give advanced placement credit for surveys of literature.

The composition program at Harvard provided the exception that improved the rule by showing the profession what happened to men of letters who devoted their careers to paper grading.[19] As Katherine Adams has discussed, and Brereton has documented, Harvard had one of the most extensive writing programs in the country, but it was already positioned as a service unit. According to Wendell Berry's contribution to *English in American Universities* (which is excerpted in Brereton), more than half of English enrollments were in composition, as seems to have been the case in the other institutions that provided detailed enrollments. Then as now, composition was largely taught by paraprofessional instructors. While Hill was a founder of the Associated Press, his journalistic background gained him little credibility in the English department at Harvard, for he and his colleagues in composition had to work longer to be promoted (see Simmons, "Constructing Writers"). According to Graff, such professors carried on the gentleman amateur tradition of Harvard literati such as Longfellow and Lowell, meaning that they wrote for broader and less scholarly audiences (*Professing* 87). Hill and others who taught in the program published influential textbooks, and also introduced creative writing workshops that were imitated at Iowa and elsewhere. Such creative writing courses became a common part of composition offerings in the following decades. At Harvard as elsewhere, advanced writing courses developed out of the forensics programs that had required students to deliver orations to the assembled college.[20] From its move to the first year in 1885, a theme writing course dominated by mechanical concerns was the base of the program. Harvard's version of composition was famous for emphasizing impromptu themes drawn from daily life that were meant to imitate how journalists learned to write from writing on the job.

Such teaching duties carried little prestige and a lot of work. Even a national leader such as Scott complained of the "Sisyphean labors" of grading three-thousand essays a year, with many written "crudely, some execrably" (Payne 120). In his contribution to *English in American Universities*, Scott acknowledged that students needed the individual attention that he felt Channing's generation had been able to provide, but "now the hungry generations tread us down" (Payne 122). Faced with too many students with too many problems, the profession understandably chose to divert its focus to higher purposes. If it had concentrated on such basic problems, as many a teacher selflessly did, the discipline would not likely have gained much respect even if it had succeeded at overcoming them. Writing and reading were generally seen to be rudimentary skills that were always in need of repair, meaning that teachers could gain little recognition even if they succeeded at the impossible task of fixing them to the public's satisfaction. In any case, the challenges of gaining professional standing for work with literacy were not confined to composition, and they were only compounded by dismissing them there because the leadership of the profession became divorced from the work of practitioners.

How Work with Literacy Became Isolated
from Language Studies and Public Discourse

Questions about teaching did not go unanswered so much as unasked, at least among those who looked to MLA rather than NCTE as the center of the profession. This failure to attend to the basic work of the profession is understandable, given the quite different opportunities facing teachers and researchers. From the origins of English departments, composition has been consigned to "temporary" instructors—lecturers, junior faculty, women instructors, and graduate students, who were assigned heavier loads at lower pay.[21] The temping out of composition has shaped the development of the whole discipline because composition has been the largest area of work in English departments since they were built upon it. This professional pyramid freed scholars from worrying about teaching, and left teachers with little time to worry about anything else. The "creation of the underclass" of composition instructors laid the foundation for the "profession of literature" (Connors 172; see also Susan Miller, *Textual Carnivals*). Professors assumed that they would not have to teach writing if school teachers did their job. Introductory courses in literature as well as composition would be eliminated by raising standards to force high schools to do general education (see Hughes). By mirroring the attitudes of careerist students that general education was a waste of time for professionals, English professors subordinated liberal to professional education in ways that undercut their institutional work.

William Lyon Phelps was one of the best known proponents of the idea that it was a "hideous waste" of expertise to assign a man who had studied at an institution such as Harvard "to correct spelling, grammar, paragraphing," a job at which "any primary school-ma'am would probably have been more efficient" (rptd. in Graff and Warner 160). After graduate studies at Harvard, Phelps spent a year correcting some eight hundred themes a week before leaving Harvard to join the faculty at Yale in 1892. Yale resisted public calls to require composition, and Phelps gained national attention when he claimed that Yale's students wrote better than Harvard's without having been taught composition. Phelps's criticisms were especially damning because he taught at the leading institutions on both sides of the "composition question," and he was known for his teaching, especially his famous Chautauqua lectures. He took pride in startling his students by lecturing in a conversational manner after observing how the "icily contemptuous" style of his own professors had taken the joy out of the classroom. Ironically, Phelps felt that his success as a teacher actually lessened his chances of promotion. He reported that he was threatened with dismissal in 1895 for teaching the first modern novel course in America— not because the course had failed, but become its popularity was demeaning to an institution such as Yale. At Yale, Lounsbury's philologically oriented survey of literature served as an alternative to first-year composition courses. Lounsbury haughtily noted that "there is but one way of keeping certain people from writing wretchedly, and that is by keeping them from writing at all" (rptd. in Brereton 282). Lounsbury and likeminded New Humanists such as Charles Osgood at Princeton dismissed calls in "the popular press" to teach composition because they saw it as too "technical" and too concerned with the "worship of 'the Average'" to be a "liberal study" (Lounsbury 264; Osgood 233, 235). Such attitudes had a pervasive impact because faculty in elite institutions shaped the ethos of graduate programs, and through them the curricula of public institutions of learning across the country.

Such faculty members were taught to leave composition courses to be defined by handbooks, readers, and exercise manuals that gave overworked teachers material that was easy to teach, though often pointless to learn (see Connors, *Composition-Rhetoric*, especially 232–40). This project had little place for a civic sense of rhetoric concerned with debating public controversies. Faced with endless stacks of papers, teachers were left to their own devices and came to view the civic purposes of rhetoric as a footnote to the teaching of "exposition" as the model for academic discourse. A standard text for teaching exposition for over forty years was Fulton's popular *Expository Writing* (1912). According to Fulton, the "dispassionate and unbiased" style of exposition could be enlivened by signs of "the writer's personality," but the style of exposition was distinct from the rigor of the scientist and the passion of the "reformer." To master such differences, students were taught to model their thinking on the sort of essays that Fulton's *Expository Writing* set as models: Arnold's "Racial Elements of English Character," Brander Matthews's "Americanisms," and essays that applied evolutionary doctrines to "Progress and Poverty" and "The Migration of the Races of Men."

William James's frequently anthologized "The Social Value of the College-Bred" encapsulates how such courses helped aspiring professionals who were not well bred appear well read. James advised students that a college education would help them distinguish themselves by the distinctions they made. According to James, "as a class, we college graduates" must be able to distinguish ourselves to serve as models for the less educated, and thereby ensure that "our" culture "has spreading power" (rptd. in Fulton 30). The "spreading power" of James's essay is evident in the circulation of the piece. It was first published in the popular *McClure's Magazine*, and then it was widely anthologized to become a touchstone of the literate culture for students seeking access to that culture. James notes that the distinctive functions of higher education were being appropriated by the very magazines that circulated his essay, because they had become a "popular university" with "new educational power." As a Harvard don lecturing popular audiences on the virtues of the educated, James and his essay provided students with a model for how to distinguish themselves in a class that granted access to professional advancement to those who could demonstrate their mastery of such distinctions.[22]

Expository essays presented students with a highly formalized but purportedly transparent set of conventions that value self-restraint and impartiality. Yet even within such incapacitated forms lay opportunities to articulate more integrated approaches to English studies. Some of these possibilities are evident in John Genung's textbooks, which represented rhetoric as "the constructive study of literature" (140). In *The Study of Rhetoric in College*, Genung expanded literary studies to include not just journalism but also students' essays, which were "to be treated not as school-boy task-work, but as earnestly meant literature" (156). Genung is often identified as just another one of the textbook writers who promoted "current-traditional rhetoric," but rather than running students through exercise routines, he promoted "laboratory" methods for literary study that at least in principle treated students as authors. As an ordained minister and a German-trained PhD whose handwriting was so elegant that it was reportedly used in the manufacture of typefaces, Genung marks the transition from antebellum preachers of sentiment to credentialed critics of literature. From an oratorical sense of literature that included journalism and composition, Genung held forth the possibility of viewing a student writer as "an originator, not a mere absorber, of thought." Such possibilities arise whenever teachers of literacy recognize that "other studies are something to know; this is something to do" (135). While that "something" is often re-duced to basic skills, the inability of such categories to encompass the prag-matics of literacy is what gives work with them such power, and possibility.

While first-year composition courses were often overwhelmed by oppres-sive workloads and debilitating purposes, some English departments developed wider programs of work with writing. In the first decades of the twentieth cen-tury, some three hundred colleges developed writing majors or minors. Creative writing courses were especially common in women's colleges according to Adams's *A Group of Their Own*, which provides a general history of advanced writing courses and an account of the spread of creative writing workshops that significantly differs from Myers's analysis.[23] Courses in writing fiction, poetry, and journalism became a common supplement to literature and com-position offerings in many departments of English, and in the departments that were beginning to break off from them. The rhetoric department that Scott established at Michigan in 1903 was one of the more notable. Before being reabsorbed into English at his retirement in 1926, it developed the sort of "vertical curricula" in writing that Crowley has called for, and which has recently reemerged in independent writing programs and broadly based Eng-lish departments (Crowley, *Composition* 263; also Shamoon, Howard, and Jameson). Scott's department was the first to teach newspaper writing, accord-ing to Stewart and Stewart. Like most such programs, Scott's department was understaffed and overloaded, offering fifteen courses, which ranged from first-year composition through journalism courses to seminars on rhetoric and the teaching of composition (see Stewart, "Harvard's Influence"; also Berlin, *Rhetoric and Reality* 55–56; and Adams, *Progressive Politics* 65). Other notable programs existed at Mount Holyoke, which offered a major in rhetoric and some of the first courses in journalism, playwriting, and the teaching of rhetoric, according to Wozniak (122–23).[24] Such accounts expand the picture provided by Payne's survey to show that as the discipline was narrowing its focus to litera-ture, some departments were developing courses in business and technical writ-ing, newspaper and magazine journalism, other forms of public address, and even English as a second language.

Journalism connected creative writing with what was taught in other com-position courses—until journalists left university English departments, along with rhetoricians concerned with public speaking. Already by 1893, a survey found separate speech departments and programs in fifty-two institutions (Gray, "Some Teachers and the Transition to Twentieth-Century Speech Edu-cation" 423). A noted step in the growing independence of speech was taken in 1914, when the organization that would become the Communications Association of America was founded by seventeen members of the NCTE Public Speaking Section, with twelve of the seventeen coming from large public universities in the Midwest (see Rarig and Greaves). The departure of rhetoricians interested in public speaking further isolated those who remained in English departments. As speech departments left the humanities to take up the methods of the social sciences, rhetoric became a marginal concern on both sides of the modern divide between the arts and sciences.[25] When journalism followed the trajectory of speech, composition became confined to academic and personal forms of writing with little sense of the genres that bridged the two domains. As Katherine Adams discusses, journalism was generally seen as a trade by English professors, and then as now, those concerned with creative writing sharply distinguished it from "mere" journalism. Some early journalism programs offered writing courses for business and science, according to Adams, but journalism departments soon rose above such service duties and joined with other "content" disciplines in looking to English to teach the formalities of writing (see Cunliffe). The departure of journalism and speech left composition largely defined by such service duties, including business and technical writing courses that were often even more formalistic and less respected than basic composition courses.

By distancing itself from journalism and composition, creative writing became something more refined and less broadly engaged than what it might have become if more productive use had been made of its potential to bridge literary and literacy studies. Some sense of what that might have been is provided by D. G. Myers's argument that creative writing emerged to foster creative reading in an effort to teach literature from a writer's point of view. In addition to its origins at Harvard, Myers identifies creative writing with broader trends in Progressive education. According to Myers, "creative writing was first taught under its own name in the 1920s" in Progressivists' reforms of high schools, most notably by "*the* pioneer of creative writing," Hugh Mearns (187).[26] Mearns studied at Harvard with Wendell, Baker, and William James (who made him promise not to get a PhD). Mearns was recruited to teach in the laboratory school run by Columbia's Teachers College, with which Dewey had been involved. In an era when Robert Frost clubs were helping to popularize creative writing classes, Mearns gained a national reputation for promoting workshop methods in collections such as the Progressive Education Association's *Creative Expression*, written by Gertrude Hartman.[27] From such sources (which he often pointedly critiques), Myers argues that literature presents distinctive pedagogical challenges because it represents "a fusion of knowledge and practice" that has to be experienced to be understood (12). This "constructivist" approach to literary study is identified by Myers as a humanistic alternative to our discipline's emphasis on formal analysis. Myers at points strains to distance creative writing from composition in ways that suit current hierarchies better than his historical sources, but he is right that a more holistic sense of knowledge in the making is needed to bridge the opposition of interpretation and composition that has divided the discipline (9, 172).

Such divisions widened when the departure of journalism left composition and creative writing with little in common (except students). The chasm that opened up between the two was paralleled by the gaps in language studies left by linguists' movement to form an autonomous discipline. Works on philology such as Lounsbury's *History of the English Language* had founded English studies on the history of Anglo-Saxon, with literature largely studied to document the historical development of linguistic laws. Changes in language were understood to be embedded in broader cultural developments. However, philologists were generally not interested in pedagogy, and teaching held even less interest for linguists. Such considerations generally become secondary when a subject is defined as a rule-governed system, for then teaching and learning become merely a matter of memorizing the rules. Linguistic formalism compounded this tendency. According to Matthews's *Grammatical Theory in the United States*, linguistics is founded on the assumption that "the study of formal relations can and should be separated from that of meaning" (3). As linguists worked to establish a scientific footing for their discipline, and critics set out to study literary texts as objects unto themselves, literary and linguistic studies became defined in terms that had nothing to do with each other. Professors of literature such as Brander Matthews rejected the idea that linguistics and literature have "any necessary connection" because "one falls in the domain of science and the other in the domain of art" (340). For their part, linguists responded that they would no longer be "subsidiary . . . to the study of literature, or paired with it as 'the linguistic side' of philology," as Bloomfield proclaimed in 1925 at the founding of the Linguistic Society of America, which drew more of its founding members from English departments than any other discipline ("Why a Linguistic Society?" 4).

Andresen details how linguistics, English, and anthropology followed diverging "arcs of development" in the first quarter of the twentieth century (though linguistics departments did not appear even in research universities until after World War II). Even before the establishment of structuralism as the model for linguistics, the discipline was invested in what Andresen has characterized as a "neogrammarian, mechanical conception of language" that divorced language studies from social contexts and educational applications (37). The purposes and needs of language users became irrelevant to the study of language, much as the popular motivations and uses of literature became peripheral to its profession. The practical limitations of linguistic formalism are evident in Bloomfield's vision of how linguists' "professional consciousness" would serve the "public interest" ("Why" 69). Bloomfield looked down on teachers who "do not know what language is, and yet must teach it." However, when he turned to explain how making a science of language would improve its teaching, he treated learning as a transparent process not worth examining (69). Ignoring matters of intention, use, and meaning, Bloomfield discussed the acquisition of literacy as a process of rote mastery to be made more efficient through "purely formal exercises," with pedagogical activities such as storytelling dismissed because the "practical and cultural values of reading can play no part in the elementary stages" ("Linguistics and Reading" 263–64). Bloomfield set out this formalist model with all the certainty of a believer speaking to the faithful. He did not feel a need to cite any educational research because "the facts which have been set forth" were obvious, at least to those who understood language to be a self-enclosed system (264).

As linguists moved to the boundaries of the field and then beyond them (along with journalists and rhetoricians working with public speaking), English studies lost contact with the anthropological conceptions of culture that had been provided by philology, and would later reemerge with cultural studies. Linguistics lost a broadly based institutional engagement with the pragmatic challenges that language learners pose to language theories. These losses are evident in the absence of linguists from the largest organization of teachers of language in North America, the National Council of Teachers of English. In the 1920s, as linguists began setting out their own programs of research, NCTE's Committee on Grammar Terminology carried on an incessant discussion of how to teach grammar. In response to the overwhelming pressures on teachers to concentrate on syntactic proprieties, researchers argued that teaching formal grammar apart from students' writing had little impact on it or them. The contributions of the few linguistically informed participants provide a sense of the educational impact that might have been achieved if there had

~been a critical mass of pedagogically oriented linguistic researchers (Connors, *Composition-Rhetoric* 156–70). Most notable were three of Scott's students: Gertrude Buck (who was very involved with the NCTE grammar committees), Charles Fries (whose publications included *The Teaching of the English Language*), and Sterling Leonard (whose most relevant work was his posthumously published *Current English Usage*). Leonard's "How English Teachers Correct Papers" was exactly the sort of linguistically informed and pedagogically oriented research that was sorely needed by overworked teachers. Limited as it was, this sort of research could not hope to redress the impact of prescriptive handbooks of grammar, which according to a survey in 1927 were the only textbooks used in 40 percent of midwestern composition programs (Connors, *Composition* 147).

There is perhaps no starker indication of just how isolated the most commonly taught English courses were than the fact that so many apparently had students read nothing more than a handbook of syntactic conventions. National surveys show that most composition courses were staffed by teachers who were "inexperienced, unfitted by nature for the work, ill-trained, and sometimes, in addition, reluctant and disaffected" (Scott, Thomas, and Manchester 593). That was in 1918. As early as the 1890s, teaching assistants had begun to be used to staff composition courses in universities, and at the turn of the twentieth century, such programs began to be led not by researchers on teaching writing, but by administrators whose scholarly interests lay elsewhere.[28] Commentators estimated that most English professors began their careers teaching first-year composition without having received any training for "such utilitarian work" (Thomas, "Training for Teaching Composition in Colleges" 456). Professional groups such as The Committee on the Labor and Cost of English Teaching repeatedly recommended the teaching loads that have been proposed for almost a century now—sixty students per instructor (Hopkins, "Good Composition" 4). Connors has argued that some of the more dubious practices in composition can be attributed to the heavy teaching loads, including the emphasis on personal experience essays that could be proofread more efficiently than those on sensitive political issues. Connors concludes that such practices have remained impervious to critique simply because they work so efficiently, though the work they do is not really to teach writing as a meaningful act, as Sharon Crowley and Susan Miller have argued. Many of the problems confronted by composition teachers were worsened by their isolation from work in other areas of the field. Insofar as the discipline did not prepare graduates to teach, did not support research on teaching, and did not secure workloads that provided time for teachers to reflect upon their work, college English adopted a disciplinary economy that reduced its learning capacity and public agency. A broader perspective on the field may help us to reimagine its possibilities.

The Pragmatics of Making a Difference

I will reassess those possibilities by examining the disciplinary alternatives that emerged at institutions that served students quite different from those attending a university such as Harvard. The establishment of research as the chief distinction among classes of faculty and institutions was not as inevitable as researchers tend to assume. The classification of higher education institutions by research hierarchies has played into the tacit conservatism of professionalism by reinforcing the tendencies of public universities to look up to elite institutions for models, rather than taking a broader accounting of their functions and potentials. Up to the middle of the twentieth century, research universities largely served to prepare educators for other schools and colleges, because even in the sciences there was little demand for researchers as researchers until after World War II.[29] Research hierarchies provided a reward system that disoriented professors in disciplines such as English from coming to terms with their broader work, which often differed dramatically from how the field of study was represented in scholarly journals. As part of the most broadly based discipline in the academy, English graduate programs were guided by professional priorities that were especially ill suited to the possibilities that arose as higher education expanded to include underrepresented groups, particularly the normal schools that were evolving into colleges. As literature became defined by less didactic and more professional purposes, teaching largely remained identified with character formation, which was understood to be women's work, and therefore unworthy of professional attention. While the discipline has tended to define its history by the professionalization of literary studies, it is the failure of teaching to achieve professional standing that has had a more pervasive impact on practitioners, and on our students— especially those who come from backgrounds that differ from those traditionally valorized by studies of the Anglo-Saxon character of English literature.

Too often such students enter the field hoping to learn how to teach for a living, and then graduate from it having seen it ignore both their traditions and their aspirations.

While professional leaders such as Phelps noted that it was a waste of expertise to assign researchers with graduate degrees to teach introductory courses, most saw that as a problem in teaching assignments and not graduate preparations. Some did perceive that graduates of research institutions were not being prepared to teach in more accessible colleges. The most famous reaction against the requirement of the PhD for college teaching jobs was William James's "The PhD Octopus." According to James, requiring PhDs for college teaching positions was merely a marketing ploy. James's response resonates with Burke's research that the rise of research institutions was not simply an effort to secure outside funding. Research funding was quite limited outside such areas as agriculture until after World War II, while the cost of building research infrastructures was quite high. The classification of colleges and universities by their research missions was integral to the market logic of the American higher-educational system. Before American universities and colleges were ranked by their research funding, an emphasis on research helped universities distance themselves from teaching institutions, and thereby compete for better classes of students. By distancing themselves from teachers, professors were able to improve their professional standing, and this professional hierarchy mirrored the tendency of the higher-education market to dismiss teaching to lower-class institutions that served students who looked to teaching as an opportunity to advance themselves.

These institutional economies gave rise to conflicted professional value systems, as can be seen in the deliberations of the Pedagogy Committee of the MLA, and after it was closed, in Fred Newton Scott's work with the Central Division of MLA and then the NCTE. An editorial in the second volume of the *English Journal* in 1913 signed F. N. S notes that PhDs are "as a rule elaborately mistrained for the subject they are fated to teach," because they are "trained as if they were to lecture on obscure problems of English literature to small groups of graduate students" (Editorial 456).[30] One of the projects that was begun in the Central Division of the MLA in 1912 and then completed by the NCTE was The Committee on the Preparation of College Teachers of English, which surveyed 52 heads of graduate departments, 87 college presidents, and 190 recent PhDs (with 28, 87, and 135 responding, respectively). Most of the recent PhDs felt basic changes were needed. While department heads were more satisfied with the status quo than college presidents, 40 percent of the former and 50 percent of the latter agreed that more attention to teaching was needed ("Report of the Committee on the Preparation of College Teachers of English"). Why then was it not instituted?

Assorted organizations were setting out models for how to prepare teachers in graduate programs. For example, in an NCTE session in 1912 on "The Preparation of College Instructors in English," a Harvard composition professor outlined a practicum that worked in tandem with first-year writing courses to prepare graduate students to run workshops, respond to drafts, and conference with students, while also improving their own writing (see Greenough, "Experiment"). One respondent from a small college criticized the research orientation of graduate studies, and another respondent from a midwestern university proposed needed changes in fellowships, hiring, and promotion criteria. This session and other articles in *English Journal* show that people recognized that graduate programs ignored most of the work of the field. As one article noted, "teaching is likely to be looked upon as an avocation" that provides a scholar with "an opportunity to follow his vocation" (Cox 208).[31] Given the actual duties of professors, such conceptions of the work of the profession are rather curious. Specialized publications aimed at other experts need not have become the only model for the scholarly work of the discipline. In addition to the writings of professors of journalism and creative writing, the articulation efforts of public universities had yielded publications on teaching, and other models were put forward for applied scholarship that served to articulate the values and methods of literary and literacy studies to broader audiences. In an article in *English Journal* in 1916, Noble outlined how to teach graduate students to do research for literature courses, including writing introductions for textbooks and other works aimed at general audiences. Rather than fostering specializations in minor areas, this research agenda was explicitly intended to prepare graduate students to articulate the public relevance of the humanities (670).

The clearest example of how the priorities of the profession disoriented practitioners from the broader potentials of their field of work is provided by those colleges that were evolving from teaching institutions into research institutions. Much like college entrance exams, normal schools provided the discipline with broad opportunities to articulate its methods and values to the rest of the educational system. Following trends that began in the nineteenth century, "normals" were evolving from two-year to four-year institutions. As noted in the last chapter, normal schools and teachers colleges opened up access to women, people of color, laborers, and foreign-born students (see Burke 228). Normal schools were instrumental in enabling high school teachers to earn college degrees, with up to 90 percent having earned such degrees, according to a national survey, in 1915 (Baker et al. 328). As they evolved into state universities, the traditional purposes of teachers colleges came into conflict with their academic aspirations (see Borrowman). The impact of these conflicts is detailed in Jewett's examination of the development of English curricula in teachers colleges in the first quarter of the twentieth century. Drawing on a survey of catalogs between 1900 and 1925, Jewett documents how the disciplinary priorities of research institutions were imitated by colleges with broader purposes. Most courses came to focus on literature. Instruction in rhetoric virtually disappeared as composition courses became relentlessly mechanical, with courses in argument offered by fewer than 20 percent of the seventy-one colleges in the 1925 sample (151–52). What Jewett found most problematic was the lack of attention to preparing students to teach. Few methods courses were offered, and few course descriptions even mentioned teaching. In Jewett's assessment, this inattention to students' professional duties undermined the standing of the work of the field.

The alienation of the profession from the pedagogical processes involved in sustaining it is evident in how teaching remained largely a mystical matter of character formation, even after literature began to be characterized in more professional terms. In the early *PMLA* issues that I have already discussed, some of the advocates of the "aesthetic standpoint" discussed literature in moralistic categories drawn from Ruskin and Arnold, but those modalities changed as the methods of study became more specialized (see Fruit; also Graff, *Professing Literature* 81–118). Discussions of teaching began in a similar mode, with exhortations to serve as "ministers to the soul of the inner man" (Fruit 29). Distancing the teaching of literature from such oratorical exhortations was doubly difficult because literature was traditionally identified with a didactic stance (and professors did after all teach for a living). To avoid getting too explicit about teaching (and thereby sounding like educationalists), professors often invoked the eloquence of the selfless teacher. Even as professors adopted the professional personae of scholars and critics, even more progressive educators often continued to characterize teaching as a calling "akin to the ministry" (Scott, "Undefended" 55).[32]

While the traditional tendency to represent professors of English as preachers of virtue still shaped how the values of literature were characterized, preaching and teaching had a broader historical association that was complicated by several developments in this period. As detailed in Burke's study of the social backgrounds of faculty members and students, teaching had replaced preaching as the principal means for lower-class students to gain social status through education. At the same time, such service work was traditionally understood to be women's work, as social work had become in sociology, counseling had become in psychology, and nursing had become in medicine. In part, these disciplinary distinctions were a reaction to the fact that minorities, laborers, and women were entering higher education in rising numbers, often to become teachers. Most Morrill Act institutions had become coeducational by the last quarter of the nineteenth century. The highest concentrations of women were often in teacher preparation departments, which contributed to a 50 percent increase in the number of women in college in the last decade of the nineteenth century.[33] According to Williams's "The Intellectual Progress of Colored Women," "thousands" of women of color were able to gain an education in order to become educators: "it is almost literally true that, except teaching in colored schools and menial work, colored women can find no employment in this free America" (rptd. in Ritchie and Ronald 185). As Katherine Adams has discussed in *A History of Professional Writing Instruction in American Colleges*, these professional choices expanded somewhat as the demand for writers for print media increased. Those options had also begun to change with the Second Morrill Act in 1890, which made specific provisions for funding African American institutions, though those provisions had a vocational emphasis that dampened the development of more academic programs.

A study of the opportunities open to students and teachers from marginalized backgrounds provides an alternative historical frame of reference for considering how literacy and literacy studies developed in the Progressive era. Some research has been done to expand our history from such universities as Harvard to institutions such as Northeast Oklahoma State University, which evolved from Northeastern State Normal School. That school had itself evolved from the Cherokee Female Seminary that was founded by the tribe in 1857 to educate teachers in a curriculum modeled upon that of Mount Holyoke Seminary. The "seminary" approach to English studies deemphasized political debates in favor of a belletristic approach that was closer to *Godey's Lady's Book* than to the rhetorics that had taught men to speak with power (see Ricks). If one looks past what was taught to what was learned, one can move beyond viewing such instruction as merely indoctrination. As Miheusuah discusses in

Cultivating the Rosebuds: The Education of Women at the Cherokee Female Seminary, 1851–1909, the seminary gave thousands of Native American women the chance to learn how to earn a living through education by writing for the college newspaper, speaking in literary societies, and organizing themselves. Participating in literary and debating societies was particularly useful to students from underrepresented backgrounds because they could gain experience speaking with others whose backgrounds differed from those represented in English literature classes. Such groups provided women and people of color with networks to sustain them when they graduated and sought to enter professions that were often unresponsive if not openly hostile (see Adams, *A Group of Their Own*).

Even institutions that taught the same groups of students sometimes offered very different learning experiences, as evident in the case studies of Radcliffe and Vassar by Simmons's "Radcliffe Responses to Harvard Rhetoric" and JoAnn Campbell's account of Gertrude Buck's teaching at Vassar. Radcliffe students were originally taught by Harvard professors such as Barrett Wendell, who combined a stifling emphasis on stylistic proprieties with a patronizing chauvinism that led him to grade students on their "charmingly feminine" style (qtd. in Simmons 272). As Simmons details, some students retreated to their journals to critique his "absurdly stiff way of thinking" (qtd. in Simmons 273). As one student wrote, first-year composition "does not teach us to write, it teaches us not to write. It is not a path to future composition courses; it is a stumbling block, over which most of us get so bumped and battered & discouraged, that we let English class alone through college" (Simmons 279). Students learned to make more productive use of their experience in the composition, literature, and creative writing classes at Vassar (see Ricks). Drawing upon her studies with Scott and Dewey, as well as her experience in Baker's playwriting workshop at Harvard, Gertrude Buck and her colleagues developed a pragmatic approach to rhetorics and poetics that treated creation and reception as transactional processes. As evident in writings ranging from "Recent Tendencies in Teaching English Composition" to *The Social Criticism of Literature*, Buck was a leading proponent of a pragmatic philosophy of English studies that, according to Campbell, provided a "civic" alternative to formalist approaches to composition and criticism (xli).

Campbell's collection includes Buck's scholarship, creative writing, and textbooks along with institutional reports that document how the efforts of such committed teachers were limited by the teaching loads that pressed teachers to confine themselves to the basics. The reports of Buck and her chair and life partner, Laura Wylie, document how their department's creative initiatives were overwhelmed by teaching loads of as many as seven courses per faculty member a semester in the years that Buck taught at Vassar, from 1897 to 1922. Buck and her collaborators acknowledged that teaching composition presented laborious challenges that made it difficult to offer specialized courses. Instead of responding as professors at Stanford and other elite institutions did, Buck and Wylie persisted with a "laboratory" approach that emphasized revisions and conferences, and they also engaged in articulation programs with colleagues in high schools. Buck and her coworkers did research to show that they taught more students at lower costs than other disciplines, but their requests for additional faculty were repeatedly denied. Buck was able to sustain her outreach commitments by creating a noted community theater group, but she was unable to continue the playwriting she did in Baker's workshop. Baker later wondered what it must have meant to her to "put aside her own play writing, when she had had as much success as that, and give out richly to the people who wanted to write" (qtd. in Campbell 159). Buck's workload reportedly contributed to her early death in 1922. Such selfless devotion was commonly expected from female teachers. Buck's uncommon vision provides a powerful example of how prevailing attitudes undermined the professional capacity of English studies by imposing workloads that left generations of female teachers with little time to write and thereby shape the discipline's sense of purpose.

The sort of alternatives that were lost to the discipline is evident in Susan Kates's account of the "activist" approach to rhetorical and cultural studies that was developed by reformers in colleges for women, people of color, and laborers. Kates provides three case studies: Mary August Jordan's career at Smith College from 1884 to 1921, Hallie Quinn Brown's teaching at Wilberforce University from 1893 to 1923, and a group of teachers at Brookwood Labor College from 1921 to 1937. Kates's creative reconstruction defines this activist tradition by a shared commitment to replacing proscriptive standards with an attention to how language differences embody social experiences. This critical engagement with social experience was developed by assigning the student to address the political problems of his or her particular social group in order to teach him or her how to speak to its needs. As Kates notes, such an approach was consistent with Progressive pedagogy and the integrally related reforms of Progressive journalists and activists. Central to this tradition in college English studies was a shared vision of teaching literacy and literature as a means to civic engagement. That vision provided an alternative to stressing stylistic proprieties and self-restraint. For example, Jordan wrote for popular magazines and home instruction manuals as well as scholarly publications, and she drew upon Lounsbury's descriptivist approach to linguistic change to challenge the emphasis on grammatical niceties that restricted less-educated people's opportunities to gain access to higher education, and through it to positions of public authority. On these and other points, Jordan argued that women's colleges should break from the dominant tradition: "Why insist upon sharing the wreck of educational dogma? Why insist upon ranking as 'advantages' the under-inspiration of our over-examined young men? . . . The student's mind is a republic of powers, not a receiving vault" (qtd. in Kates 31).

As Kates discusses, this alternative tradition developed a critical engagement with pedagogy that was opposed to the prevailing disciplinary paradigm, which Kates identifies with Freire's conception of "banking" approaches to education. This critical stance on teaching and writing was developed by figures with marginal standing in the profession who developed a practically situated and politically engaged approach to teaching and writing. The values of literary studies were articulated in terms that are virtually unrecognizable to the profession in works such as Victoria Earle Matthews's "The Value of Race Literature." As exemplified in such texts, women, workers, and people of color sometimes sustained a more broadly engaged civic conception of *literature*, which Matthews defined as "all the writings emanating from a distinct class," including more oratorical genres such as "History, Biographies, Scientific Treatises, Sermons, Addresses, Novels, Poems, Books of Travel, miscellaneous essays and the contributions to magazines and newspapers" (126). In contrast with the concentration on aesthetic genres that emerged from the opposition of belletristic to utilitarian values within the profession, Matthews identified literature with a very different class affiliation: not with the learned or educated classes, but with the class with whom she identified as an African American woman. Such class identifications are part of what got left out of literacy studies as they came to concentrate on a modern conception of literature.

These figures and the broader Progressive tradition provide a historical alternative for assessing how literary studies came to be defined by middle-class professionalism. Figures such as Brown and Matthews were community-based intellectuals. Like their predecessors in the antebellum period, women and African American teachers and writers depended for their income and identity on networks of lectures, magazines, and reform societies of the sort that educators had looked to before professors came to locate their work within specialized disciplines (see Logan 20–21).[34] These informal educational networks were often more accessible to teachers and others with limited credentials than professional associations, which often required intellectuals from marginalized backgrounds to give up their identifications with their own communities in order to speak as experts. The difference between what professions professed and provided to outsiders is set out in Martha Carey Thomas's "Should the Higher Education of Women Differ from That of Men?" (1900). Thomas argued that colleges violated their own professional values by admitting women to graduate study and then denying them college teaching jobs. Critiques of middle-class professionalism became more pointed with the emergence of labor colleges in the 1920s, which drew upon their own networks of unions, workers' educational groups, and radical periodicals. As Kates details, while such colleges were not free of sexism or racism, they did offer a civic vision concerned with teaching students to use "the working class vernacular" to address racial, gender, and class oppression.

These trends can be broadly identified with the Progressive movement of the first decades of the twentieth century. "Progressivism" served as a unifying but ill-defined ideology for coalition building among educators, journalists, social workers, and activists, who ranged from socialists to reformers simply seeking to check the excesses of capitalism. However defined, the Progressive era saw the most pervasive leftist politics in American history, with thirty-three cities governed by socialist mayors in 1912, when almost a million voted for a socialist presidential candidate, and again two decades later for socialist and communist presidential candidates (Leitch 3). The Progressive movement in education was closely identified with the work of John Dewey. In two hugely influential books, *Democracy and Education* and *Experience and Education*, Dewey set out a philosophy of education as a model for democracy. Dewey's educational philosophy was integral to his vision of democracy as a "way of life" characterized by collaborative inquiries into the potentials of experience. To explore those potentials, students undertook collaborative projects that drew on varied disciplines to address social issues and community needs. In opposition to the increasing specialization of academic disciplines, Progressives organized education not around subject areas but around students' developmental levels and social experience. In some respects, Progressive education attempted to break out of the routines of classroom instruction by looking back to the informal social networks that had shaped learning and literacy before schooling became state mandated. In other respects, Progressive educators looked forward to the student-centered models of learning that gained resurgence in the 1960s, and which played a vital role in the process movement in composition studies. Within the context of the second quarter of the twentieth century, the Progressive movement is significant because it posed a historical alternative to the disciplinary professionalism that would come to define college English studies. The distinctive methods and values of Progressivism were founded not on the mastery of an autonomous body of knowledge, but on the collaborative work of learning and teaching. Not surprisingly, Progressivism was especially popular among those who worked with teachers, particularly professors of education in state universities and normal schools. On the other hand, Progressive doctrines were often dismissed by "content" faculty, who felt threatened by the lack of respect that was shown to their distinctive forms of disciplinary expertise.

These opposing responses unfortunately played into deepening divisions in college English studies by providing a unifying ideology to those concerned with teaching, writing, and teacher training—and a unifying point of opposition for those who looked down on them. The former group looked to NCTE for models of the "experience curriculum" and the "project method," and the latter identified with MLA, where Dewey and Progressives were often attacked for contributing to the decline of the humanities in a commercial age. Humanists and social scientists were at the time fighting a "border war" over whose expertise would hold sway in the literate public sphere (see Wilson). One front in that conflict was over control of public schools. As discussed in the last chapter, liberal arts proponents did not get very involved in that conflict, but losing it reinforced their shared opposition to Dewey as a proponent of the expanding influence of the social sciences. Dewey provoked such reactions by publishing popular articles arguing that "only the gradual replacing of a literary by a scientific education can assure to man the progressive amelioration of his lot." Dewey's "Science and Education" appeared in *Scientific Monthly*, sandwiched between articles on synthetic rubber and genetics (55). Progressives were comfortable with such popular venues, as were the courses they helped to popularize in journalism and creative writing.

Progressives viewed creativity as part of everyday experience and expression, as Dewey detailed in *Art as Experience*. Dewey argued that concentrating aesthetics on "works of art" creates a "chasm between ordinary and aesthetic experience" that opens a gulf between artistic creation and purposeful action (10–12). Dewey saw art not as an object but an experience. The artistic experience was distinguished by a "degree of completeness" in the transactions among "sense, need, impulse and action" (26, 25). On these and other points, Dewey set out an alternative to the conception of literature that was being instituted in English departments. In opposition to that conception, Dewey argued that "assuredly there is a lack of imagination implied in the current identification of the humanities with literary masterpieces; for the humanism of today can be adequately expressed only in a vision of the social possibilities of the intelligence and learning embodied in the great modern enterprises of business, law, medicine, education, farming, engineering, etc." (156). Such doctrines directly challenged New Critics' efforts to demarcate literature as a specialized domain of aesthetic experience. Dewey's social-constructivist vision of the humanities was broadly consistent with the disciplinary trends that emerged with the pragmatic turn in the 1990s, though his standpoint is pointedly opposed to the positions staked out by the best-known neopragmatist, Stanley Fish, as I will discuss after reviewing the school of criticism that first instituted a modern sense of literature as a discipline unto itself.

"Criticism, Inc."

While "the New Criticism" is usually used to refer to the generation of John Crowe Ransom and his contemporaries, they were not the first to use the term to argue that literary works should be studied as self-contained artifacts. As I have discussed, that line of thinking is evident in the surveys of curricula included in Payne's *English in American Universities* and in other early-twentieth-century statements on the purposes of modern literary studies. In 1910 in a talk entitled the "New Criticism," J. E. Spingarn had set out the basic idea that historical and psychological considerations distract "interest from the work of art to something else" (44). Spingarn called for critics to dispense with classical authorities, romantic "abstractions," rhetorical precepts, and "moral judgment" to concentrate on how an artist's intentions are realized in the work itself (52–61). Literary criticism was positioned in a comparable way by John Crowe Ransom's ironically titled "Criticism, Inc." in 1939. Ransom positioned literary critics as outsiders to both the academy and the popular culture because they stood aloof from public tastes and were opposed to the mindset of scientists, scholars, and educators. Such oppositions helped to justify the institution of New Criticism as the discipline's distinctive methodology and ideology (as will become more fully apparent when I review the evolution of undergraduate and graduate programs of study in the next chapter). Ransom wrote in the urbane style of the literary magazines that remained a professional mainstay until specialized journals proliferated, but "Criticism, Inc." is a carefully calculated piece of professional maneuvering. Ransom maintained that if "criticism" is to "become more scientific," it must be "seriously taken in hand by professionals . . . which means that its proper seat is the universities" (455). A year later Ransom pronounced that "The Age of Criticism" had come (4). It arrived as English departments were trying to make sense of sharp increases in students and faculty. In 1925, reflecting back over this "revolution" in English departments, Fred Lewis Pattee noted that "nothing in American educational history—in all its areas a most sensational field— has been more sensational than the growth of English departments everywhere during the last two decades" (205).[35] After World War II, literary criticism completed its rise to become a recognized academic specialty, "a profession that one can practice with self-respect and a serious sense of responsibility" (Hyman 7).[36] No longer accepting "its traditional status as an adjunct to 'creative' or 'imaginative literature,'" criticism had become a "methodological art: the criticism of criticism" (Glicksberg 55). The New Criticism was instrumental in distancing literary studies from the more politically engaged schools of criticism that were popular in the Progressive era—those of "Leftists, or Proletarians," whom Ransom dismissed for being as didactic as belletristic moralists (457).[37]

While teaching the public to improve its taste was a longstanding duty of the critic, the New Critics professionalized that role by offering more rigorous analytical methods that explicitly distanced literature from its educational uses, while providing a methodology that proved very effective in translating the work of the profession into a method of instruction. Ransom and other New Critics, such as Allen Tate, openly expressed "contempt" for "educationists" such as Dewey (Tate 474). In his landmark essay "The Present Function of Criticism," Tate positions literary criticism in opposition to the "rise of the social sciences and their influence in education." For Tate, the "coming of the slave society" is nowhere more apparent than in "the intellectual movement variously known as positivism, pragmatism, [or] instrumentalism" (474). Tate scorned the "vulgarity of the 'utilitarian attitude'" and noted that there is "but a step from the crude sociology of the normal school to the cloistered historical scholarship of the graduate school" (474). As is suggested by such positionings, Tate, Ransom, and other literary critics were maneuvering for standing in graduate programs, in part by positioning themselves above the teaching of teachers, as Tate himself did in 1939 when he moved from the Women's College of North Carolina to Princeton University (a move followed by other leading New Critics teaching in such provincial towns as Nashville and Baton Rouge). New Criticism came to define college English studies because its interpretive methods proved to be highly effective in pedagogical practice, though part of the effect was to divorce the field of study from the field of work. The New Criticism reacted against the mass culture's encroachment on the literate tradition by creating methods that enabled literature to be taught on a massive scale. The contradictions between the purposes and functions of the New Criticism worked to set the critical apparatus of the profession in opposition to its institutional base.[38]

New Criticism set out a less rhetorical and more "objective" conception of literature by concentrating on "the nature of the object rather than its effects upon the subject." The "personal" responses of readers were to be excluded along with other extraneous "Historical," "Linguistic," and "Moral studies" (Ransom 462–64). According to Gerald Graff's *Professing Literature*, the New Critics succeeded in expunging "the genteel schoolmarm theory of literature, which had defined literature as a kind of prettified didacticism," and replaced it with a "theory of the radical 'autonomy' of the imagination" (5). As detailed in Wellek's defensive postmortem in 1978, New Criticism in the end became identified with a formalist methodology with scientific pretensions—little more than a "pedagogical device, . . . explication de texte" (55). As Wellek notes in his attempt to repudiate such claims, the charge that New Criticism made a science of literature is ironic, for Tate and others viewed "scientism" as "a spiritual disorder" (Tate, "Present Function" 469). However, Tate and other New Critics did define the object of study as "the specific objectivity" of the literary work, "an objectivity that the subject matter, abstracted from the form, wholly lacks" (Tate, "Miss Emily" 14). By defining their studies in such terms, literary critics internalized the logic that they opposed in an effort to make criticism rigorously methodical in order to compete with the standing of the sciences. These formalist tendencies have been examined by Graff, who attributes them to the "routinization" of New Critics' methods in general education ("'Who Killed Criticism?'" 126). With the title "Criticism, Inc.," Ransom plays off of the irony inherent in the project of making literature into a profession with an anticommercial ethos, for as Ransom discusses, English departments, like "any other going business," must secure their "proprietary interest" by becoming more scientific in order to compete with history and philology (458).

The broader irony of the New Criticism is that it came to have a pervasive impact on specialized literary studies because its methods were effective in teaching general education. As Graff discusses in *Professing Literature*, the New Criticism became influential just as general education programs were being set up to deal with the broader classes of students graduating from high schools and returning from the war (162–79).[39] The New Criticism provided methods of close reading that students could use to write passable analyses even if they did not know much more about literature than the text in front of them. These methods were justified by the assumption that giving students direct contact with a masterpiece would enable them to appreciate its powers. That assumption was popularized not just by New Critics but by other general education reformers, such as Mortimer Adler, who were concerned with teaching basic literate strategies to broader classes of readers. Self-instruction manuals such as Adler's *How to Read a Book* and I. A. Richards's *How to Read a Page* become popular when literacy and the literate are expanding and new classes of readers have to be taught how to read appropriately. The close reading strategies that came to be identified with the New Criticism were connected with the new pedagogy in Richards's *Practical Criticism*. Richards analyzed the failings of several hundred students' explications of unattributed poems, much as the Harvard reports had done to establish composition as the only universally required course in the undergraduate curriculum. Richards understood that poems are defined in part by "the quality of the reading we give them," but he did not take into account how this fact made literary modes of reading dependent upon context (349). His students understandably resorted to "stock responses" because they were denied details on "authorship, period, . . . or the hint of a context" (315). Richards attributed his students' failings to the limitations of their reading skills rather than to how his assignments limited the transactional dynamics of reading texts against contexts, including the questions that one is asked to read for (see Graff, *Professing Literature* 177).

While Richards undertook the sort of research on students' reading and writing that was needed to expand the base of literary studies in a more broadly engaged manner, his account of his students' illiteracies unfortunately provides a telling example of how formalist approaches divorce reading and writing from the contexts in which they function, as New Criticism tended to do by ignoring the challenges of teaching literature to students from varied backgrounds. Richards and other New Critics idealized the wholeness of experience to be realized in close readings of literature, but their approach discouraged students from connecting their responses to their own experiences. While many professors of literature have complained about "the poverty" of students' "literary experience," Richards was one of the few to try to study the sources of that problem, and he was widely condemned as a positivist for doing so (*Practical* 312). The potentials and limitations of Richards's writings are important to consider because he was one of the few figures in our history to publish influential works in all four corners of our field—in English education, applied linguistics and world Englishes, literary and cultural studies, and writing, including poetry and plays as well as rhetoric and composition.[40] If other English professors had taken up his wide-ranging research on teaching and the uses of literacy, the formalist tendencies of the New Criticism might have been called to account against studies of how students interpret what they read in the contexts of what they have learned and experienced. Unfortunately, the pedagogy of the New Criticism systematically ignored students' learning experiences by dismissing educational work and concentrating on formal explications of isolated texts.

As the New Criticism came to define the profession's higher purposes, its broader responsibilities were being redefined by the Progressive movement. Experience was set out as a key concern of New Critics as well as Progressives in two texts published in 1938: Dewey's *Experience and Education*, and the best-known statement of the New Criticism, Brooks and Warren's textbook, *Understanding Poetry*, which set out the assumption that "the poem itself is an experience" (32). Both New Critics and Progressives responded to the challenges of teaching literacy to broader classes of students by focusing on the experience of making sense of the printed page, but New Critics and Progressives diverged on how broadly they engaged with that experience. For Progressives, it was a guiding principle that "subject matter" was secondary to "pupil needs" (Seely 11–12). As Angus and Mirel have discussed, the Progressives' "most extensive revisions appeared in English" (30). The "experience curriculum" was organized around interdisciplinary "projects" and themes that undermined the autonomy of individual disciplines. Such themes as "Health" and "Vocation" were set out in the influential *Cardinal Principles of Secondary Education* (1918) to map out inquiries that left literature as a matter for the "Worthy Use of Leisure" or "Ethical Character."[41] Instruction in reading and writing was redirected away from introducing students to literature toward using it to introduce them to social issues, making literature sometimes merely "an adjunct to sociological exploration" according to Moulton (60). As a result, in the 1930s the "experience curriculum" was cited some two hundred times in NCTE journals, and not once in those of the MLA. Dewey acknowledged that the weakest aspect of Progressivism was its treatment of "intellectual subject matter," but he identified the liberal arts with passive methods of instruction and an indifference to practical applications that were "out of touch with all the conditions of modern life" (*Experience* 78).

The most broadly encompassing efforts to reform the discipline in the 1930s were undertaken by the Curriculum Commission and related NCTE committees. NCTE worked with interdisciplinary groups such as the National Education Association and the Progressive Educational Association to produce conferences and publications, aiming to foster collaborations among a broad range of teachers and professors of English and education. Drawing on classroom research and reports from teachers in schools and colleges, several influential committee reports were published: Oscar Campbell's *The Teaching of College English*, Hatfield's *An Experience Curriculum in English*, Broening's *Conducting Experiences in English*, and *A Correlated Curriculum* by Scott's student and NCTE president, Ruth Mary Weeks.[42] These efforts were all based on the assumption that "experience is the best of all schools" (Campbell, *Teaching* 20). They were also specifically intended to respond to high schools' being "dominated" by the "college entrance requirements" set out by the College Entrance Examination Board. The CEEB provoked such responses by replacing essays on literature with objective tests that "called into question the presumed centrality of literacy, as it was defined by departments of English" (Trachsel 103). High school English courses were redefined by the dual purposes of teaching communication as an aid to "social activities" and providing "indirect (vicarious) experiences where direct experiences are impossible" (Hatfield 3). The "dynamic philosophy of English as experience" and "the passion for life that literature itself exemplifies" were intended as an "emotional prophylactic" to the rising influence of the mass media—radio, film, and "the pulps" that fostered a "revulsion to the classics" (Broening 4–5; Campbell 11). "Intensive" reading in literary classics was balanced with extensive readings guided by students' interests to encourage "healthful" leisure and to "discipline . . . unruly, unsocial emotions" (Campbell 53–55).

A comprehensive assessment of the teaching of English in college is provided by the companion volume to Hatfield's *Experience Curriculum*, Oscar Campbell's *The Teaching of College English*. The collection surveys the broader work of the field, including articulations between high schools and colleges, composition and general education courses, introductory surveys of literature, undergraduate majors, and graduate programs, which like other levels of the curriculum were judged by how well they integrated "humanistic, cultural, and practical" concerns (128). Articulation became even more important as community colleges increased from 1.9 percent to 17.6 percent of college enrollments between 1918 and 1940, with three-quarters of community colleges still located in high schools in the 1930s (Levine 162; Campbell, *The Teaching of College English* 32). As disciplines and students became more diversified, Campbell and other Progressives looked to "correlation" to redress specialization by fostering interdisciplinary collaborations on literacy and literary studies. Other formative trends were addressed in ways that might have moved the discipline along a very different trajectory. Creative writing and composition courses were related by their shared concern for transactional work with reading and writing. Surveys of literature were criticized for failing to engage students in ways that could make literature a "criticism and revelation of life" (58). Undergraduate programs were examined against the fact that many majors intended to teach and teachers require distinctive training (59). On this and other points, *The Teaching of College English* surveyed the field with an eye to students' needs and purposes. Campbell and his collaborators responded to many of the same institutional conditions as the New Critics, but Progressives responded to these pressures with an interdisciplinary vision of collaborative learning that was meant to enlist faculty in other disciplines in becoming "teachers of composition" in order to reduce the overwhelming workloads faced by teachers of English (7).

Conclusion: Why College English Didn't Become a More Progressive Discipline

According to Graff, "what was needed" in this formative phase of the institutionalization of English studies was not just new methods of literary criticism but "hard thinking and open debate about the larger cultural situation of literary studies," for a "gulf had developed" between literary studies and literate society (*Professing* 96–97). If one positions modern literary studies within the broader history of literacy studies, one can see that the configuration of literature as a self-contained object of study paralleled the rise of linguistics to become an autonomous science that was unconcerned with practical questions about how language is learned and used. These trends distanced the basic work of the discipline from its higher purposes by reducing teacher education and writing and language instruction to merely methodical matters. Composition courses were further marginalized by the distinction between creative and technical writing that arose out of literary critics' hostility to practical applications and popular journalism. As a result of these trends, the profession failed to realize the historical possibilities arising from its expansive articulation apparatus, including its broad base in public education, its central role in college admissions, its interdisciplinary involvement with writing to learn and learning to write, and the traditional emphasis on journalism, rhetoric, and public address that had positioned the discipline to speak for the political reforms of the Progressive era. While politically oriented critics did engage literary studies with the issues of the day, the New Critics were instrumental in distancing the intellectual concerns of the discipline from the historical changes that were reconfiguring its institutional base.

The loss of literary studies' "sovereignty" in the correlated curriculum of high schools led some to ask "Is English on the Way Out?" (Henry). Henry was not alone in concluding that the discipline was in a "dire predicament" because "mass education is being tried at the secondary level," and "liberal education" cannot be conveyed to "a throng disqualified by verbal incompetency, congenital defects, undernourishment, brutalization, experiential limitations, and harsh economic uncertainty" (Henry 284). Insofar as "English-as-a-course and mass education" were fundamentally "incompatible," the discipline was going to be forced to play "second fiddle to the militant social-science groups that had suddenly decided to save democracy" (286). Such anxieties were often vented on ceremonial occasions such as MLA conventions, as in Prokosch's presidential address, "Treason within the Castle." Positioning English departments as bastions of the culture of the book, Prokosch called for efforts to buttress the "scientific character of our departments" to defend the discipline against students looking to major in English as a refuge from the rigors of linguistics or foreign languages (1324). In response to the encroachments of Progressivism, the MLA established The Commission on Trends in Education Adverse to the Teaching of Modern Languages and Literatures. The commission was responding to the same trends as the NCTE curriculum committees that I have discussed, but it did little to come to terms with the expansion of print and new media, or to prepare broader classes of students to address the social problems of the time. In its preliminary statement of its findings in 1939, the commission criticized the lack of discipline of educators and education students, and blamed trends in general education for being "menacing to our subjects and to the humanities in general" (Doyle 1350).

Such hostilities were due in part to the fact that humanists were losing influence to the social sciences, as Elizabeth Wilson has discussed.[43] Insofar as Progressives tried to make education into a social science, they were perceived to be antihumanistic. Progressives responded by arguing that if literature "needs defending," as presumed by the MLA Commission on Trends in Education, then programs of study for English majors need to be made more broadly suited to students' needs, and "learned societies" should become more than "curators of relics" and become more involved with "general education and even pedagogy" (Basler 63). The NCTE did sponsor just such broadly based research on pedagogy, but many of the accounts of the social purposes of English studies that emerge from those surveys suffer from the limited conception of literature and literacy that almost inevitably arises when literary critics, compositionists, linguists, and English education specialists fail to confer.[44] The weaknesses in Progressives' accounts of the social purposes of education are particularly crucial because Progressives defined literary and literacy studies by their social uses. These limitations can be seen in influential accounts of Progressive reforms of high school English studies such as Roberts, Kaulfers, and Kefauver's *English for Social Living*. Surveys of literature are replaced with "problem-solving" courses in which students select readings to advance collaborative projects (255). As Moulton discusses, similar texts such as *Educating for Peace* (1940) and *Pupils Are People* (1941) defined literary studies by the "instrumental" purposes of enhancing individual development and addressing social problems. Such purposes might have been more richly defined if humanists had become more broadly engaged in deliberations with teachers on the politics of the liberal imagination.

One of the contemporaries of the New Critics did provide models and methods for engaging in collaborations with sociologists and educators on literary and literacy studies—Kenneth Burke, whose rhetorical criticism was concerned with "Literature as Equipment for Living," which was exactly the sort of terminology commonly used by Progressives. Because Burke routinely transgressed the disciplinary distinction between literary and rhetorical criticism, he was a "taxonomical embarrassment" to most professors of English (Gabin 203). Politically oriented commentators such as Hyman recognized that academic specialists could only make use of parts of Burke because he ranged so freely across linguistics, philosophy, literature, and anthropology that he had "no field, unless it be Burkology" (359). Like the Progressives, Burke developed an interdisciplinary perspective concerned with the social sources and political uses of interpretation, and "symbolic action" more generally. Like the New Critics with whom he was sometimes identified, Burke was concerned with how formal elements of texts embody the psychological and cultural dynamics of interpretive experience. Unlike the New Critics, and like the Progressives, Burke saw poetics as integrally related to rhetoric's traditional concern for the situated dynamics of civic action. Burke's rich engagement with the pragmatics of symbolic action provides perhaps the best example of how much the discipline lost by reducing rhetoric to methods for teaching marginalized courses in syntactic proprieties, while at the same time isolating literary studies from the social uses of literacy.

As is powerfully evident in Burke, rhetoric might have provided categories for articulating the civic values of collective deliberations on public issues, but rhetoric had become so confined to the mechanics of teaching composition and so shrouded in formalism that textbooks such as Manly and Rickert's *The Writing of English* (1919) presented rhetoric as an "extinct art," belonging "to the past as much as the toga and the snuffbox" (rptd. Brereton 431). Even a creative thinker with an expansive and integrated view of the discipline such as I. A. Richards characterized rhetoric as "the dreariest and least profitable part of the waste that the unfortunate travel through in Freshman English" (*Philosophy* 3). As a result of these institutional constraints and professional attitudes, the productive capacities of rhetoric were ignored, and rhetoric became at best an aid to the "study of misunderstanding and its remedies," and as such merely an ancillary to the interest in semantics popularized by the postwar communications movement (3). New Critics dismissed rhetoric's traditional concern for intentions and effects as "fallacies" that end up in "impressionism and relativism" because they mislead the "objective critic" by confusing a poem with its results, "what it *is* and what it *does*" (Wimsatt 32, 21). In one of the major works of the New Criticism, Wimsatt's *Verbal Icon*, Aristotle's *Rhetoric* is identified with a "pragmatic" concern for purposes and audiences that is set apart from a distinctly "literary" approach, which is by definition concerned with the form of the work itself (xv; see also Abrams). The formalist presuppositions of the New Criticism make it the epitome of the "transparent" disciplinarity that Russell has discussed as a characteristic feature of how academics in this period were composing highly rhetorical practices that depended on not appearing rhetorical to achieve their effects.[45]

The professional opposition of literary criticism to the Progressive movement presented virtually insurmountable barriers even to those who attempted to engage literary studies with educational work. One of the most influential attempts was published by the Progressive Educational Association in the same year as Dewey's *Experience and Education* and Brooks and Warren's *Understanding Poetry*. Louise Rosenblatt's *Literature as Exploration* was one of the most promising efforts to bridge the concerns of New Critics and Progressives. Her interdisciplinary approach to literary studies drew from Dewey's *Art as Experience* as well as Richards's *Practical Criticism*. In a foreword to the fifth edition (published by MLA in 1995), Wayne Booth concluded that no "literary critic of this century has enjoyed and suffered as sharp a contrast of powerful influence and absurd neglect as Louise Rosenblatt" (vii). While the book "influenced more teachers" than perhaps any other work on literature, "the world of literary criticism and theory has only recently begun to acknowledge" that the work was not just "a valuable guide to pedagogy in secondary teaching" (viii). Literary critics could ignore Rosenblatt because she studied students' responses in order to teach "emancipated youth" to develop a "critical" stance on stock responses and "anachronistic emotional attitudes" (212). Rosenblatt's use of literature to contribute to "growth in the social and cultural life" aligned her with the Progressives who threatened to make literature into a social science (v). The reaction to that threat overshadowed any attempt to build on Rosenblatt's efforts to study the transactions between readers and texts in the manner that Richards had undertaken. As a result, according to Booth, the New Critics failed to recognize and avoid "the excesses that result when this or that element in the rhetorical transaction is turned into an exclusive center" (viii).

In the year that Rosenblatt published *Literature as Exploration*, she was invited to contribute to the committee that grew out of the MLA's Commission on Trends in Education. She reported being surprised at the invitation, for "this was the very university establishment whose influence on the teaching of literature in colleges and schools I was seeking to combat" ("Retrospect" 101). The report of the committee on "The Aims of the Teaching of Literature" responded to "the insistent current demand that literary study should primarily inculcate 'social values'" by identifying literary study as a means to educate "richly endowed and self-reliant individuals, sensitive to the individual lives of their fellow men and to their own personal potentials" (1368). This "rugged individualism on the plain of the spirit" is the point of departure for the committee's discussions of "*Literature as Delight*," "*Literature as Imagina-*

tive Experience," and "*Literature as Document.*" Literature is presented as part of "the living tissue of its society" and a means to foster "empathy" (1368–70). This pronouncement on the "service which the study of literature can render individuals in a democratic state" is seen by Elizabeth Wilson as an example of how the humanities came to terms with the social sciences by giving an imaginative tenor to the liberal individualism that bridged the professional aspirations and political functions of academic specializations. Such reforms were facilitated by Progressive educators and other social workers. Like the other liberal accommodations of the Progressive movement, what was lacking in reader-response criticism was the civic engagement with symbolic action that is evident in Burke and several of the other "New Rhetoricians" whom I will discuss in the next chapter.

5

At the Ends of
the Profession

The mode of being of the new intellectual can no longer consist
in eloquence, which is an exterior and momentary mover of
feelings and passions, but in active participation in practical life,
as constructor, organizer, "permanent persuader" and not just
a simple orator (but superior at the same time to the abstract
mathematical spirit); from technique-as-work one proceeds to
technique-as-science and to the humanistic conception of history,
without which one remains "specialized" and does not become
"directive" (specialized and political).

Antonio Gramsci,
Selections from the Prison Notebooks, 10.

IN *THE FORMATION OF*
College English, I drew upon Gramsci's theories much more explicitly than I
have here. His perspective has shaped the framework that I have used to examine how literacy and literacy studies have evolved in conjunction with the
elaboration of civil society, including the institution of professionalism as the
unifying ideology of the middle classes. One of Gramsci's best known concepts is his definition of "organic" intellectuals by their integral involvement
with the lived experience of a group, as distinguished from "traditional" intellectuals, such as educators and clerics, who occupy institutional positions from
which they profess to speak disinterestedly for the common good. In the passage quoted above, Gramsci pushes that distinction to argue that intellectuals
must be engaged with "practical life" to influence political developments.
Gramsci identifies a "humanistic" stance with an "active participation" in history in the making. This conception of humanism and the humanities can help
us assess how the discipline has responded to the practical bent of modern
education. By 1950, almost 60 percent of seventeen-year-olds were graduating

from high school, and in 1965, over 40 percent of eighteen- to twenty-four-year-olds were in college (Charles Andersen 418, 435). Majors in English rose apace, and then they suddenly collapsed. Undergraduate and graduate degrees in the field both dropped by about 50 percent from 1972 to 1980.[1] At century's end, English departments were producing 20 percent fewer graduates than in 1972, despite a 50 percent increase in college graduates. These declines contributed to a collapse in professional jobs and an increase in "temporary" positions to cover the composition courses that departments had come to depend upon to maintain themselves. Rather than blaming the decline of literary studies on the "New Vocationalism" as Godzich and others have, I want to use Gramsci's articulation of a "humanistic conception of history" to reflect upon what we are to make of recent developments in literacy and literacy studies.

As discussed in the previous chapter, vocationalism has been a unifying point of opposition for the profession since literary critics first secured their standing in higher education by setting themselves above "educationalists" and social scientists. That opposition can be seen as an example of how "traditional" intellectuals reacted against the elaboration of the technical and managerial expertise that universities began to produce in the Progressive era, as the Ehrenreichs and others have discussed.[2] The "professional-managerial classes" were provided with a general education in cosmopolitan values by English departments. However, as the technical and managerial classes developed their own "organic" intellectuals after World War II, they began to articulate their status in terms of specialized expertise rather than as a general professional ethos. With that transition, the culture of expertise came to replace the humanistic "cultural capital of the old bourgeoisie" (Guillory 45). As Guillory and others have discussed, our profession has recently developed its own class of technicians (compositionists) to administer its basic services. Unfortunately, such accounts generally seek to defend the status of literary studies in a space apart, and offer little help in considering more "practical" conceptions of the humanities such as Gramsci's.

Of course much depends upon how we relate literacy studies to "practical life." Throughout the history of the liberal and mechanical arts, humanists have looked down upon vocationalism. Since at least the Yale Report in 1828, humanists have complained about students being too concerned with working for a living (see *Reports on the Course of Instruction*). Such complaints have been concentrated on classes of students deemed unworthy of liberal education. In the Progressive era, this hierarchy was used to dismiss such "pragmatic, utilitarian disciplines" as education and engineering. Veblen and his like-minded contemporaries assumed that academics should keep their distance from public education, especially "'university extension,' and similar excursions into the field of public amusement" (*Higher Learning* 34). This stance divorced traditional intellectuals from the work they did in the credentialing of the professional and managerial classes. Because college English has traditionally been defined in the studiously impractical ways that Veblen advocated, departments of English have been ill-prepared to articulate the values of their work. That problem was exacerbated by the historic drop in majors and jobs in the 1970s. As in previous periods, the antivocationalism of the humanities was marked by disdain for those students who looked to education as a means to social advancement. As discussed in previous chapters, the aspirations of women, workers, and people of color have been channeled into vocational tracks that were deemed to be worthy of them. Teaching for a living might have gained more socioeconomic standing if our discipline had invested its intellectual capital in developing humanistic approaches to teaching and writing at work. In the heyday of the research university, tracking the less worthy into classes on teaching methods and the mechanics of writing helped to contain the forces for change that new classes of students brought to our field. Our indifference to these changes has exacerbated the problems that have beset our field over the last decades.

The marginalization of teaching and writing served to underwrite the aspirations of English departments in the "the golden age" of the research university. That era is surveyed from a quite different standpoint from Veblen's in Clark Kerr's tellingly entitled *The Uses of the University*.[3] In Kerr's vision, the "multiversity" would be a center of human resource development for the "knowledge economy," with research parks to channel expertise into the private sector.[4] Kerr provides an incisive assessment of the accountability and efficiency measures that did not really take hold until after the explosive growth of the 1960s. Kerr looked to the rise of the research university as an international institution intertwined with the growth of multinational corporations. As president of the largest university system in America, the University of California, and chairman of the Carnegie Commission, Kerr was instrumental in accounting for the establishment of the research university as the center of higher education. That standpoint can be very disorienting when considering the work of English departments. In fact, by 1980 fewer students were attending research universities than community colleges, which enrolled one in three college students. "Junior colleges" helped to uphold the research hierarchies of the profession by providing masses of students with low-cost composition and literature courses. When we expand our field of vision to community colleges (and high schools), the historic scope of our field of vision expands dramatically, and we are challenged to assess what our profession has made of its expansive educational capacities.

In this chapter, I will survey several historical junctures where developments in our field have converged with broader trends. Such shifts in a field of cultural production occur, according to Bourdieu, as a result of "change in the power relation which constitutes the space of positions" (*Logic* 32). Adopting the humanistic stance set out by Gramsci may enable us to focus on the socio-institutional junctures where those changes are articulated. At such sites, disciplinary trends often work in tandem with social movements that can be enlisted to advance broader reforms—if institutional resources can be marshaled by practitioners. Institutional resources, social movements, and disciplinary trends provide the means, opportunities, and justifications for historical change in higher education. When social, institutional, and disciplinary trends converge in a particular area, that conjunction can take on considerable historical power.

Each section of this chapter is focused on how a particular area of the field took on critical importance in successive decades in the last half of the twentieth century. In the decade after World War II, the profession was hard-pressed to disarticulate its higher purposes from its massive service functions. To serve the exploding numbers of students, general education programs were established that laid the groundwork for the rise of the profession. In the 1960s, English departments sought to claim some of the federal funding that flowed into education in the post-Sputnik era, and notable disciplinary, social, and institutional possibilities emerged around English departments' partnerships with schools. These initiatives presented a historic opportunity to establish an integrated field of work that reached from grammar to graduate school. Unfortunately, these efforts largely ended with the collapse of funding, jobs, and majors at the end of the 1960s. In the 1970s, pressures built up to restructure programs of study to address students' changing needs and aspirations. While English curricula proved to be remarkably resistant to change, writing studies emerged as a recognized area of graduate studies. Unfortunately, the challenges posed by writing, and the teaching of writing, were contained by establishing separate programs rather than by revising shared assumptions. The rift between composition and literary studies in the 1980s was part of a series of shifts in "power relations" that also contributed to the turn to theory and the "culture wars." These developments were shaped by what Ira Shor has characterized as the "conservative restoration." That restoration contributed to broad declines in educational access. In retrospect, we can see such steps as the cutting edge of the privatization of public learning that has restructured education and civil society. While the discipline has not traditionally concerned itself with these broader socio-institutional trends, the pragmatic turn in the 1990s has opened up a field of vision in which such matters as "English Only" movements and the deprofessionalization of teaching are coming to be seen as integral to the concerns of college English studies. I hope that my historical survey will contribute to this pragmatic reassessment by highlighting some of the historical junctures where the discipline has confronted the forces at work at the ends of the profession.

From Social Reconstruction to Life Adjustment in Postwar General Education

Disciplinary historians such as Gerald Graff have examined how the postwar growth of general education programs enabled the profession to expand and consolidate its institutional position (see also Connors and Russell). The formalism of New Criticism provided methods for handling less literate students without having to come to terms with the challenges their experiences posed. Formalist approaches to teaching reading and writing helped consolidate a disciplinary economy that transferred the values of literacy in use to the higher purposes of the profession. Intellectual and institutional resources generated by general education enrollments were invested in building up a research mission that lacked the external sources of support that other disciplines drew upon. In their absence, English and other humanities disciplines came to depend upon cheaply delivered general education courses to support research workloads for selected faculty. Those faculty formed the leadership of the profession and shaped its sense of purpose through their control of graduate programs, journals, and the rest of the profession's articulation apparatus. The research agendas of those faculty shaped the graduate programs that produced the teachers to cover the discipline's service. This political economy depended upon the use value of utilitarian offerings, and reacted against that dependence with an anti-utilitarian stance that identified literary studies as the real work of the discipline.

In the postwar years, the public's sense of the humanities came to be defined, according to Veysey, by the "outpouring" of books on general education that characterized the humanities by their opposition to the methods of the social sciences (57). Perhaps the most influential was the presidential commission's six-volume report, *Higher Education for American Democracy*. That report concluded that "general education is liberal education with its matter and method shifted from its original aristocratic intent to the service of democracy" (rptd. in Hofstadter and Smith 2:990). The commission identified English as particularly fundamental to the humanities. The commission's vision of the humanities was shaped by an earlier report, *General Education in a Free Society*, which was produced by a Harvard committee that included I. A. Richards. According to that report, instruction in the humanities reveals "an organic process, which is the American, and, more broadly, the Western evolution" (rptd. in Hofstadter and Smith 2:958). By serving as a "secular continuation of the Spirit of Protestantism," this humanistic "heritage" would inoculate students against the "hostility to tradition" that was endemic to "the scientific attitude," especially "pragmatism" (rptd. in Hofstadter and Smith 2:957, 960). As Graff has discussed, this ahistorical traditionalism set up the context for the rise of New Criticism, which served to "rescue tradition from the jaws of history" by providing a methodology for reading texts as literary embodiments of humanistic ideals divorced from their political sources and functions (*Professing* 171; see also Said).

These reports located English studies at the center of general education, but that position threatened to define the profession by the service work that aspiring departments were using to raise their profiles.[5] To advance such aspirations, university administrators supported the founding of community colleges as a means to download general education, especially the instruction of the less advantaged. Community colleges typically cost less than half of the in-state tuition of a public university. Higher education was stratified largely by the costs of the competing private and public institutions that make up the American system. The expansion of the postwar period was fueled by an explosion in federal funding, which was largely divided between funds for individual research projects and direct grants to students. Rather than investing in the instructional infrastructure, this funding system reinforced the competitive ethos of higher education by setting individual students and faculty members in direct financial competition with each other.[6] Universities began to become dependent upon the entrepreneurial activities of star researchers, while students' competition for access to elite institutions was given the appearance of a meritocracy by admissions tests of basic skills. Like the "external funding" that drove research priorities in many field, those tests were not controlled by disciplines, but were drawn up by a large corporation that tested students not on their content mastery, as in Germany, Britain, and other countries, but on their general aptitudes in ways that systematically compounded academic achievements with cultural backgrounds (see Trachsel). This laissez-faire educational economy has fostered the popular impression that Americans of ability who are willing to work are free to rise to achieve their potential. By displaying the semblance of a meritocracy that provides equal opportunities for individuals to advance from class to class according to their abilities, higher education has legitimized the inequalities that people confront when they leave the classroom and enter the "real world'" (see Karen).

These trends shaped the rise of New Criticism, which became the methodology that defined the discipline. As Cain has discussed, in the 1940s New Criticism became "an established practice, and by the early 1950s it was 'the Establishment' itself." Cain and others have noted that the methods of New Criticism had a "democratic" appeal because they helped broader classes of "students learn to read" (101). Of course the subtleties of literary explications are most accessible to those who can read between the lines to appreciate nuances that are often lost on the less sophisticated. Many professors who came into the profession in the 1950s have recounted how they learned a new mode of reading by teaching that "sacred textbook *Understanding Poetry*" (Ohmann, *English in America* 79). New Criticism served the needs of the profession by promising to transform its distinctive expertise into a remedy for nothing less than the ills of the age. In reassessing the promise of New Criticism to heal a culture infected by a market mentality, Ohmann has suggested that "a general principle of ideology is helpful: a privileged social group will generalize its own interests so that they appear to be universal social goals" ("Teaching" 92). According to Ohmann, this principle applies to the close reading strategies that divorced texts from their social sources and political purposes in ways that were consistent with bourgeois assumptions that culture is apolitical. In their efforts to strip literature of its ideological trappings and social functions, Ohmann's generation was sometimes disconcerted to discover how readily students accepted cosmopolitan critiques of conventional assumptions. From a distance, we can see that such reactions were not really all that surprising coming from those seeking to rise above their provincial origins and acquire the sensibilities of liberally educated professionals.[7]

New Criticism provided English departments with a means to teach reading to students who were not well versed in literature, but the discipline also faced encroachments on its institutional base by interdisciplinary approaches to teaching writing that undercut literary hierarchies. According to Crowley's *Composition in the University*, the communications movement was the first time that English departments' "ownership" of composition was challenged by those "who had sufficient clout to divert it from its humanist moorings in literature and current traditional pedagogy" (156). Descriptions of several dozen communications programs were collected and edited by Earl James McGrath in 1949. As U.S. Commissioner of Education, McGrath was an early advocate of bilingual education and other efforts to expand the international reach of research universities. Communications courses were a basic part of the general education programs that were hastily put together to handle the million veterans who were sent to college in 1945 (Miller, *The Meaning of General Education* 115). McGrath and other contributors drew broadly on Progressive efforts to use the "experiences of students as vehicles of instruction" (vi). Many "communications" programs were defined by studies of mass communications, while some were defined simply by the four communication skills of listening, speaking, reading, and writing, or more generally by structuralist models of language as a system of communications. Virtually all emphasized semantics, with semiotics sometimes used to frame studies of "symbolic transformation" and the "economical gestalt of the symbolic process" (Grey 11). Semiotic models were sometimes drawn from texts such as Ogden and Richards's *The Meaning of Meaning* (1949) and Charles Morris's *Signs, Language, and Behavior* (1946), but the general source was American structural linguistics, along with related trends in cultural anthropology and social psychology. The Progressivist synthesis of scientific methods and social-expressivist objectives is evident in the McGrath collection's conclusion that communications courses shared a common base in "a biological-psychological-anthropological idea of communication as the process of self-realization in expressive interaction with society" (Shoemaker 243).

This fusion of scientism and expressivism was consistent with some of the best and worst tendencies of Progressivism. Progressives often turned to science to provide the sort of objective tests and tracking mechanisms that dominated the four-skills program at Iowa State University that is described in McGrath's collection. All incoming students were run through a weeklong gamut of tests and were then prescribed a complex array of tracks, labs, and clinics to treat their individual needs. The Progressive tradition is better represented in the program at Dewey's former institution, Columbia University's Teachers College. That program drew upon a set of sources that included not only Dewey but the other pragmatists who provided a rich semiotic framework that few Progressive educators had really drawn upon: James, Peirce, Mead, and Morris, as well as Suzanne Langer. From these sources and work in structural linguistics, the program professed to teach semiotic analyses of "scientific, social, and artistic symbols," with short documentaries used to help students relate symbolic interpretations to social interactions in the highly mediated urban landscape (Grey 14). In this and other programs, one can see how structuralist linguistics served to provide a model for studying mass communications, with semantics used to teach students to maintain a critical disengagement from mass propaganda. The critical possibilities of such approaches were muted by the blurring of social reconstructionist purposes into life adjustment models that is evident in the "student-centered" program at Drake University. Rather than seeking to prepare students to confront social problems, "the Reconstructionist school of educational thinking" at Drake was based on the assumption that "each student is an environment," and the teacher's task is to help students "adapt" to their individual potentials and needs (Dunn 89).

The communications movement was sometimes described as the "linguistic communications" movement, and as such, it represents the broadest effort in the history of college English studies to apply linguistics to general education. In the 1950s, linguistics was well on its way to defining itself as an "autonomous" science, though even a decade later there were only fifteen separate linguistics departments (Joos 15). The rise of linguistics was fueled by work with foreign languages during World War II, and after it by America's rise to international dominance. A related source of funding came from evangelical efforts to codify the languages of isolated peoples so that they could be converted. These internationalist resources led linguists to give more attention to applying their expertise to teaching English as a foreign language (EFL) than to the challenges of bilingual education—even though about 11 percent of Americans spoke English as a second language in 1960.[8] The organization of Teaching English to Speakers of Other Languages (TESOL) helped coordinate the creation of twenty-two certificate programs by the end of the 1960s (see Matsuda). According to Hymes and Fought, the postwar generation was the first to "seek and secure positions as linguists, not for their knowledges of languages," but for their distinctive methodologies (64, 117). Those methods shifted from genealogical to structuralist models of linguistic systems, a shift that paralleled the Progressive tendencies in the communications movement (Hymes 311). Progressives had repudiated prescriptivist approaches to teaching writing, and conservatives responded by condemning the communications movement as an alliance of permissive linguists and Progressive educators who were unconcerned with maintaining the standards of the literate culture (see de Mordaunt).

Such reactions played into the interdepartmental politics that brought an end to the communications movement in the organization to which it gave its name—the Conference on College Composition and Communication. CCCC was founded in 1949 by the NCTE after a joint conference with the Speech Association on first-year composition and communications courses. Plenary speakers included the leading figure in EFL, Harold B. Allen (who would become the first president of TESOL). Speakers represented the innovative communications programs at Teachers College and Minnesota, but according to other reports from the conference, some communications courses seem to have amounted to little more than some concepts from structural linguistics combined with semantic analyses of "mass media of communication." For example, in his talk on English A at Northwestern, Wallace Douglas praised the "linguistic communication" approach for giving students a "feeling for the ideals of scientific humanism" (31, 26). Such positions helped justify the efforts of humanists to reclaim the "turf" of first-year courses for literary studies, as Crowley and Heyda have discussed. The debates between advocates of communications and composition in *College Composition and Communication* did seem to come down to the "*control of the class hours*" (Tuttle). English departments won out as communications expanded its field of study into organizational and media studies. First-year communications courses dwindled, and instruction shifted away from media studies and semiotics to become more aligned with English departments' opposition to the "increasing mechanization and materialism of present day life," especially the "colossus of modern technology" (Edman 17).[9]

As composition became consolidated as an area of service work in English departments, and linguistics began to move out of English departments (at least in leading research universities), some of the concerns of communications courses became redefined by the conjunction of composition and rhetoric. One of the "New Rhetoricians," Richard Weaver, was the second speaker at the conference that led to the establishment of CCCC. Speaking from a classical conception of rhetoric, he expressed a traditional humanist's disdain for composition courses that operate as "a service station" to provide skills instruction in a "businesslike" manner (15). It had been arranged for James McCrimmon to speak before Weaver, and McCrimmon used Weaver's recently published *College English* article "To Write the Truth" to castigate his absolutism before he even had a chance to speak. Weaver's talk was at odds with the functionalist stance that McCrimmon set out, and which the conference followed through on. Weaver's invocation of a Platonic conception of rhetoric is nonetheless notable, both because his tenor was so discordant with the occasion, and because he gave classical rhetoric the pride of place that it would gain as composition moved up to become an area of graduate study in the 1970s. In contrast with the conservative assumptions of classicists such as Weaver, communications models sought to advance Progressive attempts to use "contemporary materials of local community life" to teach "communication skills in varied mediums" (Shoemaker 243).

The founding of CCCC was an important step toward gaining professional recognition for those who published on composition. As Goggin has discussed, the organization and its journal were instrumental in building a research mission upon the teaching of composition. A later president of the organization, David Bartholomae, characterized its role as providing teachers with a forum in which they could play a different part from those professors who lectured on "an attenuated humanistic tradition" to students who sat passively wondering how it related to their needs and goals (41). In the early years, the organization was centered on improving the teaching of composition and the workloads of those who taught it, including the challenges faced by community college faculty. The organization held regular workshops on "The Status in the Profession of the Composition Teacher." A national survey by that title in 1953 reported that training was rarely provided because it was assumed that composition was merely an "apprenticeship" that would be left behind by those who were capable of rising to more rewarding work in literature. The rest were consigned to teach composition—lots of composition. CCCC repeatedly called for revamping this job system. For example, as president of CCCC in 1952, Don Allen visited forty-seven departments to ask chairs why they assumed that literary studies "automatically" prepared one to teach composition. Allen reported that he received a hostile response from those who assumed that only someone from education would think that teachers needed training. In most departments, such training was confined to a few staff meetings, though Allen did find better support and workloads in the communications programs he visited.[10]

English departments' approach to general education mirrored the workings of the stratified educational market by exploiting the efforts of broader classes of teachers, and enabling a select few to demonstrate their worth in its terms and thereby rise to positions of privilege. The rest were then left to do the basic work that provided the institutional legitimization for the prevailing hierarchies. This professional economy was consolidated by making composition into an area of managerial expertise, and by creating methods for literary studies that could be upheld as research, while also doing double duty as an efficient means to handle class work. These developments were consistent with trends in other disciplines. A rich set of contrasts is provided by Bender and Schorske's *American Academic Culture in Transformation: Fifty Years, Four Disciplines*, which includes analyses and reflections of prominent figures in economics, English, political science, and philosophy. In each field, the 1950s saw a transition away from questioning first principles to concentrate on formal methods, as evident not just in New Criticism but also in the turn away from pragmatism in philosophy and the turn to behaviorism in economics and political science. At the "end of ideology," each discipline settled down to refine its methods with what promised to be unending funding (Bender and Schorske 32). As Bender and Schorske note with some surprise, all the contributors to the collection ignore the impact of broader social movements and discuss their disciplines as autonomous and self-authoring. Such a stance is not really surprising because turning a blind eye to the social forces at work in a discipline enables insiders to presume that they have justly earned their rewards, while looking at a discipline from farther afield challenges traditional intellectuals to question the ends of the profession.[11]

English Education in the "Golden Age" of the Profession

A dramatic sense of what class work looked like from the other side of the podium in 1962 is provided by Leslie Fiedler's "On Remembering Freshman Comp." Fiedler's essay on his class as a freshman composition student was the lead article in a special issue of *College Composition and Communication* on "The Experience of Freshman English." That issue echoes with a fading sense of the "experience curriculum" as inflected by a 1960s sense of *experience*. Looking back to taking a composition class in 1938 in a New York University classroom, Fielder remembered sitting beside others whose speech betrayed the Yiddish rhythms of their homes: "here or nowhere our (approximately) Anglosaxon [sic] mentors had decided, we would be convinced we spoke a common tongue with them: a language capable of uttering only the most correctly tepid Protestant banalities no matter what stirred in our alien innards" (2). Fiedler describes how his class was berated by his midwestern TA, who paused in the middle of his insults to explain his sarcasms. Fielder imagined that the TA wanted to ensure that his students felt the sort of biting humiliation he had been subjected to by his own professors. Six years after this rite of passage, Fiedler himself stepped up to the podium to teach composition as a graduate student at Wisconsin. Fiedler sardonically remembered teaching from mimeographed copies of the communications theories that S. I. Hayakawa had distilled from the works of Alfred Korzbski. Few descriptions of first-year composition capture its transcultural politics more richly than Fiedler's description of how an "urban Jew" ended up teaching English to midwestern farmers through the semantic theories propounded by a Polish engineer and popularized by a Japanese immigrant (who went on to become a senator and a leading proponent of English-only initiatives). The ironies at issue are compounded by the fact that Fiedler's cutting recollection is followed by an article by Hayakawa himself in which he blithely details how first-year semantics courses move students beyond provincial commonplaces to acquire a more cosmopolitan mindset.

Fiedler was one of the more iconoclastic figures to gain professional prominence in the "golden age" of the research university. From the start of his career, he adopted the position of an outsider in works such as *What Was Literature?* Success came readily to his generation. The demand for faculty far outstripped production. Only one-quarter of new English professors had PhDs in 1960, as compared to one-third in 1953 (Grommon). The enrollment pressures had a leveling effect, with two-thirds of faculty teaching some composition, and many teaching mostly composition (Kelly; Weingarten et al.). Such teachers called upon researchers to consider the needs of the diverse students who made it into college in the 1960s as a result of the fourfold increase in federal aid. With the end of segregation, students of color rose to become 8.4 percent of enrollments by 1971 (Andersen; Lucas, *American Higher Education*). More traditional professors responded to such trends by calling for the abolition of composition as a distraction from the higher purposes of English departments. With a confidence buoyed by increasing enrollments, the chair of Freshman English at the University of Michigan proposed eliminating composition altogether, despite his acknowledgment that it accounted for most of his department's enrollments. If composition could be dispensed with, his department would be able to quit hiring teachers who dragged down its reputation because they "have not published much," including faculty in English education who worked with local schools (Steinhoff 25). Despite the general attitude that education was a distraction to the profession, over 90 percent of PhDs in English were becoming educators—more than in any other field (Allen). These studiously impractical attitudes prevented aspiring departments from exploiting the booming educational economy to claim professional support for teachers. At no time in its history did the discipline have a better opportunity to improve the standing of the nearly one million English teachers working in American schools (Squire, "English"). In 1965, half of all first-year college students wanted to become teachers, and 12 percent hoped to teach in college.[12] More students chose English than any other major because it seemed to promise the sort of opportunities most students cited when surveyed about they wanted from life—an opportunity to help others while also being "original and creative" (Andersen 102–03).

A historic opportunity to restructure the field of work came in the 1960s, when millions of dollars in federal funding were secured to improve the teaching of English. Those resources were used to articulate an integrated vision that bridged schools and colleges.[13] The NCTE and the MLA first attempted to secure major foundation grants with conferences on "Basic Issues in the Teaching of English" in 1958, and then in 1961 NCTE followed up to gain federal funding with *The National Interest and the Teaching of English*.[14] In response to the question "*What Is English?*" the Basic Issues conferences defined the discipline as a "*sequential and cumulative*" program of study in literature, language, and composition. While this "triad" in principle centered on literature, it was estimated that in practice new professors spent about 90 percent of their early years teaching composition, while graduate programs had almost no courses "dealing primarily with language and rhetoric" (Squire, *National* 9). To gain public support, *The National Interest* argued for the economic benefits of improving literacy (Squire, *National* 23). The "startling deficiencies" in teacher preparation were the "greatest single weakness," and they arose in part from a lack of "articulation" with schools (Squire, *National* 47, 33). The report promised to address this need and cited research showing that doubling school writing assignments reduced student failures by two-thirds. Statistics were enlisted to demonstrate that improving writing instruction would save ten million dollars a year—the costs of providing remedial writing courses to 20 percent of all first-year college students (Squire, *National* 92–93, 113). The report concluded with a pitch to allow English departments to compete for the funds going to the social and natural sciences under the National Defense Education Act of 1958, which in the wake of Sputnik had concentrated on math, science, and technologies of instruction. On this and other points, one can see how the discipline tried to rearticulate the distinction between content disciplines and teaching methods that had enabled English professors to distance their humanistic concerns from teacher preparation, but which had also come to undercut their ability to claim resources for work with new technologies and public education.

The Education Commission set aside four hundred thousand dollars in 1961 to improve reading, writing, and speaking skills. With a couple of million more in 1962, "Project English" followed up on the *National Interest* proposals to set up teams of professors and teachers to work with schools in teacher institutes and regional curriculum centers to develop an "integrated English program" ("Project English" 40). According to Erwin Steinberg, the second coordinator of Project English, twelve curriculum centers were established, including one at Teachers College, where "comparative linguistic and cultural studies" were applied to teaching ESOL to multilingual speakers. Another center, at Hunter College, developed the noted "Gateway English" program for students in "urban slums" (Steinberg, *Curriculum* 58). Gateway English was a rare effort to get English professors involved with impoverished schools to respond to the view that literature was "suspect" because its study excluded the traditions of people of color, which were not deemed to be literary (Steinberg, *Curriculum* 52). Before the creation of the National Writing Project in 1974, Project English was the only national program to enlist professors in collaborations with teachers in summer institutes and collaborative research aimed at developing curricula to meet the developmental needs of students. These materials provided a coordinated, research-based attempt to work through the possibilities of new linguistic models, advance studies of the rising interest in rhetoric and writing, and build on the research on the teaching of literature that had been undertaken by Richards and Rosenblatt. For an all-too-brief historical period, Project English provided resources to build disciplinary collaborations with the schools that bridged the boundaries of literature, linguistics, writing studies, and English education.

One research study funded by Project English was Braddock, Lloyd-Jones, and Shoer's landmark *Research in Written Composition*, which reviewed several thousand empirical studies in the hope of establishing scientific principles for the teaching of writing. *Research in Written Communication* has been cited as one of the two studies that make 1963 the beginning of modern research on composition, according to Stephen North.[15] The other was Kitzhaber's *Themes, Theories, and Therapy: Teaching Writing in College*, which took its title from the confused array of composition programs that Kitzhaber surveyed. With funding from the Carnegie Foundation, Kitzhaber reviewed syllabi from ninety-five institutions and conducted an in-depth study of student writing at one institution, Dartmouth. While he used quite traditional measures, Kitzhaber found that writing improved in the first year, but then it declined in later years because little writing was assigned after first-year composition, even in an elite institution such as Dartmouth. The basic structure of composition seems to have become fairly consistent with the fading of communications (which was still found in six institutions, though half of those were seen to be moribund). While remedial courses were declining, they were enrolling about 15 percent of students in half of the programs. Approximately 75 percent of students were placed into standard composition courses, with about 80 percent of those courses beginning with personal narratives. The first semester was commonly devoted to language study and the second to literature (though one-quarter focused the second course on rhetoric or logic). In addition to "a lot of impromptu writing" (to limit plagiarism), eleven essays were commonly written in the first semester and ten in the second, including a research paper (25). Kitzhaber concluded that a common theoretical paradigm was needed to reduce the "bewildering" range of aims and methods. Other than "a desiccated rhetorical doctrine," Kitzhaber found no conceptual coherence in the handbooks and anthologies used in the programs (16). The lack of a unifying conceptual vision for composition studies undercut varied aspects of English studies, as is evident in Kitzhaber's recommendations that improving the course depended upon changing teacher assignments and training, broadening graduate and undergraduate curricula, and reassessing the general teaching of reading and writing.

These and other attempts to expand collaborations among teachers and professors were often guided by the idea that structuralism was about to lead to major advances in teaching. However, structuralism gave rise to a confusing array of generative and transformational models that left those arguing for the broader usefulness of linguistics lamely trying to justify a discipline that could not seem to agree upon its basic elements, and often dismissed its practical applications (see Sledd's "Plea for Pluralism" and Fries's "Advances"; also Crowley's "Linguistics" and Faigley 80–84). Just as it was being left behind in linguistics, structuralism was generating models of learning and literacy that were having an interdisciplinary impact. Brunner's "spiral curriculum" provided the model that Project English proponents used to articulate the methods and "principles of order" that set out to structure English studies as a unified field (Kitzhaber, "Rage" 1218).[16] As in the communications movement, structural linguistics provided categories for making sense of social conventions that had been called into question by a "communications revolution" that deepened anxieties among "literary people" that new media were threatening to create a "standardized mass society" (Muller 8). "Mediation" was set out as a distinctive concern of structuralism in Hartman's "Structuralism: The Anglo-American Adventure," which reviewed how structuralism had shifted the focus of study from texts to contexts by popularizing the idea that "societies are systems" (149). Structuralism's guiding concern for systems of signification became unsustainable with the transition from structuralism to poststructuralism. At the conclusion of the noted Yale Colloquium in 1966, J. Hillis Miller observed that the antinomies of structuralism "melt into each other," and are therefore meaningless apart from the system of signification that is set up to establish a presumed set of differentiations (562).[17]

In the same year that J. Hillis Miller characterized structuralism in terms that would postdate it, a three-week conference of fifty American and British educators was held at Dartmouth that is commonly identified as a signature event for the emergence of the process model in composition studies. Kitzhaber opened the conference with a talk entitled "What Is English?" He assumed that this question had been fully answered by the integrated and cumulative models developed by Project English. James Britton responded by shifting the basic focus from what English should be to what students should be doing. With that shift, the discussion took on a process orientation that the American participants had not anticipated. This basic shift in focus proved to have tremendous generative power when Dixon's account of the conference, *Growth through English,* popularized what came to be known as the "personal growth" model. That model had so many striking continuities with Progressives' efforts to organize curricula around students' experiences that it is ironic that the model was set out by British educators. Kitzhaber never did understand how the "neo-Progressivism" of Dartmouth was able to revive process models that he identified with "life adjustment" units on "understanding our neighbors." However, he did recognize that the British were reacting against a school system that was "dominated" by state examinations that stratified schools by the class of students attending them (1216; see also Mullen 12–13). American researchers such as Kitzhaber were trying to institute a structured field of work within a disjointed educational system, while Dixon, Britton, Moffett, and others appealed to British teachers who worked within a much more regulated system. The British "neo-Progressives" captured the spirit of the 1960s by noting that "learners are born free, but are everywhere in chains" (Dixon 111). According to Harris's insightful analysis in "After Dartmouth," the content-centered model of Project English was swept aside by an engaging vision of composition as a "teaching subject" that challenged research hierarchies by locating the making of knowledge in classroom transactions (634).

American educators viewed the politics of the discipline differently because American education did not have content-based standards to unify the field of study set out in schools and colleges, while British reformers were attempting to move English studies away from a more academic model of the discipline. British figures such as James Britton maintained that English should be about "experience rather than knowledge," in part because they recognized that the working-class experience had been devalued by the culture of schooling (87).[18] The tracking of "culturally different" students was discussed at Dartmouth, but according to the American appointed to publish an account of the conference, Herbert Muller, the matter was not resolved because "the trouble remains that these youngsters are in fact backward" (29). While American participants were nervous about what Muller characterized the "revolt of Negroes," American education was not seen to suffer "the social inequality that had long dominated British education" (25). Muller noted that Americans generally believed in "the democratic fallacy—the popular notion that all middle-class Americans are properly entitled" to a college "education whether or not they have the intellectual capacity for it" (31–32). In stating that "fallacy" in those terms, Muller aptly characterized the American tendency to assume that "all middle-class Americans" pretty much includes all Americans. American education was not seen to be classless by other reformers. In his article survey-ing the changes between the Basic Issues conferences in 1958 and the Dart-mouth Conference in 1966, Marckwardt noted that "the rediscovery of the American lower class" was disabusing educators of the notion that "we were simply one vast and relatively undifferentiated middle class" (10–11). Progres-sivists' concerns about the class politics of American education were reemerg-ing. From their national survey of high schools, Squire and Applebee concluded that "the most pressing failing" of curricula was the lack of attention to the experience of students in the "lower tracks" (30). Along those same lines, the editor of the *English Journal* responded to repeated requests for advice on teach-ing "culturally disadvantaged" students by criticizing the tracking that stratified students by their "socio-economic background" (Burton 14).

One area where American and British class politics had a differing impact on English studies was in creative writing. Dixon and other American advo-cates of personal growth such as James Moffett and Donald Murray empha-sized "creative expression" in ways that have been criticized for demarcating the personal from the political (see Berthoff's "The Problem"; and Berlin's *Rhetoric and Reality*). This criticism is well founded and can be extended back to the reader-response theories of Louise Rosenblatt. On the other hand, in valuing the generative capacities of students' individual experience, Rosen-blatt's transactional model can also be seen as "a humanistic alternative to the excesses of close reading" (Clifford 38). Perspectives on such alternatives were shaped by the differing class experiences in American and British classrooms. In 1968 Dixon identified self-expression and classroom dramatizations of daily life as strategies for enabling working-class children to connect with their home cultures and regional dialects (99; see also Muller 32). Expressive writing is given primacy in Britton's influential "Writing to Learn and Learning to Write" (with the comparativist perspective of Edward Sapir cited as a guiding author-ity). However, Britton's theories look to social transactions as the ends of dis-course in ways that are broader than the "interior view" adopted by American "expressionists" such as Donald Murray (see, for example, Murray's "Teach Writing as a Process"). Whatever their limitations, such efforts to foster cross-fertilizations among studies of literature and writing contributed to the peda-gogical popularity of creative writing.[19] At the college level, in the 1960s creative writing became a national movement—a "minor commercial phenomena" that traditionalists saw as a rather "shabby" business only "remotely" related to literary studies (Freedman 128). As those relations became better instituted, the pedagogical uses of creative writing came to be looked down upon by those who did not see student writing as having the creative capacities of literature.

The pedagogical continuities between creative writing and composition in the 1960s had the same sort of potential that the communications movement had in the 1950s—the potential to shift the structural framework for the discipline (see Gallagher and Mayers). That potential was complicated by the renewal of interest in rhetoric in composition studies. That interest is documented by works such as Martin Steinmann's *The New Rhetorics*, which collected popular articles into an emerging canon of categories and concerns. The lead piece was Booth's "Revival of Rhetoric," which set out the sense of the time that something historic was beginning to take hold in the field. One of the historical trends that the collection aptly documents is the assumption that structural linguistics provided the expertise that would renew rhetoric by offering generative models of communications, as discussed in the chapters by Ohmann, Young and Becker, Christensen, Sledd, and others. This faith in the promise of structuralism would prove to be less generative than the rediscovery of rhetorical invention. Classical strategies for exploring what was assumed in varied domains provided heuristics that proved to be very useful in making sense of the explosion of knowledge that gave rise to intertextual models of reading and writing.[20] In retrospect, we can see that rhetoric was not well-enough positioned to break down the divide that had been set up by polarizing writing studies into the truly creative and merely technical. From that polarized perspective, a rhetorical conception of *techniques of invention* appeared to be an oxymoron, insofar as inventive processes were by their nature unmethodical, and therefore largely unteachable. The alliance of rhetoric with the teaching of composition and structural linguistics only confirmed its irrelevance to creative writing.

Such attitudes had a divisive impact at a historical juncture of considerable significance. The rediscovery of the art of invention was part of a workshop approach to teaching that opened up generative capabilities at the same time that the discipline was expanding its structural capacities. An expansive survey of the field at the end of the 1960s is provided by Lois Josephs and Erwin Steinberg's *English Education Today*. This collection introduced teachers to a field of boundless possibilities with surveys of high school curricula, an excerpt from Brunner's structuralist paradigm, materials from Project English centers and Basic Issues conferences, and articles following up on Dartmouth to discuss how to teach creative reading and writing. Curricula for the "talented" and "disadvantaged" are included, along with writings by Cleanth Brooks and Neil Postman, Kitzhaber and Dixon, and Rosenblatt and Braddock to provide teachers with a multivalent but integrated view of the field. This field of vision documented the historic possibilities that were opening up to teachers. The collection shows how the formalism of the 1950s had been replaced by a process-oriented approach, not only in the teaching of writing and generative linguistics, but also in transactional approaches to literature. These approaches acknowledged that "underprivileged" students were not culturally deprived but politically oppressed. This expanding awareness was vital because the formalist presuppositions of traditional models of content mastery prevented practitioners from coming to terms with the critical potentials of the social experiences of broader classes of students. Those formalist presuppositions have historically exacerbated the oppressive workloads that have been imposed on teachers of gateway courses. As I will discuss in the next section, content-mastery approaches to teaching have tended to concentrate class time on formal instruction in literature, writing, and grammar. Very little time ends up being left for workshopping writing or for reading. By default, writing ends up being the work left to be done at the end of the day. Teachers are left alone to spend their "free" time commenting on papers after students have completed their writing on their own. [21] This "process of teaching writing by correction—or instruction after the fact and after the act"— would prove to be particularly debilitating in confronting the collaborative capacities of the interactive technologies that began to redefine literacy in the 1960s (Applebee, "A Record of English Teaching Today" 14).

The Crisis in Literacy and Literary Studies in the 1970s

The historical potentials of articulation in the 1960s take on clearer significance when contrasted with the "uses of bad publicity" against the discipline in the culture wars of the 1970s and 1980s (Graff). At the same time that the profession was confronted with a collapse in majors and jobs, it faced public assaults on its credibility and a back-to-basics movement that undercut its educational base. The number of graduates with majors in English was cut in half (from 63,976 in 1972 to 32,541 in 1980). Doctorates followed in a parallel drop (from 1412 in 1973 to 714 in 1983): "the job market changed suddenly and completely," leaving few tenure-track positions and lots of work for overloaded composition teachers (Wilcox 11). Much of the disabling discontinuity between that work and those positions had been set out by the discipline itself. The profession had long ignored the fact that many undergraduate and most graduate students will teach for a living. The pressures to attend to that fact were contained within a job system that downloaded the most challenging teaching onto paraprofessionals, technical colleges, and service courses. If the profession had confronted those challenges, they might not have grown to crisis proportions. As noted by John Fisher, when the bottom first dropped out of the job market, professional leaders were slow to react because those in "distinguished departments" could afford to ignore such problems.[22] As the crisis deepened, some leaders began to call for redefining the field in terms of literacy studies, but the same forces that pressed for reform also stiffened resistance to it.

Those forces are most evident in the back-to-basics movement that sought to reestablish a deference to literate conventions at an elemental level. Access to education had expanded, and many homes had more televisions than toilets. Print was about to be transformed by the "personal" computer, which Apple began selling in 1977. The anxieties of the time made for front-page homilies such as *Newsweek*'s "Why Johnny Can't Write" in 1975. The lack of respect for traditional conventions was blamed on permissive educators who had failed to maintain discipline (see Faigley 61–66). The back-to-basics movement gave rise to the first wave of high-stakes testing initiatives that undercut teachers' professional autonomy by pressing them to teach to tests of minimum competencies, which were imposed on thirty-eight state systems by 1985 (see Apple). *A Nation at Risk* in 1983 was one of several clarion statements by Reagan administration figures seeking to establish their political standing by attacking Progressive educators for a "homogenized, diluted, and diffused" curriculum that imposed an "unthinking, unilateral educational disarmament." Declines in SAT scores and increases in the "functionally illiterate" provided all the proof that was needed that the public had become "scientifically and technologically illiterate." These literacy campaigns worked to reinforce the anxieties of white middle-class males about affirmative action, economic decline, and a loss of public respect for their values. Such anxieties had often been invoked to expand support for public education, but in the 1980s, they were used to justify its privatization. *A Nation at Risk* cited Gallup polls that showed education was still viewed by most Americans as a higher funding priority than national defense. Those priorities shifted decisively in the Reagan era. Higher education came to be represented more as a private benefit than a public duty, resulting in a shift in funding from public grants to personal loans and the elimination of many access and research programs established to make public education more responsive to the experiences of underserved populations.

In retrospect, we can see that literacy was not so much declining as diversifying, as commentators began to use the term "literacies" to refer to professional, scientific, and technological skills. Literacy became pluralized in discussions of the need to provide workers with the technical skills needed to compete in the global economy. The impact of new economies and technologies of literacy is documented by such studies as the National Adult Literacy Survey, which came to define *literacy* as something more than the ability to read. Such surveys expanded definitions of *literacy* to include "document" and "quantitative" literacies that encompass the abilities to interpret texts and process information to solve technical problems. As discussions expanded still further to include "information literacy" and "computer literacy," *literacy* began to change much faster than literacy studies, in part because the emphasis on minimum standards and basic skills undermined the transactional approaches to literacy and learning that Progressives had begun to develop. Those approaches were needed to address the demands and potentials of interactive technologies of literacy. This lag is evident in Arthur Applebee's surveys of curricula, textbooks, and instructional practices in 1984 and 1993. Applebee found that three-quarters of English classes continued to be devoted to talking about literature, with the teacher doing most of the talking. "Discussions" of literature tended to be recitations of readings of isolated texts in the outmoded manner of New Criticism, leaving little time for work with writing (*Literature in the Secondary School* 50). Teachers served primarily as examiners of writing, which was "more likely to be assessed than . . . taught" (*Contexts* 184). Applebee's studies also show that there was no cause to worry that the classics were being pushed aside by multiculturalism. About the only classic to lose standing was *Silas Marner*. In fact, of the fifty most assigned books in the 1980s, only one was by a woman and two were by minority writers (*Literature* 82).

Attacks on multiculturalism were clearly a response to expansions in educational access, and such reactions were successful to a significant degree, not just in rolling back affirmative action but in broadly reducing the access of poorer students.[23] While more women than men were attending higher education in the 1980s, the access of lower-class students to upper-class institutions decreased after 1975 as costs outstripped grants, and grants shifted from needs-based to merit-based criteria in response to middle-class anxieties about being priced out of the best schools (see Karen; Garcia et al.; and Faigley 248). In 1975 the maximum Pell Grant covered 84 percent of the costs of an average public four-year institution (and only 38 percent of a private institution). Twenty years later, the largest available Pell Grant paid only 34 percent of the costs of a typical public institution (and 13 percent of a private one). This change was compounded by the income disparities that expanded in the Reagan-Bush era. An average public four-year institution cost 42 percent of the income of those coming from the poorest third of families in 1972, while in 1992 that same institution cost such families 62 percent of their annual income. Those in the richest third saw no such proportional increase, with the cost of a public institution remaining stable at 7 percent of their family incomes (Garcia et al. 7). While the percentage of high school graduates attending college rose from 51 percent in 1975 to 62 percent two decades later, the period saw an historic "political mobilization by dominant groups to maintain their relative exclusivity in elite higher education" (Karen 194).[24] In these ways, widened access worked in concert with deepening stratification to increase the numbers of poor and minority students in college, and to track those students into less prestigious institutions.

The stratification of higher education and the diversification of literacy and the literate were compounded by the differentiation of disciplines to undermine the standing of the humanities in ways that conservatives effectively exploited. In the 1960s many universities raised their profiles by expanding their research efforts. In the 1970s and 1980s, federal funding for basic research began a steady decline in real dollars outside defense-related areas, with particularly marked decreases in funding for research on education and social issues. Unlike the post-Sputnik era of Project English, public anxieties were not translated into increased public funding for education. The prevailing political forces promoted the idea that educators had wasted the resources that had been given to them. Decreases in funding for instruction increased entrepreneurial efforts to deploy university resources to develop business "partnerships." Between 1980 and 1984 such initiatives resulted in the establishment of some two hundred projects just in the area of biotechnology, yielding over $335 million a year in licenses and patents by 1996 (Cohen, *The Shaping of American Higher Education* 415). These trends resulted in marked increases in the salary differentials for fields where the indirect costs of research yielded funds not vested in the instructional infrastructure. This internal divesture in the humanities was compounded by an historic shift in the professional classes away from the "humanistic" idealism of the 1960s as the pressing social concerns shifted from social and cultural issues to economic anxieties that helped justify state divestures in public institutions (Brint 14). These shifts helped redefine the priorities of students: in 1970 only 39 percent of students stated that they had come to college to become "very well off financially," but by 1987 77 percent were selecting that purpose as a primary life goal (Faigley 247). These shifts also helped shape conflicts within the profession. Unfortunately, leftists and traditionalists have both attributed the humanities' loss of influence to vocational attitudes without giving much attention to how the discipline might have intervened in the political and institutional forces at work.[25]

Such reactions help to explain why the basic changes in literacy that were emerging at this time did not bring broader reforms in literacy studies. A detailed portrait of the field before the crash in jobs and majors is provided by the surveys that had been undertaken to find ways to handle the tripling of majors in the 1960s—a decade that was soon looked back upon as a "golden time" (Kellogg). Allen's *The PhD in English and American Literature* documented a 50 percent growth in the rise of PhD programs in the 1960s, from 81 in 1960 to 124 in 1969. Burgeoning doctoral programs established the research credentials of departments in state colleges seeking to raise their standing.[26] Allen's study was sponsored by the MLA with foundation funding to examine why doctorates were taking an average of ten years in English—more than in any other field (with six years the average in the humanities). ABDs were apparently fanning out from doctoral departments to meet the demand for instructors, with about half of all doctoral students not completing their degrees. Allen concluded that "colleges depend for their teaching staffs on ABDs and teachers not yet that far advanced" (83). Allen noted that the discipline was even more culpable because it had not trained those teachers for the work they were doing, and hiring procedures did not include any attempt to document the quality of that work (117, 79; see also Wilcox 30).[27] Allen called upon professors to "face the fact that society has always supported them because they are teachers," but his study shows that the profession was already structured as a pyramid scheme with a large base of lowly paid instructors handling the most labor-intensive courses (89). Nonetheless, through the sixties most faculty entered the profession through its base, and thereby gained at least a passing familiarity with the challenges posed by introductory courses. This pattern shifted in the 1970s as beleaguered departments downloaded composition courses onto a caste of teachers with few chances of moving up to positions within the profession.

The deepening dependence on teachers without professional benefits was compounded by the tendency to look down upon education as a service function, as is documented by Wilcox's *Anatomy of College English*. Wilcox's study provides particularly timely benchmarks because the crash in jobs and majors came between the beginning of his survey of four-year departments in 1967 and its publication in 1973.[28] As with Allen's study, the problems that Wilcox surveyed were changing as he examined them. Wilcox perceived that rising enrollments would finally make it possible to eliminate "that monster, freshman English," which accounted for 40 percent of all enrollments (ix). However, hopes to eliminate such courses receded when enrollments dropped and departments came to depend upon composition to avoid "decimation" (Hunter 2; see also Simeone). Wilcox was surprised to find that "few if any *major* renovations" had been implemented in majors since the 1930s because he perceived that curricula had long lacked any basic coherence (156). English departments commonly offered a hodgepodge of courses without any cumulative sequencing, with sophomores commonly taking a "masterworks" course, an advanced composition course, and sometimes a public speaking course. Then students moved through overlapping courses that did not follow any logical sequence, including uncoordinated surveys of British and American literature, genre courses such as "Modern Poetry," period courses such as the "Romantic Movement," and courses on individual writers, most commonly Chaucer, Shakespeare, and Milton. Most departments also offered a couple of courses in "Literary Composition," one on critical methods, and another in the history of English and/or an introduction to linguistics.[29] In the boom years, departments worried less about curricular coherence than covering classes, which was cited as a problem by more than half of the departments in 1967. Finding teachers ceased to be a problem after the "panic" years of 1969 and 1970, which brought the "most dramatic, the most far-reaching, and the most significant change to occur in the history of college English" (Wilcox 13).

Despite the historic drops in majors and jobs, the curriculum remained largely unshaken. This resistance to change was built into the field coverage model. As discussed in Graff's influential *Professing Literature*, the popular and professional controversies of the time were accommodated by simply adding a course in theory, film, ethnic literature, or feminism. By confining such trends to an isolated course, departments were able to sustain programs of study that had grown increasingly incoherent since New Critical methods were overlaid on historical surveys that rarely provided any theoretical rationale for studying literature historically. These unexamined contradictions deepened as critical methods became more contested with the turn to theory (Graff, *Professing* 226–46). This "contradictory mixture of historicism and formalism" served as a "residual paradigm" from the 1930s through at least the 1970s (Waller 32). While there were repeated calls for more attention to linguistics and composition, most undergraduate majors only included an isolated course or two, and graduate programs often gave even less attention to writing, teaching, and language studies. Such limited reforms are remarkable, given the intensifying institutional pressures that faculty were facing to acknowledge that their jobs depended on teaching and teachers. Majors rose and fell in the 1960s and 1970s in tandem with changes in certification requirements and enrollments in education (see ADE 2001–02 Ad Hoc Committee on the English Major). Wilcox found that in a given institution, the number of English majors was often smaller than that of English education majors, which were offered in 85 percent of public institutions. However, many departments seemed to "discharge this responsibility blindly" (110). Most did not establish the partnerships with schools needed to supervise student teachers, with the excuse commonly being that faculty did not want to work with schools and teachers, which is not surprising given the training that most faculty had received and the rewards and support that were offered for such work.

Wilcox's survey helps to explain why departments were not forced to diversify their offerings by the historic drop in majors in the 1970s, for he found that even beyond first-year classes, 55.8 percent of students who enrolled in English courses were not majors (116). Wilcox found that 81.7 percent of institutions "require or encourage" a year of English beyond the first year, and a third year was commonly taken in 43.1 percent of institutions (presumably liberal arts colleges) (116). Fewer than a quarter of departments distinguished courses for majors and nonmajors. These statistics demonstrate that undergraduate courses were largely serving a general education function even when the percentage of graduates in English was at its highest point in history (8 percent), making English one of the three largest majors in over three-quarters of studied institutions (Wilcox 129). Even in the heyday of the profession, English departments were largely about general education, not just in composition courses but in their general undergraduate offerings.

This institutional reality helps to explain why departments tried to consign their service function to composition courses in order to prevent the profession from becoming defined by that function. The discounting of service work upheld the higher purposes of the profession in the "golden age" of the research university. However, English departments might have established a more solid footing for themselves if they had taken a fuller accounting of the values of their services when there was funding available to support their work with general education, including teacher training and articulation. Instead, professional leaders often looked down upon the populations that the profession depended upon. Concerns were expressed at the time that over two-thirds of majors in coeducational institutions were women, because "docile young ladies" were seen to be "dutiful but somewhat dull pupils" who made English look like an "effeminate discipline, fit only for women who intend to teach" (Wilcox 129–30). Such attitudes are an important counterpoint to claims by the current leadership of the profession that English majors dropped not as a result of "developments internal to the field" but because career opportunities for women expanded (ADE Committee on the Major 2002, 73). One can only wonder what might have developed if the discipline had attended to the needs of female and working-class students by diversifying offerings to expand students' career options and improving the professionalization of teachers. As has become increasingly apparent as more and more teaching jobs have been temped out of the profession, the declining fortunes of the discipline have been due not just to the drops in majors but also to the general degradation of teaching as a profession—a decline that the profession had itself helped justify by temping out its work with general education, including teaching and articulation with schools.

By devaluing its broader obligations to general education, the profession failed to develop the broader educational engagements that might have enabled it to anticipate and respond to the changes in literacy that contributed to the collapse of jobs and majors in the 1970s. Canonical readings and modes of reading were losing their representative authority with the diversification of the literate and the rise of interactive modes of literacy that did not respect the autonomy of individual authors and texts. Commentators such as Armstrong recognized that traditional curricular structures had become unsustainable: "once there is no longer agreement about what it means to read, then 'reading' itself must be studied as an issue in its own right." The turn to theory made modes of reading into a subject of study, but Derrida, de Man, and other leading theorists wrote in a notoriously inaccessible style for a diminishing "coterie" of experts who were markedly indifferent to the experiences of the less literate (Cain xiv). Readers' responses were examined in a polemical style that was calculated to engage broader audiences by neopragmatists such as Stanley Fish. Like other reader-response critics, Fish's *Is There a Text in This Class?* focused on the pragmatics of reading in the assumption that "the experience of the reader, rather than the 'text itself,' was the proper object of analysis" (21).[30] Unlike earlier pragmatists such as Rosenblatt, Fish did not concentrate on the personal dynamics of readers' responses because he worked from the postmodern assumption that "selves are constituted by the ways of thinking and seeing that inhere in social organizations" (336). From this perspective, literature becomes a "*self-consuming artifact*" that was defined by a distinctive "way of reading" that enacts "a community agreement about what will count as literature, which leads the members of the community to pay a certain kind of attention and thereby to *create* literature" (*Is There a Text?* 40, 97). This pragmatic conception of "interpretive communities" is what was lacking in the research of Richards and Rosenblatt, and it quickly became a locus for social constructivist accounts of literacy, including Bizzell's noted "Cognition, Convention, and Certainty" in 1982 (103).

Transactional accounts of literacy and the literate were responding to the same changes that conservatives were attempting to contain. The cultural and cognitive dimensions of literacy had begun to be studied in the 1960s as people began to have second thoughts about the traditional assumption that literacy was a universal good because it was instrumental to modernization (see Faigley). By the 1980s, the assumption that literacy distinguished "savage" and "civilized" mentalities largely went "out of fashion," in the academy if not in the popular press (Kaestle 16). Beginning with such works as Febvre and Martin's *L'Apparition du livre* in 1958, the "culture of the book" became seen not as a transhistorical given but as a distinct social construction that raised questions about textuality, technology, and the politics of literacy itself (see, for example, Davidson; also Bazin). What came to be known as the "new literacy studies" emerged from the historical juncture where literacy was pluralized. With the proliferation of literacies, literary studies turned theoretical, and literate anxieties turned political. The Center for the Book was established in 1979 by the Library of Congress, which proclaimed 1987 the "Year of Reader." That same year Hirsch published his *Cultural Literacy* and Bloom condemned public illiteracy in *The Closing of the American Mind.* The literacy campaigns of the time were clearly an attempt to preserve the classics of the culture of the book against transactional modes of literacy that challenged traditional literary conventions, including the basic assumption that "the first requirement of a work of art . . . is that it should *do* nothing" (Tompkins 210). As discussed in Tompkins's "The Reader in History," such assumptions had become unstable with the theoretical shift to examine the effects of texts on readers. However, according to Tompkins, literary studies generally failed to shift its focus of study and remained locked into formalist explications that take "meaning to be the object of critical investigation" because, unlike rhetoricians, literary critics continued to "equate language not with action but signification" (203).

While reader-response criticism and the expanding research on literacy had the potential to redefine the working assumptions of the discipline, the collapse in consensus on the methods of New Criticism seems to have combined with the downturn in jobs to create a "spiritless stalemate" in departmental deliberations upon curricula (Kinnaird 758). Commentators recognized that the profession was being subjected to forces that were beyond its control, though some also realized that it had weakened its position by failing to attend to the needs of teachers and community colleges (see Standley). As president of ADE in 1977, Alan Hollingsworth gave an address starkly entitled "Beyond Survival" that was addressed to chairs "who wish to save their departments from the extreme erosion or outright collapse that many English departments have undergone" (7). According to Hollingsworth,

> it is not that lots of writing sections should not be offered as inexpensively as possible. My point is that unless a composition program is embedded in a sufficiently rich matrix of literature, literary criticism, and language study, it may be cut off from the engendering insights of hundreds of years of literature, literary study, and language theory. (7)

Hollingsworth saw no contradiction between his assumptions that writing should be taught on the cheap and that it was enriched by being allowed to keep company with literary studies—and he was one of the more Progressive commentators on English departments. He maintained that a "research-based, theory-based, experience-based" approach to teaching writing was vital to connect research and teaching, bridge the divide of literature and composition, and get faculty involved in mentoring TAs. On this and other points, Hollingsworth responded to the crisis by concluding that "departments interested in literature must help to create and sustain a truly literate reading public," in part by articulating a "true and democratized literacy" in collaboration with schools.[31]

The conflicted assumptions underlying such proposals document why the virtual collapse of the field did not change its structure, because the trends that pressed for change also raised resistance to it. In 1971 as secretary of English for the MLA, Michael Shugrue gave a talk entitled "The English Profession in the 1970s" that surveyed how disciplinary hierarchies were being undercut by the mass media, reductive accountability pressures, and feminists' critiques of canonical assumptions. Shugrue proposed shifting the discipline's focus from literary to literacy studies in order to develop partnerships with schools, attract broader classes of students, and prepare graduates for varied careers. Other reform proposals, such as those of John Gerber in 1977, also recognized that drops in majors and positions were due to broad changes in literacy and education that called upon professors to attend to the conditions and consequences of their work. Such pragmatic responses often treated the discipline's service mission as the key to revamping programs of study around the practical benefits it provided. Such proposals tried to harness the power of the uses of literacy to build public support, expand programs, and open up new career opportunities. To reformers, this response was simply common sense. To traditionalists, it threatened to overturn the profession by subordinating its higher purposes to its basic uses.[32] Such anxieties were not ill founded. The instrumental powers of literacy have such popular appeal that they challenge the profession's sense of itself in ways that have been contained by confining writing and teacher training to service courses.[33] In retrospect, we can see how such hierarchies have limited the discipline's learning capacities at critical phases in its development, for a discipline cannot expect to learn from the work it ignores. As changes in literacy deepened, the discipline could no longer maintain its critical distance, and practically engaged alternatives began to emerge in more broadly based departments.

The Strategic Possibilities of Rhetoric
in the Curricular Revisions of the 1980s

The crisis in the standing of the profession continued into the 1980s. Undergraduate and doctoral degrees in English were both cut in half by 1983, when tenure-track jobs began a new five-year drop of 40 percent. When discussions in MLA forums considered how to respond to the collapse of the academic job market, they tended to focus on ways to find places for traditionally trained doctorates, and rarely advanced practical proposals for revamping training, even though traditional curricula provided no preparation directly relevant to nonacademic jobs (see Woodruff, "The PhD"). One trend that proved undeniable was hiring in rhetoric and composition. Only 5 percent of new positions were in composition and technical writing in the fall 1971 postings in the MLA's Job List, but by 1979 those areas accounted for 23 percent of all positions. This trend contributed to the spread of graduate programs in rhetoric and composition, as documented by the national surveys of curricula that I will review in this section. Following on the hiring of writing specialists, undergraduate curricula began to include more writing, language, and rhetoric courses. These reforms were significantly more common in public institutions, especially broadly based departments that attended to the needs of English education students. The diversification of curricula further increased the demand for rhetoric and composition specialists, but the shift in hiring did not really change the professional economy of the discipline. The temping out of general education had laid the groundwork for the historic increases in non-tenure-track faculty and union activity that date from the 1970s. As with other leading trends, unionization was more common in public institutions because faculty members in less elite institutions were quicker to see collective action as a means to deal with the collapsing conditions of the time (see DeCew 11–15). Critics recognized that the crisis had been produced by graduate programs that supplied too many cheaply paid TAs and too many traditionally trained graduates, who ended up in teaching jobs for which they were not well trained or paid (Cutts). Some recognized that ignoring teaching actually reinforced the standing of elite graduate programs that imposed "narrow and rigid canons of professionalism," because ignoring such duties meant that the graduate curriculum could not be held accountable to preparing students to teach and organize themselves (Woodruff, "Only Connect").[34]

The disconnect between elite graduate programs and the needs of more accessible institutions explains why repeated surveys of graduates documenting the need for more attention to teaching and writing resulted not in broad curricular reforms but in the establishment of more vocationally oriented programs of study in rhetoric and composition, which were much more likely to be introduced into public institutions than in the graduate programs that the profession looked to for leadership.[35] The first graduate programs in rhetoric and composition were founded in the 1970s in land-grant universities such as Ohio State University, and in other institutions, such as Texas Women's University, that were peripheral to the profession's sense of itself. Most of the sixteen programs established in the 1970s were in public universities with large general education writing programs. In an ADE survey of 356 departments undertaken in 1983–84 by Bettina Huber and Art Young, 52 percent of departments with PhD programs offered graduate degrees in creative writing, 45 percent offered them in rhetoric and composition, and 12 percent in technical communication. Sixty percent of departments that offered creative writing also had programs in rhetoric and composition. More than half of public institutions offered graduate studies in creative writing (56.4 percent) and in rhetoric and composition (50.3 percent). These rates were over three times that of private institutions (15.7 percent for both areas). This difference can be attributed to the fact that writing courses made up 71.8 percent of undergraduate classes in public institutions, as compared to 53.8 percent in private, according to a survey in 1991–92 by Huber that was published in 1996. Departments that diversified graduate and undergraduate offerings saw increased enrollments. Programs in technical communication saw the greatest proportional growth. Huber and Young conclude that majors in such areas increased enrollments by attracting "new constituencies for English studies." The growth in such areas is also significant because technological innovations were almost entirely confined to writing courses, which accounted for 96.6 percent of courses using computers in 1991 (Huber, "Undergraduate").

Such technological changes helped to advance ongoing revisions of undergraduate curricula. Those revisions are documented by surveys conducted by the ADE in the 1980s that provide telling details on how reforms were shaped by the differences among PhD, MA, BA, and AA departments. In the national sample drawn up with a grant from the NEH to assess evolving trends, 43 percent of the departments included other disciplines, such as philosophy or foreign languages (Huber and Young). In departments offering majors, 85 percent offered traditional English majors, 51 percent offered English education, 33 percent offered creative writing, and 28 percent offered technical communication majors. Journalism majors were included in 34.9 percent of departments in BA/MA departments, with 21.7 percent of those same departments also offering speech, and 65.1 percent offering linguistics (much higher than in PhD departments, where only 12.6 percent offered journalism, 8.1 percent offered speech, and 52.3 percent offered linguistics). Such institutional differences are vital to consider because researchers tend to conceive of English as a departmentalized discipline. While that model may fit the realities of research universities, it can distract faculty in interdisciplinary departments from thinking about how to harness institutional resources to develop curricula suited to the distinctive needs of their students. Many departments have had the potential to develop majors combining various types of writing and media, because 80.2 percent of the departments surveyed in 1984 offered creative writing courses, 61.4 percent offered technical writing, 52.7 percent business writing, 43.3 percent speech, 43.2 percent linguistics, 38.5 percent journalism, and 35 percent film. From her research on different types of departments, Huber concluded that a critical nexus for curricular innovation was centered at the conjunction of writing, language studies, and English education offerings, because departments that were more involved in training teachers generally offered and required significantly more language, rhetoric, and writing courses.

Such institutional differences shaped the reforms of undergraduate curricula that followed upon the diversification of graduate programs and faculty hiring. Using roughly the same sample of over 350 that was used by previous ADE studies, in 1984 Huber and Laurence found that general education requirements in literature had dropped significantly since Wilcox's study. Thirty-six percent of institutions were found to have no requirements, and most others required such courses only for some majors. From these findings, the authors concluded that "more fundamental than the highly publicized debate about canonical and noncanonical literature may be the question of the place [of] literature of any sort—ancient or modern, classic or contemporary, elite or popular, canonized or otherwise." Following the turn to theory, more attention was reportedly being given to theory in undergraduate courses in 87.2 percent of departments. Between 1980 and 1985, 36.8 percent of departments had added professional and technical writing courses, the greatest area of increase. A substantial portion, 28.7 percent, of departments added courses in women writers, 28.4 percent added upper-division rhetoric and composition, 23.6 percent added film, 21.3 percent ethnic literature, and 19.6 percent creative writing, with creative writing majors in 55.5 percent of departments in 1984–85. However, only 18.1 percent of PhD institutions had technical writing majors, as compared to 35.1 percent of MA and 38.3 percent of BA institutions. These distinctions are significant because they indicate the differing resources for reforming literacy studies that have been available in a BA or PhD department. For example, a department that offered majors other than English was far more likely to require writing and linguistics courses than even very large departments that presumably had more resources to expand programs of study. As a result of such institutional differences, 15.5 percent of joint programs required advanced courses in rhetoric, as did 13.7 percent of departments in midsized public institutions, but only 2.9 percent of departments in the largest institutions (Huber, "Undergraduate").

As documented by such surveys, specialized English departments have presented different possibilities for innovation than those that still include journalists and rhetoricians who teach public address. Unfortunately, new faculty have been discouraged from considering the potentials of working in a more broadly based department by being trained in research departments where collaborations on teaching are not rewarded. Prevailing reward systems teach graduate students that general education has marginal professional standing. Departments with research missions have generally sustained them by assigning first-year courses to non-tenure-track faculty (who in 1999 were teaching 94.1 percent of first-year courses in doctoral departments and 57.8 percent of those in baccalaureate departments).[36] While only 31 percent of the undergraduate courses in doctoral departments are taught by tenure-track faculty, their graduate students will likely go on to more broadly engaged departments, including baccalaureate departments where 59 percent of all undergraduate courses were taught by tenure-track faculty in 2000 (ADE Committee on the Major 78). While many faculty members will spend most of their time teaching general education, they are often prepared to assume that duty by studying in departments where fewer professors have traditionally been involved in general education. As a result of this discontinuity, when faculty make the transition from a graduate program to a more comprehensive department, they are likely to see the greater involvement of tenure-track faculty in general education as an obligation that would be better assigned to adjuncts to avoid distracting professors from their real work. Such trends spread across the country in the 1970s and 1980s as the declining job market brought faculty with more research credentials to more teaching-oriented institutions.

These trends undercut the institutional impact of the turn to theory that "destabilized" traditional methods and objects of study (Huber, "A Report" vi). Literary critics ranging from Wayne Booth through J. Hillis Miller to Terry Eagleton looked to rhetoric to provide an integrative paradigm for work with reading and writing. Such proposals were undermined by the professional anxieties that deepened as jobs for compositionists rose and openings for critics declined. In 1979, J. Hillis Miller observed that "in the area of expository writing a large industry is being mobilized to create a new discipline." With more than stylistic echoes of Matthew Arnold, Miller's "The Function of Rhetorical Study at the Present Time" concluded that rhetoric was "the key" to lock writing instruction to literature and thereby prevent "pragmatic programs in expository writing" from rising up and leaving literary studies behind. According to Miller, composition and literature were both passing through "a 'paradigm shift' from a referential or mimetic view of language to an active or performative one." In the same year as Miller's article, Culler called upon graduate programs to "rethink" the basic relations of rhetorics and poetics because the demarcation of literature had become unsustainable as a result of assaults on the canon. For Miller, and for other theorists such as de Man and Culler, rhetoric was largely to be confined to the figurist elements of discourse that had been identified with deconstructionism.[37] Culler perceived that changes in literacy were leaving literature in "a very problematic role in the cultures in which our students live" ("Rethinking the Graduate Curriculum" 20). According to Miller and Culler, that problematic position called for reorganizing programs of study around the transactional relations between literature and other modes of representation, including the mass media. Culler and Miller concluded that surveys of masterworks were based on tropes that had exhausted their uses, on both a theoretical and pragmatic level, but neither Culler nor Miller critiqued those hierarchies.

Such hierarchies loomed over the subordination of the teaching of writing to rhetoric, for the rise of graduate programs and tenure-track jobs for researchers threatened to reproduce the prevailing subordination of teaching to research within writing studies. Some graduate programs in the area were established from former English education programs, and the energy that went into developing research programs almost inevitably distracted from less professionally rewarding collaborations with school teachers. That work shaped several of the most noted contributions to the early development of rhetoric and composition—including Emig's *Composing Processes of Twelfth Graders* and Britton's *The Development of Writing Abilities (11–18)* (see Gallagher 179). Graduate programs in rhetoric and composition were clearly a direct response to the need to prepare teachers of composition, but ironically, that need was not seen to be primary in most of those programs. In a survey in 1986, only 19 percent of graduate programs in rhetoric and composition identified pedagogy as primary to curricula. Pedagogy was not seen to be any more primary than history, which was also cited by 19 percent of respondents. Twice that percentage looked to theory as central (Huber, "A Report" 152). Given such priorities, rhetoric and composition ran the risk of reproducing the very hierarchies that leading figures such as Maxine Hairston were criticizing to persuade compositionists to leave English departments. On the other hand, the theoretical and historical emphases of graduate programs show how reductive and professionally self-serving it has been for commentators such as Guillory and Godzich to reduce rhetoric and composition to a technical and vocational mindset.

In the theoretical orientation of graduate programs, as in the technical emphases of basic composition courses, one can see that the drive to abstract scholarship from practical applications follows the general tendency of professionalism to divorce the higher purposes of disciplines from the technical expertise of practitioners. While this tendency may encourage us to focus on the dissemination of theory down to practitioners on the ground in the field, we need to devote far more of our institutional and intellectual resources to investigating how disciplinary innovations are constrained by institutional factors such as class size and teacher turnover. Such factors limit the impact of the theoretical innovations that we often use to define developments in the field. For example, the process movement in the 1970s and 1980s had a broader impact on pedagogy than perhaps any other trend. However, like previous trends such as the New Criticism, the process movement was often reduced in practice to a mechanistic model that worked against its own theoretical premises. The most detailed picture of the impact of the process movement on teaching is provided by the surveys that Applebee reported in *Contexts for Learning to Write* in 1984. Applebee found that overworked teachers and over-tested students tended to treat the writing process as a sequence of mechanical steps such as filling out thesis statements because classroom routines provided little sense of the generative potentials of writing for different audiences, situations, and purposes (188). As Crowley has discussed, the applications of the process model often amounted to little more than mixing personal writing into the formalism of current-traditional rhetoric (*Composition in the University* 197–214).

The institutional and ideological forces that have worked to reduce writing to a technical skill have set critics and compositionists at odds in ways that might have been more productively addressed if rhetoric had achieved the integrative role that had been envisioned for it. A glance across the divide between the arts and sciences may be helpful in assessing the forces that shaped the institutional transmission of theoretical innovations. In speech communications, rhetoric was also invoked by critics against more technical and applied concerns, but rhetoric did not have the same integrative possibilities in communications because aspiring social scientists felt little need to turn to the classical tradition to legitimize their rising concerns.[38] On other points, rhetorical studies did parallel trends in English. The counterparts to Project English and the Dartmouth Conference were the two NEH-funded conferences held by the National Developmental Project on Rhetoric in 1970. Leading figures wrote position statements that provide counterpoints to the trends that shaped the turn to theory in English studies. In Becker's "Rhetorical Studies for the Contemporary World," the transition from structuralist to poststructuralist models is framed not by literary or linguistic theories, but by information science. Despite the differences in theoretical sources, this institutional transition also followed upon a perceived "knowledge explosion" that made texts too richly interconnected to be studied as autonomous objects. According to Becker, individual texts and authors ceased to be the primary objects of study as scholars expanded their frames of reference to examine the symbolic economies through which information became diffused through social relations (33).

While Becker's vision stood far afield from the rise of deconstruction, rhetoric was positioned by the National Development Project on Rhetoric in ways that offer a broader sense of rhetoric's historical potentials than the more self-serving aspects of Miller's and Cullers's perspectives on rhetoric. One of the contributors to the New Criticism, Richard McKeon, delivered an influential plenary entitled "The Uses of Rhetoric in a Technological Age: Architectonic Productive Arts" (see also McKeon's "Criticism and the Liberal Arts"). To mediate the institutional oppositions of interpretive and productive arts, McKeon looked to rhetoric for heuristics to investigate the transactions of "knowing, doing, and making" (50). McKeon reviewed Aristotelian modes of inquiry that move from experience through art to science, with politics providing the civic purposes for practical wisdom in political action. McKeon also reviewed Ciceronian attempts to mediate the dualism of "words and actions," and the Renaissance shift to the humanist distinction of "art and nature." According to McKeon, in the age of science the driving opposition becomes "values and facts." This opposition emerges from the "separation of theory and practice by the constitution of a technology which is theory applied, the *logos* of *techne*" (54). Rather than assuming a critical distance from technological rationality, McKeon concluded that "the architectonic productive art in an age of technology is obviously technology itself given a rhetorical transformation" (52). On this and other points, McKeon set out generative topoi that positioned rhetoric as a humanistic philosophy of practical engagement with technological change. If such a standpoint had been adopted, English departments might have been able to break down the disabling dualism between the truly literary and the merely technical, and thereby become critically engaged with the technologies that were transforming literacy (see Kinney and Miller).

Looking back through the categories that McKeon provided, we can see that the diversification of graduate programs and the introduction of technical writing and computer technologies was part of a transition in literacy studies in which the operative distinction was ceasing to be that between the two cultures of the arts and sciences, as C. P. Snow had framed it in 1959. The opposition had shifted to that between literary and technical intellectuals. As noted in the introduction, these groups have been identified as *critical* and *technocratic* intellectuals by Guillory and other literary critics. Unfortunately, that self-serving opposition does not have much potential for developing humanistic modes of practical engagement with the technological and social changes that are transforming literacy, the literate, and literacy studies. Ever since the *Reports on the Course of Instruction in Yale College* almost a century ago, literary critics have buttressed their positions by dismissing teaching and general education as accommodations to the prevailing vocationalism without acknowledging how such a position undercuts the institutional foundations and political potentials of the humanities.

A sense of how those potentials were shaped by converging social, disciplinary, and institutional trends is provided by a retrospective account of the founding of one of the most noted graduate programs in rhetoric and composition, the PhD program in rhetoric established at Carnegie Mellon University in 1980. "Planning Graduate Programs in Rhetoric" was published in 2000 by two of the founders, Richard Young and Erwin Steinberg (previously mentioned as a coordinator of Project English and coeditor of *English Today*). Young and Steinberg advised those planning to advance institutional reforms to look to the strategic potentials that arise at places where expanding disciplinary trends converge with social needs and institutional resources. Young and Steinberg report that they sought to relate research on the composing process (particularly the emphasis on invention) with the need to teach students how to write, and with CMU's strengths in research on cognition and communications. Linda Flower and other researchers at CMU advanced cognitive research on the writing process that was among the most influential work done in the 1980s, and the English department at CMU also developed one of the most richly theorized undergraduate curricula in the field (see Waller). Flower's research shifted in the 1990s to focus on community literacy. That area of study has gained the same sort of strategic importance that graduate programs in rhetoric and composition had in the 1980s as a result of the rising importance of writing at work and the expanding potentials of interactive technologies (see Faigley and Miller). Responding to trends that shaped the rise of rhetoric and composition, many English departments are currently expanding their engagements with outreach and service learning as universities attempt to account for their public benefits against forces that are working to reduce those benefits to merely economic terms.

These developments can be identified with the innovations that I have explored in previous sections through the wide-ranging contributions of Erwin Steinberg, particularly his "Applied Humanities" in 1974. Like other reformers in the 1960s and 1970s, Steinberg called for the discipline to reengage with writing for the public. Like advocates of media, ethnic, and women's studies, Steinberg argued for expanding interdisciplinary engagements in popular media, ethnic cultures, and urban problems. Following through on the projects he had undertaken with Project English, Steinberg called upon English professors to move past the ends of the profession to collaborate with schools and become community ethnographers and pop culture critics. Steinberg saw that the discipline had mawkishly imitated the research hierarchies of the sciences and had thereby lost its institutional footing as professors had come to look down upon general education, articulation, and teacher preparation. He recognized that while the sciences had instrumental benefits to justify their research, humanists did not, making teaching vital to the viability of the discipline in a way that it was not in the sciences. As Steinberg recognized, while research hierarchies have served science well, they have come to exclude the humanities in ways that call for a broad reassessment of the disabling tendency of professions to divorce their higher mission from their practical applications. The sort of articulation projects that Steinberg developed, and which his successors at Carnegie Mellon have advanced, set out a vision of the humanities as integrally involved with community issues.

Conclusion: A "Humanistic Conception" of
"An Active Participation in Practical Life"

Throughout the last half of the twentieth century, English departments struggled to come to terms with the "communications revolution" created by film, television, and computer technologies. As with earlier transformations of literacy, that revolution first restructured the field of literacy studies at its base, in exploding general education programs. A communications movement emerged that challenged English departments' control of literacy instruction in colleges. As with earlier transitions in the history of literacy and literacy studies, the expansion of access to higher education and the spread of the mass media created a sense of crisis. A back-to-basics literacy campaign attempted to reestablish a respect for order at an elemental level. The convergence of these political, educational, and technological forces shaped the rise and fall of the profession. Majors and tenure-track positions were cut in half, while deprofessionalized teaching jobs nearly doubled. Professional leaders in elite institutions faced less pressure to rethink traditional hierarchies, because these trends strengthened the stratification of higher education, while also expanding its base to accommodate expanding classes of lower-class students.[39] More accessible departments expanded programs of study. Departments in public institutions were more likely to diversify graduate programs, and public institutions that attended to English education were more likely to require language, rhetoric, and writing courses. These innovations have been pivotal to the development of the discipline, because writing courses have been centers of work with new technologies. That work is vital to the sort of humanistic engagement with the changes that I have identified with Gramsci at the opening of this chapter.

At this and other critical junctures in its development, the profession has weakened its ability to articulate the values of its work by discounting teaching, teacher training, and writing at work. The articulation apparatus of the discipline was not vital when literature could be upheld as an autonomous area of study. For most practical purposes, the traditional conception of literature as an end in itself came to an end in the "culture wars" of the 1980s. A more pragmatic stance began to emerge in the movements that I have surveyed in this chapter. The attempts of more conservative elements in the profession to contain this pragmatic turn is pointedly documented in the ADE Committee Report on the English Major in 2002. That committee was set up after another downturn of graduates from English departments between 1993 and 1997. Instead of repeating earlier surveys to document continuing reforms, the committee actually argued that the "flight of students from English" was a "healthy correction" because "selectivity" was more important than "popularity," given the disorienting "demand for Vocationalism" (84, 77). Such an assessment made sense from the perspective of those who worked in highly selective institutions, who could afford to look down on the vulgarity of the public in the ways that literary critics often have. This standpoint is clear in David Laurence's editorial in the *ADE Bulletin* issue that contains the committee's report. Laurence maintains that "a specific and valuable sort of uselessness characterizes true engagement in the learning that serious consideration of literature uniquely affords" (4). To preserve this "uselessness," Laurence's committee recommended that departments limit pragmatic reforms to "minor" accommodations to new technologies and limit writing courses to avoid risking "curricular integrity."

More integrative visions of the converging potentials of the four corners of the field were put forward by the contributors to the *ADE Bulletin* issue. After an introductory article by Culler on how majors could be structured around methods of rhetorical, cultural, and literary analysis, revisions of undergraduate curricula are described by faculty members from such institutions as Louisiana State, Montclair State, Bronx Community College, and the University of Houston. In such accounts, one can see how reforms tend to emerge at several junctures where expanding disciplinary trends converge with social and institutional needs: gateway courses where faculty have to articulate their methods to those who do not share their assumptions, internships that provide contacts with public constituencies, English education majors that call for collaborations with schools, capstone courses where students reflect upon what they can do with what they have learned, and outcomes assessments that challenge departments to document what students have learned to do. Several contributors discuss how their departments had developed more collaborative, research-based reforms in an effort to break out of the field-coverage model that had been caught up in "replicating" the specialized expertise of faculty (Moffat 13). Rather than dismissing vocationalism, contributors maintained that students' needs and goals present challenges that professors "ought to welcome" (Shepard 26). To explore those challenges, Beidler reported on surveys of his department's graduates on what they found most beneficial in their studies: 69.7 percent cited learning to write, while 22 percent cited literary appreciation, with most respondents citing how these skills had helped them get a job (31).

According to contributors to the special issue on the English major, their departments had developed majors in "reading, interpreting, and writing about texts" in response to "the culture wars, critical theory, poststructuralism, and the reemergence of Marxist social criticism" (Schwartz 16). A powerful retrospective on those movements is provided by the final article in the issue,

J. Hillis Miller's "My Fifty Years in the Profession." According to Miller, the theoretical turn in the 1970s had been "a sign" that the "social function of literature" had changed with the spread of mass media. Miller perceived that media, ethnic, and women's studies were part of an effort to rediscover "the social utility" that was lost as "the study of canonical works" became a "minor form" in an "electronic age" (65). Miller's eulogy for what he elsewhere characterized as the "culture of the book" openly confronts the historical forces that the ADE Committee on the Major's report attempted to contain in limited accommodations to popular needs. In an earlier issue of *ADE Bulletin*, Miller had discussed how a "crisis in representation" had made it impossible to continue to read classical texts as synecdoches for an author and his era. As a result of the political, cultural, and technological forces that converged in that crisis, the requirements for traditional literature majors became increasingly incoherent, and the humanities lost their authority to represent the public in universalist terms (Miller, "Literary Study" 32, 31). Miller calls for a retreat into an ill-defined "new university of dissensus" as the only defense against programs that teach "communication skills" to "technocrats in the service of transnational corporations" (33). On this and other points, Miller conveniently ignores how such programs had underwritten literary studies throughout his half-century career (33).

In the last decades of his career, Miller observed that literary studies had seen a "massive shift to cultural studies" ("Literary" 32). Cultural studies came to provide broadly engaging conceptions of literacy that were not limited to the bookishness of literary studies. This impetus can be traced back to the concerns of the founders of the Birmingham School: Hoggart's *Uses of Literacy*, Thompson's *Making of the English Class*, and Williams's *Long Revolution*, which are concerned with the social sources and political implications of literacy in everyday life. In America as in Britain, the shift to transactional models of cultural and literacy studies was a response not simply to interactive technologies, but to shifting cultural economies. The classroom came to be seen as a "contact zone" that was connected to other sites where culture is transacted. As Pratt discussed in her influential article on the topic, in the 1980s "imagined national syntheses that had retained hegemonic force began to dissolve." Groups "with histories and lifeways different from the official ones began insisting on those histories and lifeways *as part of their citizenship*, as the very mode of their membership in the national collectivity" (39). The folkways of oppressed peoples came to be seen as dramatic enactments of the "radical contingency" of human understanding—epitomized not by critics realizing the wholeness of their individual experience through a self-controlled reading of a book, but by the everyday experience of peoples for whom such verities held little practical relevance. As discussed in Kent's "Self-Conscious Writers and Black Traditions" in 1972, African Americans had an "uncertain and ambiguous relationship to all cultural institutions," including "the high ground of humanism," insofar as it stands aloft from the "gritty" realities of working people (76–78). For students from such backgrounds, the professed "uselessness" of literature seems calculated to offer nothing more than what they have learned to expect from education and the educated (Laurence 4).

According to J. Hillis Miller, the "massive shift to cultural studies" occurred as a result of the television generation's having joined the professoriate. At Birmingham and elsewhere, cultural studies circulated through the same sort of informal educational exchanges as the semiotic models that were first established as methods of study in the communications movement. As in the extracurricular networks of the previous century, these informal teacher networks have also broadcast the ethnographic methods that have become part of ethnic, media, and women's studies, along with complementary modes of inquiry such as service learning, community literacies, and social movement studies. As in the Progressive movement, these modes of collaborative inquiry are defined not by individual close readings, but by the transactional pragmatics of collective experience. For Progressives, the historical models for that experience have been the shared traditions of women, workers, and people of color. These methods have often been guided by the desire to enter into broader coalitions with those groups in order to make public universities into something more than an oxymoron. Stuart Hall has stated that his basic goal for the Centre at Birmingham was to educate "organic intellectuals." Gramsci was very attuned to the tensions that arise when one understands intellection as imbedded in the lived experience of a community, and then tries to combine this "humanistic" understanding with an attention to the fact that "school is the instrument through which intellectuals of various levels are elaborated" (Gramsci 10). Hall acknowledged how problematic such ethnographic ambitions are, but he held them out as a hopeful vision of how the work of education could help people to develop collective agency.

Through cultural studies and other wide-ranging collaborative projects such as community literacy, we are coming to understand that articulation, general education, and the teaching profession are integral parts of literacy and literary studies. In 1989, Richard Lanham recognized that the "real question for literary study now is not whether our students will be reading Great Traditional Books or Relevant Modern ones in the future, but whether they will be reading books at all" (265). Lanham called upon the profession to move beyond its "craft-guild" investment in print to "think constructively about the electronic word" in order to develop "more agile, capacious, and hopeful" engagements with technological changes in literacy (288). Our ability to develop that more expansive field of vision has been undercut by efforts to divorce the higher purposes of the profession from our basic work in general education. Those efforts have become unsustainable as teaching has become increasingly deprofessionalized. Our discipline has been complicit with that historical trend. If we can recognize that complicity, we may be able to confront the forces at work at the ends of the profession. We need to form coalitions with the English teachers who are struggling to resist the forces that are reducing our studies to basic skills courses. Decades ago, at another critical juncture in the history of our work, proponents of Project English imagined that school-college partnerships could build "a critical, professional public" by establishing school-college partnerships of a "hitherto undreamed of scale" (Marckwardt 11). That dream is still imaginable, though its pragmatics will take a lot of work.

Conclusion

WHY THE PRAGMATICS OF
LITERACY ARE CRITICAL

> The literary historian of the future will have to widen his vision
> and take into . . . account such factors as the invention of the
> rotary press, the state of general education and enlightenment,
> the constant cheapening of the processes of printing, the
> increasing ease of travel and communication, the distribution of
> surplus wealth and leisure, the introduction of the typewriter,
> the distributions of bookstores and circulating libraries, the
> popularization of the telephone, motor car, movies, and radio,
> and legislative attitudes toward such questions as censorship,
> international copyright, and a tariff on foreign books.
>
> Harry Clark in 1928, "American Literary History
> and American Literature," 23.

IN 1928, CLARK ENVISIONED
a future in which the history of literature would be studied against changes in
literacy, education, and mass media. Clark's sense of history was shaped by
the profound social and technological changes of his time. Technologies figure
prominently in his set of historical benchmarks, and for good reason. In the
decade in which he published "American Literary History and American Literature," radio networks were formed, the first talking film was made, the television tube was invented, and signals began to be transmitted. Clark recognized
that these media would transform literary studies, but he underestimated the
profession's ability to maintain literary and linguistic studies as autonomous
fields of expertise. Those enclaves of expertise have been broken down as market forces have undercut the ethos of professionalism, and the "personal computer" has transformed our personal, political, and professional lives. Literature,
language, and literacy have lost their autonomy, and more transactional and
networked conceptions of cultural and literacy studies have gained currency.

"New Literacy Studies" has opposed the "autonomous" models of literacy that New Critics used to demarcate literary texts from their social contexts. Networked modes of reading have gained currency with the diversification of literacies and the rise of intertextual modes of cultural studies. Those trends are pressing us to rethink the history of literacy and literature in ways much like those that Clark envisioned. We have come to understand that literatures have evolved in tandem with broader historical transitions that have redefined literacy and the literate as access to education has expanded, the public has become more diversified, and the standing of the literate has become more contested.

At pivotal junctures in the history of literacy, new conceptions of literature have emerged out of the sort of conjunctions of social and technological changes that confronted Clark. In the colonial period, religious literature was upheld as the highest object of study in a scribal curriculum in which students were taught to recite traditional assumptions and then deduce their individual obligations from them. In Revolutionary America, English studies adopted a more oratorical sense of literature as the educated were pressed to persuade colonials that they shared a national identity. In the antebellum period, the penny press and common school established the modern identification of literacy with schooling. Literacy expanded to more diverse classes of readers, and literature adopted a more belletristic tenor as it became caught up in efforts to teach readers that they could distinguish themselves by learning to make literary distinctions. The antebellum period was a transitional phase in the development of literacy as well as literature. The effort to codify a national language and literature was informed by a "civic professionalism" that shaped the evolution of republicanism into the more specialized forms of professionalism that would became the unifying ideology of the "managerial-professional classes" with the rise of the research university. In tandem with these historical transitions in literature and the literate, modes of literacy instruction shifted from syllogistic disputations to forensic debates to belletristic essays. Each genre served a representative function in the classroom and in the forums that the literate moved into upon graduation. A deductive epistemology bridged classroom recitations with the sermons that graduates preached to the converted. Forensics helped prepare graduates for the political debates of the time, while belletristic essays helped the literate to see their efforts at self-improvement as a means to social progress.

The historical developments that contributed to the institutionalization of a modern conception of literature provide a broader frame of reference for assessing the rise of the profession. In the Progressive era, college English studies began to be divided up into distinct areas of expertise as critics and linguists consolidated their professional standing by positioning their concerns above work with teaching and writing. That hierarchy has broken down as the model of autonomous disciplines has lost its representative authority to the logic of market relations. As Ohmann discussed in "Teaching and Studying Literature at the End of Ideology," "the origins of our present malaise" lie "in the core of our earlier beliefs" (95). The divorce of intellectual inquiry from pragmatic considerations had traditionally been a mainstay of the liberal arts, and that otherworldliness served to distinguish academics from those who labor for a living. Such liberal arts hierarchies contributed to the depoliticized outlook of the middle classes by distancing the culture of professionalism from popular politics. As autonomous disciplines, the fields of literary and linguistic studies had clearly drawn boundaries, but those borders have become harder to defend as enclaves of expertise have been broken up by market forces. According to Richard Lanham, social, technological, and institutional changes are pressing the profession to address the "problems in the social and educational structures that sustain literary culture, problems that, taken together, we have come to call the 'literacy crisis'" (Lanham, "The Rhetorical Paideia" 132).

Faced with this crisis, those of us who work in more publicly accessible institutions should consider how literacy studies can provide an integrative framework for harnessing the converging potentials of work with teaching, writing, language, and literature.[1] The collapse of majors and jobs in the 1970s pressed our profession to invest more of its intellectual capacities in its institutional responsibilities, and we are now facing a comparable collapse in jobs and funding. The culture of the book is a particular historical conjunction that has begun to be formally studied.[2] The pressures on English departments are intensifying as tenure-track faculty are being replaced by part-time and "temporary" teachers. In response to these pressures, the profession has become more pragmatic about teaching, writing, and interactive technologies. This pragmatism has been critiqued as an accommodation to vocationalism by humanists, but such divisive reactions offer little help or hope. More promising opportunities will open up if we can work to connect our classroom discussions with broader deliberations on language, literature, and culture, as Mary Louise Pratt has discussed in "Building a New Public Idea about Language." I will draw on such accounts at the end of this conclusion, when I turn to examine the pragmatic capacities of broadly based departments of literacy. Before considering those potentials, I will first review the case studies that I have examined in previous chapters. Then, in the second section, I will follow through from the last chapter to assess how English majors have come to give more attention to writing in response to the spread of interactive literacies that have shifted our standpoint to a more writerly perspective on literacy studies. Such trends need to be assessed with an eye to how they can help us focus our collective energies on supporting those who teach most of the labor-intensive writing courses in the field with few benefits and little pay. We will be best able to develop broad coalitions to improve teaching conditions if we define the profession in ways that include those who work in all four corners of our field.

Critical Junctures in the History of Literacy and Literacy Studies

The relations of literacy and literacy studies have been transformed by the convergence of social, institutional, and technological developments that have changed learning and the learned. Syllogistic disputations lost their educational preeminence when the learned could no longer deduce authoritative truths from received traditions in a manner that appeared natural to the literate public. The colonial curriculum was as closed as the isolated communities in which graduates preached the Word to the converted. Knowledge circulated through face-to-face exchanges and gained authority from those who had it. Literacy functioned as a "technology of the self" that was learned by heart by reducing all that was known to hierarchies that could be memorized and recited. Learning and the learned adopted a more oratorical register with the social diversification that contributed to the Great Awakening's debates over the representative authority of clergy. Those debates expanded the influence of popular oratory and the circulation of the periodical press. The spread of print contributed to the formation of English as a subject of formal instruction in higher education. The consummate man of print, Benjamin Franklin, was instrumental in establishing the college in Philadelphia that included the first professorship devoted to teaching English. In the decades after the American Revolution, public schooling made literacy second nature and literature a school subject. The penny press and common school established the foundations for the institution of a national literature and language. Professors of English participated in informal cultural economies that were more expansive and inclusive than has been perceived by research on English studies as a professional field of study.

The colonial period provides the starkest example of the need to assess what goes on in the classroom against what graduates do when they leave it. While the communities served by early college graduates tended to be more literate than their British counterparts, books were rare, and instruction concentrated on reducing them to synopses that could be memorized and recited. Scribal literacy tended to be devoutly deductive, introspective, and arhetorical. Pneumatics, *technologicae*, and other mental sciences had an experiential orientation that proved to be responsive to the experimental impetus of the "new learning."[3] *Experimental* conceptions were also applied to the religious experience. Within the covenanting tradition, individuals had to give a convincing narrative of their conversion experience to be admitted to the church. Most graduates thus preached to closed interpretive communities that shared a closely knit set of beliefs from which their duties could be deduced. Persuasion was little studied or valued because biblical truths were seen to be self-evident to any person of faith. This system of beliefs and practices broke down as successive generations became unwilling to bare their souls in public. Communities became more factionalized and argumentation became more accepted, as documented by Lockridge's ethnographic study of a representative New England town. Individual religious differences were accommodated in higher education by replacing theology and logic with moral philosophy and rhetoric at the pinnacle of the curriculum. In response to evangelical critics and the encroachment of state authorities, educators distinguished between the public and private institutions of education, most notably in the famous Dartmouth case that first established that distinction in the higher-education market.

As the "circle of knowledge" broke up in the scribal curriculum and the closed communities where graduates preached, republicanism came to provide a unifying ideology for the expansion of learning and the learned. New colleges established professorships devoted to teaching English in order to compete for students and secure popular support. The first was at the College of Philadelphia. It was a hybrid institution that included academies for boys and girls, as would many of the colleges that sprung up in the provinces in the antebellum period. Franklin proposed to offer an "English education" in "useful" knowledge that would challenge the traditional subordination of mechanical to liberal arts, and so it is not surprising that the first "Professor of the English Tongue and Oratory," Ebenezer Kinnersley, was better known as a scientist than critic. Like many other forgotten contributors to our field of work, Kinnersley devoted most of his time to teaching writing and reading to underprepared students. The best known of the first generation of professors of rhetoric was John Witherspoon, who graduated alongside Hugh Blair at Edinburgh before emigrating to serve as president of the struggling college in Princeton where he taught rhetoric and moral philosophy.[4] Like the Scottish émigré who served as the first president of the College of Philadelphia, William Smith, Witherspoon was a conduit for Scottish theories of moral philosophy, rhetoric, and belles lettres. The most noted compositions to follow from that convergence were the *Federalist* essays that Witherspoon's student James Madison composed to defend the moderate and self-balanced virtues of representative self-governance.

While literacy was more politicized in Revolutionary America than in the rest of the British cultural provinces, Scottish works on rhetoric and moral philosophy provide rich sites for assessing how literacy studies were transformed by the transition from the ancients to the moderns (see Miller, *The Formation of College English*). Perhaps the richest are those of the first theorist of "consumer society," Adam Smith, who was one of the first to teach college English courses (see also Court; Crawford). Smith apparently took the rhetorical figure of the "impartial spectator" from the foreword to an edition of the *Spectator*. His discussions of the second self who monitors social interactions and personal reactions provide a dynamic sense of the dialectical consciousness of the cultural outsiders who studiously refashion their responses to conform to conventions that were commonly acquired as part of the natural upbringing of an English gentleman. From its origins, college English has taught aspiring provincials how to distinguish themselves by adopting cosmopolitan tastes. Before they could formalize polite proprieties for their students, Scottish professors had to first teach themselves how to speak English with propriety. In their studious self-fashionings lie many telling lessons on how instruction in literacy works to instill representative forms of self-governance. We have come to understand those workings differently in recent decades. We have come to acknowledge that it is schooling as much as literacy that instills the self-restraint and abstract thinking that distinguish the literate (see Daniell). From that knowledge, we have come to rethink the critical capacities of the dialectical consciousness of those with dual cultural identities, ranging from North Britons to African Americans. The dialectical workings of the self as other have shaped college English since its founding, and they remain critical to the introductory class work that is the most challenging and least respected part of our field.

The professions loom larger in America than they do in Britain, in part because America has historically lacked a cosmopolitan center or literary gentry. Drawing upon the conception of "civic professionalism" propounded by Bender, we may characterize the community-based intellectuals of the antebellum period who participated in informal cultural networks comprised of lyceums, teachers' institutes, and literary and scientific societies. These associations contributed to the greatest proportional growth in the numbers of colleges in American history. While those colleges have traditionally been criticized as elitist and antiquarian, Colin Burke's research shows that antebellum professors were more productive and their students more diverse than has been recognized. Struggling institutions in the backcountry brought a semblance of advanced education to rural communities. Such institutions provide a vital opportunity to consider how the field has been shaped by the "extracurriculum." This term has been used by Anne Ruggles Gere to characterize the wide-ranging associations that students and faculty have engaged in beyond the confines of formal instruction and professional duties. Student associations shaped the origins of college English studies in the eighteenth century, and in the nineteenth, lyceums, teachers' institutes, and literary and scientific societies provided vital collaborative learning opportunities for women, minorities, and others with limited access to class work with literacy. When these cultural networks are viewed as part of the educational infrastructure of the time, we can see that many antebellum colleges were more broadly engaged with their local communities than many English departments in research universities today.

These extracurricular networks provide an alternative frame of reference for thinking about possibilities represented by local book clubs, writing groups, community lecture series, and teachers' associations. Research universities have generally ignored local schools and communities because service has even less standing in higher education than teaching. This mindset may have advanced the scholarly aspirations of English departments, but it has undercut the aspirations of workers, women, and people of color who look to teaching as a means to improve their standing. English is the most broadly based discipline in the academy. Insofar as our discipline has failed to attend to its broader responsibilities, we have left them open to reactionary groups to wage literacy campaigns that have worked to limit access to education. Such campaigns predate the profession. The first back-to-basics effort in American higher education was the Yale Report in 1828. The Yale Report upheld the classics as an essential prerequisite to preserve the "present state of literature" against the encroachment of "*mercantile, mechanical,* or *agricultural*" studies and students. This response would not be the last time that literary studies were set in opposition to utilitarian concerns to buttress the defenses of a receding tradition. From a distance, we can see just how reactionary such hierarchies have been. Confining the literary experience to the classics has incapacitated work with literacy by divorcing its higher values from its practical uses. As noted many times in preceding chapters, literary critics have often expressed disdain for "educationalists." Such disdain has not served educators well, including those who teach literature.

The four corners of the field did not become professionalized until the Progressive era, when distinctions were instituted that set literary critics above journalists, linguists above grammarians, creative writers above compositionists, and professors above educators. Those distinctions were organized in diverging ways by the Modern Language Association and the National Council of Teachers of English. The former was founded as a scholarly association in 1883, and the latter was originally envisioned as a congress of teachers' associations in 1911. After the MLA closed down its pedagogy section and set itself above such pragmatic concerns as teaching loads, the NCTE was founded to serve as a "progressive" forum where teachers could organize themselves to address those concerns. As represented in the MLA and professed by New Critics, the profession of the discipline was set in opposition to the Progressive educators who were reforming its institutional base. Progressive teachers were denigrated as allies of the social scientists (with whom literary critics were fighting a "border war" for cultural authority). The NCTE's "experience" curriculum was exactly the sort of Deweyan initiative that threatened to undermine the autonomy of literary studies. A transactional approach to literature was formulated by Rosenblatt's *Literature as Exploration* in 1938, which was published by the Progressive Educational Association. Unfortunately, such Deweyan approaches often valorized "rugged individualism on the plain of the spirit," in part because the civic vision of rhetoric was so enmeshed in the formalities of composition that a rhetorician such as Burke appeared to be little more than an idiosyncratic iconoclast with limited relevance to the concerns of the discipline.

Teachers and professors of English would have been better served by the NCTE and MLA if such professional organizations had invested more of their efforts in raising the professional status of teaching. Even today, few professors see teachers as coworkers. Most of us know specialists "in our area" from across the country better than we know the teachers from down the street. This basic fact, perhaps more than any other, highlights the cosmopolitanism of English studies, in the sense that Gramsci set out. Professions function as cosmopolitan enterprises that work to abstract people from their local communities by teaching them to identify with more broadly defined and less deeply rooted values. No discipline is more central to the relations of schools and colleges than college English, much as it has sought to ignore that fact. Professors have looked to impose entrance exams to force schools to teach writing, but such efforts have only reinforced perceptions that the largest area of work in our field does not belong in college. While all professions tend to consign their more onerous duties to paraprofessionals, the distancing of literary studies from the teaching of writing was central to the disarticulation of college from high school studies that helped to privatize the assessment of incoming students.[5] As a result of this development, the largest networks of teacher workshops in the country are now controlled not by our discipline but by the College Board's Advanced Placement program, which downloads college credits onto high school courses to outsource general education. This trend can be tracked back to the marginalization of writing courses by the exclusion of journalists and rhetoricians interested in public address. The same forces are at work in the discipline's limited attention to media studies, new technologies, and workplace literacies. Our historical failure to make good use of the discipline's extensive articulation apparatus has become more pressingly apparent as support for traditional forms of research has become restricted to disciplines that pay dividends. These and related trends can best be addressed by adopting a more pragmatic stance on the economic and technological forces that are reshaping the institutional base of our field.

That base is shifting at an elemental level as changes in literacy redefine what it means to be literate. National surveys of literacy such as the National Assessment of Adult Literacy have examined three distinct types of literacy. The ability to interpret expository readings, or *information literacy*, has long been fundamental to English studies. English departments have generally ignored *document literacy*—the ability to make sense of graphic texts—and *computational literacy*, which is defined as the ability to interpret readings with quantitative data. Geographical and numerical forms of literacy have become important as literacy has become mediated in new ways. Literary works are no longer seen to be autonomous and neither are literary workers. Teachers of literature have come to acknowledge that "the Gutenberg Age" has come to an end with the breakdown of literature departments and other "print-based institutions" (Kernan 9, 12). An elegiac tone has been set by works such as Sven Birkerts's *Gutenberg Elegies: The Fate of Reading in an Electronic Age*, which characterized the digitalization of literacy as a shift from well-bound works of literature to intertextual networks where individual expressions become information nodes that are not experienced as embedded in distinct histories but as unfolding simultaneously in an interactive manner—more like cruising channels than reading a page. While books were traditionally identified with their authors' characters, the death of the "author function" ended the intimate communion of writers and readers. Reading ceased to be an act of isolated devotion, and writing shifted from self-consciously literary styles to more functional and transparent modalities as print gave way to texts that combine images, sounds, data banks, and interactive modes of correspondence.

English departments are still trying to figure out what to do with these literate forms and functions, which Bazin has termed "metatextuality" and "metareading" (154, 158). In the last chapter, I discussed how McKeon conceived of rhetoric as "a productive architectonic art" that could be used to explore the generative capacities of interactive technologies and cultural economies.[6] The topoi of rhetoric have proven productive in teaching students how to read as writers by attending to how genres shape the relations of readers and writers. Many writing programs draw upon rhetoric for metacognitive heuristics to help students reflect upon how they think about writing and reading for varied purposes in differing situations, including those that will not be confronted in English classes. Rhetorical analysis can help students critique how experiences and expectations become codified in the conventions of genres to shape what can be assumed, and what cannot be questioned. Such critiques have become the guiding concern of critical pedagogy, which has generative continuities with rhetoric's traditional concern for civic action. Action and reflection have been configured as integral to purposeful literate praxis by Paulo Friere (75n). Other heuristics for fostering metacognitive reflections upon literacy can be drawn from the interpretive categories that have been developed to teach imaginative literature, linguistic codes, and reflective inquiry in the classroom. Work in the four corners of the field can be brought together under the paradigm of literacy studies, which centers our collective attention on work with reading, writing, language, and teaching. Literacy studies can provide an expansive and integrative framework for reforming programs of undergraduate studies.

Literary and Literacy Crises, or What's an English Major For?

The profession's reaction to the transformation of literacy by new media can be traced back to the postwar communications movement in first-year literacy courses. English departments responded by consolidating their institutional base. Some professional recognition was granted to composition, and New Criticism came to demarcate the discipline's distinctive methods and objects of study. Programs of study entered a critical phase in the 1970s, when dramatic declines in jobs and majors pressed for reexaminations of traditional assumptions. The field coverage curriculum contained these pressures within isolated accommodations, as Graff has discussed. As majors and jobs continued to drop, the profession became even more dependent upon its service function, and graduate studies in teaching writing were introduced. As rhetoric and composition rose to become the largest area of hiring in the 1980s, some of those who were hired were able to look beyond first-year writing courses to help expand the curriculum. To assess how the curriculum has changed since earlier surveys, I have studied the online catalog of a representative sample of 257 four-year institutions' English majors.[7] To provide a context for that study, I will note two recent reports that have attempted to build a sense of crisis about changes in literacy, and a third that offers more positive possibilities. The changes come to the fore at curricular sites where collaborations seem most promising for those of us who work with literature, language, writing, and English education. Such collaborations can be brought into a cohesive vision by coordinating our varied programs of study around a shared concern for literacy.

One of the most striking aspects of our undergraduate programs of study is how they have retained traditional structures despite historic changes in guiding assumptions. As discussed in the last chapter, courses on critical theory, media studies, and women writers were added to curricula in the 1980s, along with more technical and other writing courses. Few efforts were made to resolve the contradictions among the methods of New Criticism, the historical structure of traditional survey courses, and the turn to theory. According to Cain, the formalist methods of New Criticism continued to hold sway long after they were repudiated in the scholarship, because they were not seen as the "legacy of a particular movement" but as "the natural and definitive conditions for criticism."

> Nobody, today, questions the place of literature in the curriculum, but few can give any reasoned justification for it. To the outsider the objectives seem undefined, the methods disorganized, the content in continual flux, and the results very difficult to evaluate. In short, there is no clear public image of the teaching of English literature. Its entrenchment in the curriculum is too often based wholly on tradition. (251)

If Cain is right about our field of study, then we need to reflect upon how this state of affairs contributed to not just the decline of majors and jobs, but to the discipline's inability to articulate what it is about, and for. Few professors have felt a need to resolve the discontinuities between what they write and what they teach because teaching is not viewed as a form of scholarly inquiry. While professors may feel pressured to keep up with research trends, few have felt the need to research curricula in other institutions, or to consider curricula in light of students' changing needs.

The marginal standing of teaching helps to explain why the theoretical challenges of the 1970s were rarely translated into new programs of undergraduate study.[8] One proposal for curricular reform was Scholes's *Textual Power: Literary Theory and the Teaching of English*. Scholes acknowledged that the "apparatus" of the discipline needed to be rebuilt from the bottom up, because it was founded upon binaries that had broken down—most notably the hierarchies of literature and "non-literature," consumption and production, and the academic and "real" worlds (10). According to Scholes, once the autonomy of literature was called into question, the boundaries of study came to seem contrived, and "then any text may be studied in an English class" (18). Scholes set about redefining the field as "textual studies," centered on the study of genre—the "network of codes" that had been conceptualized by Foucault and studied by such cultural ethnographers as Geertz (2, 3). Scholes was responding to the loss of faith that took hold in the profession as majors dwindled, and professors became "scared to death that our temples will be converted into movie theaters" (13). He realized that the rising "demand for more composition courses" would not overturn professional hierarchies, because that demand was channeled into departmental economies that appropriated the values of literacy in use to sustain the higher purposes of literary studies (6). For an alternative framework, Scholes developed a pedagogically engaged vision of the transactional relations of writing and reading, which he further elaborated in his coauthored *Text Book*. To break out of the "institutional sedimentations that threaten to fossilize" college English, Scholes looked to the classroom as a site of collaborative inquiry, with the model being the stance of the reader as composer of meaning. From this stance, students could achieve the "textual power" of critical interpretation as well as the practical art of effective communication (30).

Such attempts to revise majors in the 1980s were shadowed by the popular perception that literacy was in a critical state. This literacy crisis was fomented by *A Nation at Risk*, which has served as a point of departure for two recent attempts to launch new literacy campaigns: *Reading at Risk: A Survey of Literary Reading in America*, published by the National Education Association in 2004, and *The Neglected "R": The Need for a Writing Revolution*, published in 2003 by the National Commission on Writing that was set up by the College Board to justify the expenses of adding a written portion to its SAT exams.[9] The National Commission on Writing called for doubling the amount of student writing and engaging higher education in improving teacher training and writing instruction—all for the purpose of enabling education to serve "as an engine of opportunity and economic growth"(3). While the College Board's commission called for a renewed emphasis on writing as vital to American business, *Reading at Risk* attempted to raise public concern over the decline of "literary reading." The report was based on census questions in 1982, 1992, and 2002 that asked people if they had read a play, a book of poetry, or a novel, including "popular genres." With over seventeen thousand respondents in the 2002 sample alone, these surveys provided broad evidence of accelerating drops in the reading of literature: in 1982, 56.9 percent of respondents reported that they had read a work of literature within the previous year, while in 2002 only 46.7 percent had done so—a decline of almost 20 percent in as many years (2). Given this trend, it was concluded that the reading of literature "is fading as a meaningful activity." The steepest declines were among minorities, males, and the young. While 51.4 percent of whites reported reading a literary work in 2002, only 26.5 percent of Hispanics had done such reading. While women's rate of reading only declined from 63 percent in 1982 to 55 percent in 2002, the rate of literary reading among men dropped precipitously (from 49.1 percent to 37.6 percent). The sharpest drop was the 28 percent decline among college-aged readers (eighteen to twenty-four years old). In 1982 that group reported the highest rate of reading literature (59.8 percent), but in 2002 only 42.8 percent of college-aged readers read literature apart from school assignments—the lowest rate of literary reading of any group.[10]

One of the many striking aspects of these two reports is how they mirror the profession's tendency to divorce the practical functions of writing from the cultural values of reading in a way that incapacitates both. The discipline has not really come to terms with the fact that the interactive technologies that are often identified with the decline of reading have popularized writing in ways that could expand programs of study. One of the few positive findings in *Reading at Risk* was that creative writing courses had been taken by 13.3 percent of the respondents, which adds up to some twenty-seven million Americans. Among the respondents, 7 percent reported having written a poem, story, or play in the last year (4). While the reading of literature was significantly more common among richer white respondents, writing literature was not as stratified by income levels and was about as common among African Americans (7.4 percent) as whites (7.6 percent). Creative writing was most common among college-aged respondents (with 12.7 percent having written a poem, play, or story in the last year). This age group was also found to be more likely to attend poetry readings than most other groups (18–19). These findings underline the importance of moving beyond the debilitating divisions between literature and writing within the field to become more broadly engaged with such community-building efforts as writing groups and reading series. Literary studies have been and can be invigorated by treating literature as something that people compose collaboratively from their collective experiences. This Progressivist conception of literature presents a less exclusive and more engaging model of the discipline because it highlights the civic benefits of its literary emphases. While the reading of literature has declined significantly from 1982, college graduates were then spending almost one-quarter of their time on the job writing (Faigley and Miller), and writing has taken on expanded significance as computers have become almost as common as televisions in American homes (see Yancey).

As traditional conceptions of literature lose their currency to more interactive forms of literacy, basic reforms of undergraduate programs appear more and more inevitable. We have little information on what reforms have occurred in the last two decades because the ADE 2001–02 Ad Hoc Committee on the English Major decided to devote its efforts to defending the traditional major rather than repeating earlier surveys of undergraduate curricula. Those surveys found that writing majors and courses were increasing. To see if that trend has continued, I have conducted a review of the English majors of a representative sample of 257 four-year institutions with Brian Jackson.[11] Professional and other "noncreative" writing concentrations were found in 85.7 percent of the departments that offer multiple minors, emphases, or alternate majors (which were available in two-thirds of the departments in our sample). Related changes in the traditional major are harder to calculate but appear mixed. While writing courses have increased, only 31.5 percent of majors explicitly require writing courses, and 28.8 percent require linguistics or language courses (as compared to 42.2 percent and 39.2 percent in Huber's survey in 1991–92). However, grammar and teaching methods courses seem to be much more widely offered, with the former now in 45.9 percent of departments and the latter in 42 percent of departments. Perhaps our most significant finding has been that business, technical, and other writing majors and minors have spread through the field to become even more common than creative writing concentrations, with 46.9 percent of departments that have majors, minors, or emphases offering them in creative writing, and 85.7 percent offering other writing concentrations. Crucial links between developments in creative and other writing studies are provided by courses in creative nonfiction and journalism, which we found in 32.7 percent and 30.7 percent, respectively, of all our departments (see Winterowd, *Rhetoric*; Bishop, "Suddenly").

Such statistics inevitably gloss over the distinctive potentials of the majors offered by varied types of departments. In significant numbers of institutions, English is not a departmentalized discipline, for 17 percent of the departments in our stratified sample offer journalism and communications majors, though only 8.2 percent of the departments offer linguistics majors.[12] The general lack of attention to language studies may well be the greatest weakness in majors, for language courses are fundamental to teaching writing and literature, especially to future teachers. According to Huber, language studies have been integral to the reforms that have built upon coursework in teacher education and the demand for writing courses in more broadly based institutions. Writing courses make up almost three-quarters of all undergraduate English courses in public institutions, and that fact has made public institutions more responsive to related reforms of undergraduate curricula, and to graduate studies in rhetoric and composition. Creative writing concentrations are most common in research universities, while technical and other "noncreative" writing concentrations are generally more common in those types of institutions that are less likely to offer such creative writing studies.[13] This pattern is less clear-cut than the one reported by Huber ("Undergraduate"), for she found that technical communication majors were consistently less common in doctoral than masters institutions, and most common of all in baccalaureate departments. That finding suggests that English studies are being revised in differing ways to suit the needs of students in more broadly based institutions, as has occurred at other transitional points in the development of our field, beginning with the origins of English studies in provincial colleges that were more accessible than the centers of English education. This broader history of the teaching of English provides a context for reflecting on the spread of technical and other writing courses, which were the first to include work with the technologies that are transforming literacy.

As I have discussed in previous chapters, more transactional models of literacy studies have developed in response to more interactive technologies of literacy. The potentials of these expanding changes emerge most clearly at junctures where work in the four corners of the field may be brought together to advance cumulative innovations in undergraduate programs of study, most notably the emphasis on craft in creative writing and composition courses; the related articulation efforts in composition and English education; the attention to multilingualism that should be a shared concern in English education, ESOL, and language courses more generally; and ethnographic studies of literature, language, and learning that highlight the critical potentials that emerge at these and other junctures in undergraduate programs. Ethnography exemplifies the modes of civic engagement that are emerging from our converging interests in service learning, community literacies, and social movement studies. In these and other areas, the distinctions between service, teaching, and research are becoming blurred in ways that open up possibilities to rearticulate the practical values of our work with undergraduate education.

Almost a century ago, speech and journalism moved out of university English departments, and the remnants of rhetoric's concern for public address were divided up between the two cultures of composition and creative writing. In smaller and more teaching-oriented institutions, the discipline did not become as departmentalized, and tenured faculty have remained more broadly involved in first-year courses.[14] Such departments may be best able to break down the dysfunctional dualism of the truly creative and the merely technical by drawing journalism, communications, and media studies into courses on

writing for the public. Such an orientation could be vital to preventing technical writing majors from becoming mere accommodations to vocational pressures. Those pressures are often stronger in more accessible institutions. Such
factors may help to explain why technical writing courses and majors have
been more common in baccalaureate and masters departments. In such departments (perhaps more than in specialized research universities), those who
work with writing may be brought together around a shared concern for craft.
As Mayers has discussed, "craft criticism" has become a converging point of
discussion among varied schools of creative writing as an extension of workshop methods. These discussions could be enhanced by drawing upon composition research and literary theories. Of course creative writers have generally
kept their distance from writing about theory, research, and pedagogy out of
fear of becoming more academic and less creative (see Bizzaro, "Research").
On the other hand, unlike other English professors, creative writers are sometimes involved in the sort of writing groups and public reading series that provide community-based alternatives to disciplinary professionalism. Many such
challenges and possibilities may open up if we can advance the sort of rapprochement in writing studies that Wendy Bishop spent her career working for.

Creative writing courses grew out of the teaching of composition, and their
institutional base was laid upon the teaching of creative writing in Progressive
high schools, as has been discussed by Myers. The discipline's inability to work
with high schools helped reduce composition to gatekeeper courses dedicated
to technical concerns. Such courses are even more marginal to majors than the
English education tracks that often amount to training students to be critics,
and then sending them to an education department to talk about teaching.
Insofar as teaching commonly offered status only to those who had none,
aspiring institutions and faculty have traditionally worked to distance themselves from the teaching of teachers. Teaching and writing were pushed to the
boundaries of universities to protect them from being bogged down by the
problems of public schools. Maintaining a critical distance from such problems served professors of English well until higher education became more
fully integrated into the market economy. The most promising model for how
to confront market forces at a grassroots level is provided by the "sustained
and sustaining" teacher networks of the National Writing Project (Gallagher
83; see also Gomez). The writing project carries on the extracurricular traditions of antebellum lyceums and teachers' institutes. These associations (along
with community reading and writing groups) exercise the sort of collective

energy that the discipline needs to bring into undergraduate programs, both to build public support for its work and to help students see that work as a collective enterprise rooted in the traditions of diverse communities. Service learning, student teaching, and internships are vital to developing undergraduate majors involved with community and school networks that are supported by Writing Projects.

Such collaborations are fundamental to the Progressive tradition in English studies. For all its limitations, the Progressive movement provides a case study in how to develop programs of study that involve coalitions with teachers, journalists, public agencies, and community organizers. One area where such coalitions need to be developed is in the making of public language policies. Almost one in five Americans now speaks a language other than English at home, according to the *Chronicle of Higher Education* (August 27, 2004, 4). Working in a state where "English Only" laws were passed without any coordinated response from professors of English, I have often wondered why we do not see such issues as part of our concerns. My department has strong programs in English as a second language, and my colleague Roseann Gonzalez has been involved in addressing public language policies through her writings and community work. Nonetheless, here as elsewhere, collaborations are limited by the fact that ESOL tends to have little to do with bilingual education, even though the programs are housed in adjacent buildings. The institutional gap between the two areas grew as public universities moved away from public schools and adopted an internationalist orientation that served the economic and political agendas that fueled the rise of the research university. In response to continuing cuts in public funding, many universities have taken a new interest in outreach and partnerships with local schools. While "content" disciplines see themselves as having little to do with education, colleges of education have long been more ethnically diverse than the humanities, and that fact alone makes them important to those of us who are committed to recruiting students and faculty from underrepresented groups. Local schools are where such efforts need to begin, and they ought to be seen as part of the political base and disciplinary mission of English departments.[15]

The hierarchies that have divided our field of study and restricted our abilities to articulate its values have begun to show the stress of a system facing a critical overload. The junctures where stress becomes apparent present opportunities to raise questions about working assumptions. The prevailing research hierarchy has become increasingly unstable because it has failed to account for the work of undergraduate education. The accountability pressures that may seem threatening to traditional academics open up possibilities to reposition the civic values of our work with outreach and general education. A mode of inquiry well suited to these challenges is ethnography, as demonstrated in its uses in community literacy and other areas that are expanding our field of vision.[16] Ethnography treats research, teaching, and service as integral to collaborative inquiries into how the beliefs of communities speak to their needs and potentials. As such, it expands upon the transactional dynamics of reader-response criticism that can be traced back to Rosenblatt's discussions of how the literary experience contributes to "the growth in the social and cultural life of a democracy" by helping peoples understand the practical potentials of their differing experiences (v). Such "cultural transactions" can, according to Pratt, be identified as a process of translation if we assume an ethnographic stance that does not impose equivalences upon the "fractures and entanglements" involved in making sense of differences ("Contact Zones" 32–33). While undergraduate courses in practice often uphold the cosmopolitan values of keeping a critical distance from local engagements, ethnography assumes that we must become involved with lived communities to understand the values of their experiences. As such, ethnography provides a model for how undergraduate studies should try to relate to the communities we need to help represent in higher education, and also perhaps for how our professional leadership should relate to the basic work of practitioners in the field.[17]

Such locally engaged, transactional approaches to research, teaching, and service are likely to continue to spread through undergraduate programs of study, because these approaches are outgrowths of the basic changes in literacy and literacy studies that have been working up through our field. For over two decades now, rhetoric and composition has been one of the largest areas of hiring in English departments. Positions for people with expertise in the area increased as writing programs became vital to the viability of English departments, and graduate programs grew up to provide that expertise. As their numbers increased, faculty in rhetoric and composition have developed courses to bridge the gap between their graduate and first-year commitments (see O'Neill et al.; see also Shamoon et al.). In reaction to the collapse of the job market, other areas of graduate study have also adopted a more pragmatic engagement with teaching, and that engagement will likely spread to undergraduate programs. Programs of study have traditionally worked to reproduce the disciplinary expertise of faculty, without attending to the fact that few of our students will write for *PMLA* or other scholarly publications. However, departments are being pressed to account for their undergraduate majors in ways that create opportunities for us to rearticulate our practical values. Accountability and assessment pressures need to be creatively harnessed to redress the "proletarianization" of the basic work of the field that followed upon the distancing of its professional concerns from the "lay" experience (Horner 173). Such critical possibilities can best be achieved by focusing our intellectual energies on institutional opportunities to organize broad coalitions with our coworkers.

Organizing Teaching

The limitations of disciplinary professionalism have been compounded by divisions within the discipline that have weakened its ability to articulate the values of its work against the forces that have undermined the teaching profession. The social standing of literary studies has become further eroded as the "managerial and professional classes" have "splintered" (Brint 11). Divisions between traditional and technical intellectuals have been reproduced within the field in the opposition of literary and literacy studies that has been exacerbated by the rising attention to technical writing, computer technologies, and the management of writing programs. These areas have gained ground in the field as departments find that they cannot preserve their resource base while continuing to ignore the expansive duties that those resources have been committed to support. Our historic engagements with schools, college admissions, and general education combine with our traditional concern for writing for the public and interpreting the civic values of literature to provide an expansive articulation apparatus that needs to be enlisted in supporting teaching. We teach skills and aptitudes that are highly valued in utilitarian as well as humanistic terms. We need to do a better job of articulating our values in order to confront the historical trends that have undermined the professional status of teaching. In the same decades when English majors and jobs collapsed, teachers lost even more of their professional autonomy as their work came to be defined and evaluated by "public" accountability forces (see Herbst). These trends appear unrelated to the concerns of the discipline when it is defined as a field of study rather than as a field of work. Redefining our field by work with literacy can help us organize our collective energies around a shared concern for improving support for public education.

Employment in our field has become so degraded that the profession's ability to sustain itself is threatened.[18] In the last three decades, the numbers of part-time faculty doubled as state funding decreased and general education enrollments increased. By 1999 most English classes were being taught by non-tenured faculty and graduate students, according to the Association of Departments of English Ad Hoc Committee on Staffing. Even while detailing how widely the undergraduate duties of faculty vary in different sorts of departments, the committee maintained that American higher education "forms a single system" that requires "identical commitments to scholarship and teaching" (9). While the committee failed to consider the discontinuities between the research institutions that trained faculty and the teaching institutions that hired them, it did acknowledge that

> the institutionalization of a multitiered faculty sharply divided in its levels of compensation and security of employment, in its quality and conditions of work, and in its reward for teaching or research . . . threatens the communication of basic intellectual and academic values. Put at risk is the capacity of the academic profession to renew itself and pass on to the future the ideal of the scholar-teacher—the faculty member who, while pursuing new knowledge, takes active responsibility for the institution, the department, and all parts of the curriculum. (4)

While the ideal of the "scholar-teacher" can strengthen calls for collective action, it has traditionally served to organize the field around a professional hierarchy in which research departments maintain their preeminence by training faculty to look up to the profession as the center of their intellectual work and down on service to local communities and institutions as a time-consuming distraction. This is the "single system" of values that unifies disciplinary professionalism, and it is breaking down.

That system has been at least partially responsible for having set up the professional economy that is now collapsing around us because disciplinary professionalism disoriented departments from applying their research capabilities to their institutional responsibilities in ways that might have strengthened the standing of teaching. This disorientation is evident in reports such as that from the 1997 MLA Committee on Professional Employment (Guillory and Laurence). Here too, American higher education is characterized as an undifferentiated system represented by the research university. Its conflict-ing instructional needs and research priorities are discussed in the section of the report attributed to John Guillory and David Laurence (1162–65). Their analysis is skewed by their presumption that rising research revenues served to underwrite the access of "increasingly ill-prepared" students (1164). Pre-cisely the opposite dynamic has prevailed in English departments, and it is rather incredible that professional leaders have refused to acknowledge that fact. Our funding comes not from research but from teaching. It has been easy to ignore how teaching assistantships enabled the growth of research-oriented graduate programs because those programs have ignored the work done by those teachers. By assuming that research resources fueled educational access, the MLA Committee failed to consider how research in our field has depended upon teaching for funding.

Such committees were formed partially in response to the pressure of Cary Nelson and other faculty and graduate student activists who have called upon the MLA to do more than report on the workloads of underpaid teach-ers. Such activism provides a powerful counterpoint to the sense of unreality that permeates MLA recommendations that departments transform adjunct jobs into tenure-track lines and provide all new graduate students with fel-lowships. Such proposals are not simply unrealistic; they do not offer any real sense of how such goals could be achieved, other than by raising enroll-ment ceilings and reducing graduate offerings to move faculty into the lower division. While the call to service is important in assessing the profession's efforts to come to terms with working conditions, these committee reports are marked by the sort of disengagement from institutional work that char-acterizes most traditional academic discourse. This disengaged reportorial stance sharply contrasts with the case studies in labor organizing provided by books such as Nelson's 1997 *Will Teach for Food: Academic Labor in Crisis*. Nelson and others such as Eileen Schell have called for the profession to invest its critical capacities in the pragmatics of coalition building and labor organizing to address the needs of the part-time faculty and graduate stu-dents who teach most English courses. Unfortunately, these teachers' work with basic literacy is sometimes shown the same lack of respect by Nelson and related figures, such as Bérubé, as has been shown by other leaders in MLA.[19] This dismissive attitude to composition and general education shapes discus-sions of such vital concerns as the professionalization of graduate students, for it tends to be presumed that the question is when to begin scholarly publishing, not how to prepare teachers to approach education as a collective undertaking (see Nelson 2000).

Nelson and Bérubé have characterized first-year courses as "Rhet/Comp Droid assembly lines" where "warm freshman bodies [are] processed" (Bérubé 135). Such assessments, according to Richard Miller, show a "vested interest in remaining wholly ignorant of what goes on in composition" (96).[20] Miller has himself been attacked by those in literary studies, such as Marc Bousquet, who have depicted composition as a "managerial science" concerned with overseeing teaching. Such divisive infighting is the sort of jockeying for position that is to be expected as historical pressures undercut some areas of our field and open up others. All of us who have positions that provide time to do research are complicit with "academic capitalism," an institutional economy in which competing groups of employees maneuver for advantages, often by banking on the labors of those who lack the standing to engage in such maneuvers.[21] As Rhoades has discussed, tenure-track faculty are being challenged by new classes of "managerial professionals," many of whom occupy hybrid staff positions that combine administrative and teaching duties, often without the benefits of tenured faculty (272). Writing program administrators occupy such positions in departments that reduce composition to a service function. In such departments, administering a writing program is generally a managerial role that can be filled by anyone willing to show up for meetings, including untenured professors pressed into such service. As discussed in previous chapters, traditionalists have defined literary study by its "uselessness," and then pressed others into service, thereby confirming that their own concerns are merely vocational. This professional economy has imposed heavy workloads on new teachers and their supervisors, and it has pressed them to embrace the virtues of efficiency just to manage the loads. Prevailing hierarchies are then reinforced by dismissing efforts to manage the dualisms that structure basic work, as I have discussed further in "Managing to Make a Difference."

Rather than setting our areas of work in opposition, we need to change how the political economy of disciplinary professionalism excludes the majority of our coworkers from full standing in our field, and also isolates all of us from the rest of the educational system. The writings of Nelson, Schell, and others on labor organizing should become central to our field of study because they address issues that are vital to our field of work. Composition provides a case in point for studies in the political economy of professionalization. As Ohmann, Sledd, and others have long discussed, composition has "made little if any improvement in who does the front-line work," despite its "instituting the usual apparatus (journals, conferences, a professional society, and graduate programs and degrees), bringing a great advance in theoretical sophistication, and winning job security and good compensation for advanced practitioners" (Ohmann, *Politics* 43–44). As a result of this professional apparatus, credentialed specialists in composition have been able to claim the same status as other disciplinary professionals, including being able to claim to represent the work of teachers. As part of their professional rise, compositionists have become more theoretical and less interested in classroom research, following a pattern that saw linguistics shed its concern for language learning, literature distance itself from teaching reading, and creative writing divorce itself from work in journalism. All these trends have been shaped by the same forces that press teachers to seek status by leaving the classroom to move up to administration. In response to these professional tendencies, the four corners of the field have dropped pragmatic concerns that have gained critical importance as the hierarchies that have structured the discipline's development begin to crumble at their base, making it critical to develop a more inclusive conception of our field of work.

Disciplines lose the capacity to learn from the work that they chose to ignore. English studies have lost the opportunity to learn from the generations of teachers who have been denied positions that provide the time needed to step back from their daily duties to contribute to deliberations in the field. A sense of this loss emerged in the 1970s as the discipline found it hard to renew itself by hiring its graduates. As thousands of PhDs were temped out of the profession, faculty began to ask, "what is the meaning to the academic world of a whole generation lost to it?" (Hunter 8). Part of this "lost generation of humanists" was surveyed in a study entitled *PhDs—Ten Years Later*, which focused on 6000 doctoral graduates in 6 fields from 61 universities between 1982 and 1985, including 1217 PhDs in English (see Nerad and Cerny, "Rumors"). Of that number, 814 responded. This response rate is notable because the 33 percent who could not be found or were unwilling to discuss their jobs were probably less successful than those who responded. Of the respondents, 53 percent were tenured 10 years after graduation, and 5 percent more were in tenure-track jobs. Fifteen percent were non-tenure-track faculty, and 16 percent were in nonacademic jobs. Of the rest, 5 percent were unemployed, and the final 6 percent were either working both inside and outside academia or did not provide details on their work. All these groups tended to be "highly critical" of their doctoral programs for not preparing them to seek jobs and work inside and outside academe (8). Nerad and Cerny recommended revising graduate programs to provide students with the skills needed in academic and nonacademic jobs. This outcomes orientation has become increasingly common as the discipline has been confronted by the accountability pressures that are also forcing undergraduate programs to attend to the "skills" that the discipline has traditionally chosen to ignore.[22]

Nerad and Cerny concluded that "if PhD programs in English continue to train their graduates solely for the future professoriate, then doctoral programs need to reduce their enrollments" (11). Reducing and eliminating graduate programs have been commonly proposed by professional reports.[23] What is less often considered is what would be entailed in expanding graduate programs to prepare students for a wider range of jobs, and also to prepare them to approach teaching as a collective enterprise. Few attempts have been made to research the experiences of graduates (other than isolated departmental reviews that tend to be filed away after serving their immediate functions). No department that I know of has yet tried to revise its graduate or undergraduate programs with an eye to preparing students for life after graduation.[24] The skills that Nerad and Cerny recommended are those needed by editors and managers (the two most common jobs for PhDs who do not teach). Given the state of not just the profession but the professions, the skills that need to be taught include not just writing and researching but organizing. Our undergraduate and graduate students are looking at the downside of a trend that has undercut the best entrenched profession in America: while 90 percent of doctors were self-employed in 1985, almost 40 percent had become HMO employees by 1998 (Cohen, *The Shaping of American Higher Education* 294). Such trends are transforming the work of college graduates, and our discipline cannot afford to continue to ignore them in its programs of study. While institutional conditions became a subject of study with the pragmatic turn in the profession, we are only beginning to publish research such as the collections I have cited, and we have not yet followed through to translate this research into programs of instruction—outside courses on writing program administration, which too often assume the managerial standpoint that Bousquet and others have so aptly critiqued.

We need to acknowledge that labor organizing is essential to translating professional proposals into practical action.[25] Senior faculty in research universities tend to see a union as a threat to the research hierarchy that has rewarded them for working within it. The professional apparatus of graduate programs, research journals, and scholarly associations has been unsupportive of efforts to organize its material base, despite how dependent the profession is on that base, because unions provide locally situated associations that compete with traditional priorities in the reward systems that structure academic work.[26] These and other lessons have become clear from graduate union organizing at institutions such as Yale, and from related efforts within the MLA professional hierarchy by figures such as Nelson. Part-timers have enabled English departments to "cover" general education and defend the privileges of research faculty, and it is hard to break out of such exploitative hierarchies to build a sense of common cause, as needs to be done to organize and sustain unions, according to Lovas (198–99). Rather than looking at each other as competing for diminishing resources, such coalitions should look to the experience of the 63 percent of full-time faculty in public institutions who are union members, for unionized faculty tend to make 30 percent more than unorganized faculty, according to Rhoades (9–10, 78). Decades of work have gone into organizing efforts by groups such as adjunct faculty in the University of California system (see Tingle and Kirscht). We need to develop ways to understand and reward this service as integral to our teaching and research efforts. For example, Daniel, Blasch, and Caster have discussed ways to increase the visibility of labor groups on campus by integrating labor concerns into instruction and other intellectual work as part of an effort to promote the values of coalition politics against the corporate discourse that has become endemic in institutions of public learning.

English departments have the potential to develop a broad articulation apparatus to address this agenda and related equity issues. We are the only discipline that teaches all undergraduates, including our future coworkers in local schools. Many of the outcomes initiatives that are emerging in undergraduate and graduate programs involve surveying graduates, creating internships, community boards, and other partnerships with public constituencies that can extend the powerbase of English departments (see, for example, Dorothy Baker). Public discussions of higher education are often monopolized by university administrators, but labor organizers have found that they can be quite effective at challenging that monopoly (see, for example Tingle and Kirscht 226). This strategy extends to state educational systems. Official articulation channels serve to ease the transfer of any and all credits, including those generated by dual enrollment programs that may have "delivered" credits without involving disciplinary faculty. Alternatives are not hard to imagine. Teacher educators have sketched them out many times, as in a workshop on "Articulating High School and College Work" at CCCC back in 1951, which called for setting up community reading and writing groups, statewide associations of professors and teachers with conferences and exchange programs, publications of high school and college writings developed by practitioners rather than corporations, and information networks to share resources. Some elements of these collaborative networks are common in comprehensive departments of English. If we look to them for disciplinary models, we can develop broader conceptions of where our discipline may be headed, and how we can get there by bringing our wide-ranging areas of work into a coherent paradigm that addresses the needs of our public constituencies.

Realizing the Pragmatic Potentials of Departments of Literacy

I look past the profession to the broader history of literacy and literacy studies because I believe that focusing on the interactions between the two can help us to make the best use of the technological, institutional, and social changes that are transforming our field of work. The changes facing the discipline do not follow from the history of ideas contained within it, but from trends that have been most clearly evident in our basic service work. If we want to see the shape of things to come, we need to look not up but down. As I have tried to show, the professional apparatus of the discipline has largely been invested in hierarchies that have maintained a conservative standpoint on the diversification of literacies. In benchmark studies such as the National Assessment of Adult Literacy, *literacy* has been expanded to include not just the interpretation of prose texts but also textual layouts and quantitative data. This extension to visual and informational literacies has inevitably felt threatening to those whose cultural capital is invested in traditional forms of literacy. The resultant sense of crisis has often fueled literacy campaigns that have pressed teachers to concentrate on the "basics" and ignore the critical possibilities that open up as conventions are called into question. Those possibilities can be difficult to realize in the sites where they emerge most pointedly. Introductory courses in research universities are commonly assigned to novices who may be struggling to master the very conventions that they are pressed to teach, while those who work in teaching institutions often have workloads that leave little time in their workdays for reflection. With the time that I myself have been granted, I have tried to write a history that does justice to the work of such teachers, and addresses the pragmatic possibilities that are opening up in broadly based departments that include all four corners of the field.

Such departments generally have a marginal standing in our professional discourse. It is thus significant, but not surprising, that when one of our leading professional organizations publishes an issue surveying disciplinary trends, such as the *ADE Bulletin* 2003 issue on "The English Major," most of the most promising innovations do not come from major doctoral programs. When called upon to report from the hinterlands of the profession, representatives from teaching institutions characterize themselves "not so much as specialists in a particular subdiscipline of English studies," but "as well informed readers facilitating student encounters with various texts in order to inculcate a love of reading and language, and a care for culture that will persist throughout students' lives" (Evans 208). According to such reports, teaching departments can provide "a sense of being involved in a common enterprise." Such departmental cultures can seem rather provincial to newly minted PhDs who think of "themselves as much more specialized members of a profession" (208). Their research training has taught them to adopt a more cosmopolitan and less locally situated vision of their work. As Bourdieu has discussed, institutionalized "fields of cultural production" provide practitioners with a "*space of possibles*" that shapes their sense of the pragmatic resources and possibilities of the situations they face by defining what problems matter and who they matter to (*Field* 176). Research universities prepare practitioners to situate their work in specialized areas of expertise and often look down upon teaching and service, while a teaching department may challenge faculty to address purposes that research departments have temped out to paraprofessionals. Because more comprehensive departments have not specialized their functions to the same degree, they may be better able to gain funding to translate adjunct positions into tenure-track lines by arguing that hiring teachers on a piecework basis does not serve the ongoing needs of students or teaching institutions (see Journet).

In departments that have come to value the pragmatic possibilities of their service mission, literary studies may become envisioned as a public works project. For example, The Institute at Temple was founded by Steven Parks and Eli Goldblatt of the English Department at Temple University as an extension of their work with New City Press and Teachers for a Democratic Culture. Journals that publicize the poetics of everyday life carry on the tradition of such student literary magazines as *Foxfire*. The work at Temple brought together poets, critical pedagogues, social activists, and others involved with literary and cultural studies. Such ethnographic collaborations build out from the reading and writing groups that are often sponsored by English departments, and frequently undertaken without such support by MFAs teaching composition off the tenure-track. Such teachers are sometimes involved in writing in local businesses, public agencies, and community settings that could become seen as part of our field of work if adjuncts were viewed as coworkers (Murphy 33). They provide a sense of the *profession of literature* that includes collaborations with communities of writers and readers, writing for the popular press and the world of work, and literatures of underrepresented groups. Such collaborative engagements provide the best way to respond to the criticisms that Watkins developed in his influential *Work Time*. According to Watkins, traditional approaches to literature often make little more than an "empty" promise, for students realize that English classes provide a space apart, where the workings of literature can be savored in ways that most people cannot, not just because they do not have the time, but because they do not have the collective investment needed to make literature matter (3, 27). As Spellmeyer has discussed, we need to develop new ways of working with "reading and writing as modes of involvement with the lived world" (285).[27]

In departments where the teaching of writing is a "common enterprise," such potentials can be enriched by breaking out of the disabling dualism of the vocational and literary that has incapacitated our discipline and reinforced the hierarchies that marginalize our basic work. Even the most incisive critics of our profession have stumbled across this dichotomy when they have tried to account for how English departments depend upon the teaching of writing and yet define themselves as being about literature. Such accounts are haunted by the practical values that have been excised from modern conceptions of literature. Ohmann faces that specter when he asks "Is the myth of our usefulness to the rest of the university and to society then totally unfounded?" According to Ohmann, not as long as we provide such practical skills as

> organizing information, drawing conclusions from it, making reports, using Standard English (i.e., the language of bourgeois elites), solving problems (assignments), keeping one's audience in mind, seeking objectivity and detachment, conducting persuasive arguments, reading either quickly or closely, as circumstances demand, producing work on request and under pressure, valuing the intellect and its achievements. (302)

This quick list of the practical values of English studies mixes job skills with an underlying critique of vocationalism in a way that provides little sense of how close reading or persuasive arguments might actually enable students to do something about the politics of "Standard English." The world in which work is produced "on request and under pressure" has been kept at a distance from how people are taught to "read closely or quickly, as circumstances demand." Critical capabilities and practical skills have been set apart in ways that incapacitated both. We need metacognitive categories for thinking through the discontinuities between academic and nonacademic writing to develop a practical understanding of the civic imagination at work.[28] Literacy studies could provide us with such a vocabulary.

Expanding our sense of the field from literary to literacy studies can help us reflect upon how the profession has marginalized work with writing and teaching in ways that have undercut our ability to articulate our practical usefulness, and thereby claim resources to support our work. Teacher education is but the starkest example of how our discipline has incapacitated itself by not investing more of our intellectual energies in learning from teaching and schooling. The possibilities of a learning-centered vision of the discipline are exemplified by the pragmatic experimentalism of a figure such as Mina Shaughnessy. Shaughnessy recognized that students' writing made their learning visible, and she built research on basic literacy on that base, as Susan Miller and others have discussed (165–69). Such possibilities have gained professional visibility at historical junctures such as the Dartmouth Conference where professors and teachers have come together to envision a field of work that includes their shared concerns; also Harris). Such possibilities have been foreclosed by the traditional tendency to distinguish the "content" of the discipline from the methods used to teach it (see Franklin, Laurence, and Welles xii). Teachers who have invested their time in learning from students have long recognized that the opposition of content and skills disables the discipline, because "other studies are something to know; this is something to do" (Genung 4–5). The Progressive tradition in English studies was centered on such assumptions, as Gallagher has discussed. Decades ago, the profession was challenged to recognize that "if poetry is not to vanish from the experience of the great majority of American secondary school pupils, their English teachers will have to become better teachers of poetry" (Grommon 280). Now that the eclipse of literature has become a real possibility, we should come to recognize that supporting teachers is vital to our field of work.

Preparing a Nation's Teachers represents a high-profile attempt to face this responsibility.[29] In the lead chapter, Donald Gray admits that because his colleagues at Indiana University "don't think of themselves as teachers who teach teachers, they pay little explicit attention to questions about pedagogy" (Gray 57). He tries to appeal to those of "us" who wonder why teachers should be of concern to "members of the MLA [who] have all been educated to use as one pure measure of professional achievement the presence of our names in the pages of *PMLA*" (1). In such remarkably unapologetic statements, the hierarchies of the profession are set out in ways that undercut the ostensible purpose of showcasing its commitment to teacher education:

> Let the secondary schools perform their traditional tasks of educating citizens in the discourse of their culture so that they can fit gainfully into it. Ours is the yet more interesting task of teaching students how to interrogate the premises of their culture so that they become skeptical citizens of it. (9)

According to self-serving premises that are shown remarkably little skepticism, literary studies "will only be confused by the introduction of instrumental, practical means and ends" (7). While Gray valorizes the uselessness of liberal education as set out by Cardinal Newman, he also expresses the profession's deepening anxieties that this tradition had exhausted its uses: "While we have neglected or disdained teacher education, it has become a discipline to whose principles and imperatives we must now accommodate our own" (3). This standpoint is divorced from that assumed by contributors from more broadly based institutions such as Illinois State University, where the challenges of teaching teachers are seen as a case in point for rethinking how majors are structured around students' learning process to prepare them for what they will do when they leave the classroom.

Such departments provide models for coming to terms with the challenges of articulating our values to public constituencies. "Having disdained popular-representation, we have predictably been inept in representing ourselves in the public sphere," according to Graff ("Preaching to the Converted" 112). Graff has offered the best-known accounts of the need to reform "the institutional patterns of daily work" for the purpose of developing more generative and integrative structures (119). Graff argued for "making the conflicts of literary studies part of the subject matter of literary education itself" (112). His institutional history of the "profession of literature" contributed to the pragmatic turn that built upon sociological research on how the power of professionals is "weakened by the insulating compartmentalization of the bureaucratic organization in which they work" (Larson 29). Our attention to the pragmatics of professionalization has helped us to see specialization as both a means to power, and a means to contain it. This recognition led to attempts to develop more integrative models, with textual studies held forth as such a model in 1980s by Scholes and others. Then in the 1990s cultural studies became an increasingly popular paradigm. I have proposed literacy studies as a model because it is expansive enough to include our coworkers in local schools, our expanding engagements with community and workplace literacies, and also the broader technological and cultural transformations that are redefining what it means to be literate. Colleagues who work with visual and information literacy have become common in comprehensive departments, and they are often involved with interdisciplinary collaborations on learning, teaching, and outreach that are being infused with efforts to develop civic models that look to public service as a means to redress the fragmentation of students' experience and the university's public mission.[30]

One source of that fragmentation is the transformation of classrooms and texts by new technologies of literacy. "The remaking of the 'modern literary system,'" according to Hesse, has advanced to the point where it no longer involves "a technological revolution (which has already occurred) but the public reinvention of intellectual community in its wake" (29). "The modern literary system" may be coming to its end as "linear and concrete literacies" are replaced by interactive technologies (Hesse 29; Zavarzadeh and Morton 67), but one need not adopt a millenarian outlook to recognize that we are facing institutional, epistemological, and technological changes that are as dramatic as those that shaped the transition from classical to modern studies. In *The Formation of College English*, I examined how the three language arts of the *trivium* were transformed by the "science of human nature" to replace rhetorics with poetics at the pinnacle of literacy studies in response to the evolution of the reading public into a modern consumer society. The spread of interactive technologies and economies is now leading to similarly fundamental and wide-ranging changes, including more transactional models of literacy studies. These models open up possibilities to develop collaborative networks that could help us break out of the disciplinary professionalism that constituted literary and linguistic studies as autonomous fields of expertise, but did little to contribute to the professional standing of teaching. Faced with a sense of the profession that does not fully include most practitioners in the field, or the courses they teach, we need to develop a vision that is both more expansive and more strategically situated.

As I have discussed, the profession has taken a pragmatic turn after decades of drops in majors and professional jobs. Faculty hiring has shifted to address areas of growth such as creative writing, ESOL, rhetoric and composition, and cultural, ethnic, and media studies, leaving some departments confused about how such areas relate to each other. Some of us have moved beyond the boundaries of English departments to set up new places to work— not just in independent writing programs, but varied interdisciplinary initiatives concerned with teaching with technology, community-based outreach projects, and partnerships with schools and workplaces. These are the practical sites where the discipline is discovering new resources to connect with broader social needs. Literacy studies provides a vision that includes the four corners of the discipline: literary and cultural studies, language studies (including ESOL, critical discourse studies, and other areas of applied linguistics), English education (including articulation and community partnerships), and writing studies (which has been incapacitated by the debilitating dualism of "creative" and "technical" writing in many departments, but perhaps less often in those where journalism and communications courses fill the curricular void between composition and creative writing). The recent turn in the profession to address the pragmatics of its interpretive assumptions and working conditions has historic potentials. It is basic to trends ranging from service learning and community literacy through work with ethnography and new media to studies of technology and social movements. These trends follow upon changes in the technologies and political economies of literacy to institute more transactional, locally situated, and practically engaged lines of inquiry. Though the pragmatic matters at issue seem clear, where these inquiries will take our work remains an open question.

NOTES

Introduction: Working Past the Profession

1. In "The Implications of the New Literacy Studies for Literacy Education," Brian Street traces a line of development that parallels my analysis. Literacy ceased being defined as an autonomous object of study as the focus shifted to the institutional and ideological contexts that shape the composition, circulation, and reception of literate practices. These trends have been articulated in complementary ways by those studying language, writing, literature, and teaching. For example, Gee's "Literacy, Discourse, and Linguistics" shows how such linguistic categories such as contact codes, interference, pidginization, and creolization can be used to examine the social practices that constitute varied literate discourses.

2. In "Arts of the Contact Zone," Pratt defines *contact zones* as "social spaces where cultures meet, clash, and grapple with each other, often in contexts of highly asymmetrical relations of power" (34). Her concept has proven useful in discussions of the classroom. See, for example, Bizzell, "Contact Zones and English Studies," and Richard Miller. Pratt has defined *transculturation* as the "processes whereby members of subordinated or marginal groups select and invent from the materials transmitted by a dominant or metropolitan culture" (36).

3. Robert Scholes is about the only historian from outside rhetoric and composition who has examined how literary studies evolved out of their opposition to writing studies. Scholes's *Rise and Fall of English* is also one of the few histories to come from any area of English studies that acknowledges that if we are to change these debilitating hierarchies, we will need to build coalitions with teachers of English in the schools.

4. DeLuca reviews how articulation theory has influenced rhetorical studies in communications, and Kimme Hea analyzes how it can be used to explore new technologies of literacy, while Griswold, McDonnell, and Nathan Wright relate those technological developments to shifting class relations in a way that is congruent with both work on social movements and new literacy studies.

5. As Scholes has discussed, the eighteenth-century "concept of belles letters . . . served as a transition . . . from an older view of literature as including all kinds of written works worthy of study, to a different view that led to a curriculum dominated by Romantic notions of genius and imagination, along with their Arnoldian development as 'high seriousness'" (12).

6. Cotton Mather's ritual pronouncement at graduation and the decision of the Harvard Corporation on the appeal of graduate tutors are reprinted in Richard Hofstadter and Wilson Smith's *American Higher Education: A Documentary History*, along with related texts that are reprinted there (18, 21–27).

7. Franklin's involvement in the establishment of the first professorship of English in America has all the rich historical resonance of the fact that one the first professors of English in Britain was Adam Smith, who taught rhetoric and belles lettres in the years that he was formalizing the political economy of consumer society. Franklin also provided formative models for the reading public, and like Smith, his models were influenced by civic humanism. According to Bender, "Franklin best represents the

activist, pragmatic, and institution-founding character of early American civic human-ism," which had an amateurish quality that proved vulnerable to rapid expansion, geographical dispersal, and social stratification ("Erosion" 86).

8. Graff recognizes the merits of the antebellum literary networks, but is finally dis-missive of the "classical college": "From the point of view of subsequent literary criti-cism, the old college's conception of literary study as an extension of grammar, rhetoric, and elocution was merely evidence of hopeless provincialism. But this modern view was formed only after literature had largely ceded to journalism and other media what-ever power it had had to shape public opinion" (50–51).

9. The evolution of English textbooks can be traced back to the eighteenth-century elocutionary anthologies that preceded the *McGuffey Eclectic Readers*, which sold hun-dreds of millions of copies. In the antebellum period, literature began to be studied in historical surveys such as Cleveland's *A Compendium of English Literature* that included selections along with biographical and historical commentary. An example of how tech-nologies shaped pedagogies is provided by how the paperback revolution of the 1920s and 1930s contributed to the close reading pedagogies of New Criticism, which set itself in opposition to the massification of literacy.

10. As Bender examines in his volume on the social histories of English and three other disciplines, between 1950 and 1970, governmental expenditures on higher educa-tion rose more than tenfold (from $2.2 to $23.4 billion), as compared to only 30 per-cent between 1970 and 2010 (21). As Kerr (*The Great Transformation*) and others have discussed, the decades after midcentury were historic not only because of the exponen-tial growth, but also because American higher education became a much more strati-fied system, with community college enrollments growing much faster between 1960 and 1980 (from 400,000 to 4 million) than higher education generally (from 3.5 to 12 million). As in the era when the research university replaced the liberal arts college as the paradigm for American higher education, social diversification and educational strati-fication were integrally involved, and they structured the work of English departments in many conflicting ways.

11. Siskin has examined how nineteenth-century print technologies generated forms of professional expertise that included literature as a "newly restricted arena for the work of writing" that excluded "women writers in startlingly systematic ways" (2). Literature became the disciplinary substructure that all areas of literate expertise "had in common —the prerequisite for entering them as autonomous professional fields" (7). This struc-ture is currently breaking down along with other elements of modern professionalism.

1. Learning and the Learned in Colonial New England

1. In his account of the development of American higher education as a competitive marketplace, Clark Kerr looks back to the adoption of Scottish governance structures as fundamental to the colonial colleges' "autonomy, diversity, flexibility, and competi-tiveness" (xii).

2. Lockridge's study complements his better-known research on colonial literacy. Lockridge's *Literacy in Colonial New England* criticizes the Progressivist assumption that print spread an optimistic faith in individual enterprise that became an instrumen-tal part of American republicanism. However, Lockridge maintains that when societies modernize, literacy is often "intimately involved in an educational subprocess which

enhances the changes in attitudes already encouraged by general changes in society. In both instances, the results are a more active, instrumental, optimistic, and widely aware consciousness particularly associated with literacy" (29). Lockridge criticizes Bailyn's argument that anxieties about the frontier experience prompted an intense concern for education, but Bailyn's analysis has served as a point of reference for later research on schooling and literacy in the colonial period (see Grubb).

3. As Perry Miller stressed, the Puritans "were in no sense pioneers of religious liberty, and when their English counterparts [under Cromwell] went whoring after this strange perversion of political orthodoxy, they resolved to stand all the more resolutely in New England for an absolute uniformity, for a rigorous suppression of all Dissent, by capital punishment if necessary" (*American Puritans* 94).

4. A record of an influential educator's reading is provided by Samuel Johnson's "Catalogue" of the books he read after he left his tutorship at Yale in 1719, through his years as a country parson, and then as the first president of King's College (now Columbia University) in 1754. Johnson read widely in the natural law tradition (Grotius and Pufendorf), the "new learning" (Newton, Bacon, Locke, and Berkeley), Scottish moral philosophers (Hume, Hutcheson, and Turnbull), and authors on rhetoric and logic ranging from Cicero and Quintilian to the Port Royalists and Isaac Watts. Johnson also read Milton, Pope, Rollin, and periodical literature such as the *Spectator, American Magazine*, and "several of the Reviews" (*Samuel Johnson* 1:497).

5. Meriwether concluded that there is "no evidence" that students spoke Latin "colloquially" or that many could write it with "any degree of ease or correctness" (92–94). The Latin of the college laws is itself sometimes corrupt. Letters from professors such as Francis Alison complained that students were admitted "who recite the classics by rote" and could not write any Latin (MS 4).

6. Whitefield's most famous imitator was Gilbert Tennent, who was known for roaring with divine laughter at the sufferings of the damned (Morgan, "Movement" 16). Whitefield noted that Tennent "learned experimentally to dissect the heart of natural man." The missionary fervor of New Lights was an inspiration to groups who had often been ignored by the clergy, including the first African American writer "of consequence," Phillis Wheatley, a slave who gained an international readership for her 1770 poem "On the Death of the Rev. Mr. George Whitefield" (22–24).

7. Alison went on to become vice-provost of the College of Philadelphia, where he taught English and moral philosophy courses based on the works of Francis Hutcheson. In a letter to President Stiles of Yale on December 12, 1767, Alison stated that when he immigrated, "there was not a College, nor even a good grammar school, in four Provinces, Maryland, Pennsylvania, Jersey and New York," and all who "made any pretensions to learning were branded as letter learned Pharisees" (Letters 15 and 17).

8. Commencement theses have been examined in detail by Thomas, Guthrie, Peaden, and Perrin. Extensive lists of theses are included in Potter's *Debating in the Colonial Chartered Colleges*.

9. Popular in library companies as well as college libraries, Ward's neoclassical *Lectures* were penned into the Yale Library Catalogue of 1755, included in Harvard's catalogue of 1765, taught at other colleges such as Brown, and often included in the catalogues of library companies. According to Guthrie, the influence of Ward's survey of classical rhetoric was "almost as complete in its time as the later domination by Whately, Campbell and Blair" (55–56).

10. Wadsworth's Commonplace Book from his junior year documents the texts on rhetoric and belles lettres that were being studied at Harvard in 1766–67. Wadsworth took notes on the works of David Fordyce, Charles Rollin, Bernard Lamy, John Ward, Philip Doddridge, John Wilkins, and James Addison.

11. The Assembly responded to Clap by cutting off Yale's annual grant in 1755. Clap was able to keep the Assembly from asserting control by threatening to appeal to London, raising anxieties that the government might look into the ambiguities in the charter of the colony as well as that of the college. Clap was finally forced to resign in 1766 after students destroyed the college and drove off the tutors before walking out. The Assembly then intervened to reestablish public control (see Herbst, *Crisis* 114–19).

12. This incorporation of higher education into the market economy in terms of "corporate privileges" was consistent with emerging trends in copyright and property law (Crane 67). This case also helped establish the internal political economy of American universities by investing control in boards of lay administrators rather than in the faculty, as was the tradition in many European educational systems (see Rudolph 210–11).

2. Republican Rhetoric

1. The College of Philadelphia was built upon the curricular reforms at Aberdeen. Franklin's "Proposals Relating to the Education of Youth in Pennsylvania" drew on two works by Aberdeen moral philosophers, George Turnbull's *Observations upon Liberal Education* and David Fordyce's *Dialogues Concerning Education*. The curriculum that William Smith implemented was modeled on his own studies at Aberdeen under Alexander Gerard (see Miller, *Formation* 146).

2. The decline of religious literature is also evident in publication rates. According to the subject categories in Evans's bibliography, theological works accounted for 34.63 percent of all American publications between 1730 and 1750, as compared to 11.45 percent on political science and law. Theological works accounted for 29.37 percent of publications between 1765 and 1773, and then declined by two-thirds to only 9.89 percent between 1774 and 1778 (see Tanselle 327–29).

3. Henretta estimates the population at 250,000 in 1700; 570,000 in 1725; 1,170,000 in 1750; 2,500,000 in 1775; and 5,300,000 in 1800 (*Evolution* 11). Hofstadter details how the middle and southern colonies became diversified via German, Dutch, Scots, and Scots-Irish immigrants, as well as African slaves. The last was the largest group and comprised over 20 percent of the population by 1770. Smith and Franklin were especially anxious to assimilate Germans because 100,000 had immigrated by the Revolution, making them one-third of the population of Pennsylvania (Hofstadter, *America at 1750: A Social Portrait* 66–67, 17–30).

4. Recommended readings included works by Watts and Locke in logic, a wide range of scientific texts, and the full republican corpus in moral philosophy, ranging from civic humanists such as Cicero through Commonwealth men such as Harrington and Sidney to natural law theorists from the Continent (Pufendorf and Grotius) and Britain (Locke and Hutcheson). Bacon and Newton were foundational authors in these studies. The use of the *Preceptor* editions of these works connects these reforms with the expansion of the reading public because *The Preceptor, Containing a General Course of Education* was a popular self-instruction manual edited by one of the leading publishers —a self-educated former apprentice, Robert Dodsley.

5. Franklin's *Observations, Relative to the Intentions of the Original Founders of the Academy in Philadelphia* (1789) recounted the forty years he had spent trying to promote English studies as an alternative to the classics (*The Complete Works* 10:95–108; also Montgomery 250–51).

6. Wilson soon moved on to study and practice law. He served in the Continental Congress and become a leading architect of the Constitution and a justice of the Supreme Court. Wilson returned to Philadelphia to deliver one of the first college courses on the law in 1790, when the college had been reorganized by the republican legislature as the University of Pennsylvania.

7. Dennis Barone has published Jasper Yeates's notes from Smith's "Course of Lectures on Rhetoric" from 1760 along with an introduction on his life, the college, and the sources of his teaching.

8. The links between moral and natural philosophy were part of the college's debts to reformers at Aberdeen. A good example of such Newtonian approaches to politics and ethics is provided by Samuel Jones's notebook from Francis Alison's course on "Practical Philosophy." Notes on the "Law of Nature" from Alison's moral philosophy course are included side by side with lectures on "A System of Nature" from a natural science course.

9. In the *Introduction to Philosophy* (first published in the *Republic of Letters* in 1731), Johnson complained that students learned only a "smattering in a few of the Latin classics" and remained "scandalously ignorant" of Greek. He recommended requiring a "good competency" in both Latin and Greek for entering students, though he was hard pressed to admit less-qualified students to build enrollments at King's, which only graduated about five students annually up to the Revolution (*Career and Writings* 2:315). Another professor at New York in 1785 complained that it was absurd to lecture students on the "beauties of the classics" when students could not even understand them (qtd. in Roach 17, 18).

10. Longaker aligns Johnson's writings and teachings with Smith's belletristic approach by their shared conservative loyalties, religious affiliations, and class identifications (140–62).

11. The impact of print on concepts of usage is evident in Witherspoon's comments on punctuation. According to Witherspoon, punctuation only became an issue as more people began writing for the press. Witherspoon noted that only periods were commonly used in letters, though other punctuation marks were useful to indicate pauses in texts to be read (244). These comments situate Witherspoon at the juncture where scribal modes of literacy began to be assessed against the regularities of print.

12. Hutcheson was studied at Philadelphia, Princeton, King's, Brown, and Harvard. The only other work to have such influence was a similar Scottish text, David Fordyce's *Elements of Moral Philosophy*, which was widely available in the *Preceptor* (1748). The *Preceptor* passed through eight editions in a half century, and *Elements*, published as an independent work in 1754, then went through multiple editions also.

13. According to Wills, "those who think Jefferson had to derive his natural right of revolution from Locke have no direct textual parallels to draw on. But the parallels within the Scottish school are everywhere" (238). Hutcheson's general assumption that virtue should be measured according to "the greatest happiness for the greatest numbers" became "a touchstone for enlightened thought" (Hutcheson, *Inquiry* 180). As Wills discusses, Jefferson's debts to Hume, Smith, Ferguson, Kames, and especially

Hutcheson are well documented in his accounts of his studies and libraries (see also Hamowy).

14. This passage from the course of lectures that Madison studied with Witherspoon encapsulates the principle of the balance of powers that is set out in the most noted essays in the history of American political literature, Madison's *Federalist* essays. Witherspoon himself spoke on "that enlarged system called the balance of power" in a speech in Congress supporting the Articles of Confederation (151).

15. Alison's students included five signers of the Declaration, while the two major proposals and the compromise plan for the Constitution were all put forward by Princeton graduates, who outnumbered the graduates of Yale and Harvard combined at the Constitutional Convention (Norris 73). Witherspoon's most influential student was Madison, who stayed on after graduation to study with Witherspoon and in the process became Princeton's first graduate student (Thorp et al. 6–9).

16. After studying with a Scottish clergyman, Jefferson studied at William and Mary with another Scot, William Law. Jefferson wrote in his *Autobiography* that Law's instruction in "Ethics, Rhetoric and Belles Lettres" "probably fixed the destinies of my life" (3, 2). Like William Smith, Law had studied at Marischal College in Aberdeen in the early 1750s, when Alexander Gerard was reforming the curriculum according to new logic to move through an inductive study of the arts and sciences to culminate with studies of "moral science" (see Miller, *Formation* 146). Law had studied with William Duncan, whose *Elements of Logic* provided the inductive argumentative framework for the Declaration of Independence, according to Howell.

17. The fifth colonial newspaper was also published without governmental approval. That paper, James Franklin's *New England Courant*, departed from its predecessors by being modeled on the essays of the *Spectator* rather than on the reportorial style of early English newspapers such as the *London Gazette*. Benjamin Franklin's essays by his nom de plume, Mrs. Silence Dogood, were published anonymously in his brother's paper. Those essays and other pieces satirized learned pretensions and affected manners as well as the government. The *Spectator* was also the model for the next American newspaper, the *New-England Weekly Journal* (1727).

18. I will discuss several *American Magazine*s that can be distinguished by their dates: *American Magazine; or a Monthly View of the Political State of the British Colonies* (1741); *American Magazine and Historical Chronicle* (1743–46); *American Magazine and Monthly Chronicle* (published by William Smith 1757–58); *American Magazine or General Repository* (1769); and finally, Noah Webster's *American Magazine* (1787–88). Each was short-lived because the ideological and commercial infrastructure for a national reading public was only emerging.

19. The cultural interactions entailed within the pairing *rhetoric and belles lettres* are all the more notable because, as the *OED* documents, *belles letters* was pivotal to the eighteenth-century transition from broadly humanistic conceptions of literature as all eloquent writings to the narrower conception that distinguished imaginative literature by its distinctive emotional effect. In the nineteenth century, *belletristic* became distinguished from *aesthetic* by a stylistic conception of literature identified with provincial tastes.

20. Alison made these comments in a letter of February 17, 1757, to Ezra Stiles, one of many he wrote to the conservative president of Yale (Alison Letters, Presbyterian Historical Society).

3. When Colleges Were Literary Institutions

1. Burke concluded that 241 colleges were established in this period. Burke and his research team only counted institutions that actually offered instruction, rather than all that were chartered, as had been done by Tewksbury and the others who provided the inflated numbers of failed colleges. According to Burke's research, 70 percent of antebellum colleges persisted into the twentieth century (14).

2. Andresen distinguishes Webster's "political conception of language" from Grimm and Bopp's mechanistic model of language change. Andresen rereads this "hinge period" in linguistics to identify Webster with the origins of sociolinguistics and language education, which have been ignored in the history of linguistics in the same ways literacy has been ignored by literary studies (68–119).

3. For example, Miller's *Letters from a Father to his Son in College* also combines patriarchal condemnations of the penny press and popular novels with advice on how to become a discerning reader by forgoing "instruction without labour" in lyceums and magazines and focusing instead on such "English classics" as Bacon, Shakespeare, Milton, Addison, Pope, Johnson, Hume, and Beattie (160, 151; see also Robbins).

4. These academies emphasized English studies. For example, the stated mission of Mount Holyoke was to prepare "female teachers" and "qualify ladies for other spheres of usefulness" by providing "a solid, extensive, and well-balanced English education, connected with that general improvement, that moral culture, and those enlarged views of duty, which will prepare ladies to be *educators* of children and youth, rather than to fit them to be mere teachers as the term has been technically applied" (qtd. Smallwood 88–89). For a study of how the highly gendered approaches of seminaries and normal schools both opened up and limited education for women, see Ricks. Most women in college in the latter half of the century attended normal schools. Harmon provides a case study of the largest of those, Illinois State Normal University (founded 1857), which educated over twenty-four thousand teachers by the end of the century (over half of them women), though only 7 percent stayed long enough to graduate. Another case study is provided by Miheusuah's analysis of the Cherokee Female Seminary at Park Hill, Indian Territory, which was modeled on Mount Holyoke.

5. Such self-reports were undoubtedly skewed by the desire to appear literate. Other benchmarks are provided by signature rates, with 42 percent of army enlistees unable to sign their names in 1800, dropping to 25 percent in 1850 and just 7 percent in 1895. This sample is biased downward and can be contrasted with signatures on wills, which represent a more select group. From a meta-analysis of several samples of wills from 1800, Stevens found between 70 percent and 90 percent percent able to sign (101).

6. After graduating from Washington College in 1826, William Holmes McGuffey served as president of Cincinnati College and Ohio University, and at his death in 1845, he was chair of mental and moral philosophy at the University of Virginia.

7. Propounded in terms that are meaningless to students, such distinctions as these have served to instill anxieties about correctness that have made generations of composition students into nonwriters:

> *Will*, in the first person singular and plural, intimates resolution and promising; in the second and third person, only foretells; as, "I will reward the good, and will punish the wicked;" "We will remember benefits, and be grateful." "Thou wilt, or he will, repent that folly;" "You or they will have a pleasant walk."

Shall, on the contrary, in the first person, simply foretells; in the second and third persons, promises, commands, or threatens; as, "I shall go abroad," "We shall dine at home;" "Thou shalt, or you shall, inherit the land," "Ye shall do justice, and love mercy;" "They shall account for their misconduct." (Murray 90).

8. Schultz contrasts these textbooks with the better-known works that established composition as a mainstay of secondary education, including Green Parker's *Progressive Exercises* (1832, with thirty-three imprints within a half century). The forerunner of these textbooks was John Walker's *Teacher's Assistant in English Composition; or Easy Rules for Writing Themes and Composing Exercises on Subjects Proper for the Improvement of Youth of Both Sexes at School* (1801, with the first American edition in 1808).

9. Two richly complementary accounts of what antebellum women made of their reading and writing are provided by Kelley's "Reading Women/Women Reading" and Eldred and Mortensen's *Imagining Rhetoric: Composing Women of the Early United States*.

10. The historians of the discipline whom I have on other points found quite incisive have depicted antebellum colleges as outmoded and elitist. Russell has sweepingly concluded that before 1850 "almost all post-elementary schools were unapologetically elitist and sectarian" (35). According to Ohmann, antebellum colleges were "little more than sectarian academies" that maintained the "traditional class structure" by perpetuating an "aristocratic tradition" (*English* 282). On this and other points, such analyses depend upon the assumption that faculty and students came from the upper classes. This assumption is not borne out by research on the period, calling into question basic assumptions about how antebellum colleges worked, and whom they worked for.

11. Hofstadter maintained that because resources had been spread too broadly, most antebellum colleges failed, as documented by Tewksbury's finding of an 80 percent failure rate among the over seven hundred colleges chartered before the Civil War. However, Burke found that Tewksbury erred in assuming that all the colleges that were chartered actually opened. Burke also researched the diverse social backgrounds of a random sample of over twelve thousand college graduates and two thousand students in professional schools in the first half of the nineteenth century. Burke's research documents how antebellum colleges expanded access, with the greatest growth in underserved regions, and expanded access for rural, poor, and women students (19).

12. Allmendinger's research on New England colleges complements Burke's national study. According to Allmendinger, common schools brought a "flood of students from poor families" into colleges. At Amherst, for example, five hundred of thirteen hundred students from 1821 to 1845 relied on charity funds intended to prepare ministers (65). Allmendinger estimates that one-quarter of New England college students relied on charity scholarships or work, while Herbst estimates that about one-third of all New England college students took leaves each year to teach (*And Sadly Teach* 22). In 1823, Harvard President Ticknor complained about "the poverty of [the] many students, who keep school" (rptd. Hofstadter and Smith 1:271). However, by 1831 only thirty-four Harvard students were still on financial aid, as a result of increases in costs and admissions requirements (Story 76).

13. In my studies of the records of antebellum students from Harvard, Yale, Princeton, Brown, and the University of Pennsylvania, I have found almost all of the notes and compositions to be in English. For example, of some 750 pages left by William Gardiner (Harvard graduate of 1816), no more than 10 pages are in Latin. Though almost 200 pages are on ancient Greek history and literature, the writings are confined

to responding to translations, not translating the texts themselves. The only Greek in the two dozen writings on Greek literature is a quote on a title page or a concluding line. On the other hand, Gardiner's notebooks include extensive work with English composition and literature, including several dozen themes, two dozen forensic disputations, and an essay of over forty pages on English and American literature. Some of these compositions are accompanied by rough drafts with brief written comments in another hand.

14. A sense of that discipline is provided by Julian Sturtevant's reflections on his studies at Yale. According to Sturtevant, Yale's "power lay in its fixed and rigidly prescribed curriculum, and in its thorough drill." Sturtevant (who was president of Illinois College from 1844 to 1876) recounted being taught by graduate tutors who were "excellent drill-masters," though "they could hardly be said to teach at all." Remembering one of his few lessons with a professor, Sturtevant recounted how a coauthor of the Yale Report (James Kingsley) dismissed students' translations by noting, "Young gentlemen, you read Latin horribly and translate it worse." Kingsley also reportedly stated, "Young gentlemen, you have been reading one of the noblest productions of the human mind without knowing it." Sturtevant ironically added that students "might justly have retorted . . . 'whose fault is it?'" given how rarely they saw faculty in the classroom (rptd. Hofstadter and Smith 1:275).

15. The Yale Report can be read as one of the reactionary responses to the populist politics of the Jacksonian period, as discussed in Kerber's chapter on "Salvaging the Classical Tradition" in *Federalists in Dissent*. To explain their loss of power to Democratic-Republicans, conservative republicans looked to the Augustan eras of Rome and Britain for models of the disintegration of democracy into demagoguery.

16. The creation of the University of Michigan paralleled Jefferson's unsuccessful efforts to create a state educational system in Virginia. In New York and then Michigan, Henry Tappan attempted to create a state system of education culminating in a research university. As Bender discusses, Tappan's *University Education* (1851) positioned universities as the cosmopolitan centers of the antebellum networks of literary societies, schooling systems, and lyceums.

17. In *The Shaping of American Higher Education*, A. M. Cohen reviews the libraries of thirty-three antebellum colleges of varied sizes and regions. In ten the literary societies had larger holdings than the college, and in eight the societies' were at least three-quarters the size of the colleges' (91–92). On the topics debated in such societies, see David Potter.

18. Fitch's writings include two books of forensic debates from his junior and senior years, class notes, a diary recording his studies, and a notebook on his independent reading. His fourteen junior-year compositions range from three to over ten pages, while his senior essays run to over twenty pages. Brackett wrote ten essays and nine forensic disputations for the professor of rhetoric and English literature (course created in 1850). Ten essays are extant from his sophomore physiology course and nine from his junior history course. According to the university laws for Brown of 1852–53, Brackett was required to deliver weekly declamations in his first two years. He also had to write essays every two weeks in his second and third years, and deliver an original oration monthly in his last two years. Cash awards were given for the best essays in each area of study: modern and classical literatures, rhetoric, history and moral philosophy, natural philosophy, engineering, and "chemistry applied to the arts."

19. In the curricula of thirty-five eastern colleges between 1850 and 1860, Wozniak found that one-third required compositions every semester. On average, students wrote compositions in over three-quarters of their semesters (Wozniak 36–37).

20. The place of elocution in the curriculum can be traced back to the first American edition of Sheridan's *Rhetorical Grammar* in 1783, printed under the supervision of the professor of English and oratory at the University of Pennsylvania. Sheridan's *Lectures on Elocution* was reprinted at Providence in 1796 (see Benzie). The scientific aspirations of the speech department were first set out in *The Philosophy of the Human Voice* by Benjamin Rush's nephew James Rush (see Wozniak, Hochmuth and Murphy, and Connors).

21. The most popular American-authored rhetoric was *A Practical System of Rhetoric*, by Samuel Newman, who served as professor of rhetoric and oratory at Bowdoin College from 1824 to 1839 (see Kremers; Carr, Carr, and Schultz 48). Newman's textbook went through sixty editions and printings. A student of Goodrich's, Henry N. Day, published *Elements of the Art of Rhetoric*, the "most original" textbook of the time, according to Connors (221). Blair also shaped the next generation of textbooks, including Quackenbos's *Advanced Course of Composition and Rhetoric*, which had an extensive apparatus of exercises on syntax along with guidelines for compositions and advice for teachers on correcting papers—all laid out to provide an efficient pedagogy for overworked writing teachers.

22. Clark and Halloran argue that the "tendency to ground rhetoric in the private experience of the individual" marks the historical transition from the neoclassical rhetorics of Witherspoon and Adams through the belletristic emphasis on taste to the literary orientation that emerged with Channing (17).

23. While previous generations had taught students with little access to print and largely uncontested power to speak for the public, Channing lived in a world of print, in which "opinions are constantly coming to us from . . . all parts of the world, through many channels, and we are thus enabled to instruct ourselves, and to think liberally and independently on all subjects, and especially on the opinions that are most current at home, and which the ancient orator might have appealed to with unresisted and terrible power. In the ancient republics, the orator might control the audience, but now we see the audience controlling him" (16–17).

24. Nietz details how English textbooks evolved from readers with literary excerpts, through histories that surveyed periods and genres, to the anthologies that instituted a modern sense of literature. One of the first advanced readers was Lindley Murray's *English Reader* (1799). Early histories of literary genres included John Dunlop's *History of Fiction* (1814), Walter Scott's *Biographical and Critical Notices of Eminent Novelists* (1825), and John Hart's *Class Book of Poetry* (1844). Scott's textbook is a good example of how surveys of literature evolved in tandem with increased access to literature, for the text was part of the popular reprint series *Ballantyne's Novelists Library*. A more comprehensive survey was provided by Robert Chambers's *Cyclopaedia of English Literature* (1843–44) and Samuel Goodrich's *Literature, Ancient and Modern, with Specimens* (1845). Among the more popular histories of literature were Charles Cleveland's *A Compendium of English Literature* (1848) and his more advanced *English Literature of the Nineteenth Century* (1852), which developed out of his literature courses in a women's academy. Also popular in normal schools and academies were Rickard and Orcutt's *Class Book of Prose and Poetry* (1847) and William Spalding's *The History of English Literature* (1853). These evolving genres are examined in detail by Carr, Carr, and Schultz.

25. After graduating from Cambridge, Shaw went to Russia to teach English literature in St. Petersburg at the Imperial Alexander Lyceum. Despite their plodding style and deadening minutiae, Shaw's textbooks were widely used in American high schools, academies, and colleges. Redactions of Shaw's text proliferated into "Shaw's New Series of English and American Literature," a series of textbooks authored by professors who taught at Vassar and institutions such as Packer Collegiate Institute.

26. Between the first census in 1790 and the seventh in 1860, Philadelphia grew from 42,520 to 565,529, and Boston grew from 18,038 to 177,840. New York evolved from a group of towns into a city of over 1 million, with Manhattan alone growing from 33,131 to 813,669. "The result was urban chaos" (Bender 34).

27. School readers became "standardized" in the 1860s, according to Windhover, who found Longfellow to be the most popular author in the ninety anthologies she reviewed from the third quarter of the nineteenth century. Longfellow and other "school poets" such as Irving were the most anthologized authors because they provided moral platitudes that displayed "a spiritual meaning in even the smallest aspect of nature" (Windhover 31). Daniel Webster was more popular than Shakespeare, though he became more frequently anthologized when his works were included on college admissions tests in the 1870s.

28. American literature was a mainstay of antebellum readers. Textbooks on the subject included Frost's *The Class Book of American Literature* (1826), Knapp's *Lectures on American Literature* (1829), Duyckinck's *Cyclopaedia of American Literature* (1856), and Grisswold's *Poets and Poetry of America* (1842), *Prose Writers of America* (1847), and *Female Poets of America* (1849).

29. The contested class politics at work in the expansion of professionalism are pointedly addressed in *A Plan for an Industrial University for the State of Illinois* (1851) by Jonathan Baldwin Turner, who was instrumental in persuading Congressman Justin Morrill to introduce the Land Grant College Act. As a lobbyist for the Illinois Industrial Association, Turner promoted the values of "INDUSTRIAL LITERATURE" to align workers with capitalists against the monopoly imposed on higher education by the "PROFESSIONAL" class (rptd. in Crane 174). Turner assumed that only "the literary and clerical" classes really needed "to become writers and talkers." This assumption reinforced his utilitarian tendency to divorce imaginative literature from the practical needs of working people (184; see Danika Brown).

4. How the Teaching of Literacy Gave Rise to the Profession of Literature

1. A prominent example of how professors of English distinguished themselves from teachers of English is provided by James Morgan Hart's influential *German Universities: A Narrative of Personal Experience* (1874). Hart was a professor of rhetoric and philology, but in his vision of his duties, "the professor is not a teacher" because "his duty begins and ends with himself" (264). The "professor is his own master," "accountable only to himself for his opinions and mode of living" (264).

2. In 1890, high school enrollments were 298,000 (5.6 percent of 14–17 year olds); in 1900, 630,000 (10 percent); in 1910, 1 million (14.3 percent); in 1920, 2.4 million (31.2 percent); and in 1930, 4.7 million (50.7 percent) (Angus and Mirel 203). For the first time most high school teachers were college graduates—70 percent of men teachers and 53 percent of women teachers in the 1890s (Borrowman 129; Krug 187). The rise

in college attendance from 3 percent in 1890 to 12 percent in 1930 can be accounted for largely by the increases in women students, mostly in normal schools (Burke 262; Gary Miller 31).

3. David Russell examines how literate technologies shaped the formation of modern systems of expertise, as evident in the use of efficiency experts to reduce work to written routines. Such technological innovations as the invention of the typewriter in the 1870s enabled the development of complex organizations and new types of work. For example, the number of stenographers increased from 154 in 1870 to 112,000 at the end of the century.

4. As examples of the credentialing of expertise that was a key element of the professionalization of middle-class work between 1870 and 1900, Bledstein cites these statistics: certified nurses increased eleven hundred percent, veterinarians eightfold, engineers six times, architects five, and dentists fourfold (39; see also Bender).

5. By 1940, women made up 98 percent of nurses, 90 percent of librarians, 75 percent of teachers, and 64 percent of social workers. Women comprised 26.6 percent of college teachers and professors, compared to 4.6 percent of doctors and 2.4 percent of lawyers and judges. Women were also 32 percent of professional writers and 25 percent of journalists and editors (Adams, *A Group of Their Own* 155).

6. As Russell discusses, "the systematic teaching of rhetoric as public discourse— the heart of the classical liberal arts curriculum for centuries—almost passed out of the curriculum entirely." With it went the emphasis on debate and other "mechanisms for guided revision, public presentation to the academic community and extracurricular reinforcement." These structures were replaced by a "system with no formal means of guiding revision, no formal cooperation among faculty, and few opportunities for public presentation or extracurricular reinforcement" (15, 46).

7. *Articulation* is most commonly used in education for the programs in which colleges and schools confer on courses and then transfer credits. These articulation arrangements sometimes include conferences and publications that involve collaborations among professors and teachers. I will discuss the history of these partnerships in terms that draw upon a conception of *articulation* as a process of communicating to outsiders, at critical junctures, where a group or institution formalizes what it is about to those who are being subjected to its distinctive modes of expression and interaction (see Hall, "On Postmodernism" 53).

8. A standard account of the Progressive movement in education is Cremin's *The Transformation of the School: Progressivism in American Education, 1876–1957*. Progressivism was criticized by traditional academics for promoting student-centered approaches that undermined academic disciplines, and it has also been criticized for looking to social scientists and managerial expertise to check the excesses of capitalism (see, for example, Berlin's *Rhetoric and Reality*).

9. A poignant counterpoint to professors' characterizations of students' illiteracies is provided by the paper that Woolley cites as an example of the essays produced by the 15 to 20 percent of students who were placed into basic writing at the University of Wisconsin in the early decades of the twentieth century (see Brereton 491–543 for similar examples):

My object in coming to the U. was to attain a higher knowledge of education. I wish to prepare my-self for the difficulties and the environment of life. To fit my-self to be capable of mingling with educated people and converse with them. Also to be able to understand their line of argumentation in their talk. (240)

10. Most accounts agree that these recommendations helped establish the curricular preeminence of English studies, and to concentrate those studies on literature. Fitzgerald has even maintained that "English had no coherent subject matter" before the curricular debates over college entrance requirements (438).

11. Scott spent his career at the University of Michigan, where he worked with John Dewey for a time. After graduating and joining the faculty in 1899, in 1903 he set up a separate Department of Rhetoric, which included journalism. Scott was president of MLA in 1907, and he became the founding president of the NCTE in 1911. He did not confine himself to working within the discipline, for he also served as president of the North Central Association, the American Association of Colleges and Secondary Schools, and the American Association of Teachers of Journalism. His department produced twenty-three PhDs, including such reformers as Gertrude Buck, Sterling Leonard, and Charles Fries. At the instigation of Harvard-trained professors of literature and against the wishes of its faculty, the Department of Rhetoric was reabsorbed into English at Scott's retirement in 1926, much as Michigan's Composition Board was just over a half century later.

12. Loaz Johnson documents how this accreditation system evolved into the University of California's English A program (see also Stanley's *The Rhetoric of Remediation: Negotiating Entitlement and Access to Higher Education*). English A grew from 16 to 116 schools between 1888 and 1900. This articulation program was initially about more than entrance exams. In 1900, 479 out of 521 entering students were admitted by certificate rather than exam. The essay topics that Johnson includes from English A exams emphasize formal English usage and culturally sensitive topics that would have excluded students from more diverse linguistic and cultural backgrounds. (For sample essays from the 1920s, see Brereton 528–35).

13. In "Pedagogy as a University Discipline," Dewey responded by arguing that reducing the preparation of teachers to methods courses divorced teaching from the social purposes it served by eliminating coursework in theories of education, history, psychology, and sociology.

14. The first CEEB examination "was essentially designed to measure achievement in the subject of English literature" but the exams eventually gave up essays on literature as too subjective (Trachsel 78).

15. The effect of assessment measures on literary studies is examined in Ohmann's critique of how AP tests restrict the capacities of both students and literature by concentrating assessments on how well students can abstract from their felt responses with formalist categories devoid of social purpose (*English in America* 57).

16. A "Professor of English Literature" at Central High School in Philadelphia published the first article on American literature in *PMLA*. Smyth's "American Literature in the Class-room" provides a good example of how the challenges of general education gave rise to an interest in teaching literature as literature (rather than philology or history). Despite the involvement of such teachers, the MLA had a more restricted membership than other disciplinary associations such as the American Historical Association. While only one-quarter of the AHA's original membership were academics, over three-quarters of MLA members were, and that percentage increased as the group narrowed its purposes and ignored outreach, unlike the AHA (Veysey 70). Such differ-

ences show how our field was professionalized in ways that made it less accessible to teachers and writers.

17. Survey courses were also found to be standard requirements in English majors in the broader sample of one hundred English department curricula that Pohl surveyed in 1914. Pohl found that ninety-seven institutions required survey courses in the first or second year, though anxieties were frequently expressed that this historical approach did not adequately stress the close reading of individual works.

18. Another professor from Stanford, H. B. Lathrop, publicized his department's efforts to restrict access in an article in *Educational Review* in 1893. Professors had reportedly separated literature from composition, "the most appalling drudgery of a drudging profession," by implementing a separate writing exam, requiring failing students to pay for their own remediation, and following up with repeated writing tests to force out less literate students (23:293). Such efforts succeeded. Within two decades, Stanford had become an elite national university, with the highest faculty salaries and the second highest tuition in the country (Burke 225).

19. The unusual emphasis given to composition at Harvard seems to have been pressed on the faculty by outside forces. Reforms were supported by the Board of Overseers, an alumni committee that was very active in shaping curricula. This committee was quite interested in the "Department of Written English," as the Board referred to the English department in its minutes for May 27, 1885, when it made one of its many recommendations on course offerings and modes of instruction.

20. Writing-across-the-curriculum-requirements tried to fill the void created by the disappearance of forensic programs, which had required students to deliver compositions almost every semester in their careers as late as the 1860s, but which had largely disappeared a half century later, according to Wozniak's study of thirty-seven eastern colleges. Russell reported that he found the same development in a dozen midwestern institutions.

21. In the first decades of the twentieth century, the average faculty salary was about that of a "skilled industrial worker," according to Christopher Lucas (197). Connors provides particular details on college composition instructors' salaries (199–200)

22. James's distinctions were in fact used for just this evaluative purpose in this essay prompt in an examination in Subject A at the University of California in 1932:

> William James said: 'The best claim that a college education can possibly make on our respect . . . is this: that it should help you to know a good man when you see him.'
>
> What is meant by 'good man'? What are the advantages of being able to distinguish a good man from one not so good? Of what practical value is the 'critical sense'? May one not develop the power to discriminate without going to college? In what vocations would this ability be most useful? In what sense is Professor James's statement most true?

Like questions on what students read or why they came to college, this question presented many miscues for those less familiar with literate modes of decorum (see Brereton 491–545 for samples of such essays). Such students might assume that to "discriminate" was bad or that being a "good man" was a simple moral matter.

23. While their purpose was not to produce "professional story-tellers, or readymade poets," poetry and fiction workshops were a common part of the Harvard cur-

riculum, most notably Wendell's "studio course," English 5 (Copeland and Rideout 35; see also Adams, *A Group of Their Own* 44). Harvard graduates spread creative writing courses across the country, with a student of Wendell's introducing such workshops at Iowa, according to Adams. The "Technique of the Drama" workshop that George Pierce Baker began at Harvard in 1906 was another source for creative writing. After publishing several books, Baker was finally promoted to professor, and he immediately turned his attention to concentrate on his playwriting studio. Students did not receive credit for the class because it was deemed to be too "technical." Such attitudes led Baker to move to Yale, where he established the Yale Drama School in 1925 (see Myers, *The Elephants Teach* 68; also Gray 427–30).

24. Like teaching, journalism offered opportunities to women that were programmatically ignored by the profession of literature. In her comments on the journalism course at Wellesley, Bates noted that they had enabled Wellesley's graduates to gain jobs with newspapers and magazines—a major achievement given the limited options facing female graduates (Payne 145). As Adams discusses, jobs for female journalists grew with the explosion of readership: while only four monthly magazines had circulations of over one hundred thousand in 1885, twenty years later, over twenty magazines produced a total circulation of more than 5.5 million (71).

25. For an early attempt to institute speech on a scientific basis, see Frost. Such frameworks displaced rhetoric from its central role, as documented by Donald Smith's study of the courses offered by 118 institutions:

Table 1. Courses offered by 118 institutions

Courses	1900–10	1910–20	1920–30
Public speaking	58	152	164
Interpretation	37	104	167
Rhetoric	195	36	7
Elocution	289	107	4
Oratory	148	152	44

Source: Smith, Donald K., "Origins and Development of Departments of Speech."

The discipline's movement toward an interpretive stance was even more definitive than these statistics may suggest, for oratory classes were "seldom performance courses" after 1920 (465).

26. D. G. Myers cites some of the texts first used to teach creative writing: Cody's *How to Write Fiction* (1895), Barrett's *Short Story Writing* (1898), Smith's *The Writing of the Short Story* (1902), Albright's *Short Story: Its Principles and Structure* (1907), Hamilton's *Materials and Methods of Fiction* (1908), Esenwein's *Writing the Short Story* (1908), Cross's *Short Story* (1914), and Neal's *Short Stories in the Making* (1914).

27. One of many cases in which creative writing was cited as a means to teach creative reading is provided by Chandler's "A Creative Approach to the Study of Literature" (1915). The workshop pedagogy of Progressives such as Mearns defined creative expression in Deweyan terms as a means to create a collaborative understanding of experience.

28. Connors has provided the most thorough account of the development of labor conditions in composition (171–209), but they have also been critiqued by other leading histories of composition, such as Berlin's *Rhetoric and Reality* (78–80) and Crowley's

Composition in the University (118–31). Brereton concludes his collection of materials documenting the impact of these loads on students' writing by reprinting Taylor's *National Survey of Conditions in Freshman English*, which surveys how composition was left "to go through its paces with cheap labor and mass production" (557).

29. In 1918, three hundred industrial research laboratories employed some twelve hundred researchers in private corporations, while in 1940 there were still only twenty-seven thousand people employed in twenty-three hundred such labs (Levine, *The American College* 50).

30. In "English and the PhD" (1925), Harry Baker underlined that the shortcomings of the typical PhD "are best shown by his often pathetic attempts to wrestle with the problem of teaching Freshman composition," which is "the standing joke of the American university," in part because "the middle-aged doctors are not required to teach it, and the young ones teach it badly" (qtd. in Connors 198).

31. The double bind facing those who were interested in teaching is clearly evident in Cox's "What Is the Best Preparation for the College Teacher of English? Training for Teaching and Training for Research," which was delivered at a regional MLA conference and then published in the *English Journal* in 1913. Cox recounted how PhDs had begun to be hired at his institution (West Virginia University) to replace well-meaning generalists who taught literature as a means to shape character. In an effort to improve his own professional standing, Cox recounted how he had attended summer school at "one of our great universities." When he asked the head of the department why teaching was ignored, the department head indignantly responded that a PhD "is not a teacher's degree but an investigator's degree" (207). Cox found such an assessment dubious because the "lifework" of most graduates is teaching, but to avoid being confused with professors of education, Cox quickly followed up to reassure his readers that he deplored "the relative importance given to the subject of education in certain quarters" (213).

32. Writings for teachers often retained an exhortative style, as evident in Chubb's popular *The Teaching of English*, and "The Blight of Literary Bookishness" in the *English Journal* in 1914. According to Chubb, "the supreme aim of literary and linguistic training is the formation of character," and teachers should see themselves as "the radiant ideals of manhood and womanhood prefigured in Literature" (*Teaching* 380, 238).

33. The number of women in college rose from fifty-six to eighty-five thousand between 1890 and 1900, according to Kates, who examines how the studies offered to women changed as the class backgrounds of female students expanded beyond those served by such institutions as the "Seven Sisters," which were founded between 1865 and 1890—Vassar, Smith, Wellesley, Radcliffe, Mount Holyoke, Barnard, and Bryn Mawr (see also Weidner and Harmon).

34. The dependence of female and minority writers and orators upon such networks is evident in Ritchie and Ronald's collection, *Available Means: An Anthology of Women's Rhetoric(s)*. As in the antebellum period, virtually all the individuals included from the early twentieth century worked as teachers, with most moving back and forth from classroom lecterns to other public forums, often supplementing their incomes by writing for the increasing numbers of magazines and newspapers aimed at female, working-class, and minority readers. The experience of Ida Wells provides a case in point. Upon the early death of her parents, she began teaching at sixteen and then became active in her church and a teachers' lyceum, for which she edited a newsletter. When she was fired for opposing segregation, she became "one of the first women investigative report-

ers in the United States" and used her own *Free Speech and Headlight* and other Progressive periodicals to investigate the lynching of African Americans. Such efforts were also common among the Progressivist women working as social workers and teachers in settlement houses, women's groups, and expanding social service agencies.

35. The effects of this growth on the curricula are evident in surveys completed in the 1920s. Taylor's 1929 survey of over two hundred departments shows that composition had largely become confined to the first year, with 70 percent of institutions in the East using literature to teach composition, as compared to under 20 percent in the Midwest and West, where rhetoric was taught in conjunction with composition by three-quarters of departments, as compared to less than half that in the East (12–13). A. H. R. Fairchild's study of forty-eight departments suggests that the major had become pretty clearly drawn. The first year was commonly given over to composition and rhetoric, though a third of the respondents included a survey of British literature in the first year, with the rest offering it in the second year. The last years of study included a variety of courses in American literature, modern literature, the history of drama, Romantic and Victorian literature, Shakespeare, and "Old English or Chaucer or History of the Language" (153). Three departments had abandoned linguistic studies, and one-third of all the respondents noted that linguistic requirements had come to be seen as undesirable (156).

36. I will not be able to look past the New Critics to examine the more sociologically oriented critics that Hyman and later historians have looked to for alternatives to the rising influence of the New Critics within the profession. Hyman himself argued for making Marxism the "foundation" of the discipline, with "dialectical materialism" set out as an "integrative frame" for literary studies (397).

37. As Ohmann discusses, the supposedly apolitical stance of the New Critics suited the professional aspirations of faculty and students who "were trying to cut loose from their social origins and join an intellectual elite" (92).

38. Ohmann has argued that the New Critics' method of close reading "neutralizes and flattens out . . . impulses to action," instilling a political passivity well suited to an era when English professors were making the transition from poorly paid educators to well-paid professionals (90). Unfortunately, most workers in the field did not share in that transition.

39. In "The Old Professor of English: An Autopsy," Pattee commiserates on the passing of the generation who taught "an uncommercialized, unpopularized, unmodern phase of literature" (219). One can see how critics felt demeaned by teaching general education in Pattee's comments on how his Pennsylvania State University students asked, "how is this dope going to help a guy get a job and pull down a good salary?" and then returned years later as rich alumni smug in the knowledge that they made far more than he did (182–83).

40. Berthoff has maintained that Richards's protocols represent "the first genuine research in the teaching of English" ("I. A. Richards" 56). Richards assumed that the pragmatics of learning can provide insights into cognition, semiotics, and symbolic action, but at least at Cambridge, he was not challenged to consider how differing social contexts shape students' responses because he worked with male students who largely came from a narrow range of social backgrounds. This limitation is important because Richards was a founder of not just New Criticism but reader-response theory. As Spurlin discusses, many reader-response theorists followed New Critics in assum-

ing that "the text and reader alone are sufficient to define the contexts for reading," even though "readers do not operate in a vacuum" apart from "social, political, historical, and cultural conditions" (240–41).

41. The popular *Project Method* was published by William Kilpatrick, a colleague of Dewey's at Teachers College, Columbia. Students set up collaborative teams to research social issues. This methodology was similar to the community ethnographies of Ira Shor and other proponents of critical pedagogy, but the politics of the project method were accommodationist. In practice it combined "scientific management with a free-market faith in the individual" (Holt 81; see also Russell 205). The project method was widely promoted by the editor of the *English Journal*, William Hatfield, and it was a principal part of the "experience curriculum."

42. In *Conducting Experiences in English*, Broening reports on the curricula of 274 teachers, noting that "principals, supervisors, and teachers everywhere report that their courses in English are based upon the experiences of their pupils," and every textbook salesperson reportedly cited *An Experience Curriculum in English* (v).

43. According to Ross, psychology, economics, sociology, and political science began establishing specialized journals and graduate programs in the last decades of the nineteenth century (at the same time as English professors), but the social sciences only became identified as part of a coherent educational project after 1920. Larson has discussed how the social sciences advanced an "ideology of expertise" that was instrumental in reshaping public education, while at the same time "possessive individualism" became a key element in "liberal political thought," resulting in a general "impoverishment" of the public sphere (30). The Progressive movement was caught up in these trends, while literary studies were largely set in opposition to them.

44. For example, to investigate the social uses of English studies, Pendleton surveyed hundreds of teachers, graduate students, and community leaders as well as textbooks and curricula. Pendleton's *Social Objectives of School English* (1924) lists over fifteen hundred "social outcomes," with the top ranked being spelling, speaking in correct sentences, and "economy" of expression. Even the more substantive outcomes do not amount to more than reading literature for enjoyment or speaking "tactfully and efficiently," and these outcomes are characterized in moralistic qualities such as being honest, "constructive," and "alert" (36).

45. One of the more famous examples of how New Critics formalized rhetoric's traditional concern for the transactions of audiences and authors is Wimsatt's quoting J. S. Mill on how "Eloquence is *heard*, poetry is *overheard*" (xv). Such romantic mystifications distracted attention from the fact that there are few if any methodological distinctions between New Critics' works of literary and rhetorical studies, most notably Brooks and Warren's *Understanding Poetry* and *Modern Rhetoric*. *Understanding Poetry* opens with a rhetorical analysis of the "emotional appeal" and other persuasive strategies in a political speech, before turning to sermons, editorials, advertisements, and the other sorts of highly purposeful and referential texts that poetry is later positioned above by defining it according to its distinctive rhetorical effect "as a piece of writing which gives us a certain effect in which, we discover, the 'poetry' inheres" (18). This concern for readers' experiences (which is central to Progressives' accounts of literature) is obviated by a formalist methodology that brackets off authors' intentions and audiences' responses, and with them the social sources and functions of literature.

1. In assessing the following numbers from the National Center for Education Statistics, one needs to remember that *communications* (like *business*) expanded and diversified majors in ways English did not. *Communications* can often refer to a college rather than a department. Also, the NCES category 23, "English Language and Literature/Letters," counts graduates in majors that the profession has not acknowledged as part of the field, most notably the 8,340 graduates in 2000 who are included in the NCES subcategory 23.1001, "Speech and Rhetorical Studies," a category that is included in the statistics used by groups such as ADE and MLA, but which has not traditionally been recognized by those organizations as part of the field they represent (for an elaborate justification and explication, see ADE 2001–02 Ad Hoc Committee on the English Major, 87–90). When this category is combined with the 1704 graduates from writing majors, the total comprises about 20 percent of all graduates from the "field."

Table 2. Majors in English, communications, and business in U.S. colleges and universities

	1950–51	1960	1970	1980	1990	2000
Total graduates	432,058	382,440	839,730	935,140	1,094,538	1,244,171
BAs in communications	n.d.	n.d.	10,324	29,428	51,650	58,013
BAs in business	n.d.	n.d.	114,729	198,983	249,311	265,746
BAs in English	17,240	20,128	56,410	32,541	47,519	50,920
College graduates in English (%)	3.99	5.13	7.21	3.5	4.52	n.d.

Source: National Center for Education Statistics.
n.d. = No data.

2. According to Barbara and John Ehrenreich, the "professional-managerial classes" "emerged with dramatic suddenness in the years between 1890 and 1920" with the creation of social service professionals, scientific technicians, management experts, and "culture producers" for the mass media (18, 9).

3. As Kerr discusses, between 1960 and 1980, college enrollments grew from 3.5 to 12 million, with community colleges growing tenfold from four hundred thousand to 4 million students. While teacher colleges had enrolled only half a million in 1960, they evolved into comprehensive and research universities that enrolled six times that number two decades later. Federal funding rose from 300 million dollars to 10 billion dollars. Universities became entrepreneurial institutions "dominated by professional schools" with research centers, extension programs, and business partnerships that marked "the last and conclusive triumph of the Sophists over the Philosophers" (xiii).

4. According to Kerr, the "multiversity" became the leading institution in the "knowledge industry" as it came to "permeate government and business" (*Uses* 66). As Kerr observed, by the early 1960s, 29 percent of the GNP was involved in the production and distribution of knowledge, according to Machlup.

5. The dependence of English departments on cheaply provided general education courses only became a professional concern after the crash in majors and jobs in the 1970s, but the institutional economies at work date back to the expansion of the research mission in the postwar period, when research faculty workloads were instituted

that would have been prohibitively expensive if community colleges had not been used to provide general education courses staffed by teachers who were used to heavy teaching loads. Despite the fact that community colleges were the fastest-growing sector of higher education, the average cost per student rose from two thousand dollars in 1930 to five thousand dollars in 1960, then nine thousand dollars in 1990 (Kerr, *Uses* 179). This institutional economy was founded on the distinction of permanent funding vested in faculty lines from "temporary" funding dispensed to "cover" general education courses. That distinction made general education seem to be an extraneous cost that distracted from departments' core missions, rather than as a highly profitable area of instruction that subsidized the research infrastructure.

6. In the 1950s, federal funding for higher education rose from $2.7 to $6.2 billion, with the funding per student rising by 50 percent from $1159 to $1747 (Machlup 79).

7. In "Teaching and Studying Literature at the End of Ideology," Ohmann cites Trilling's recollections of how students responded when confronted with the darkest recesses of modernism. According to Trilling, students often responded "dutifully and gladly," and "the Abyss has greeted them with the grave courtesy of all objects of serious study, saying: 'Interesting am I not? And *exciting*, if you consider how deep I am and what dread beasts lie at my bottom. Have it well in mind that a knowledge of me contributes materially to your being whole, or well-rounded, men'" (qtd. 107; see also Graff's *Professing Literature* 232).

8. While some Progressive schools had promoted linguistic pluralism, bilingual education largely disappeared between the 1920s and the decade of the Bilingual Education Act in 1968, according to Andersson, who cites research from the 1950s that found that on average, students with Hispanic surnames in Texas spent three years in the first grade and usually dropped out before reaching the fifth grade. Such students were largely ignored by work in ESOL in English departments, for that work has generally had an internationalist orientation that equated ESOL with EFL and the teaching of "foreigners" (see Wilcox 60). In his foreword to the proceedings of the first TESOL conference, James Squire noted that resources were largely going into EFL, while bilingual education was just beginning to gain attention. While the array of foreign service and government agencies at the conference helps to explain that discontinuity, the continuing failure to connect ESOL with bilingual education can also be attributed to the marginalization of English education in English departments.

9. The antitechnical reaction of humanists to the communications movement is included in McGrath's collection in the polemic of Norman Foerster, who haughtily noted that communications programs were not headed by the "best minds" but by "educationists." Their administrative mindset showed "an abnormal interest in organization," resulting in "incessant staff meetings" and stifling efforts to make a science of the art of writing (202–03). Foerster lines up the points of opposition that humanist and leftist critics commonly use to distance their concerns from composition by identifying it with a managerial mentality, vocational ethos, and technological methods.

10. Allen found that TAs and new PhDs could readily assess what preparation they needed, if departments bothered to ask them. From their responses, he recommended graduate instruction in higher education (including general education, teaching in community colleges, and the pragmatics of being a professor), research on learning (assessment, classroom strategies, and cognition), language (including standard usage and language acquisition), reading theory, the teaching of literature, and recent innovations

in high school curricula, first-year composition, and "rhetorical theory" (including semantics and practical reasoning) (10–12).

11. With a career that reached back to the 1930s, M. H. Abrams was selected to assess trends in English. Its professional autonomy had been set out in Abrams's milestone *The Mirror and the Lamp,* which places the formalism of New Criticism at the end of history. Aesthetics is seen to have evolved from "mimetic" and "pragmatic" theories through "expressive" paradigms to conclude with the "objective" theories of New Criticism. Abrams plots this development using the semiotic model of the communication triangle, with I. A. Richards and Richard McKeon cited as authorities. Rhetoric is identified as the classical source of the "pragmatic" concern for audience responses. Literary critics' disdain for pragmatism is evident in how Abrams reviews "pragmatic" aesthetics without feeling any need to cite the best-known American philosopher of the twentieth century, the pragmatist John Dewey.

12. Such aspirations were still shaped by the jobs available to women, within higher education and elsewhere. A study of the careers of PhDs granted at Harvard and Radcliffe in the 1950s found that 32 percent of men and 20 percent of women went on to teach in "major" universities, with 30.2 percent of women and 12.3 percent of men staying at the instructor rank, which in English departments meant teaching composition (Grommon 485).

13. In addition to gaining federal funding for research on the discipline, the NCTE also set up a national writing competition in 1958 in which 2300 students submitted essays, with the incentive being that the NCTE would help to secure grants for college. The first year's efforts raised $852,000, according to *The National Interest and the Teaching of English* (Squire). These initiatives provided the collaborative networks that were used in the national surveys of curricula that were undertaken in the 1960s, 1970s, and 1980s (see, for example, Squire and Applebee, and Applebee's "Record," *Survey, Contexts,* and *Literature*).

14. Working from his background as a linguist, Marckwardt tried to bridge the two cultures of the NCTE and the MLA. He reported that leaders of the MLA had a "touching innocence about education" and responded with "anguished groans" to NCTE publications (8). According to Marckwardt, the participants at the conferences were only able to maintain unanimity by not raising troubling questions about whether "literature should be taught at all" in an era of "newer media of communication" (10). Such agreements were only possible, according to Markwardt, because "educationalists" were "blackballed" and New Criticism had passed "its zenith" (9, 10).

15. Another historic event in 1963 was the *Toward a New Rhetoric* CCCC convention, which included Booth's "The Rhetorical Stance" and other noted papers by Kitzhaber, Christensen, and Corbett that were published in the October 1963 issue of *CCCC.*

16. With linguistics as a model and the learning of sciences as his focus, Bruner maintained that the "principles that give structure" to a subject determine how it is to be learned. Once the "mental structure of a field of knowledge" is determined, "uneconomical" modes of instruction can be avoided, and efficient acquisitions can be made (31–32). This model represented learning as a mode of collaborative inquiry, and thereby captured the excitement associated with the process of scientific discovery. This model enhanced the professional credibility of teachers, though Harris identifies it with a "top-down" conception of the transmission of knowledge that he maintains was characteristic of Project English (see also Smagorinsky).

17. The emergence of poststructuralism is generally dated from another conference in 1966, the Johns Hopkins Conference on the Languages of Criticism and the Sciences of Man: The Structuralist Controversy, where Derrida delivered his famous "Structure, Sign, and Play in the Discourse of the Human Sciences."

18. At Dartmouth and other international conferences in the 1960s, British and Canadian participants pointedly argued that working-class students deserved more than humanistic verities and vocational skills (see Spouge; Buxton). British educational politics had their most far-reaching impact on college English in the founding of the Centre for Cultural Studies at Birmingham University in 1964. As Stuart Hall has discussed, the Centre's founder, Richard Hoggart, authored his account of working-class cultural literacy, *The Uses of Literacy*, as an extension of his experience teaching working adults. As Hall notes, the other two founding texts of British cultural studies were shaped by the articulation work that Raymond Williams and E. P. Thompson did in the 1950s. As in America, such articulation efforts were ignored by disciplinary specialists at Birmingham, who were working to raise their standing in the same ways as their counterparts at land-grant American universities. For a comparison of how literary intellectuals in Britain and America responded to the class politics of mass culture, see Lunn.

19. Squire and Applebee document the broad resurgence of interest in creative writing in the 1960s, with two-thirds of students in one survey citing creative writing as the best way they knew to improve writing (129). Such responses validated the position of Britton and others that "children learn to write above all by writing," and "what is important is that children in school should write about what matters to them to someone who matters to them" (52, 53). These points were basic to Progressive education, but that continuity was rarely cited because Progressives were held in disrepute, in part because of the "the creative writing binge" in the 1930s (Hook, "Teaching" 97).

20. On the other side of the divide between the arts and sciences, rhetoric was being revitalized as a school of criticism, with Black's neo-Aristotelian *Rhetorical Criticism* becoming the "single most important influence on rhetorical studies" in speech and communications for the "next several decades" (Leff 87).

21. Arthur Applebee's *Survey of Teaching Conditions* in 1978 cites research estimating that it took a teacher 3.5 minutes to assign a grade to a 250-word paper, and 8.6 minutes to comment upon higher-order skills. Given that formula, a teacher with 125 students would take 17.5 hours to comment upon a weekly theme. In reality, many teachers had more students and less time than that.

22. According to McLeod's "Watching Our Discipline Die" (1980), the profession showed not "much concern and almost no alarm" when the number of lecturers doubled in the California state system in the 1970s.

23. The coordinated media assault on liberal educators is evident in the bestseller standing of one of the best-known statements of the culture wars, Bloom's *The Closing of the American Mind: How Higher Education Has Failed Democracy and Impoverished the Souls of Today's Students*. The book was first listed on the *New York Times* bestseller lists even when there were only ten thousand copies of the book in print and only seven thousand had been distributed. As Davidson notes, "no one, in retrospect, quite understands how a title could be listed as a bestseller when there were not enough copies in print to qualify it for that status" (20).

24. Working with the National Education Longitudinal Study sample of students attending eighth grade in 1988 and other large representative samples, Karen provides an analysis of educational access that controls for class background, race, test scores,

and grades. This analysis shows that African Americans were being tracked into less prestigious institutions, while the access of Hispanics and women to elite institutions was shaped mostly by class, particularly the income and education of parents. Of course neither grades nor test scores can really be considered independent variables in analyses of the effects of race, class, and gender on access.

25. According to Guillory, the "failure to install the standard vernacular at lower levels" led to the rising importance of composition as a means to credential the "professional-managerial classes" (79; see also Godzich 12). The teaching of writing is also identified as a vocational accommodation in the 2002 ADE Committee on the Major, especially in its remarkably reactionary comments on the "transparently populist and egalitarian" affirmative action initiatives that led to the spread of remedial writing (77). The ADE report looks to increasing "selectivity" to uphold the discipline's literary orientation against vocationally minded students who are unprepared to appreciate the higher purposes of the profession.

26. These aspirations are evident in the shift in the largest English graduate programs: from 1955 to 1965 the top ten producers included an almost equal number of private and state universities (Allen 19–20), but in the 1970s state universities in North Carolina, Oregon, Texas, and New York rose to join the top ten, with the only private university left among the ten largest programs being Yale (MLA-ADE Survey of Doctoral Programs 1973). The research priorities of such programs had a broad impact because the ten largest programs produced 45 percent of all doctorates from 1955–65, and their graduates were recruited by more broadly based institutions seeking to raise their standing by imitating more elitist institutions.

27. As Grommon notes, this problem was systemic: until "American higher education provides effective incentives for teaching, proposals to alter the degree program so as to produce better schoolmasters are at best premature, if not quite irrelevant." By focusing on outside factors rather than on the discipline's own attitudes to "schoolmasters," Grommon could conclude that without change elsewhere, "there will be little improvement" in the attention to teaching, "no matter how much pedagogical training is forced into a Ph.D. program" (560).

28. Wilcox's National Survey of Undergraduate Programs in English was funded by the Office of Education. A thirty-nine page questionnaire was sent to three hundred departments in 1967 (with a 95 percent response rate because a check for $25 was enclosed). Site visits were made to sixty-three departments. The growth of higher education in the 1960s that so starkly contrasts with the dramatic decreases in English majors in the 1970s is evident in the increase of four-year institutions from 1320 to 1526 between the start of his study and its publication as *The Anatomy of College English* in 1973.

29. Wilcox found the failure to organize curricula more coherently to be quite notable, given how common the types of courses were: courses in individual authors were offered in 95.6 percent of departments (with one course commonly required, usually Shakespeare), American literature was offered in 94.1 percent (with one semester commonly required), genre courses in 93.4 percent (with one required course), period courses in 91.6 percent, and surveys of English literature in 78.4 percent (with two terms typically required). Also, one course was commonly offered, but not required, in linguistics (offered in 79.5 percent of departments), advanced composition (in 72.2 percent), creative writing (in 71.1 percent), and literary criticism (in 67 percent) (120, see also 140).

30. Fish's "affective stylistics" had reworked New Critical modes of reading through linguistic models, much as Ohmann had in such works as "Generative Grammars and the Concept of Literary Style," which was reprinted in the *New Rhetorics* collection (see Fish's *Is There a Text?* 73–75).

31. A sampling of responses to the "present professional crisis" from 1975 is provided by the departmental profiles in Cowan's *Options for the Teaching of English* (63). Departments' vitality varied according to such factors as their state's accreditation requirements for teachers and their willingness to expand writing offerings, with creative writing cited by several departments as being in high demand. The departments at Yale and Chicago took pride in ignoring broader social changes and preserving traditional programs of study, while departments such as those at Virginia Polytechnic and Ball State saw strong increases in majors that were raising the prestige of their departments along with that of their institutions.

32. A repositioning of the discipline as a "service profession" was set out at The ADE-MLA Wingspread Conference on Major Issues Facing the College Teaching of Language and Literature in the 1970s (1973). Gerber, Shugrue, and others at the conference developed detailed proposals for reforms based on the assumption that the demise of traditional majors might be "inevitable." Such off-putting assumptions may explain why nothing seems to have followed from the proposals. One purpose of the proposed reforms was to increase minority enrollments, which have historically been markedly lower in the humanities than in education.

33. The popular appeal of various areas of English studies is documented by a survey done by *Life* magazine that is cited by Hogan. Twenty-five hundred parents, students, teachers, and administrators were surveyed about what studies they found most useful, important, and interesting. Literature was distinguished from composition and grammar. For importance and usefulness, literature was ranked as low as hygiene, physical education, and music. On the other hand, composition and grammar were ranked among the most useful, the most important, the most difficult—and the most boring. Hogan concluded that such responses left English professors with three choices: accept the popular demise of literary studies, split up the discipline and choose sides, or weather out the storms of the time. The profession seems to have largely elected the third option in the 1970s, though the second emerged as a real possibility in the comp-lit wars of the 1980s.

34. One of the main proposals for dealing with the job crisis was to discourage rising departments from adding graduate programs. Ironically, emerging programs actually had better placement rates than elite departments according to the MLA Job Market Committee in 1979, which attributed that trend to established programs' being less responsive to changing needs (Hellstom 97).

35. Surveys of PhD graduates often found that they wished they had been able to study teaching, writing, and language. For example, Allen surveyed 1,880 PhDs who graduated between 1955 and 1965: 58.9 percent wished that they had attended a course in grammar, though only 3.6 percent had taken one (172; see Kline, Huff, and Kinneavy).

36. Wilcox found that all English faculty members had to teach first-year English in 33 percent of public and 57.4 percent of private institutions. Wilcox also found that most large public institutions used teaching assistants (with the ratio of faculty to gradu-

ate assistants being one to ten at UCLA and one to thirty at the University of Illinois) (65–66). Such departments provided models for the job system that became the norm in research universities.

37. According to Guillory, de Man's conception of "rhetorical reading" arose out of an "exhaustion in the discourse of literature" that began with the structuralist shift from aesthetic to linguistic models that identified literary qualities with the tropes of rhetoric (178, 208).

38. According to Bryant (1971), the Behavioral Conference in Communications in 1968 was a sort of coming of age for social scientists. Critical responses to those methods were reviewed in Brockriede's "Trends in Rhetoric: Toward a Blending of Criticism and Science" at the first National Developmental Project on Rhetoric in 1970.

39. The research of Astin and Oseguera shows that poorer students are less likely to enroll in selective institutions than they were in the 1970s, with last decade bringing an almost 50 percent decrease in the access of students with the lowest social economic status. Astin and Oseguera attribute the increased stratification of higher education to policy decisions made between the mid-1980s and 1990s. As a result of these trends, in 1998 a white American was almost twice as likely to earn a college degree as an African American, and three times as likely as a Hispanic American (see Andersen 23). One of the most striking aspects of such statistics is how marginally relevant they seem to be to the concerns of college English. While no discipline is more central to access to higher education, that fact is rarely factored into programs of study, including research programs as well as undergraduate and graduate programs.

Conclusion: Why the Pragmatics of Literacy Are Critical

1. As evidence of his assessment that literature as a "print institution" "lies in ruins," Kernan cited his visits to departments that had responded to drops in majors by shifting their focus from literary to cultural studies and restructuring "to teach basic writing and reading skills, creative writing, business and technical writing" (17). Others have noted that the marginal standing of such studies had long been due to "literature's refusal to soil itself by rendering service to the state—when that very refusal is the greatest service that it can render to a polity that must disguise the extraction of surplus value as cultural dynamism" (Spivak 672).

2. One of the most noted works along these lines was Watkins's *Work Time*. Watkins treated college English departments as "a site of cultural production" involved in a "complex ensemble" of socio-institutional relations that circulate cultural values through the field through the process of credentialing professionals (8).

3. In *The Formation of College English*, I explored how the three language arts of logic, rhetoric, and grammar were transformed by what Hume termed "the science of human nature." The shift from a deductive to an inductive logical framework moved moral philosophy away from theology and toward the social sciences. The process of generalizing from individual experiences was also well suited to the general shift away from initiating students into the received tradition, assimilating broader classes into education by teaching them how to make sense of their experiences in a self-controlled manner.

4. For more details on Witherspoon, see my edition of his lectures on rhetoric and moral philosophy, which also includes samples of the rhetoric that he produced as a

founder of the American Presbyterian Church and a signatory of the Declaration of Independence. Like Madison, Jefferson and Hamilton also studied rhetoric, belles lettres, and moral philosophy with Scottish college graduates.

5. Mary Trachsel concluded that as a result of its failure to address its central role in assessment, "the profession has lost considerable power to transform its professional values into public policy" (178). This failure helped to marginalize the first-year courses that are taught by teachers who have little standing in higher education, in part because their own discipline has ignored the values of their work.

6. Mailloux has more recently made the case for "cultural rhetoric" as a synthetic paradigm that offers hermeneutic strategies for making sense of cultural changes and intellectual transformations, including those that have come to the fore with postmodernism (195). Mailloux has also attempted to use this paradigm as a converging point of reference for the varied concerns of an English department.

7. This program of research has included the online catalogues and course descriptions of a 15 percent sample of 257 four-year institutions with the assistance of Matt Gonzalez, F. Vance Neil, Jennifer Walker, and Brian Jackson. We used the Carnegie Foundation's institutional categories to draw up a stratified sample to represent the broad diversity of English departments. I have published articles on this research in *Rhetoric Society Quarterly* (2005) comparing the position of rhetoric in English and communications, in *College English* (2006) briefly articulating how literacy studies can make sense of several apparently diverging trends in the field, and in *College Composition and Communications* (2007) reporting more fully on trends in undergraduate curricula than I have space to do here. The last article was coauthored with Brian Jackson, who has been a major collaborator in this research.

8. Several such majors were experimented with in the 1980s, most notably at Carnegie Mellon University, in part as an offshoot of its rise to become a center of studies of rhetoric and composition. Mailloux's "Rhetoric Returns to Syracuse: The Reception of Curricular Reform" provides a case study of another attempt to implement a major in "textual studies." The effort to synthesize cultural studies, critical theory, and rhetoric broke up when rhetoric and composition seceded to form an independent program. Scholes also elaborated a related program of studies in *The Rise and Fall of College English.*

9. To form the National Commission, the College Board gathered together school superintendents, university chancellors, and even a teacher, and then it followed through to publish glossy magazines and reports on the importance of writing to business. This effort was launched in part to disarm criticism of the timed writing task that was added to the SAT exam, along with marked increases in fees. These efforts of the College Board and its business partner, the Educational Testing Service, are but one example of how corporations are following through on the discipline's efforts to download writing instruction on the schools by outsourcing it, as for example through the use of machine-graded entrance exams.

10. *Reading at Risk* notes several related trends that have also been noted by other research on literacy. Such research has demonstrated that while the sales of books tripled in the last quarter of the last century, the numbers of people who reported having read one dropped significantly; similar trends appear in studies of magazine reading and other print literacy activities (see Stephenson 7–10; *Reading at Risk* 1). Television and computers have commonly been blamed for these trends. However, *Reading at*

Risk reports that readers of literature watched television for 2.7 hours per day, while those who did not read literature only watched about a half hour more. Also, in a Gallup survey of over 500 computer users and nonusers in 2001, there was no difference in the amount of time spent reading print—1.1 hours daily (*Reading at Risk* 15). The potential of television to increase reading has become characterized as the "Oprah" effect, for the dramatic increases in sales of the books discussed on Oprah Winfrey's televised "book clubs." Such reading groups play a vital role in supporting literary reading, and should be seen as part of expanding our work with the teaching of literature into a public works project.

11. I need to be tentative in comparing our results with the previous ADE surveys, including the one conducted by Huber in 1991–92 and published in 1996, because we surveyed online course catalogues and descriptions, while previous studies were based on surveys filled out by respondents. Also, we were unable to get clarifications on the categories that were used in previous surveys, despite several requests to ADE (see Miller and Jackson).

12. Linguistics seems to be continuing a downward trend in English departments, insofar as 19.3 percent of departments were found to include such majors in 1984–85, but only 13.4 percent had linguistics majors in 1991–92 (Huber, "Undergraduate"). Few institutions other than research universities have linguistics departments.

13. In our sample, 175 departments offer majors, emphases, minors, and concentrations. Such programs in creative and other writing areas are found in differing percentages in each of the three types of baccalaureate, masters, and doctoral institutions drawn up by the Carnegie Foundation in the latest revision of its categories in 2005: doctoral institutions have been reclassified into very high research activity, high activity, and simply "Doctoral/Research universities." Institutions that produce at least fifty masters' degrees a year are subdivided by size into large, medium, and smaller. And institutions that offer at least 10 percent of their degrees at the baccalaureate level and do not offer more than fifty masters or twenty doctoral degrees each year are categorized according to whether their degrees are in the arts and sciences, more diverse fields, or largely at the associate's level (Carnegie Foundation for the Advancement of Teaching).

Table 3. Percentage of institutions with majors, minors, and concentrations in writing in 2005

Carnegie Foundation Categories	Creative Writing	Other Writing
Baccalaureate/Associate's colleges	50	50
Baccalaureate colleges—diverse fields	26.5	73.5
Baccalaureate colleges—Arts & Sciences	46.4	100
Master's colleges and universities (smaller programs)	46.7	73.3
Master's colleges and universities (medium programs)	31.8	81.8
Master's colleges and universities (larger programs)	55.8	90.7
Doctoral/research universities	44.4	88.9
Research universities (high research)	72.7	81.8
Research universities (very high research)	81.8	100
Average	46.9	85.7

Source: Carnegie Foundation.

14. In 1999, nontenured and graduate student teachers taught 94.1 percent of first-year courses and 69 percent of all undergraduate courses in doctoral departments, while

in baccalaureate departments tenured faculty taught 42.2 percent of first-year courses and 59 percent of all undergraduate courses (ADE Committee on the Major, 78). Evans (1999) provides an engaging reflection on the values of a teaching department, while the faculty in research universities still view such departments as places where one will "disappear from the larger profession" and lose the chance of "a nationally relevant career" (Hall, "Professional Life" 194). This cosmopolitan opposition of the national profession to the local institution faces graduates when they have to decide whether to stay in a town where they may have community roots and teach (often in a community college) or move across the country to move up in the profession (if they are lucky enough to get a "real" job). This critical juncture in the careers of academics serves as a model for how professions form national labor pools that disassociate intellectuals from the social networks and public educational systems in which they might exercise practical agency.

15. For the purpose of developing a new "public idea" about the civic values of multilingualism, Pratt (*Building*) has called for developing relations with "local heritage communities" to build "pipelines" for people from those communities to develop educational expertise that builds on their linguistic and cultural resources. Such community engagements are already part of service learning and some schoolwork in English education. Those areas provide models for how students and faculty can develop a more rooted sense of how their studies of language, writing, and literature relate to the needs of local communities.

16. I have discussed the ethnographic dimensions of rhetoric and moral philosophy's traditional concern for the dynamics of mores and morals in my article "Changing the Subject" with particular reference to Gadamer's hermeneutics.

17. The application of ethnographic methods to research on teaching has been integral to the broader effort to reconceptualize teaching as a reflective process of collaborative inquiry, or "practitioner inquiry" as Horner and others have termed it (177). Louise Wetherbee Phelps has offered rich theoretical accounts of teaching as "reflection in action" (872). As with related sources in critical literacy and rhetorical studies, Phelps invokes classical conceptions of *techne* and *praxis* for models of knowledge in the making that can serve as alternatives to the disabling dualism of technical and artistic modes of knowing that have structured English studies (see also Kinney and Miller).

18. Major reports on the temping out of teaching include "MLA Statement on the Use of Part-Time and Full-Time Adjunct Faculty" (1983, revised 1987), "Statement of Principles and Standards for the Postsecondary Teaching of Writing" (1989), and "Statement from the Conference on the Growing Use of Part-Time and Adjunct Faculty" (1997), which was produced by a coalition of ten professional associations, including AAUP as well as CCCC, MLA, NCTE, and organizations from other disciplines. The Wyoming Conference in 1986 led to the passage by CCCC of the Wyoming Resolution in 1986. That resolution envisioned setting up a sanctioning system comparable to that used by AAUP, but its practical action was never enacted.

19. Such writings as Berube's *The Employment of English* and various pieces by Cary Nelson openly look down upon composition courses as ways to cover the costs of literary studies. Nonetheless, Nelson has done more than anyone else in the profession to highlight labor conditions and organize faculty and graduate students to improve those conditions.

20. As Mayers discusses, a dismissive stance toward the instructional base of English departments is also adopted by other books that can be identified with the pragmatic concern for the institutional contexts of literary studies, including Goodheart's *Does Literary Studies Have a Future* (1999), Herman's *Day Late, Dollar Short* (2000), and Williams's *The Institution of Literature* (2002). Even while professing to adopt a materialist orientation, such accounts of the field perpetuate "the fantasy that the interpretive study of literature (or even the broader domain of 'culture') can, by itself, justify the size of any given English department" (Mayers 106).

21. As has increasingly been recognized, tenure functions as a bastion of the perceived autonomy of disciplinary professionals. Amid the widespread hiring of adjuncts on a piecework basis, tenure justifies disciplinary professionals' perceptions that their work is different from other teachers'. Tenure thereby serves to "keep a whole class of employees on their best behavior" by distracting them from addressing the fact that they are not autonomous professionals but salaried employees (Huber, "Report" 124; see also Rhoades).

22. Our tendency to define our discipline's practical aptitudes in terms of *skills* is an extension of the opposition of content and methods courses that has marginalized teaching and writing. The instrumental capacities of English courses can serve as part of what Burke termed "the equipment for living" and Scholes has discussed as part of the "cultural equipment" that students "are going to need when they leave us" (*Rise* 67–68).

23. As discussed in the last chapter, research has shown that more established programs have actually been less successful at placing graduates than the emerging programs that were targeted for closure. This finding has been attributed to their being more responsive to changing needs (see Hellstom 1979).

24. I have made a case for doing so in "Why Don't Our Graduate Programs Do a Better Job of Preparing Students for the Work We Do?" (2001).

25. The NCTE was set up to deal with the labor issues that the MLA dispensed with as it narrowed its purposes to supporting research. This same dynamic is evident in the history of graduate student teachers. When they first tried to align themselves with the faculty in the colonial period, the faculty responded that tutors should be categorized as servants. Graduate students began organizing themselves almost as soon as graduate programs became organized. Local associations gave rise to the Federation of the Graduate Clubs in 1893, which began to call for better workloads, with graduate students from English being one of the largest groups (see Allen 14). The organization ended within a few years as graduate teaching assistants came to think of themselves as disciplinary professionals rather than as a labor class.

26. An alternative venue for discussions of labor organizing, school partnerships, and community outreach was provided by the online journal *Workplace*, which was cofounded by Bousquet and includes important discussions with figures such as Ohmann and Nelson.

27. This promise has powerful public appeal, which became evident in how popular creative writing was found to be in the surveys conducted for *Reading at Risk*. In a survey reported in the *Chronicle of Higher Education* asking students about what seems most essential in their lives, "writing original works" was cited by 15.4 percent of students. Such responses might figure differently if the discipline did a better job of articulating how such writing contributes to other things that students find essential, ranging from

the top ranked "raising a family" (74.8 percent), earning a living (73.8 percent), and "helping others" (63.7 percent) to other concerns that are more obviously connected with the humanities, such as "integrating spirituality into my life" (40.4 percent) and "developing a meaningful philosophy" (39.3 percent). Such popular values provide a broad foundation for civic work with writing and literature (*Chronicle of Higher Education* August 27, 2004, 19).

28. The disabling dualism of the vocational and literary also appears in what goes without saying whenever undergraduate English majors virtually apologize for having chosen the field, perhaps with a reference to parental concerns over their career options or an open expression of their own anxieties. Such students often relate how they switched from a major that left them cold to something that made sense to them. We have an obligation, I think, to provide them with better accounts than we often do of how English majors will provide them with options when they leave school.

29. The MLA established the Teacher Education Project in 1993 with funds from private foundations and federal agencies and held two meetings that led to the collection of reports on teacher education programs.

30. This civic movement has been identified with works such as *Habits of the Heart: Individualism and Commitment in American Life* (1985) and related works by such figures as Benjamin Barber (see Lucas, *American Higher Education* 281–92). Service learning has been a key element of this general movement, which has been promoted by the Carnegie Foundation through the American Democracy Project as reported in *Educating Citizens*, and the Ford Foundation through the American Commitments Project.

WORKS CITED

Abrams, M. H. *The Mirror and the Lamp: Romantic Theory and the Critical Tradition*. New York: Oxford University Press, 1953.

An Account of the Commencement in the College of Philadelphia, May 17, 1775. Philadelphia: 1775.

Adams, John Quincy. *Lectures on Rhetoric and Oratory*. 1810. Delmar, New York: Scholars' Facsimiles and Reprints, 1997.

Adams, Katherine H. *A Group of Their Own: College Writing Courses and American Women Writers, 1880–1940*. Albany: State University of New York Press, 2001.

———. *A History of Professional Writing Instruction in American Colleges*. Dallas: Southern Methodist University Press, 1993.

———. *Progressive Politics and the Training of America's Persuaders*. Mahwah, N.J.: Lawrence Erlbaum Associates, 1999.

Adler, Mortimer Jerome. *How to Read a Book; The Art of Getting a Liberal Education*. New York: Simon and Schuster, 1940.

Aikin, W. M. *The Story of the Eight-Year Study: With Conclusions and Recommendations*. New York: Harper and Brothers, 1942.

Albright, Evelyn May. *The Short-Story: Its Principles and Structure*. New York: Macmillan, 1907.

Alden, Raymond MacDonald. "The College Curriculum in Literature." *English Journal* 2.5 (May 1913): 271–82.

Alison, Francis. 23 Letters to Ezra Stiles from June 20, 1755 to October 22, 1773. Photostatic and Typed Copies. Presbyterian Historical Society, MS Al4c1–23.

———. *Moral Philosophy; In Three Books; Containing the Elements of Ethics, the Law of Nature, and Economics with Politics, to Which Is Subjoined, Communis Ethicae Compendium: or, A Compend of Ethics, In Latin*. Transcribed by Jasper Yeates. Alison Collection, Van Pelt Library. University of Pennsylvania, 1759.

———. "Philosophical Questions Reduced to a System; —And an Account of the Authors that maintain both sides of the question according to the different Hypotheses that they maintain. For the use of the students in The Academy & College of Philadelphia." Historical Society of Pennsylvania, Philadelphia. Society Misc. Col., Case 19, Box 2.

Allen, Don Cameron. *The PhD in English and American Literature*. New York: Holt, Rinehart, and Winston, 1968.

Allmendinger, David F. *Paupers and Scholars: The Transformation of Student Life in Nineteenth-Century New England*. New York: St. Martin's Press, 1975.

The American Magazine; or a Monthly View of the Political State of the British Colonies. 1741. New York: Columbia University Press, 1937.

American Magazine and Historical Chronicle. 1743–46. American Periodical Series. Ann Arbor, Mich.: University Microfilms, 1942.

American Magazine. 1787–88. American Periodical Series. Ann Arbor, Mich.: University Microfilms, 1942.

Andersen, Charles. *Fact Book on Higher Education*. 1997 ed. Phoenix: American Council on Education, 1998.

Anderson, Benedict R. *Imagined Communities: Reflections on the Origin and Spread of Nationalism.* Rev. Ed. New York: Verso, 2006.

Andersson, Theodore. "Bilingual Education: The American Experience." *Modern Language Journal* 55.7 (November 1971): 427–40.

Andresen, Julie. *Linguistics in America 1769–1924: A Critical History.* New York: Routledge, 1990.

Andrews, John. *Elements of Rhetorick and Belles Lettres.* Philadelphia: Moses Thomas, 1813.

———. *A Compend of Logick for the use of the University of Pennsylvania.* Philadelphia: Budd and Bartram, 1801.

Angus, David, and Jeffrey E. Mirel. *The Failed Promise of the American High School, 1890–1995.* New York: Teachers College, 1999.

Antczak, Frederick J. *Thought and Character: The Rhetoric of Democratic Education.* Ames: Iowa State University Press, 1985.

Apple, Michael. "National Reports and the Construction of Inequality." *British Journal of Sociology of Education* 7.2 (1986): 171–90.

Applebee, Arthur N. *Contexts for Learning to Write: Studies of Secondary School Instruction.* Norwood, N.J.: Ablex, 1984.

———. *Literature in the Secondary School: Studies of Curriculum and Instruction in the United States.* Urbana: NCTE, 1993.

———. *A Survey of Teaching Conditions in English.* Urbana: ERIC Clearinghouse on Reading and Communications Skills, 1978.

———. *Tradition and Reform in the Teaching of English: A History.* Urbana, Ill.: NCTE, 1974.

Applebee, Roger. "A Record of English Teaching Today." 1966. In *English Education Today,* edited by Lois Josephs and Erwin R. Steinberg, 18–31. New York: Noble and Noble, 1970.

Appy, Nellie. *Pupils Are People.* New York: D. Appleton-Century Co., 1941.

Armstrong, Paul B. "The English Coalition and the English Major." *ADE Bulletin* 96 (Fall 1990): 30–33

Arnold, Matthew. *On Translating Homer: Last Words.* London: Longman, Green, Longman and Roberts, 1862.

"Articulating High School and College Work." Workshop Report. *College Composition and Communication* 2.4 (1951): 21–23.

Association of Departments of English 2001–02 Ad Hoc Committee on the English Major. "The Undergraduate English Major." *ADE Bulletin* 134–35 (2003): 68–91.

Association of Departments of English Ad Hoc Committee on Staffing. "Report of the ADE Ad Hoc Committee on Staffing." *ADE Bulletin* 122 (Spring 1999): 1–24.

Astin, Alexander W., and Oseguera, Leticia. *Degree Attainment Rates at American Colleges and Universities.* Los Angeles: Higher Education Research Institute, Graduate School of Education, UCLA, 2002.

Atkinson, Paul. *The Ethnographic Imagination: Textual Constructions of Reality.* London: Routledge, 1990.

Atwill, Janet. *Rhetoric Reclaimed: Aristotle and the Liberal Arts Tradition.* Ithaca, N. Y.: Cornell University Press, 1998.

Backus, Truman J. *Shaw's New History of English and American Literature with Henry T. Tuckerman's Sketch of American Literature.* New York: Sheldon, 1874.

Bacon, Jacqueline, and Glen McClish. "Reinventing the Master's Tools: Nineteenth-Century African-American Literary Societies of Philadelphia and Rhetorical Education." *Rhetoric Review* 30.4 (Autumn 2000): 19–47.

Bailyn, Bernard. *Education in the Forming of American Society: Needs and Opportunities for Study.* 1960. New York: Norton, 1972.

———. *Ideological Origins of the American Revolution.* Cambridge, Mass.: Belknap, 1967.

Baker, Dorothy Z. "After the English Major." *ADE Bulletin* 133 (Winter 2003): 36–41.

Baker, Franklin T., et al. "Preparation of High School Teachers of English: A Report of a Committee of the National Council of Teachers of English." *English Journal* 4.5 (May 1915): 323–32.

Barone, Dennis. "An Introduction to William Smith and Rhetoric at the College of Philadelphia." *Proceedings of the American Philosophical Society* 134.2 (June 1990): 111–60.

Barrett, Charles Raymond. *Short Story Writing.* New York: Baker and Taylor & Co., 1900.

Barthes, Roland. "The Old Rhetoric: An Arde-Memoire." In *The Semiotic Challenge,* 11–94. New York: Hill and Wang, 1988.

Bartholomae, David. "Freshman English, Composition, and CCCC." *College Composition and Communication* 40.1 (February 1989): 38–50.

Basler, Roy P. "Preserving a Place for English." *College English* 2.1 (October 1940): 63–65.

Bates, Herbert. "The School and Current Fiction." *English Journal* 1 (1912): 15–23.

Bazin, Patrick. "Toward Metareading." In *The Future of the Book,* edited by Geoffrey Nunberg, 153–68. Berkeley: University of California Press, 1996.

Beadie, Nancy. "Academy Students in the Mid-Nineteenth Century: Social Geography, Demography, and the Culture of Academy Attendance." *History of Education Quarterly* 41.2 (Summer 2001): 251–62.

Becker, Samuel. "Rhetorical Studies for the Contemporary World." In *The Prospect of Rhetoric. Report of the National Developmental Project,* edited by Lloyd F. Bitzer and Edwin Black, 21–43. Englewood Cliffs, N.J.: Prentice-Hall, 1971.

Beidler, Peter G. "What English Majors Do Out There, How They Feel About It, and What We Do About It." *ADE Bulletin* 133 (2003): 29–35.

Bender, Thomas. "The Erosion of Public Culture: Cities, Discourse and Professional Disciplines." In *The Authority of Experts: Studies in History and Theory,* edited by Thomas L. Haskell, 84–106. Bloomington: Indiana University Press, 1984.

———. *Intellect and Public Life: Essays on the Social History of Academic Intellectuals in the United States.* Baltimore: Johns Hopkins University Press, 1993.

Bender, Thomas, and Carl E. Schorske, eds. *American Academic Culture in Transformation: Fifty Years, Four Disciplines.* Princeton: Princeton University Press, 1997.

Benzie, William. *The Dublin Orator: Thomas Sheridan's Influence on Eighteenth-Century Rhetoric and Belles Lettres.* Menston, Yorkshire: Scolar Press, 1972.

Berlin, James A. *Rhetoric and Reality: Writing Instruction in American Colleges, 1900–1985.* Carbondale: Southern Illinois University Press, 1987.

———. *Writing Instruction in Nineteenth-Century American Colleges.* Carbondale: Southern Illinois University Press, 1984.

Berthoff, Ann E. "I. A. Richards." In *Traditions of Inquiry,* edited by John C. Brereton, 50–80. New York: Oxford University Press, 1985.

——. "The Problem of Problem Solving." *College Composition and Communication* 22.3 (October 1971): 237–42.

Berube, Michael. *The Employment of English: Theory, Jobs, and the Future of Literary Studies*. New York: New York University Press, 1998.

Bidwell, Charles E. "The Moral Significance of the Common School: A Sociological Study of the Local Patterns of School Control and Moral Education in Massachusetts and New York, 1837–1840." *History of Education Quarterly* 6 (1966): 50–91.

Birkerts, Sven. *The Gutenberg Elegies: The Fate of Reading in an Electronic Age*. Boston: Faber and Faber, 1994.

Bishop, Wendy. "Suddenly Sexy: Creative Nonfiction Rear Ends Composition." *College English* 65.3 (2003): 257–75.

Bizzaro, Patrick. "Research and Reflection in English Studies: The Special Case of Creative Writing." *College English* 66 (January 2004): 294–309.

Bizzell, Patricia. "Cognition, Convention, and Certainty: What We Need to Know about Writing." In *Academic Discourse and Critical Consciousness*, 75–104. Pittsburgh: University of Pittsburgh Press, 1992.

——. "Contact Zones and English Studies." *College English* 56 (February 1994): 163–69.

Black, Edwin. *Rhetorical Criticism*. New York: Macmillan, 1965.

Blair, Hugh. *Lectures on Rhetoric and Belles Lettres*. 1789. Edited by Harold F. Harding. 2 vols. Carbondale: Southern Illinois University Press, 1965.

Bledstein, Burton J. *The Culture of Professionalism: The Middle Class and the Development of Higher Education in America*. New York: Norton, 1976.

Bloom, Allan. *The Closing of the American Mind: How Higher Education Has Failed Democracy and Impoverished the Souls of Today's Students*. New York: Simon and Schuster, 1987.

Bloomfield, Leonard. "Why a Linguistic Society?" *Language* 1 (1925): 1–5.

——. "Linguistics as a Science." *Studies in Philology* 27 (1930): 553–57. Rpt. in *A Leonard Bloomfield Anthology*, abridged ed. edited by Charles F. Hockett, 149–52. Chicago: University of Chicago Press, 1987.

——. "Linguistics and Reading." *The Elementary English Review* 19 (1942): 125–30. Rpt. in *A Leonard Bloomfield Anthology*, abridged ed. edited by Charles F. Hockett, 255–66. Chicago: University of Chicago Press, 1987.

Booth, Wayne. "Foreword." In *Literature as Experience*, by Louise M. Rosenblatt, vii–xiv. 5th ed. New York: MLA, 1995.

——. "The Revival of Rhetoric." *PMLA* 80.2 (1965): 8–12.

Borchers, Gladys L., and Lillian R. Wagner. "Speech Education in Nineteenth-Century Schools." In *History of Speech Education in America: Background Studies*, edited by Karl R. Wallace, 277–300. New York: Appleton-Century-Crafts, 1954.

Borrowman, Merle L. *The Liberal and Technical in Teacher Education: A Historical Survey of American Thought*. New York: Teachers College, Columbia University, 1956.

Botein, Stephen. "The Legal Profession in Colonial North America." In *Lawyers in Early Modern Europe and America*, edited by Wilfrid Prest, 129–46. New York: Holmes and Meier, 1981.

——. "Printers and the American Revolution." In *The Press and the American Revolution*, edited by Bernard Bailyn and John B. Hench, 11–57. Worcester, Mass.: American Antiquarian Society, 1980.

Bourdieu, Pierre. *The Field of Cultural Production*. New York: Columbia University Press, 1993.

———. *Practical Reason: On the Theory of Action*. Cambridge: Polity Press, 1998.

Bousquet, Marc. *Tenured Bosses and Disposable Teachers: Writing Instruction in the Managed University*. Carbondale: Southern Illinois University Press, 2004.

Braddock, Richard, Richard Lloyd-Jones, and Lowell Schoer. *Research in Written Composition*. Champaign, Ill.: NCTE, 1963.

Brandt, Deborah. *Literacy as Involvement: The Acts of Writers, Readers, and Text*. Carbondale: Southern Illinois University Press, 1990.

Brandt, H. C. G. "How Far Should Our Teaching and Text-books Have a Scientific Basis." *PMLA* 1 (1884–85): 57–63.

Brattle, William. *Compendium Logicae Secumdum Principia D. Renati Cartesii Plerumque Efformatum, et Catechistice Propositum*. Boston: 1735.

Brereton, John C., ed. *The Origins of Composition Studies in the American College, 1875–1925: A Documentary History*. Pittsburgh: University of Pittsburgh Press, 1995.

Briggs, Le Baron Russell. *Girls and Education*. Boston: Houghton, 1911.

———. *Men, Women, and Colleges*. Boston: Houghton, 1925.

———. *Schools, Colleges and Character*. Boston: Houghton, 1901.

———. *To College Teachers of English Composition*. Boston: Houghton, 1928.

Brint, Steven G. *In an Age of Experts: The Changing Role of Professionals in Politics and Public Life*. Princeton, N.J.: Princeton University Press, 1994.

Britton, James N. "Writing to Learn and Learning to Write." In *Humanity of English*, NCTE Distinguished Lectures, 32–53. Urbana: NCTE, 1972.

———. *The Development of Writing Abilities (11–18)*. London: Macmillan, 1975.

Brockriede, Wayne. "Trends in the Study of Rhetoric: Toward a Blending of Criticism and Science." In *The Prospect of Rhetoric: Report of the National Developmental Project*, edited by Lloyd F. Bitzer, Edwin Black, and Karl Richards Wallace, 123–39. Englewood Cliffs, N.J.: Prentice Hall, 1971.

Broening, Angela M. *Conducting Experiences in English*. New York, London: D. Appleton Century, 1939.

Brooks, Cleanth, and Robert Penn Warren. *Modern Rhetoric*. New York: Harcourt Brace, 1958.

———. *Understanding Poetry: An Anthology for College Students*. New York: Henry Holt, 1938.

Brown, Danika M. "Hegemony and the Discourse of the Land Grant Movement: Historicizing as a Point of Departure." *JAC* 23.3 (2002): 319–50.

Brown, Katherine. "The Controversy over the Franchise in Puritan Massachusetts, 1954–1974." *The William and Mary Quarterly* 33.2 (April 1976): 212–41.

Brown, Richard D. *Knowledge Is Power: The Diffusion of Information in Early America, 1700–1865*. New York: Oxford University Press, 1989.

Brubacher, John Seiler, and Willis Rudy. *Higher Education in Transition: A History of American Colleges and Universities*. 4th ed. New Brunswick, N.J.: Transaction, 1997.

Bruce, Philip Alexander. *History of the University of Virginia, 1819–1919*. 5 vols. New York: Macmillan, 1920–22.

Bruner, Jerome S. *The Process of Education*. Cambridge: Harvard University Press, 1960.

Buck, Gertrude. "Recent Tendencies in Teaching English Composition." *Educational Review* 22 (1901): 371–82.

———. *The Social Criticism of Literature*. New Haven: Yale University Press, 1916.

Buel, Richard, Jr. "Freedom of the Press in Revolutionary America: The Evolution of Libertarianism, 1760–1820." In *The Press and the American Revolution*, edited by Bernard Bailyn and John B. Hench, 59–97. Worcester, Mass.: American Antiquarian Society, 1980.

Burke, Colin B. *American Collegiate Population: A Test of the Traditional View*. New York: New York University Press, 1982.

Burke, Kenneth. "Literature as Equipment for Living." In *The Philosophy of Literary Form: Studies in Symbolic Action*, 293–305. 1941. 3rd ed. Berkeley: University of California Press, 1974.

Burton, Dwight L. "English Education as a Scholarly Discipline." In *The Changing Role of English Education: Selected Addresses Delivered at the Second Conference on English Education*, edited by Stanley B. Kegler, 1–15. Champaign: NCTE, 1965.

Butterfield, Lyman H. *John Witherspoon Comes to America*. Princeton: Princeton University Press, 1953.

Buxton, Earl W. "Teaching Writing in Canada." In *A Common Purpose: The Teaching of English in Great Britain, Canada, and the United States: A Report of the International Conference on the Teaching of English*, edited by James R. Squire, 100–07. Urbana: NCTE, 1966.

Cain, William E. "English in America Reconsidered: Theory, Criticism, Marxism, and Social Change." In *Criticism in the University*, edited by Gerald Graff and Reginald Gibbons, 85–110. Evanston, Ill.: Northwestern University Press, 1985.

Calhoun, Craig. "'New Social Movements' of the Early Nineteenth Century." *Social Science History* 17.3 (Autumn 1993): 385–427.

Campbell, George. *The Philosophy of Rhetoric. 1776*. Rev. ed. Carbondale: Southern Illinois University Press, 1988.

Campbell, Jo Ann, ed. *Toward a Feminist Rhetoric: The Writing of Gertrude Buck*. Pittsburgh: University of Pittsburgh Press, 1996.

Campbell, Oscar James. *The Teaching of College English*. New York: Appleton-Century, 1934.

Cardinal Principles of Secondary Education: A Report of the Commission on the Reorganization of Secondary Education, Appointed by the National Education Association. Bulletin No. 35. Washington, D.C.: U.S. Government Printing Office, 1918.

Carnegie Foundation for the Advancement of Teaching. The Carnegie Classifications of Institutions of Higher Education. 2006. http://classifications.carnegiefoundation.org/descriptions/basic.php?key=791 (accessed June 3, 2010).

Carr, Jean Ferguson, Stephen L. Carr, and Lucille M. Schultz. *Archives of Instruction: Nineteenth-Century Rhetorics, Readers, and Composition Books in the United States*. Carbondale: Southern Illinois University Press, 2005.

Chamber, Stephen, and G. P. Mohrmann. "Rhetoric in Some American Periodicals, 1815–1850." *Speech Monographs* 37 (1970): 111–20.

Chandler, Frank W. "A Creative Approach to the Study of Literature." *English Journal* 4 (1915): 281.

Channing, Edward Tyrrel. *Lectures Read to the Seniors in Harvard College*. 1856. Edited by Charlotte Downey. Delmar, New York: Scholars' Facsimiles and Reprints, 1997.

————. "'Literary Independence' Address: Before the Phi Beta Kappa Society, Harvard University. August 27, 1818." *The Key Reporter* 26.3 (Spring 1961): 2–5.

Charters, Statutes and By Laws of the University of Pennsylvania. Philadelphia: NP, 1826.

Chauncy, Charles. *A Letter from a Gentleman in Boston, to Mr. George Wishart, One of the Ministers of Edinburgh, Concerning the State of Religion in New-England.* Edinburgh: 1742.

————. *Enthusiasm Described and Caution'd Against: A Sermon Preach'd at the Old Brick Meeting-House in Boston.* Boston: J. Draper, 1742.

Cheyney, Edward Potts. *History of the University of Pennsylvania, 1740–1940.* Philadelphia: University of Pennsylvania Press, 1940.

Chubb, Percival. "The Blight of Bookishness." *English Journal* 3.1 (January 1914): 15–27.

————. *The Teaching of English in the Elementary and Secondary School.* 1902. New York: Macmillan, 1927.

Clap, Thomas. *The Annals or History of Yale-college, in New Haven, in the Colony of Connecticut, from the First Founding Thereof, in the year 1700, to the year 1766.* New Haven: 1766.

————. *An Essay on the Nature and Foundation of Moral Virtue and Obligation; Being a Short Introduction to the Study of Ethics; for the Use of the Students of Yale College.* New Haven: 1765.

Clark, Gregory. "Timothy Dwight's Moral Rhetoric at Yale College, 1795–1817." *Rhetorica* 5 (1987): 149–62.

Clark, Harry Hayden. "American Literary History and American Literature." In *Reinterpretation of American Literature: Some Contributions Toward the Understanding of Its Historical Development,* edited by Norman Foerster, 181–217. New York: Harcourt, Brace, and Company, 1928.

Clark, Gregory, and S. Michael Halloran. "Transformations of Public Discourse in Nineteenth-Century America." Introduction to *Oratorical Culture in Nineteenth-Century America: Transformation in the Theory and Practice of Rhetoric,* edited by Gregory Clark and S. Michael Halloran, 1–26. Carbondale: Southern Illinois University Press, 1993.

Clarke, James Freeman. *The Western Messenger.* Louisville, Ky.: Western Unitarian Association, 1835–1841.

Cleveland, Charles D. *A Compendium of English Literature Chronologically Arranged.* Philadelphia: Biddle, 1848.

————. *English Literature of the 19th Century.* Philadelphia: Bancroft, 1869.

Clifford, John. "Transactional Teaching and the Literary Experience." *English Journal* 68.9 (1979): 36–39.

Cmiel, Kenneth. *Democratic Eloquence: The Fight for Popular Speech in Nineteenth Century America.* New York: Morrow, 1990.

Cody, Sherwin. *How to Write Fiction.* New York: Charles T. Dillingham & Co, 1894.

Cohen, A. M. *The Shaping of American Higher Education: Emergence and Growth of the Contemporary System.* San Francisco: Jossey-Bass, 1998.

Cohen, Sol, ed. *Education in the United States: A Documentary History.* 5 vols. New York: Random House, 1973.

Coley, W. B., and Richard Ohmann. Editorial. Special Issue, "Literacy and Basics," *College English* 38.5 (1977): 441–42.

College and High School Section. "The National Council of Teachers of English: Proceedings of the Third Annual Meeting." Chicago, 1913. *English Journal* 1.3 (January
1914): 38–60.

Collins, Varnum Lansing. *President Witherspoon: A Biography.* 2 vols. Princeton: Princeton University Press, 1925.

Connors, Robert J. *Composition-Rhetoric: Backgrounds, Theory, and Pedagogy.* Pittsburgh: University of Pittsburgh Press, 1997.

———. "The Rise and Fall of the Modes of Discourse." *College Composition and Communication* 32 (1981): 444–55.

———. "Textbooks and the Evolution of the Discipline." *College Composition and Communication* 37 (1986): 177–94.

Copeland, Charles Townsend, and H. M. Rideout. *Freshman English and Theme Correcting in Harvard College.* New York: Silver and Burdett, 1901.

"Corporation Records: Minutes of the Harvard Corporation, 1643–1870." Cambridge:
Harvard University Archives. MSS. UAI 5.30.2.

Court, Franklin E. *The Scottish Connection: The Rise of Literary Study in Early America.*
Syracuse, New York: Syracuse University Press, 2001.

Cowan, Elizabeth Wooten, ed. *Options for the Teaching of English: The Undergraduate
Curriculum.* New York: MLA, 1975.

Cowie, Alexander. *Educational Problems at Yale College in the Eighteenth Century.* New
Haven: Yale University Press, 1936.

Cox, John Harrington. "What Is the Best Preparation for the College Teacher of English?:
Training for Teaching and Training for Research." *English Journal* 2 (1913): 207–14.

Crane, Theodore Pawson, ed. *The Colleges and the Public, 1787–1862.* New York: Teachers
College, 1963.

Crawford, Robert. *The Scottish Invention of English Literature.* Cambridge: Cambridge
University Press, 1998.

Cremin, Lawrence Author. *The Transformation of the School: Progressivism in American
Education, 1876–1957.* New York: Knopf, 1961.

Cross, E. A., and Elizabeth Carney. *Teaching English in High Schools.* New York: Macmillan, 1939.

Cross, Ethan Allen. *The Short Story: A Technical and Literary Study.* Chicago: A. C. Mc-
Clurg & Co., 1914.

Crowley, Sharon. "Communication Skills and a Brief Rapprochement of Rhetoricians." *Rhetoric Society Quarterly* 34.1 (2004): 89–103.

———. *Composition in the University: Historical and Polemical Essays.* Pittsburgh: University of Pittsburgh Press, 1998.

———. "Linguistics and Composition Instruction: 1950–1980." *Written Communication* 6 (October 1989): 480–505.

———. *The Methodical Memory: Invention in Current-Traditional Rhetoric.* Carbondale:
Southern Illinois University Press, 1990.

Culler, Jonathan. "Problems in the 'History' of Contemporary Criticism." *Journal of
the Midwest Modern Language Association* 17.1 (Spring 1984): 3–15.

———. "Rethinking the Graduate Curriculum." Special issue, "The State of the Discipline, 1970s–1980s," *ADE Bulletin* 62 (September–November 1979): 19–26.

Cunliffe, John W. "College English Composition." *English Journal* 1 (1912): 591–600.

Curl, Mervin James. *Expository Writing*. Boston: Houghton, 1919.

Cutts, Richard. "The State of the Profession." *ADE Bulletin* 25 (May 1970): 45–46.

Daniel, R., L. Blasch, and P. Carter. "Resisting Corporatization of the University." In *Campus, Inc. Corporate Power in the Ivory Tower*, edited by G. D. White and F. C. Hawck, 61–84. New York: Prometheus, 2000.

Daniell, Beth. "Against the Great Leap Theory of Literacy." *PrelText* 7 (1986): 181–93.

Davidson, Cathy N. *Reading in America: Literature and Social History*. Baltimore: Johns Hopkins University Press, 1989.

Day, Henry Noble. *Grammatical Synthesis: The Art of English Composition*. 9th ed. New York: Scribner and Co., 1867.

———. *Rhetorical Praxis*. New York: American Book Company, 1861.

DeBoer, John J., Walter V. Kaulfers, and Helen Rand Miller. *Teaching Secondary English*. New York: McGraw-Hill, 1951.

DeCew, Judith Wagner. *Unionization in the Academy: Visions and Realities*. Lanham, Md.: Rowan & Littlefield, 2003.

DeLuca, Kevin. "Articulation Theory: A Discursive Grounding for Rhetorical Practice." *Philosophy and Rhetoric* 32.4 (1999): 334–48.

DeMille, George F. *Literary Criticism in America: A Preliminary Survey*. New York: L. MacVeagh, The Dial Press, 1931.

Derrida, Jacques. "Structure, Sign, and Play in the Discourse of the Human Sciences." In *The Structuralist Controversy: The Languages of Criticism and the Sciences of Man*, edited by Richard Macksey and Eugenio Donato, 247–64. Baltimore: Johns Hopkins University Press, 1972.

Dewey, John. *Art as Experience*. New York: Minton, Balch & Company, 1934.

———. *Democracy and Education: An Introduction to the Philosophy of Education*. New York: Macmillan, 1916.

———. *Experience and Education*. 1938. New York: Collier, 1963.

———. *Later Works, 1925–1953*. 17 vols. Carbondale: Southern Illinois University Press, 1981–1990.

———. "Pedagogy as a University Discipline." In *The Early Works of John Dewey, 1882–1898*, vol. 5, 1896, edited by Jo Ann Boydston, 281–89. Carbondale: Southern Illinois University Press, 1969.

———. *The Public and Its Problems*. Chicago: Swallow Press, 1954.

———. "Science and Education." *Scientific Monthly* 52.1 (January 1941): 55.

Dexter, Franklin Bowditch. *Documentary History of Yale University, 1701–1745*. 1916. New York: Arno, 1969.

Dickinson, John. *Letters from a Farmer to the Inhabitants of the British Colonies in Pennsylvania*. Philadelphia: 1768.

Dixon, John. *Growth through English*. 3rd ed. 1967. London: Oxford University Press for the NCTE and MLA, 1975.

Dodsley, Robert. *The Preceptor; Containing a General Course of Education. Wherein the first principles of polite learning are laid down in a way most suitable for trying the genius, and advancing the instruction of youth*. 2 vols. London: R. and J. Dodsley, 1748.

Douglas, Wallace. "Accidental Institution: On the Origin of Modern Language Study." In *Criticism in the University*, edited by Gerald Graff and Reginald Gibbons, 55–61. Evanston, Ill.: Northwestern University Press, 1985.

———. "Power and Responsibility: English Departments and the Preparation of Teachers." *ADE Bulletin* 20 (January 1969): 3–15.

Doyle, Henry Grattan. "Some Fundamental Problems for the Modern Languages and Literatures (A Preliminary Statement for the Commission on Trends in Education)." *PMLA* 54.5 (1939): 1346–55.

Dugard, William. *Rhetorices Elementa Quaestionibus et Responsionibus Explicate.* London: 1656.

Duncan, William. *The Elements of Logick.* Edinburgh:1780.

Dunlop, John. *History of Fiction.* London: Longman, Brown, Green & Longman, 1845.

Dunn, Thomas F. "The Drake University Program in Communication." *Communication in General Education,* edited by Earl James McGrath, 89–102. Dubuque, Iowa: Brown, 1949.

Duyckinck, Evert, and George L. Duyckinck. *Cyclopedia of American Literature: Embracing Personal and Cultural Notices of Authors and Selections from Their Writings from the Earliest Period to the Present Day.* 2 vols. New York: Scribner, 1866.

Eagleton, Terry. *Literary Theory: An Introduction.* Minneapolis: University of Minnesota Press, 1983.

Easton, Morton W. "The Rhetorical Tendency in Undergraduate Courses." *PMLA* 4 (1888–89): 19–23.

"Editorial: Training and Mistraining." *English Journal* 2.7 (September 1913): 456–58.

Edman, Marion. "Suggested Methods for Realizing Our Common Goals." In *A Common Purpose: The Teaching of English in Great Britain, Canada, and the United States: A Report of the International Conference on the Teaching of English,* edited by James R. Squire, 17–23. Urbana: NCTE, 1966.

Edwards, Jonathan. *Sinners in the Hands of an Angry God.* Salem: 1786.

Ehrenreich, Barbara, and John Ehrenreich. "The Professional-Managerial Class." In *Between Labor and Capital,* edited by Pat Walker, 5–48. Boston: South End, 1978.

Eldred, Janet Carey, and Peter Mortensen. *Imagining Rhetoric: Composing Women of the Early United States.* Pittsburgh: University of Pittsburgh Press, 2002.

Emerson, Ralph Waldo. "Eloquence." In *Letters and Social Aims.* Vol. 8 of *The Complete Works of Ralph Waldo Emerson.* Boston: Osgood, 1876.

Emery, Edwin. *The Press and America: An Interpretive History of the Mass Media.* Englewood Cliffs, N.J.: Prentice Hall, 1972.

Emig, Janet. *The Composing Process of Twelfth Graders.* Urbana, Ill.: NCTE, 1971.

Ennals, Thomas. "On Ancient Eloquence." *Account of the Commencement in the College of Philadelphia, May 17, 1775.* Philadelphia: 1775.

Esenwein, Joseph Berg. *Writing the Short Story.* New York: Noble and Noble, 1918.

Everett, Edward. *Orations and Speeches on Various Occasions.* Boston: Little, Brown and Company, 1870.

Faigley, Lester. *Fragments of Rationality.* Pittsburgh: University of Pittsburgh Press, 1992.

Faigley, Lester, and Thomas Miller. "What We Learn from Writing on the Job." *College English* 44 (1982): 557–69.

Fairchild, A. H. R. "The Sequence of Courses for College and University Students Who Chose English as a Major Subject." *English Journal* 12 (1923): 153–63.

Fairchild, Edward Henry. *Historical Sketch of Oberlin College.* Springfield: Republic, 1868.

Fairchild, James H. *Oberlin the Colony and the College, 1833–1883.* Oberlin, Ohio: Goodrich, 1883.

Farnaby, Thomas. *Index Rhetoricus et Oratorius, Scholis, & Institutioni Tenerioris Aetatis Accommodatus.* London: 1672.

Febvre, Lucien, and Henri-Jean Martin. *The Coming of the Book: The Impact of Printing 1450–1800.* Translated by Davide Gerard Martin, and edited by Geoffrey Nowell-Smith and David Wooten. London: NLB, 1976.

Fiedler, Leslie. "On Remembering Freshman Comp." *CCC* (1962): 1–4.

———. *What Was Literature?: Class Culture and Mass Society.* New York: Simon and Schuster, 1982.

Fiering, Norman. *Moral Philosophy at Seventeenth-Century Harvard: A Discipline in Transition.* Chapel Hill: University of North Carolina Press, 1981.

———. "Moral Philosophy in America, 1650–1750, and Its British Context." PhD diss., Columbia University, 1969.

———. "President Samuel Johnson and the Circle of Knowledge." *William and Mary Quarterly* 28 (1971): 199–236.

Fish, Stanley. *Is There a Text in this Class?: The Authority of Interpretive Communities.* Cambridge, Mass.: Harvard University Press, 1980.

———. "Profession Despise Thyself: Fear and Self-Loathing in Literary Studies." *Critical Inquiry* 10.2 (December 1982): 349–64.

Fisher, Ann. *The Pleasing Instructor.* Boston: 1756.

Fisher, John H. "The King's English in a Working Man's World." *ADE Bulletin* 26 (September 1970): 17.

Fitzgerald, Kathryn R. "From Disciplining to Discipline: A Foucauldian Examination of the Formation of English as a School Subject." *Journal of Advanced Composition* 16 (1996): 435–53.

Fletcher, Robert Samuel. *A History of Oberlin College from Its Foundation through the Civil War.* 2 vols. Oberlin, Ohio: Oberlin College, 1943.

Flexner, Abraham. *Universities: American, English, German.* New York: Oxford University Press, 1930.

Fordyce, David. *Dialogues Concerning Education.* London: 1745.

———. *The Elements of Moral Philosophy.* In *The Preceptor; Containing a General Course of Education. Wherein the first principles of polite learning are laid down in a way most suitable for trying the genius, and advancing the instruction of youth.* 6th ed. 2 vols. London: 1765.

Franklin, Benjamin. *Autobiography.* Edited by J. A. Leo LeMay and P. M. Zall. New York: Norton, 1986.

———. *The Complete Works of Benjamin Franklin.* Edited by John Bigelow. 10 vols. New York: Putnam: 1888.

———. *Observations, Relative to the Intentions of the Origins and Founders of the Academy in Philadelphia.* 1789. Rpt. in *The Complete Works of Benjamin Franklin,* vol. 10, edited by John Bigelow, 86–115. New York: Putnam, 1888.

———. "Proposals Relating to the Education of Youth in Pennsylvania." 1749. Rpt. in *A History of the University of Pennsylvania from Its Foundation to A. D. 1770,* edited by Thomas Harrison Montgomery, 495–500. Philadelphia: Jacobs, 1900.

———. *Sketch of an English School for the Consideration of the Trustees of the Philadelphia Academy.* 1779. Rpt. in *The Complete Works of Benjamin Franklin,* vol. 6, edited by John Bigelow, 244–52. New York: Putnam, 1888.

Franklin, Phyllis, David Lawrence, and Elizabeth B. Welles. Preface. *Preparing a Nation's Teachers: Models for English and Foreign Language Programs,* edited by Phyllis Franklin, David Lawrence, and Elizabeth B. Welles, ix–xiv. New York: MLA, 1999.

Franklin, Phyllis, David Lawrence, and Elizabeth B. Welles, eds. *Preparing a Nation's Teachers: Models for English and Foreign Language Programs*. New York: MLA, 1999.

Freedman, Marcus. *Chaos in Our Colleges*. New York: David McKay, 1963.

Friend, Christy. "The Excluded Conflict: The Marginalization of Composition and Rhetoric Studies in Graff's Professing Literature." *College English* 54.3 (March 1992): 276–86.

Friere, Paulo. *Pedagogy of the Oppressed*. Translated by Myra Bergman Ramos. New York: Continuum, 1970.

Fries, Charles C. "Advances in Linguistics." *College English* 23 (1961): 37.

———. *The Teaching of the English Language*. New York: Thomas Nelson, 1927.

Frost, John. *Easy Exercises in Composition*. Philadelphia: Butler, 1843.

Fruit, John P. "A Plea for the Study of Literature from the Aesthetic Standpoint." *PMLA* 6.1 (1891): 29–40.

Fuller, Margaret Ossoli. "American Literature: Its Position in the Present Time, and Prosperity for the Future." 1846. Rpt. in *American Literary Criticism*, edited by William Morton Payne, 137–57. New York: Longman, 1904.

———. *Woman in the 19th Century*. New York: Greeley and McElrath, 1845.

Fulton, Maurice Garland. *Expository Writing: Materials for a College Course in Exposition by Analysis and Imitation*. New York: Macmillan, 1912.

Gabin, Rosalind J. "Entitling Kenneth Burke." *Rhetoric Review* 5.2 (Spring 1987): 196–210.

Gallagher, Chris W. *Radical Departures: Composition and Progressive Pedagogy*. Urbana: NCTE, 2002.

Garcia, Juliet V., et al. *Access Denied: Restoring the Nation's Commitment to Equal Educational Opportunity*. Washington, D.C.: Advisory Committee on Financial Assistance, 2001.

Garnett, James M. "The Course in English and Its Value as a Discipline." *PMLA* 2 (1886): 61–73.

Gayley, Charles Mills, and C. B. Bradley. *Suggestions to Teachers of English in the Secondary Schools*. Berkeley: University of California Press, 1894.

Gee, James Paul. Introduction. Special Issue, "Literacy, Discourse, and Linguistics: Essays by James Paul Gee," *Journal of Education* 171.1 (1989): 5–17.

———. "What Is Literacy?" Special Issue, "Literacy, Discourse, and Linguistics: Essays by James Paul Gee," *Journal of Education* 171.1 (1989): 18–25.

Geertz, Clifford. *Local Knowledge: Further Essays in Interpretive Anthropology*. New York: Basic Books, 1983.

Genung, John Franklin. *The Study of Rhetoric in the College Course*. Boston: D. C. Heath, 1892.

Gerber, John. "Suggestions for a Commonsense Reform of the English Curriculum." *College Composition and Communication* 28.4 (December 1977): 312–16.

Gere, Anne Ruggles. "Kitchen Table and Rented Rooms: The Extracurriculum of Composition." *CCC* 45.1 (February 1994): 75–92.

Glicksberg, Charles I. *American Literary Criticism, 1900–1950*. New York: Hendricks House, 1951.

Godzich, Wlad. *The Culture of Literacy*. Cambridge, Mass.: Harvard University Press, 1994.

Goggin, Maureen Daly. *Authoring a Discipline: Scholarly Journals and the Post–World War II Emergence of Rhetoric and Composition*. Mahwah, N.J.: Lawrence Erlbaum Associates, 2000.

Goodheart, Eugene. *Does Literary Studies Have a Future?* Madison: University of Wisconsin Press, 1999.

Goodrich, Chauncy. *Select British Eloquence: Embracing the Best Speeches Entire of the Most Eminent Orators of Great Britain for the Last Two Centuries*. 1852. Indianapolis: Bobbs-Merrill, 1963.

Goodrich, Samuel G. *Literature, Ancient and Modern, with Specimens*. Boston: Bradbury, Soden, & Co., 1845.

Gomez, Mary Louise. "The National Writing Project: Staff Development in the Teaching of Composition." In *On Literacy and Its Teaching: Issues in English Education*, edited by Gail E. Hawisher and Anna O. Soter, 68–83. Albany: State University of New York Press, 1990.

Graff, Gerald. "Academic Writing and the Uses of Bad Publicity." In *Eloquent Obsessions: Writing Cultural Criticism*, edited by Marianna Torgovnick, 208–20. Durham: Duke University Press, 1994.

———. *Clueless in Academe: How Schooling Obscures the Life of the Mind*. New Haven: Yale University Press, 2003.

———. "Preaching to the Converted." In *English Inside and Out: The Places of Literary Criticism*, edited by Susan Gubar and Jonathan Kumholtz, 109–21. New York: Routledge, 1993.

———. *Professing Literature: An Institutional History*. 20th Anniversary Edition. Chicago: University of Chicago Press, 2007.

———. "'Who Killed Criticism?' in Retrospect." In *The New Criticism and Contemporary Literary Theory*, edited by William J. Spurlin and Michael Fischer, 125–29. New York: Garland, 1995.

Graff, Gerald, and Michael Warner, eds. *The Origins of Literary Studies in America: A Documentary Anthology*. New York: Routledge, 1989.

Graff, Harvey J. *The Legacies of Literacy: Continuities and Contradictions in Western Culture and Society*. Bloomington: Indiana University Press, 1987.

Graham, Patricia A. *Progressive Education: From Arcady to Academe*. New York: Teachers College Press, 1967.

Gramsci, Antonio. *Selections from the Prison Notebooks*. Edited and trans. by Quentin Hoare and Geoffrey Nowell-Smith. London: 1971.

Gray, Donald. "Introduction: What Happens Next? And How? And Why?" In *Preparing a Nation's Teachers: Models for English and Foreign Language Programs*, edited by Phyllis Franklin, David Lawrence, and Elizabeth B. Welles, 1–11. New York: MLA, 1999.

Gray, Giles Wilkeson. "Some Teachers and the Transition to Twentieth-Century Speech Education." In *History of Speech Education in America: Background Studies*, edited by Karl R. Wallace, 422–46. New York: Appleton-Century-Crafts, 1954.

Grey, Lennox. "'No Signs, No Symbols! Use *A-B-C*s' A Problem of Practical Definition." In *Communication in General Education*, edited by Earl James McGrath, 1–17. Dubuque, Iowa: Brown, 1949.

Greenough, Chester Noyes. "An Experiment in the Training of Teachers of Composition for Work with College Freshmen." *English Journal* 2 (1913): 109–21.

———. "The New Plan of Admission in English to Harvard College." *English Journal* 1 (1912): 364–74.

Greenough, Chester Noyes, and Frank W. C. Hersey. *English Composition.* New York: Macmillan, 1917.

Griffin, Edward M. Introduction. *A General Idea of the College of Mirania,* v–xv. New York: Johnson Reprint, 1969.

Griswold, Wendy, Terry McDonnell, and Nathan Wright. "Reading and the Reading Class in the Twenty-First Century." *Annual Review of Sociology* 31(2005): 127–41.

Grommon, Alfred, ed. *The Education of Teachers of English for American Schools and Colleges.* New York: Appleton-Century-Crofts, 1963.

Grubb, F. W. "Growth of Literacy in Colonial America: Longitudinal Patterns, Economic Models, and the Direction of Future Research." *Social Science History* 14.4 (Winter 1990): 451–82.

Guder, Darrell L. "The Story of Belles Lettres at Princeton: An Historical Investigation of the Expansion and Secularization of Curriculum at the College of New Jersey with Special Reference to the Curriculum of English Language and Letters." PhD diss., University of Hamburg, 1964.

Guillory, John. *Cultural Capital: The Problem of Literary Canon Formation.* Chicago: University of Chicago, Press, 1993.

Guillory, John, and David Laurence. "The History of the Job Crisis in Modern Languages." Modern Language Association, December 1997. http://www.mla.org/resources/documents/rep_employment/prof_employment/prof_employment6 (accessed April 12, 2010).

Guthrie, Warren. "The Development of Rhetorical Theory in America: The Dominance of the Rhetoric of Style, 1635–1730." *Speech Monographs* 13 (1946): 14–32.

———. "The Development of Rhetorical Theory in America, 1635–1850: II." *Speech Monographs* 14 (1947): 38–54.

———. "The Development of Rhetorical Theory in America: Domination of the English Rhetorics." *Speech Monographs* 15 (1948): 61–71.

———. "The Development of Rhetorical Theory in America 1635–1850: V, The Elocution Movement—English." *Speech Monographs* 18 (1951): 17–30.

———. *The Development of Rhetorical Theory in America, 1635–1850.* Evanston, Ill.: Northwestern University Press, 1940.

———. "Rhetorical Theory in Colonial America." In *History of Speech Education in America: Background Studies,* edited by Karl R. Wallace, 48–59. New York: Appleton-Century-Crafts, 1954.

Habermas, Jurgen. *The Structural Transformation of the Public Sphere: An Inquiry into a Category of Bourgeois Society.* Cambridge, Mass.: MIT Press, 1989.

Hall, David. "The Politics of Writing and Reading in Eighteenth-Century America." In *Cultures of Print: Essays in the History of the Book,* 151–69. Amherst: University of Massachusetts Press, 1996.

———. "The Uses of Literacy in New England, 1600–1850." In *Printing and Society in Early America,* edited by William Joyce, David D. Hall, Richard D. Brown, and John B. Hench, 1–47. Worcester, Mass.: American Antiquarian Society, 1983.

Hall, Donald E. "Professional Life (and Death) under a Four-Four Teaching Load." In *Profession 1999,* 193–203. New York: MLA, 1999.

Hall, G. Stanley. "On the History of American College Textbooks and Teaching in Logic, Ethics, Psychology, and Allied Subjects." *Proceedings of the American Antiquarian Society* 9 (1894): 137–74.

Hall, Stuart. "On Postmodernism and Articulation: An Interview with Stuart Hall." *Journal of Communication Inquiry* 10 (1986): 45–60.

———. "The Emergence of Cultural Studies and the Crisis of the Humanities." Special Issue, "Humanities as Social Technology," *October* 53 (Summer 1990): 11–23.

Hamilton, Clayton Meeker. *Materials and Methods of English*. New York: Baker and Taylor & Co., 1908.

Hamowy, Ronald. "Jefferson and the Scottish Enlightenment: A Critique of Gary Will's *Inventing America: Jefferson's Declaration of Independence*." *William and Mary Quarterly* 36 (1979): 503–23.

Hancock, John. *The Danger of an Unqualified Ministry*. Boston: 1743.

Harmon, Sandra D. "'The Voice, Pen, and Influence of Our Women Are Abroad in the Land': Women and the Illinois State Normal University, 1857–1899." In *Nineteenth Century Women Learn to Write*, edited by Catherine Hobbs, 84–102. Charlottesville: University Press of Virginia, 1995.

Harris, Joseph. "After Dartmouth: Growth and Conflict in English." *College English* 53.6 (October 1991): 631–46.

———. *A Teaching Subject: Composition Since 1966*. Upper Saddle River, N.J.: Prentice Hall, 1997.

Hart, James Morgan. "The College Course in English Literature: How It May Be Improved." *PMLA* 1 (1884–85): 84–95. Rpt. in *The Origins of Literary Studies in America: A Documentary Anthology*, edited by Gerald Graff and Michael Warner, 34–38. New York: Routledge, 1989.

———. *German Universities: A Narrative of Personal Experience*. New York: 1874.

Hart, John. *A Class Book of Poetry*. Philadelphia: Butler, 1857.

Hartman, Geoffrey. "Structuralism: The Anglo-American Adventure." *Yale French Studies* 36/37 (1966): 148–68.

Hartman, Gertrude, Ann Shumaker, and Progressive Education Association (U.S.). *Creative Expression: The Development of Children in Art, Music, Literature, and Dramatics*. New York: John Day Co., 1932.

Hatfield, Walter W. *An Experience Curriculum in English*. New York: Appleton-Century Company, 1935.

Havemann, Ernest, and Patricia S. West. *They Went to College: The College Graduate in America Today*. New York: Harcourt, Brace, 1952.

Hays, Edna. *College Entrance Requirements in English: Their Effects on the High School, An Historical Survey*. New York: Teachers College, 1936.

Heath, Shirley Brice. *Ways with Words: Language, Life, and Work in Communities and Classrooms*. New York: Cambridge University Press, 1983.

Henretta, James A. *The Evolution of American Society, 1700–1815: An Interdisciplinary Analysis*. Boston: D.C. Heath, 1973.

Henry, George H. "Is English on the Way Out?" *English Journal* 31.4 (October 1945): 284–93.

Herbst, Jurgen. *And Sadly Teach: Teacher Education and Professionalization in American Culture*. Madison: University of Wisconsin Press, 1989.

————. *From Crisis to Crisis: American College Government, 1636–1819.* Cambridge, Mass.: Harvard University Press, 1982.

Herman, Peter C. *Day Late, Dollar Short: The Next Generation and the New Academy.* Albany: State University of New York Press, 2000.

Hesse, Carla. "Books in Time." In *The Future of the Book,* edited by Geoffrey Nunberg, 21–36. Berkeley: University of California Press, 1996.

Heyda, John. "Fighting over Freshman English: CCCC's Early Years and the Turf Wars of the 1950s." *College Composition and Communication* 50.4 (June 1999): 663–81.

Hiner, N. Ray. "The Cry of Sodom Enquired Into: Educational Analysis in Seventeenth-Century New England." In *The Social History of American Education,* edited by B. Edward McClellan and William J. Reese, 3–22. Champaign: University of Illinois Press, 1988.

Hirsch, E. D. *Cultural Literacy: What Every American Needs to Know.* Boston: Houghton Mifflin, 1987.

Hochmuth, Marie, and Richard Murphy. "Rhetorical and Elocutionary Training in Nineteenth-Century Colleges." In *History of Speech Education in America: Background Studies,* edited by Karl R. Wallace, 153–77. New York: Appleton-Century-Crafts, 1954.

Hofstadter, Richard. *America at 1750: A Social Portrait.* 2nd ed. New York: Vintage, 1973.

————. *The American Political Tradition and the Men Who Made It.* New York: Knopf, 1948.

Hofstadter, Richard, and Wilson Smith, eds. *American Higher Education: A Documentary History.* 2 vols. Chicago: University of Chicago Press, 1961.

Hogan, Robert F. "The Future of the Profession." *ADE Bulletin* 22 (September 1969): 43–48.

Hoggart, Richard. *Uses of Literacy: Aspects of Working-Class Life with Special References to Publications and Entertainment.* London: Chatto and Windus, 1957.

Hollingsworth, Allan M. "Beyond Survival." In *Profession 1977,* 7–11. New York: MLA, 1977.

Hollis, Karyn L. *Liberating Voices: Writing at the Bryn Mawr Summer School for Women Workers.* Carbondale: Southern Illinois University Press, 2004.

Holt, Mara. "Dewey and the 'Cult of Efficiency': Competing Ideologies in Collaborative Pedagogies of the 1920s." *Journal of Advanced Composition* 14 (1994): 73–92.

Hook, J. N. *The Teaching of High School English.* 3rd ed. New York: Ronald Press, 1965.

————. "Teaching Oral and Written English in the United States." In *A Common Purpose: The Teaching of English in Great Britain, Canada, and the United States: A Report of the International Conference on the Teaching of English,* edited by James R. Squire, 95–99. Urbana: NCTE, 1966.

————. *Writing Creatively.* Boston: Heath, 1963.

Hopkins, Edwin M. "Can Good Composition Teaching Be Done Under Present Conditions?" *English Journal* 1.1 (February 1912): 1–8.

————. *The Labor and Cost of the Teaching of English in Colleges and Secondary Schools with Especial Reference to English Composition.* Chicago: NCTE, 1923.

Horner, Bruce. *Terms of Work for Composition: A Materialist Critique.* Albany: State University of New York Press, 2000.

Hosic, James F. "The Influence of the Uniform Entrance Requirements in English, A Brief Chapter of Educational History, Together with a Summary of the Facts So Far

Obtained by a Committee of the National Education Association and a List of References." In *English Problems*. 1912. *English Journal* 1 (1912): 95–121.

Howell, Wilbur Samuel. *Eighteenth-Century British Logic and Rhetoric*. Princeton: Princeton University Press, 1971.

———. "The Declaration of Independence and Eighteenth-Century Logic." *William and Mary Quarterly* 18 (1961): 463–84.

Huber, Bettina J. "The Changing Job Market." In *Profession 92*, 59–73. New York: MLA, 1992.

———. "Undergraduate English Programs: Findings from an MLA Survey of the 1992–93 Academic Year." *ADE Bulletin* 115 (Winter 1996): 34–73.

———. "A Report on the 1986 Survey of English Doctoral Programs in Writing and Literature." *The Future of Doctoral Studies in English*, edited by Andrea Lunsford, Hilene Hoglen, and James F. Slevin, 121–75. New York: MLA, 1989.

Huber, Bettina J., and Art Young. "Report on the 1983–84 Survey of the English Sample." *ADE Bulletin* 84 (Fall 1986): 40–61.

Huber, Bettina J., and David Laurence. "Report on the 1984–85 Survey of the English Sample: General Education Requirements in English and the English Major." *ADE Bulletin* 93 (Fall 1989): 30–43.

Huber, Bettina J., Denise Pinney, and David Laurence. "Patterns of Faculty Hiring in Four-Year English Programs: Findings from a 1987–88 Survey of Job Information List Advertisers. *ADE Bulletin* 99 (Fall 1991): 39–48.

Hughes, Hellen Sord. "The Prescribed Work in College English: Its Relation to the Secondary Schools." *English Journal* 11 (1922): 199–213.

Humphrey, David C. "Colonial Colleges and English Dissenting Academies: A Study in Transatlantic Culture." *History of Education Quarterly* 12 (1972): 184–97.

———. *From King's College to Columbia, 1746–1800*. New York: Columbia University Press, 1976.

Hunt, Isaac. *An Humble Attempt at Scurrility: in Imitation of Those Great Masters of the Art, the Rev. Dr. S——th; the Rev. Dr. Al——n; the Rev. Dr. Ew——en; the Irreverend D. J. D——ve; and the heroic J——n D——n, Esq.; Being an Answer to the Observations on Mr. H——'s Advertisement By Jack Retort, Students in Scurrility, Quilsylvania*. Philadelphia: Anthony Armbruster, 1765.

———. *The Substance of an Exercise, Had This Morning in Scurrility-Hall*. Leaflets I–VIII. Philadelphia: 1765.

Hunt, Theodore W. "The Place of English in the College Curriculum." *PMLA* 1 (1884–85): 118–32. Rpt. in *The Origins of Literary Studies in America: A Documentary Anthology*, edited by Gerald Graff and Michael Warner, 138–49. New York: Routledge, 1989.

Hunter, Paul. "Facing the Eighties." *ADE Bulletin* 62 (September 1979): 1–9.

Hutcheson, Francis. *An Inquiry into the Original of Our Ideas of Beauty and Virtue*. 3rd ed. London: NP, 1729.

———. *Short Introduction to Moral Philosophy in Three Books Containing the Elements of Ethics and the Law of Nature*. Glasgow: Robert Foulis, 1747.

———. *System of Moral Philosophy; To Which Is Prefixed Some Account of the Life, Writings, and Character of the Author by William Reichman*. London: A Millar, 1755.

Huxford, Gary. "The English Libertarian Tradition in the Colonial Newspaper." *Journalism Quarterly* 45 (1968): 677–86.

Hyman, Stanley Edgar. *The Armed Vision; A Study in the Methods of Modern Literary Criticism.* New York: A. A. Knopf, 1948.

Hymes, Dell. "De-Centering Linguistics." *Theory and Society* 7.3 (May 1979): 307–18.

Hymes, Dell H., and John G. Fought. *American Structuralism.* New York: Mouton, 1981.

Jacobs, Ida T., and John DeBoer, eds. *Educating for Peace; a Report of the Committee on International Relations of the NCTE.* New York: D. Appleton-Century Co, 1940.

James, William. "The PhD Octopus." *Harvard Monthly* 36 (1903): 1–9.

Jamieson, Alexander. *A Grammar of Rhetoric and Polite Literature: Comprehending the Principles of Language and Style,—the Elements of Taste and Criticism; with Rules, for the Study of Composition and Eloquence: Illustrated by Appropriate Examples, Selected Chiefly from the British Classics. For the Use of Schools, or Private Instruction.* 4th ed. New Haven: Maltby, 1826.

Jefferson, Thomas. *Autobiography.* New York: Capricorn, 1959.

Jewett, Ida A. *English in State Teachers Colleges, A Catalogue Study.* New York: Teachers College Press, 1927.

Johnson, Allen, et al., eds. *Dictionary of American Biography.* 20 vols. New York: Scribner's Sons, 1928–36.

Johnson, Loaz W. *The Administrative Function of English in the University of California. The Evolution of the Examination in Subject A.* Berkeley: University of California Press, 1941.

Johnson, Richard. "What Is Cultural Studies Anyway?" *Social Text* 16 (1986–87): 38–80.

Johnson, Samuel. "Autobiography." In *Samuel Johnson, President of King's College: His Career and Writings,* edited by Herbert Schneider and Carol Schneider, 1:8. New York: Columbia University Press, 1929.

———. *Elementa Philosophica: Containing Chiefly, Noetica; or Things Relating to the Mind or Understanding: and Ethica, or Things Relating to the Moral Behavior.* Philadelphia: Franklin and Hall, 1752.

———. *Samuel Johnson, President of King's College: His Career and Writings,* edited by Herbert Schneider and Carol Schneider. 4 vols. New York: Columbia University Press, 1929.

Jones, Samuel. "Samuel Jones, His Book of Practical Philosophy; viz. Ethics and the Law of Nature: Begun July 7th. Anno Dom. 1760, at the College of Philadelphia, under the Direction and Tuition of the Revrd. Mr. Francis Alison, D.D." Van Pelt Library, University of Pennsylvania, MSS 378.748 PS.14.

Joos, Martin. Preface. *Readings in Linguistics I: The Development of Descriptive Linguistics in America, 1925–56.* 4th ed. Chicago: Chicago University Press, 1966.

Josephs, Lois, and Erwin Steinberg. *English Education Today.* New York: Noble and Noble, 1970.

Journet, Debra. "Redefining the Mission of the English Department at the University of Louisville: Two Years Later." *ADE Bulletin* 128 (Spring 2001): 44–47.

Kaestle, Carl F., et al. *Literacy in the United States: Readers and Reading since 1880.* New Haven: Yale University Press, 1991.

Karen, David. "Changes in Access to Higher Education." *Sociology of Education* 75 (July 2002): 191–210.

Kates, Susan. *Activist Rhetorics and American Higher Education, 1885–1937.* Carbondale: Southern Illinois University Press, 2001.

Kelley, Brooks Mather. *Yale, A History.* New Haven: Yale University Press, 1974.

Kelley, Mary. "Reading Women/Women Reading: The Making of Learned Women in Antebellum America." *Journal of American History* 83.2 (September 1996): 401–24.

Kellogg, Robert. "The Boom Years: Graduate Education in English 1955–1968." *ADE Bulletin* 53 (May 1977): 23–26.

Kelly, George. "A Study of Teaching Conditions in Freshman Composition in 1954." *College Composition and Communication* 7 (1956): 75–78.

Kent, George E. "Self-Conscious Writers and Black Tradition." In *Humanity of English*, NCTE Distinguished Lectures, 32–53. Urbana: NCTE, 1972.

Kerber, Linda K. "Daughters of Columbia: Educating Women for the Republic, 1787–1805." In *Our American Sisters*, edited by Jean E. Freedman and William G. Shade, 137–53. Lexington, Mass.: Heath, 1982.

———. *Federalists in Dissent: Imagery and Ideology in Jeffersonian America*. Ithaca, N.Y.: Cornell University Press, 1970.

Kerr, Clark. *The Great Transformation in Higher Education, 1960–1980*. Albany: State University of New York Press, 1991.

———. *The Uses of the University*. 1963. 5th ed. Cambridge, Mass.: Harvard University Press, 2001.

Kernan, Alvin. "Plausible and Helpful Things to Say about Literature in a Time When All Print Institutions Are Breaking Down." In *English Inside and Out: The Places of Literary Criticism*, edited by Susan Gubar and Jonathan Kamholtz, 9–28. New York: Routledge, 1993.

Kilpatrick, William Heard. *The Project Method*. New York: Teachers College, Columbia University, 1922.

Kimme Hea, Amy C. "Rearticulating E-dentities of Power and the World Wide Web." *Computers and Composition* 19 (2002): 331–46.

Kinnaird, John. "What's Happening to the English Curriculum: A Survey and Some Reflections." *College English* 34.6 (March 1973): 755–72.

Kinney, Thomas, and Thomas P. Miller. "Civic Humanism, A Postmortem?" In *The Viability of the Rhetorical Tradition*, edited by Richard Graff, Arthur Walzer, and Janet M. Atwill, 141–57. Albany: State University of New York Press, 2004.

Kitzhaber, Albert Raymond. "The Government and English Teaching: A Retrospective View." *College Composition and Communication* 18 (October 1967): 228–33.

———. "A Rage for Disorder." *English Journal* 61.8 (November 1972): 1199–1200, 1209–19.

Kline, Charles R., Roland Huff, and James L. Kinneavy. "Considerations in Program Design, Training the Two-Year College Teacher." *ADE Bulletin* 48 (February 1976): 45–47.

Knox, Samuel. *An Essay on the Best System of Liberal Education, Adapted to the Genius of the Government of the United States. Comprehending Also, An Uniform, General Plan for Instituting and Conducting Public Schools, in this Country, on Principles of the Most Extensive Utility*. Baltimore: Warner and Hanna, 1799.

Kolodny, Annette. *The Land before Her: Fantasy and Experience of the American Frontiers, 1630–1860*. Chapel Hill: University of North Carolina Press, 1984.

Kremers, Marshall. "Samuel Newman and the Reduction of Rhetoric in the Early Nineteenth-Century American College." *Rhetoric Society Quarterly* 13 (1983): 185–92.

Kuklick, Bruce. *A History of Philosophy in America, 1720–2000*. New York: Oxford University Press, 2001.

Krug, Edward A. *Shaping of the American High School, 1880–1920*. Madison: University of Wisconsin Press, 1969.

Lamy, Bernard. *The Art of Speaking*. London: 1676.

Landsman, Ned C. *Scotland and Its First American Colony, 1683–1765*. Princeton: Princeton University Press, 1985.

Lane, William C. "A Manuscript Volume Recently Acquired by Harvard College." *Publications of the Colonial Society of Massachusetts* 12 (1908–09): 220–31.

Lanham, Richard A. "The Implications of Electronic Information for the Sociology of Knowledge." *Leonardo* 27.2 (1994): 155–63.

———. "The Rhetorical Paideia: The Curriculum as a Work of Art." *College English* 48.2 (February 1986): 132–41.

Larson, Magali Sarfatti. *The Rise of Professionalism*. Berkeley: University of California Press, 1977.

Lathrop, H. B. "Entrance Examinations in English at Stanford." *Educational Review* 23 (1893): 289–95.

Laurence, David. "Notes on the English Major." *ADE Bulletin* 133 (Winter 2003): 3–5.

Leff, Michael. "Rhetorical Disciplines and Rhetorical Disciplinarity: A Response to Mailloux." *Rhetoric Society Quarterly* 30 (Fall 2000):83–94.

Leitch, Vincent B. *American Literary Criticism from the Thirties to the Eighties*. New York: Columbia University Press, 1988.

Lentrichia, Frank. *Criticism and Social Change*. Chicago: University of Chicago Press, 1983.

Leonard, Sterling Andrews. *Current English Usage*. Chicago: Inland Press, 1932.

———. "How English Teachers Correct Papers." *English Journal* 12.8 (1923): 517–32.

Levine, Lawrence W. *Highbrow/Lowbrow: The Emergence of Cultural Hierarchy in America*. Cambridge, Mass.: Harvard University Press, 1988.

Levine, David. *The American College and the Culture of Aspiration, 1915–1940*. Ithaca, N.Y.: Cornell University Press, 1986.

Livingston, William, et al. "Essays from *Independent Reflector, March 22–April 19, 1753.*" In *American Higher Education: A Documentary History*, edited by Richard Hofstadler and Wilson Smith, 1:99–103. Chicago: University of Chicago Press, 1961.

Lockridge, Kenneth A. *Literacy in Colonial New England*. New York: Norton, 1974.

———. *A New England Town: The First Hundred Years, Dedham, Massachusetts, 1636–1736*. New York: Norton, 1970.

Logan, Shirley Wilson. *With Pen and Voice: A Critical Anthology of Nineteenth-Century African-American Women*. Carbondale: Southern Illinois University Press, 1995.

Longaker, Mark. *Rhetoric and the Republic: Politics, Civic Discourse, and Education in Early America*. Tuscaloosa: University of Alabama Press, 2007.

Lounsbury, Thomas R. "Compulsory Composition in Colleges." *Harper's Monthly Magazine* 123 (November 1911): 866–80.

———. *History of the English Language*. 1879. Rev. ed. New York: Holt, 1894.

Lovas, John C. "How Did We Get in This Fix? A Personal Account of the Shift to a Part-Time Faculty in a Leading Two-Year College District." In *Moving a Mountain: Transforming the Role of Contingent Faculty in Composition Studies and Higher Education*, edited by Eileen Schell and Patricia Lambert Stock, 196–217. Urbana, Ill.: NCTE, 2001.

Lowell, James Russell. "Nationality in Literature." In *Contemporary American Criticism*, edited by James Cloyd Bowman, 3–22. New York: Holt, 1926.

Lucas, Christopher J. *American Higher Education: A History*. New York: St. Martin's Press, 1994.

Lucas, Stephen E. *Portents of Rebellion: Rhetoric and Revolution in Philadelphia, 1765–76*. Philadelphia: Temple University Press, 1976.

———. "The Rhetorical Ancestry of the Declaration of Independence." *Rhetoric and Public Affairs* 1.2 (1998): 143–84.

Lunn, Eugene. "Beyond 'Mass Culture': The Lonely Crowd, the Uses of Literacy, and the Postwar Era." *Theory and Society* 19.1 (February 1990): 63–86.

Lunsford, Andrea A., ed. *Reclaiming Rhetorica: Women in the Rhetorical Tradition*. Pittsburgh: University of Pittsburgh Press, 1995.

Lunsford, Andrea, Helene Moglen, and James F. Slevin. *The Future of Doctorial Studies in English*. New York: Modern Language Association, 1989.

Lyman, Rollo Laverne. *English Grammar in American Schools Before 1850*. Washington, D.C.: Government Printing Office, 1922.

MacDonald, Victoria Maria. "The Paradox of Bureaucratization: New Views on Progressive Era Teachers and the Development of a Women's Profession." *History of Education Quarterly* 39.1 (Winter 1999): 427–53.

Machlup, Fritz. *The Production and Distribution of Knowledge in the United States*. Princeton: Princeton University Press, 1962.

Maclean, John. *History of the College of New Jersey: 1746–1854*. New York: Arno, 1969.

Madison, James. *The Federalist*. Edited by Jacob E. Cooke. Middletown, Conn.: Wesleyan University Press, 1961.

Mailloux, Steven. *Reception Histories: Rhetoric, Pragmatism, and American Cultural Politics*. New York: Cornell University Press, 1998.

———. "Rhetoric Returns to Syracuse: The Reception of Curricular Reform." In *Reception Histories: Rhetoric, Pragmatism, and American Cultural Politics*, 151–81. Ithaca, N.Y.: Cornell University Press, 1998.

March, Francis A. "1892. Recollections of Language Teaching." *PMLA* 115.7 (December 2000): 1738–41.

———. *Method of Philological Study of the English Language*. New York: American Book Company, 1865.

Marckwardt, Albert Henry. *Linguistics and the Teaching of English*. Bloomington: Indiana University Press, 1966.

Martin, Terrence. *The Instructed Vision: Scottish Common Sense Philosophy and the Origin of American Fiction*. Bloomington: Indiana University Press, 1961.

Mather, Cotton. *Magnalia Christi Americana*. 2 vols. Hartford, Conn.: Silas Andrus, 1820.

———. *Manuductio and Ministerium*. 1726. New York: Columbia University Press, 1938.

Matsuda, Paul Kei. "Composition Studies and ESL Writing: A Disciplinary Division of Labor." *College Composition and Communication* 50.4 (1999): 699–721.

Matthews, Brander. "Can English Literature Be Taught?" *Educational Review* 22 (April 1892): 337–47.

Matthews, P. H. *Grammatical Theory in the United States from Bloomfield to Chomsky*. Cambridge Studies in Linguistics. Cambridge: Cambridge University Press, 1993.

Matthews, Victoria Earle. "The Value of Race Literature: An Address Delivered at the First Congress of Colored Women of the United States." 1895. In *With Pen and Voice: A Critical Anthology of Nineteenth-Century African American Women*, edited by Shirley W. Logan, 126–48. Carbondale: Southern Illinois University Press, 1995.

Mattingly, Paul H. *The Classless Profession: American Schoolmen in the Nineteenth Century.* New York: New York University Press, 1975.

May, Henry F. *The Enlightenment in America.* New York: Oxford University Press, 1976.

Mayers, Tim. *(Re) Writing Craft: Composition, Creative Writing, and the Future of English Studies.* Pittsburgh: University of Pittsburgh Press, 2005.

Mayo, Elizabeth. *Lessons on Common Things.* Edited by John Frost. Philadelphia: Lippincott, 1857.

McGrath, Earl James, ed. *Communications in General Education.* Dubuque, Iowa: W. C. Brown, 1949.

McGuffey, William Holmes. *McGuffey's Fifth Eclectic Reader.* New York: American Book Co., 1920.

McHenry, E., and Shirley Brice Heath. "The Literate and the Literary: African-Americans as Writers and Readers: 1830–1940." In *Literacy: A Critical Sourcebook,* edited by Ellen Cushman et al., 261–74. Boston: Bedford/St. Martin's, 2001.

McKeon, Richard. "Criticism and the Liberal Arts: The Chicago School of Criticism." In *Profession 82,* 1–18. New York: MLA, 1982.

———. "The Uses of Rhetoric in a Technological Age: Architectonic Productive Arts." *The Prospect of Rhetoric,* edited by Lloyd F. Bitzer and Edwin Black, 44–63. Englewood Cliffs, N.J.: Prentice-Hall, 1971.

McLachlan, James. "The Choice of Hercules: American Student Societies in the Early 19th Century." In *The University in Society,* edited by Lawrence Stone, 2:449–94. Princeton: Princeton University Press, 1974.

McLachlan, James. *Princetonians: 1748–1768.* Princeton: Princeton University Press, 1976.

Mcleod, Dan. "Watching Our Discipline Die." *ADE Bulletin* 66 (Winter 1980): 34–35.

McMahan, Anna Benneson. *The Study Class: A Guide for the Student of English Literature.* Chicago: McClurg, 1899.

Meranze, Michael. *Laboratories of Virtue: Punishment, Revolution, and Authority in Philadelphia, 1760–1835.* Chapel Hill: University of North Carolina Press, 1996.

Meriwether, Colyer. *Our Colonial Curriculum, 1607–1776.* Washington, D.C.: Capital Publishing, 1907.

Miheusuah, Devon A. *Cultivating the Rosebuds: The Education of Women at the Cherokee Female Seminary, 1851–1909.* Urbana: University of Illinois Press, 1993.

Miller, Gary E. *The Meaning of General Education: The Emergence of a Curriculum Paradigm.* New York: Teachers College Press, Teachers College, Columbia University, 1988.

Miller, J. Hillis. "The Function of Rhetorical Study at the Present Time." *ADE Bulletin* 62 (September 1979): 10–18.

———. "Literary Study in the University without Idea" *ADE Bulletin* 113 (Spring 1996): 30–33.

———. "My Fifty Years in the Profession." *ADE Bulletin* 133 (Winter 2003): 63–66.

Miller, Perry. *The American Puritans, Their Prose and Poetry.* Garden City, N.Y.: Doubleday, 1956.

———. *The New England Mind: From Colony to Province.* 1953. Cambridge: Harvard University Press, 1962.

Miller, Richard E. "Fault Lines in the Contact Zone." *College English* (April 1994): 389–408.

Miller, Samuel. *Letters from a Father to His Son in College*. Philadelphia: Presbyterian Board of Publication, 1852.

Miller, Susan. *Rescuing the Subject: A Critical Introduction to Rhetoric and the Writer*. 2nd ed. Carbondale: Southern Illinois University Press, 2003.

———. *Textual Carnivals: The Politics of Composition*. Carbondale: Southern Illinois University Press, 1991.

Miller, Thomas P. "Blair, Witherspoon, and the Rhetoric of Civic Humanism." In *Scotland and America in the Age of Enlightenment*, edited by Richard Sher and Jeffrey Smitten, 100–14. Princeton: Princeton University Press, 1990.

———. "How Rhetorical Are English and Communications Majors?" *Rhetoric Society Quarterly* 35.1 (2005): 91–112.

———. "Managing to Make a Difference." In *Field of Dreams: Independent Writing Programs and the Future of Composition Studies*, edited by Peggy O'Neill, Angela Crow, and Larry W. Burton, 253–267. Logan: Utah State University Press, 2002.

———. "Changing the Subject." In *Realms of Rhetoric: Inquiries into the Prospects for Rhetoric Education*, edited by Joseph Petraglia, 73–89. Albany: State University of New York Press, 2003.

———. *The Formation of College English: Rhetoric and Belles Lettres in the British Cultural Provinces*. Pittsburgh: University of Pittsburgh Press, 1997.

———. "What Should College English Be . . . Doing?" *College English* 69.2 (November 2006): 150–55.

———. "Why Don't Our Graduate Programs Do a Better Job of Preparing Students to Do the Work We Do?" *Writing Program Administration* 24 (2001): 41–58.

Miller, Thomas P., and Brian Jackson. "What Are English Majors For?" *College Composition and Communication* 58.4 (June 2007): 682–708.

Miller, Thomas P., and Joseph Jones. "Working through our Histories." *College English* 67.1 (March 2005): 421–39.

Minutes of the Trustees of the College, Academy and Charitable Schools. Vol. 1. 1749–1768. Wilmington, Del.: Scholarly Resources, Inc., 1974.

Minutes of the Trustees [of the] University of Pennsylvania. Vol. 2. "College and Academy of Philadelphia, 1768–1791." University of Pennsylvania Archives.

"MLA Statement on the Use of Part-Time and Full-Time Adjunct Faculty Members." Modern Language Association. February 1994. http://www.mla.org/statement_faculty (accessed April 2010).

"MLA-ADE Survey of Doctoral Programs in English." *ADE Bulletin* 36 (March 1973): 31–33.

Moffat, Wendy. "Figure and Ground: The Transformation of the Dickinson College English Department's Faculty and Curriculum." *ADE Bulletin* 133 (2003): 11–15.

Montgomery, T. H. *A History of the University of Pennsylvania from Its Foundation to AD 1770*. Philadelphia: Jacobs, 1900.

Moore, Kathryn McDaniel. "The War with the Tutors: Student-Faculty Conflict at Harvard and Yale, 1745–1771." In *The Social History of American Education*, edited by B. Edward McClellan and William J. Reese, 39–51. Champaign: University of Illinois Press, 1988.

Morgan, Edmund S. "The American Revolution Considered as an Intellectual Movement." In *Paths of American Thought*, edited by Arthur M. Schlesinger, Jr., and Morton M. White, 11–33. Boston: Houghton-Mifflin, 1963.

Morison, Samuel E. *Harvard College in the Seventeenth Century*. 2 vols. Cambridge, Mass.: Harvard University Press, 1936.

Morris, Charles. *Signs, Language, and Behavior*. New York: G. Braziller, 1946.

Morton, Charles. *Compendium Physicae with Introduction by Samuel Eliot Morison*. Vol. 33 of *Publications of the Colonial Society of Massachusetts*. Boston: Colonial Society of Massachusetts, 1940.

———. *The Spirit of Man*. Boston, 1692.

Mountford, Roxanne. "The Feminization of Rhetoric?" *Journal of Advanced Composition* 19 (1999): 485–92.

Muller, Herbert J. *The Uses of English*. New York: Holt, Rinehart, & Winston, 1967.

Murray, Donald M. "Teach Writing as a Process Not Product." 1972. In *Cross Talk in Comp Theory: A Reader*, edited by Victor Villanueva, 3–6. Urbana: NCTE, 1997.

Murray, Lindley. *English Grammar. Adapted to the Different Classes of Learners with an Appendix, Containing Rules and Observations for Assisting the More Advanced Students to Write with Perspicuity and Accuracy*. 1824. Delmar, New York: Scholars' Facsimiles and Reprints, 1981.

Murray, Lindley, ed. *The English Reader: Or Pieces in Prose and Poetry Selected from the Best Writers*. New York: Collins, 1812.

Myers, D. G. *The Elephants Teach: Creative Writing since 1880*. Englewood Cliffs, N.J.: Prentice Hall, 1996.

Myers, Miles. *Changing Our Minds: Negotiating English and Literacy*. Champaign, Ill.: NCTE, 1996.

National Center for Education Statistics. http://nces.ed.gov.

National Commission on Excellence in Education. *A Nation at Risk: The Imperative for Educational Reform: A Report to the Nation and the Secretary of Education, United States Department of Education*. Washington, D.C.: The Commission: Superintendent of Docs., U.S. Government Printing Office distributor, 1983. http://www.ed.gov/pubs/NatAtRisk/index.html (accessed August 1, 2004).

The National Commission on Writing. The Neglected "R": The Need for a Writing Revolution. 2003. http://www.writingcommission.org/prod_downloads/writingcom/neglectedr.pdf (accessed March 27, 2007).

"National Council of Teachers of English Proceedings of the First Annual Meeting, Chicago, December 1 and 2, 1911." *English Journal* 1 (1912): 30–45.

National Council of Teachers of English and Ruth Mary Weeks. *A Correlated Curriculum; a Report of the Committee on Correlation of the NCTE, Ruth Mary Weeks, Chairperson. A Publication of NCTE*. New York: D. Appleton-Century Co, 1936.

Neal, Robert Wilson. *Short Stories in the Making*. New York: Oxford University Press, 1914.

"Negro Higher Education as Seen through the Antebellum Black Press." *Journal of Blacks in Higher Education* 20 (Summer 1998): 36–38.

Nelson, Cary. *Will Teach for Food: Academic Labor in Crisis*. Minneapolis: University of Minnesota Press, 1997.

Nerad, M., and J. Cerny. "From Rumors to Facts: Career Outcomes of English Ph.D.s." Special Issue, *The Communicator* XXXII (Fall, 1999): 1–12.

————. 2000. "Improving Doctoral Education: Recommendations from the Ph.D.s— Ten Years Later Study." *The Communicator* XXXIII (Fall 2000): 2.

New England's First Fruits. London: 1643.

Newman, John Henry. *The Idea of a University.* 1852. www.newmanreader.org/works/ idea.

Newman, Samuel P. *A Practical System of Rhetoric.* New York: Dayton and Newman, 1834.

Nietz, John. *The Evolution of American Secondary School Textbooks before 1900.* Rutland, Vt.: Tuttle, 1966.

Noble, A. B. "The Preparation of College Teachers of English." *English Journal* 5 (1916): 665–70.

Norris, Edwin Mark. *The Story of Princeton.* Boston: Little, Brown, 1917.

North, Stephen M. *The Making of Knowledge in Composition: Portrait of an Emerging Field.* Upper Montclair, N.J.: Boynton/Cook Publishers, 1987.

Ogden, C. K., and I. A. Richards. *The Meaning of Meaning: A Study of the Influence of Language upon Thought.* London: Routledge and K. Paul, 1949.

Ogren, Christine A. *The American State Normal School: An Institution of Great Good.* New York: Palgrave Macmillan, 2005.

Ohmann, Richard. *English in America: A Radical View of the Profession.* Hanover: Wesleyan, 1976.

————. *Politics of Knowledge: The Commercialization of the University, the Professions, and Print Culture.* Middletown, Conn.: Wesleyan University Press, 2003.

————. *Selling Culture: Magazines, Markets, and Class at the Turn of the Century.* London: Verso, 1996.

————. "Teaching and Studying Literature at the End of Ideology." In *The New Criticism and Contemporary Literary Theory*, edited by William J. Spurlin and Michael Fischer, 75–100. New York: Garland, 1995.

Oleson, Alexandra, and Stanford C. Brown, eds. *The Pursuit of Knowledge in the Early Republic: American Scientific and Learned Societies from Colonial Times to the Civil War.* Baltimore: Johns Hopkins University Press, 1976.

O'Neill, Peggy, Angela Crow, and Larry W. Burton, eds. *Field of Dreams: Independent Writing Programs and the Future of Composition Studies.* Logan: Utah State University Press, 2002.

Osgood, Charles G. "No Set Requirement of English Composition in the Freshman Year." *English Journal* 4 (1915): 231–35.

Ota, Thomas. "The Teaching of Rhetoric in the United States during the Classical Period of Education." In *A History and Criticism of American Public Address*, edited by William Norwood Brigance, 193–212. New York: Russell and Russell, 1960.

Ota, Thomas. "The Theory and Practice of Disputation at Yale, Harvard, and Dartmouth, from 1750 to 1800." PhD diss., State University of Iowa, 1941.

Paine, Thomas. *Common Sense. The Essential Thomas Paine.* New York: New American Library, 1969.

Pancoast, Henry S. "College Entrance Requirements in English." *Educational Review* 22 (February 1892): 132–44.

Parker, Richard Green. *Progressive Exercises in Composition.* Baltimore: Cushing and Sons, 1832.

Parker, William Riley. "Where Do English Departments Come From?" *College English* 28 (1967): 339–51.

Parrillo, Vincent N. "Diversity in America: A Sociohistorical Analysis *Sociological Forum.*" Special issue, *Multiculturalism and Diversity* 9.4 (December, 1994): 523–545.

Pattee, Fred Lewis. *Tradition and Jazz.* New York: Century, 1925.

Payne, William Morton. *American Literary Criticism.* New York: Longman, 1904.

———. *English in American Universities.* Boston: D. C. Heath, 1895.

Peirce, Benjamin. *A History of Harvard University from Its Foundation, in the year 1636, to the Period of the American Revolution.* Cambridge, Mass.: Brown, Shattuck, and Co., 1833.

Peirce, Charles Sanders. *Collected Papers of Charles Sander Peirce.* Edited by Charles Hartshorne and Paul Weiss. 6 vols. Cambridge, Mass.: Harvard University Press, 1931–35.

Pendelton, George S. *Social Objectives of School English.* Nashville, Tenn.: George Peabody College for Teachers, 1924.

Perlman, Joel, R. Silvana, R. Siddali, and Keith Whitescarver. "Literacy, Schooling, and Teaching among New England Women, 1730–1820." *History of Education Quarterly* 37.2 (Summer 1997): 117–39.

Perrin, Porter G. "The Teaching of Rhetoric in the American Colleges before 1750." PhD diss., University of Chicago, 1936.

Phelps, Louise Wetherbee. "Practical Wisdom and the Geography of Knowledge in Composition." *College English* 53 (1991): 863–85.

Pocock, J. G. A. "Empire, Revolution and an End of Early Modernity." In *Varieties of British Political Thought, 1500–1800,* edited by J. G. A. Pocock, 283–320. Cambridge: Cambridge University Press, 1993.

———. *Politics, Language, and Time: Essays on Political Thought and History.* New York: Atheneum, 1971.

Pole, J. R. *Political Representation in England and the Origins of the American Revolution.* London: Macmillan, 1966.

Potter, David. *Debating in the Colonial Chartered Colleges: An Historical Survey, 1642–1900.* New York: Teachers College, Columbia University, 1944.

Potter, David. "The Literary Society." In *History of Speech Education in America: Background Studies,* edited by Karl R. Wallace, 238–58. New York: Appleton-Century-Crafts, 1954.

Potter, Thomas, and Gordon L. Thomas. *The Colonial Idiom.* Carbondale: Southern Illinois University Press, 1970.

Pratt, Mary Louise. "Arts of the Contact Zone." *Profession* 91 (1991): 33–40.

———. "Building a New Public Idea about Language." *Profession* (2003): 110–19.

"Project English." *College Composition and Communication* 13.1 (February 1962): 39–42.

Prokosch, Eduard. "Treason within the Castle." *PMLA* 52 (1937): 1320–27.

Quakenbos, G. P. *Advanced Course of Composition and Rhetoric: A Series of Practical Lessons on the Origin, History, and Peculiarities of the English Language, Punctuation, Taste, the Pleasures of the Imagination, Figures, Style and Its Essential Properties, Criticism, the Various Departments of Prose and Poetical Composition: Illustrated with Copious Exercises. Applied to Self-Instruction, and the Use of Schools and Colleges.* New York: Appleton, 1866.

Quincy, John. *Remarks on the Nature and Probable Effects of Introducing the Voluntary System in the Studies of Latin and Greek, Proposed in Certain Resolutions of the President and Fellows of Harvard University Now under the Consideration of Its Board of Overseers, and Also on the Present State of the Latin Department in That Institution.* Cambridge, Mass.: John Owen, 1841.

Quincy, Josiah. *The History of Harvard University.* 1840. 2 vols. New York: Arno Press, 1977.

Ransom, John C. "Criticism, Inc." 1938. In *American Literary Criticism, 1900–1950,* edited by Charles I. Glicksberg, 453–67. New York: Hendricks House, 1951.

Rarig, Frank M., and Halbert S. Greaves. "National Speech Organizations and Speech Education." In *History of Speech Education in America: Background Studies,* edited by Karl R. Wallace, 490–517. New York: Appleton-Century-Crafts, 1954.

Reading at Risk: A Survey of Literary Reading in America. Research Division Report #46. Washington, D.C.: National Endowment for the Arts, 2004. http://www.arts.gov/pub/ReadingAtRisk.pdf (accessed December, 21 2005).

Reading on the Rise: A New Chapter in American Literacy. Washington, D.C.: National Endowment for the Arts, 2009. http://www.arts.gov/research/readingonrise.pdf (accessed June 15, 2010).

Reed, Henry. *Lectures on English Literature, from Chaucer to Tennyson.* 2 vols. Philadelphia: Parry and Macmillan, 1855.

Reese, William. *The Origins of the American High School.* New Haven: Yale University Press, 1995.

Reid, Ronald F. "The Boylston Professorship of Rhetoric and Oratory, 1806–1904: A Case Study in Changing Concepts of Rhetoric and Pedagogy." *Quarterly Journal of Speech* 45 (1959): 239–57.

Reingold, Nathan. "Definitions and Speculations: The Professionalization of Science in America in the Nineteenth Century." In *The Pursuit of Knowledge in the Early Republic: American Scientific and Learned Societies from Colonial Times to the Civil War,* edited by Alexandra Oleson and Stanford C. Brown, 33–69. Baltimore: Johns Hopkins University Press, 1976.

Report of the Committee on Secondary School Studies Appointed at the Meeting of the National Education Association, July 9, 1892 with the Reports of the Conferences Arranged by This Committee and Held December 28–30, 1892. Washington, D.C.: United States Bureau of Education, 1893.

"Report of the Committee on the Preparation of College Teachers of English." *English Journal* 5.1 (1916): 20–32.

Reports on the Course of Instruction in Yale College by a Committee of the Corporation, and the Academical Faculty. New Haven: Hezekiah Howe, 1828.

Rhoades, Gary. *Managed Professionals: Unionized Faculty and Restructuring Academic Labor.* Albany: State University of New York Press, 1998.

Richards, I. A. *How to Read a Page; A Course in Effective Reading, with an Introduction to a Hundred Great Words.* New York: W. W. Norton, [1942].

———. *Practical Criticism: A Study of Literary Judgment.* New York: Harcourt Brace, 1929.

Rickard, Truman, and Hiram Orcutt, eds. *Class Book of Prose and Poetry; Consisting of Selections from the Best English and American Authors.* Boston: R. S. Davis, 1850.

Ricks, Vickie. "'In An Atmosphere of Peril': College Women and Their Writing." In *Nineteenth Century Women Learn to Write*, edited by Catherine Hobbs, 59–83. Charlottesville: University Press of Virginia, 1995.

Ritchie, Joy, and Kate Ronald, ed. *Available Means: An Anthology of Women's Rhetoric(s)*. Pittsburgh: University of Pittsburgh Press, 2001.

Roach, Helen P. *History of Speech Education at Columbia College, 1754–1949.* New York: Bureau of Publications, Teachers College, Columbia University, 1950.

Robbins, Sarah. *Managing Literacy, Mothering America: Women's Narratives on Reading and Writing in the Nineteenth Century.* Pittsburgh: University of Pittsburgh Press, 2004.

Roberts, Holland D., Walter Vincent Kaulfers, and Grayson Kefauver. *English for Social Living, A Program including 25 Statements of Practice by Teachers in the Field.* New York, London: McGraw-Hill, 1943.

Roberts-Miller, Patricia. *Voices in the Wilderness: Public Discourse and the Paradox of Puritan Rhetoric.* Tuscaloosa: University of Alabama Press, 1999.

Robertson, Linda R., Sharon Crowley, and Frank Lentricchia. "The Wyoming Conference Resolution Opposing Unfair Salaries and Working Conditions for Post-Secondary Teachers of Writing." *College English* 49 (1987): 274–80.

Rosenblatt, Louise M. *Literature as Exploration.* 1938. 5th ed. New York: MLA, 1995.

———. "Retrospect." *Voices From the Middle* 12.3 (1995): 13–19.

Rossiter, Clifford Lawrence. *Seedtime of the Republic: The Origin of the American Tradition of Political Liberty.* New York: Harcourt Brace, 1953.

Ross, Dorothy. "American Social Science and the Idea of Progress." In *The Authority of Experts: Studies in History and Theory*, edited by Thomas L. Haskell, 157–75. Bloomington: Indiana University Press, 1984.

Rouse, P. Jay. "Margaret Fuller: A Rhetoric of Citizenship in Nineteenth-Century America." In *Oratorical Culture in Nineteenth-Century America: Transformation in the Theory and Practice of Rhetoric*, edited by Gregory Clark and S. Michael Halloran, 110–36. Carbondale: Southern Illinois University Press, 1993.

Royster, Jacqueline Jones, ed. *Southern Horrors and Other Writings: The Anti-Lynching Campaign of Ida Wells, 1892–1900.* Boston: Bedford, 1996.

Rudolph, Frederick. *The American College and University: A History.* New York: Vintage, 1962.

Rudy, Willis. *The Evolving Liberal Arts Curriculum: A Historical Review of Basic Themes.* New York: Teachers College, Columbia University, 1960.

Rush, Benjamin. *Essays, Literary, Moral and Philosophical.* 2nd ed. Philadelphia: Thomas and William Bradford, 1806.

———. "Thoughts upon Female Education." 1787. In *Essays, Literary, Moral and Philosophical*, edited by Michael Meranze, 34–43. Schenectady, New York: Union College Press, 1988.

———. "Thoughts upon Female Education, Accommodated to the Present State of Society, Manners and Government in the United States of America." 1787. In *Essays on Education in the Early Republic*, edited by Frederick Rudolph. Cambridge, Mass.: Belknap Press of Harvard University Press, 1965.

Rush, James. *Philosophy of the Human Voice.* Philadelphia: 1827.

Russell, David. *Writing in the Academic Disciplines, 1870–1990: A Curricular History.* Carbondale: Southern Illinois University Press, 1991.

Russell, James E. "College Entrance Requirements in English." *Educational Review* (June 1892): 74–77.

Said, Edward W. "Opponents, Audiences, Constituencies, and Community." *Critical Inquiry* 9.1 (September 1982): 1–26.

Salvatori, Mariolina Rizzi, ed. *Pedagogy: A Disturbing History, 1819–1929.* Pittsburgh: University of Pittsburgh Press, 1996.

Scholes, Robert. *Textual Power: Literary Theory and the Teaching of English.* New Haven: Yale University Press, 1985.

———. *The Rise and Fall of English: Reconstructing English as a Discipline.* New Haven: Yale University Press, 1998.

Scholes, Robert, Nancy R. Comley, and Gregory L. Ulmer. *Text Book: An Introduction to Literary Language.* New York: St. Martin's Press, 1988.

Schultz, Lucille M. *The Young Composers: Composition's Beginnings in Nineteenth-Century Schools.* Carbondale: Southern Illinois University Press, 1999.

Scott, Frank W., Joseph M. Thomas, and Frederick A. Manchester. "Preliminary Report of the Special Committee on Freshman English." *English Journal* 7.9 (November 1918): 592–99.

Scott, Fred Newton. Editorial. *English Journal* 27 (1913): 456–59.

———. "Efficiency for Efficiency's Sake." Presidential Address of the North Central Association of Colleges and Secondary Schools. 1914. In *The Standard of American Speech and Other Papers,* 48–60. Boston: Allyn and Bacon, 1926.

Scott, Fred Newton, and Joseph Villiers Denney. *Composition-Literature.* Boston: Allyn and Bacon, 1902.

———. *The New Composition-Rhetoric.* Boston: Allyn and Bacon, 1911.

Scott, Sir Walter. *Biographical and Critical Notices of Eminent Novelists.* Boston: Wells and Lily, 1829.

Schwager, Sally. "Educating Women in America." Special Issue, "Reconstructing the Academy," *Signs* 12.2 (Winter 1987): 333–72.

Seely, Howard Francis. *On Teaching English.* New York: American Book Company, 1933.

Sensabaugh, George F. *The Study of English in California Schools.* Stanford: Stanford University Press, 1952.

Shamoon, Linda K., Rebecca Moore Howard, and Sandra Jameson, eds. *Coming of Age: The Advanced Writing Curriculum.* Portsmouth, N.H.: Boynton/Cook Publishers, 2000.

Shaw, Thomas B. *Outlines of English Literature.* Edited by William Smith. New York: 1867.

Shepard, Alan. "Gumbo? On the Logic of Undergraduate Curricula in English Studies." *ADE Bulletin* 133 (Winter 2003): 25–28.

Sheridan, Thomas. *Rhetorical Grammar.* Philadelphia, 1783.

———. *A Course of Lectures on Elocution.* Yorkshire: Scholar Press, 1792.

Shils, Edward. *The Calling of Education: The Academic Ethic and Other Essays on Higher Education.* Chicago: University of Chicago Press, 1997.

Shoemaker, Francis. "Self-Realization, Communication, and Aesthetic Experience." In *Communication in General Education,* edited by Earl James McGrath, 231–44. Dubuque, Iowa: Brown, 1949.

Shor, Ira. *Critical Teaching and Everyday Life.* Chicago: University of Chicago Press, 1987.

Shumway, David. *Creating American Civilization: A Genealogy of American Literature as an Academic Discipline*. Minneapolis: University of Minnesota Press, 1994.

Simeone, William. "The Plight of a Department of English in the Seventies." *ADE Bulletin* 41 (May 1974): 30–32.

Simmons, Sue Carter. "Constructing Writers: Barrett Wendell's Pedagogy at Harvard." *College Composition and Communication* 46.3 (October 1995): 327–52.

———. "Radcliffe Responses to Harvard Rhetoric: 'An Absurdly Stiff Way of Thinking.'" In *Nineteenth Century Women Learn to Write*, edited by Catherine Hobbs, 264–92. Charlottesville: University Press of Virginia, 1995.

Siskin, Clifford. *The Work of Writing: Literature and Social Change in Britain, 1700–1830*. Baltimore: Johns Hopkins University Press, 1998.

Sizer, Theodore R. *The Age of Academies*. New York: Teachers College, Columbia University, 1964.

———. *Secondary Schools at the Turn of the Century*. Westport: Greenwood Press, 1976.

Sledd, James. "A Plea for Pluralism." *College English* 23.1 (October 1961): 15–20.

Sloan, Douglas, ed. *The Great Awakening and American Education: A Documentary History*. New York: Teachers College Press, 1973.

Smagorinsky, Peter. "*Growth through English* Revisited." *English Journal* 91.6 (July 2002): 23–29.

Smallwood, Mary Lovett. *An Historical Study of Examinations and Grading Systems in Early American Universities: A Critical Study of the Original Records of Harvard, William and Mary, Yale, Mount Holyoke, and Michigan from Their Founding to 1900*. Cambridge, Mass.: Harvard University Press, 1935.

Smith, Adam. *An Inquiry into the Nature and Causes of the Wealth of Nations*. Philadelphia, 1816.

Smith, Donald K. "Origins and Development of Departments of Speech." In *History of Speech Education in America: Background Studies*, edited by Karl R. Wallace, 447–70. New York: Appleton-Century-Crafts, 1954.

Smith, Lewis Worthington. *The Writing of the Short Story*. Boston: D.C. Heath & Co., 1902.

Smith, William. "Account of the College, Academy, and Charitable School of Philadelphia in Pennsylvania." 1759. In *Life and Correspondence of the Rev. William Smith, D.D.*, edited by Horace Smith, 1:54–64. Philadelphia: S. A. George, 1879–80.

———. *A Brief View of the Conduct of Pennsylvania for the Year 1755*. London: Griffiths, 1756.

———. *A General Idea of the College of Mirania: With a Sketch of the Method of Teaching Science and Religion, in the Several Classes: And Some Account of Its Rise, Establishment and Buildings, Address'd More Immediately to the Consideration of the Trustees Nominated by the Legislature, to Receive Proposals, &C. Relating to the Establishment of a College in the Province of New York*. New York: Parker and Weyman, 1753.

———. *Discourses on Several Public Occasions During the War in America: Preached Chiefly with a View to the Explaining the Importance of the Protestant Cause, in the British Colonies: and the Advancement of Religion, Patriotism and Military Virtue: Among Which Are a Discourse on Adversity, And Also a Discourse on Planning the Sciences, and the Propagation of Christianity in the Untutored Parts*. London: Millar, Griffith, and Keith, 1759.

———. *Discourses on Public Occasions in America*. 2nd ed. London, 1762.

———. *General Idea of the College of Mirania*. In *Discourses on Several Public Occasions During the War in America*, 39–106. 1753. London: 1759.

————. *Account of the College and Academy of Philadelphia*. In *Discourses on Several Public Occasions During the War in America*, 107–28. London, 1759.

————. *A General Idea of the College of Mirania*. 1753. New York: Johnson Reprint, 1969.

————. *Life and Correspondence of the Rev. William Smith*. Edited by Horace Wemyss Smith. 2 vols. Philadelphia: S. A. George, 1879–1880.

Smyth, Albert. "American Literature in the Class-room." *PMLA* 3 (1887): 238–44.

Snyder, K. Alan. *Defining Noah Webster: Mind and Morals in the Early Republic*. Lanham: University Press of America, 1990.

Soltow, Lee, and Edward Stevens. *The Rise of Literacy and the Common School in the United States: A Socioeconomic Analysis to 1870*. Chicago: University of Chicago Press, 1981.

Spalding, William. *History of English Literature*. New York: D. Appleton & Co, 1889.

Spellmeyer, Kurt. *Common Ground: Dialogue, Understanding, and the Teaching of Composition*. Englewood Cliffs, N.J.: Prentice Hall, 1993.

Spingarn, Joe Elias. *Creative Criticism: Essays on the Unity of Genius and Taste*. New York: Holt, 1917.

Spivak, Gayatari Chakravorty. *In Other Worlds: Essays in Cultural Politics*. New York: Methuen, 1987.

Spouge, William T. "Teaching Written and Oral English in Nonselective Secondary Schools." In *A Common Purpose: The Teaching of English in Great Britain, Canada, and the United States*, edited by James R. Squire, 83–94. Urbana, Ill.: NCTE, 1965.

Spurlin, William J., and Michael Fischer, eds. *The New Criticism and Contemporary Literary Theory: Connections and Continuities*. New York: Garland, 1995.

Squire, James R. "English at the Crossroads: The National Interest Report Plus Eighteen." *English Journal* 51.6 (1962): 381–92.

————. Foreword. *On Teaching English to Speakers of Other Languages*. Conference on Teaching English to Speakers of Other Languages. Tucson, 1964. Urbana, Ill.: NCTE, 1965.

————. *The National Interest and the Teaching of English*. Champaign, Ill.: NCTE, 1961.

Squire, James R., and Roger K. Applebee. *High School English Instruction Today: The National Study of High School English Programs*. New York: Appleton-Century-Crafts, 1968.

Standley, Fred L. "The Curriculum and Placement: An Overview." *ADE Bulletin* 36 (March 1973): 34–36.

Stanley, Jane. *The Rhetoric of Remediation: Negotiating Entitlement and Access to Higher Education*. Pittsburgh: University of Pittsburgh Press, 2010.

"Statement from the Conference on the Growing Use of Part-Time and Adjunct Faculty." American Association of University Professors. September 1997. http://www.aaup.org/AAUP/issues/contingent/conferencestatement.htm (April 12, 2010).

"Statement of Principles and Standards for the Postsecondary Teaching of Writing." *Conference on College Composition and Communication*. October 1989. http://www.ncte.org/cccc/resources/positions/postsecondarywriting (April 12, 2010).

Steinberg, Erwin. "Applied Humanities?" *College English* 35.4 (January 1974): 440–50.

————. *Curriculum Development and Evaluation in English and Social Studies*. Pittsburgh: Carnegie Institute of Technology, 1964.

Steinhoff, William. "Some Remarks on the Future of the Required Course in Freshman Composition." *College Composition and Communication* 12.1 (1961): 23–26.

Stevens, Edward. "The Anatomy of Mass Literacy in Nineteenth-Century United States." In *National Literacy Campaigns: Historical and Comparative Perspectives*, edited by Robert F. Arnove and Harvey J. Graff, 99–122. New York: Plenum, 1987.

Stewart, Donald. "Harvard's Influence on English Studies: Perceptions from Three Universities in the Early Twentieth Century. *College Composition and Communication* 43 (1992): 455–71.

Stewart, Donald C., and Patricia L. Stewart. *The Life and Legacy of Fred Newton Scott.* Pittsburgh: University of Pittsburgh Press, 1997.

Story, Ronald. "Harvard Students, the Boston Elite, and the New England Preparatory System, 1800–1870." *History of Education Quarterly* 15.3 (Autumn 1975): 281–98.

Street, Brian. "The Implications of the New Literacy Studies for Literacy Education." *English in Education* 31.3 (Autumn 1993): 26–39.

———. "What's 'New' in New Literacy Studies? Critical Approaches to Literacy in Theory and Practice." *Current Issues in Comparative Education* 5.2 (2003): 77–91

Stuckey, J. Elspeth. *The Violence of Literacy*. Portsmouth, N.H.: Boynton/Cook Publishers, 1991.

Tanselle, Thomas G. "Some Statistics on American Printing, 1764–1783." In *The Press and the American Revolution*, edited by Bernard Bailyn and John B. Hench, 315–63. Worcester, Mass.: American Antiquarian Society, 1980.

Tate, Allen. "Miss Emily and the Bibliographer." 1940. In *The New Criticism and Contemporary Literary Theory*, edited by William J. Spurlin and Michael Fischer, 7–18. New York: Garland, 1995.

———. "The Present Function of Criticism." 1940. In *American Literary Criticism, 1900–1950*, edited by Charles I. Glicksberg, 471–81. New York: Hendricks House, 1951.

Taylor, Warner. *A National Survey of Conditions in Freshman English*. Madison: University of Wisconsin Bureau of Educational Research, 1929.

Teaford, Jon. "The Transformation of Massachusetts Education, 1670–1780." *History of Education Quarterly* 10.3 (Autumn 1970): 287–307.

Tennent, Gilbert. *The Danger of an Unconverted Ministry*. Boston: 1742.

Tennent, Gilbert, and Samuel Davies. *A General Account of the Rise and State of the College Lately Established in the Province of New Jersey*. New York: 1752.

Tewksbury, Donald G. *The Founding of American Colleges and Universities before the Civil War*. 1932. Hamden, Conn.: Archon, 1965.

Thomas, J. M. "Training for Teaching Composition in Colleges." *English Journal* 5 (1916): 447–57.

Thomas, Martha Carey. "Should the Higher Education of Women Differ from that of Men?" Address to the Association of Colleges and Preparatory Schools of Middle States and Maryland, November 30, 1900.

Thompson, Edward Palmer. *Making of the English Working Class*. Middlesex: Penguin Books, 1975.

Thorp, Willard, et al. *The Princeton Graduate School: A History*. Princeton: Princeton University Press, 1978.

Tingle, Nicholas, and Judy Kirscht. "A Place to Stand: The Role of a Union in the Development of a Writing Program." In *Moving a Mountain: Transforming the Role of Contingent Faculty in Composition Studies and Higher Education*, edited by Eileen E. Schell and Patricia Lambert Stock, 218–32. Urbana, Ill.: NCTE, 2001.

Tompkins, Jane. "The Reader in History: The Changing Shape of Literary Response." In *Reader-Response Criticism: From Formalism to Post-Structuralism*, edited by Jane Tompkins, 201–32. Baltimore: Johns Hopkins University Press, 1980.

———. *Sensational Designs: The Cultural Work of American Fiction, 1790–1860*. New York: Oxford University Press, 1985.

Tough Choices or Tough Times. The Report of the New Commission on the Skills of the American Workforce. National Center on Education and the Economy: San Francisco: Jossey-Bass, 2007.

Trachsel, Mary. *Institutionalizing Literacy: The Historical Role of College Entrance Examinations in English*. Carbondale: Southern Illinois University Press, 1992.

Trumbull, John. *Poetical Works*. 2 vols. Hartford: Goodrich, 1820.

———. *Progress of Dullness*. Cambridge, Mass., 1772.

Tucker, Louis Leonard. *Puritan Protagonist: President Thomas Clap of Yale College*. Chapel Hill: University of North Carolina Press, 1962.

Turnbull, George. *Observations upon Liberal Education*. London: A. Millar, 1742.

Turner, William L. "The College, Academy and Charitable School of Philadelphia: The Development of a Colonial Institution of Learning, 1740–1779." PhD diss., University of Pennsylvania, 1952.

Tuttle, Robert E. "Composition vs. Communication—the Wrong Debate." *College Composition and Communication* 7.4 (1956): 205–10.

Veblen, Thorstein. *The Higher Learning in America: A Memorandum on the Conduct of Universities by Business Men*. 1918. New York: Sagamore Press, 1957.

———. *The Theory of the Leisure Class: An Economic Study of Institutions*. New York: Modern Library, 1934.

Veysey, Laurence R. *The Emergence of the American University*. Chicago: Chicago University Press, 1965.

Villanueva, Victor. *Bootstraps: From an American Academic of Color*. Urbana, Ill.: NCTE, 1993.

Waller, Gary F. "A Powerful Silence: 'Theory' in the English Major." *ADE Bulletin* 85 (Winter 1986): 31–35.

Walker, Jeffrey. *Rhetoric and Poetics in Antiquity*. Oxford University Press, 2000.

Walker, John. *Teacher's Assistant in English Composition: Easy Rules for Writing Themes and Composition Exercises on Subjects Proper for the Improvement of both Sexes at School*. Boston: Buckingham, 1810.

Walsh, James J. *Education of the Founding Fathers of the Republic: Scholasticism in the Colonial Colleges*. New York: Fordham University Press, 1935.

Ward, John. *A System of Oratory, Delivered in a Course of Lectures Publicly Read at Gresham College*. London: 1759.

Warner, Michael. *The Letters of the Republic: Publication and the Public Sphere in Eighteenth-Century America*. Cambridge, Mass.: Harvard University Press, 1990.

Warren, James Perrin. *Culture of Eloquence: Oratory and Reform in Antebellum America*. University Park: Pennsylvania State University Press, 1999.

Watkins, Evan. *Work Time: English Departments and the Circulation of Cultural Value*. Stanford: Stanford University Press, 1989.

Watts, Issac. *Logick: or, The Right Use of Reason in the Enquiry after Truth*. Philadelphia, 1789.

Wayland, Francis. *The Elements of Moral Science*. Boston: Gould, Kendall, and Lincoln, 1841.

———. *Thoughts on the Present Collegiate System in the United States*. Boston: Gould, Kendall, and Lincoln, 1842.

Weaver, Richard. "To Write the Truth." *College English* 10.1 (1948): 25–30.

Webster, Noah. *An American Dictionary of the English Language. By Noah Webster . . . Thoroughly Revised, and Greatly Enlarged and Improved, by Chauncey A. Goodrich . . . and Noah Porter*. 1841. Springfield, Mass.: Merriam, 1872.

———. *A Collection of Essays and Fugitive Writings. 1790*. Delmar, New York: Scholars' Facsimiles and Reprints, 1977.

———. *A Collection of Papers on Political, Literary and Moral Subjects*. 1843. New York: Franklin, 1968.

———. *Grammatical Institute of the English Language, Comprising an Easy, Concise, and Systematic Method in Education, Designed for the Use of English Schools in America. In Three Parts. Part I. Containing a New and Accurate Standard of Pronunciation*. Hartford: Hudson and Goodwin, 1783.

———. "Letter to a Young Gentleman Commencing His Education." 1823. *A Collection of Papers on Political, Literary, and Moral Subjects*. New York: Webster and Clark, 1843.

———. *Letters*. Edited by Harry R. Warfel. New York: Library Publishers, 1953.

Weidner, Heidemarie Z. "Silks, Congress Gaiters, and Rhetoric: A Butler University Graduate of 1860 Tells Her Story." In *Nineteenth-Century Women Learn to Write*, edited by Catherine Hobbs, 248–63. Charlottesville: University Press of Virginia, 1995.

Weingarten, Samuel, et al. *English in the Two-Year College. Report of a Joint Committee of the National Council of Teachers of English and the Conference on College Composition and Communication*. Champaign, Ill.: NCTE, 1965.

Wellek, Rene. "The New Criticism: Pro and Contra." 1978. In *The New Criticism and Contemporary Literary Theory*, edited by William J. Spurlin and Michael Fischer, 55–72. New York: Garland, 1995.

Wheatley, Phillis. *Poems on Various Subjects, Religious and Moral*. London: A. Bell, 1773.

Wigglesworth, Edward. *A Seasonable Caveat against Believing Every Spirit: with Some Directions for Trying the Spirits, Whether They Are of God. Given in Two Public Lectures in the Hall of Harvard College at Cambridge, N. E. April 22 and 29, 1735*. Boston: 1735.

Wigglesworth, Michael. *The Day of Doom; or, A Poetical Description of the Great and Last Judgment: with other Poems*. New York: American News Company, 1867.

———. *God's Controversy with New-England*. Cambridge: Chadwyck-Healey, 1992.

———. "Prayse of Eloquence." In *The Colonial Idiom*, edited by David Potter and Gordon L. Thomas, 8–12. Carbondale: Southern Illinois University Press, 1970.

Wilcox, Thomas. *The Anatomy of College English*. San Francisco: Jossey-Bass, 1973.

Wilensky, H. L. "The Professionalization of Everyone?" *American Journal of Sociology* 70 (September 1964): 137–58.

Williams, Fannie Barrier. "The Intellectual Progress of the Colored Women of the United States since the Emancipation Proclamation." In *Available Means: An Anthology of Women's Rhetorics*, edited by Joy Ritchie and Kate Ronald, 180–87. Pittsburgh: University of Pittsburgh Press, 2001.

Williams, Jeffrey. *The Institution of Literature*. Albany: State University of New York Press, 2002.

Williams, M. Atkinson. *Report on the Teaching of English in the United States.* London: Swan Sonnenschein, 1908.

Williams, Raymond. *Culture and Society, 1780–1950.* New York: Columbia University Press, 1983.

———. *The Long Revolution.* New York: Columbia University Press, 1961.

Wills, Garry. *Explaining America: The Federalist.* Garden City, New York: Doubleday, 1981.

———. *Inventing America: Jefferson's Declaration of Independence.* Garden City, New York: Doubleday, 1978.

Wilson, Elizabeth. "A Short History of a Border War: Social Science, School Reform, and the Study of Literature." *Poetics Today* 9.4 (1988): 711–35.

Wimsatt, William K. *The Verbal Icon: Studies in the Meaning of Poetry.* Lexington: University of Kentucky Press, 1954.

Windhover, Ruth. "Literature in the Nineteenth Century." *English Journal* 68.4 (1979): 28–33.

Winterowd, W. Ross. *The Rhetoric of the 'Other' Literature.* Carbondale: Southern Illinois University Press, 1990.

Witherspoon, John. *The Selected Writings of John Witherspoon.* Edited by Thomas P. Miller. Carbondale: Southern Illinois University Press, 1990.

Woodruff, Neal. "Only Connect." In *Profession 77,* 54–59. New York: MLA, 1977.

———. "The Ph.D. and the Future." *ADE Bulletin* 49 (May 1976): 21–23.

Woolley, Edwin C. "Admission to Freshman English in the University." *English Journal* 3 (1914): 238–44.

Worthen, Richard. "Implications of the NCTE-CCCC Status Survey on English in the Two-Year College." In *Research and the Development of the English Programs in the Junior College,* 21–27. Champaign, Ill.: NCTE, 1965.

Wozniak, John M. *English Composition in Eastern Colleges, 1850–1940.* Washington, D.C.: University Press of America, 1978.

Yancey, Kathleen Blake. *Writing in the 21st Century: A Report from the National Council of Teachers of English.* Urbana, Ill.: NCTE, 2009.

Young, Richard E, and Erwin R. Steinberg. "Planning Graduate Programs in Rhetoric." *Rhetoric Review* 18.2 (Spring 2000): 390–402.

Zavarzadeh, Mas'ud, and Donald Morton. "A Very Good Idea Indeed: The (Post) Modern Labor Force and Curricular Reform." In *Cultural Studies and the English Classroom,* edited by James A. Berlin and Michael J. Vivion, 66–82. Portsmouth, N.H.: Boynton/Cook-Heinemann, 1992.

Zebroski, James Thomas. *Thinking through Theory: Vygotskian Perspectives on the Teaching of Writing.* Portsmouth, N.H.: Boynton/Cook Publishers, 1994.

Zboray, Ronald J. *A Fictive People: Antebellum Economic Development and the American Reading Public.* New York: Oxford University Press, 1992.

INDEX

belles lettres: and concept of literature, 114, 118–19, 251n5, 256n19; expressive value of, 81; oratory vs., 95; repudiation of, 118, 120; and taste, 79–80

Bender, Thomas, 88, 224, 251n7, 252n10; *American Academic Culture in Transformation*, 184

Berkeley, George, 65

Berry, Wendell, 142

Bérubé, Michael, 239–40; *The Employment of English*, 278n19

bilingual education, 235, 270n8

Bilingual Education Act, 270n8

Birkerts, Sven, *Gutenberg Elegies*, 227

Birmingham School, 215–16, 272n18

Bishop, Wendy, 234

Black, Edwin, *Rhetorical Criticism*, 272n20

Blair, Hugh, 18, 49, 69, 118, 223, 260n21; *Account of the College*, 60; *Lectures on Rhetoric and Belles Lettres*, 112, 114

Bloom, Allan, *The Closing of the American Mind*, 201, 272n23

Bloomfield, Leonard, 148, 149

books: in colonial colleges, 16–17, 25–27, 32, 34–35, 68; and the comparative method, 68; oral approach to literature vs., 15–16; popularity of, in nineteenth century, 19. *See also* reading habits

Booth, Wayne, 171, 207; "Revival of Rhetoric," 192

Botein, Stephen, 82

Bourdieu, Pierre, 3, 176, 245

Bousquet, Marc, 240, 242, 279n26

Boylston Professor of Rhetoric and Oratory, Harvard College, 51, 112, 113

Brackett, John, 113, 259n18

Braddock, Richard, 193; *Research in Written Composition*, 188

Bradford, William, 78–79

Bradley, C. B., *Suggestions to Teachers of English in the Secondary Schools*, 133

Brattle, William, "Compendium of Logick," 35–36

Brereton, John C., 142

Briggs, Le Baron, 131, 139

Brint, Steven G., *In an Age of Experts*, 21

Britton, James, 20, 189, 190; *The Development of Writing Abilities*, 208; "Writing to Learn and Learning to Write," 191

Broening, Angela M., *Conducting Experiences in English*, 166

Brooks, Cleanth, 193; *Understanding Poetry*, 165, 171, 179, 268n45

Brookwood Labor College, 157

Brown, Hallie Quinn, 157, 158

Brown, Richard D., *Knowledge Is Power*, 31, 58, 78 ⁓

Brown University, 41, 44, 104, 108–10. *See also* College of Rhode Island

Bruner, Jerome S., 189, 192, 271n16

Buck, Gertrude, 150, 156–57, 263n11

Burke, Colin B., 89, 104–5, 128, 152, 155, 224, 257n1, 258n11

Burke, Kenneth, "Literature as Equipment for Living," 169–70

Cain, William E., 179, 229

Campbell, George, 114; *Philosophy of Rhetoric*, 101

Campbell, JoAnn, 156

Campbell, Oscar, *The Teaching of College English*, 166–67

Cardinal Principles of Secondary Education, 165

Carnegie Foundation, 188, 277n13, 280n30

Carnegie Mellon University, 211, 276n8

Carr, Jean Ferguson, 12, 94; *Archives of Instruction*, 112

Carr, Stephen L., 12, 94; *Archives of Instruction*, 112

CCCC. *See* Conference on College Composition and Communication

Center for the Book, 201

Centre for Culture Studies at Birmingham University, 215–16, 272n18

certification systems, 141, 263n12

Channing, Edward, 102, 115–16

Chauncy, Charles, *Enthusiasm Described and Caution'd Against*, 42

Cherokee Female Seminary, 155

Child, Francis, 112

Chronicle of Higher Education (newspaper), 279n27

Chubb, Percival, 15–16; *The Teaching of English in the Elementary and Secondary School*, 15

Church of England, 73. *See also* Anglican Church

Cicero, Marcus Tullius, 63; *De Oratore*, 48

"circle of learning," 33, 40

civic engagement, teaching literature as means to, 157–58, 236

civic professionalism, 88

Clap, Thomas, 44, 46, 51, 54, 254n11; *The Religious Constitution of Colleges*, 54

Clark, Gregory, 260n22

Clarke, John, *Letters to a Student in the University of Cambridge*, 49

class: in America, 95; American education and, 190–91; colonial colleges and, 57;

curriculum and, 261n29; literary studies and, 158; teaching and, 90, 97. *See also* middle class

classical languages, 33–34, 49, 96, 105–6, 109, 122–23, 255n9

Cleveland, Charles D., *A Compendium of English Literature*, 252n9

close reading, 164, 179

Cmiel, Kenneth, 11, 95; *Democratic Eloquence*, 95

Cohen, A. M., 259n17

collaboration: importance of, 10; in literary societies, 59, 70–71, 110; in literary studies, 228, 230, 246; Progressivism and, 159–60, 166–67, 235; with schools, 13, 130–37, 187–88, 202, 212, 217; with those outside the academy, 14, 88, 216–17, 224, 246

College, Academy, and Charitable School of Philadelphia, 18–19, 25, 47, 52, 56–58, 60–63, 71–74, 83–86, 110, 221–23, 253n7, 254n1, 254n4, 255nn5–6, 255n12

College Board, 226, 230, 276n9

College Composition and Communication (journal), 182, 185

college English studies: in accessible students, 106; classics replaced by, 110, 126; current status of, 1–2, 6, 23, 220, 237–38; curriculum of, 198; debilitating attitudes and actions in, 5, 23, 128–30, 143, 151, 175, 186, 194, 197, 200–205, 210–17, 224–25, 229, 238–39, 241; decline of, 193–94; discipline of, 3; divisions in, 129, 138, 148, 160, 184, 233, 237, 246, 280n28; general areas of, 2; hierarchies in, 10–11; histories of, 2, 6–14; institutional practices in, 7–8; introduction of, 47–52; as literacy studies, 2–3, 5–6, 15–23; mapping the field of, 137–43; New Criticism and, 163; origins of, 84, 96, 100; pedagogy in, 195; pragmatic approaches in, 7–11, 151–61, 177, 244–50; pragmatic approaches to, 203, 213–14; profession of, 3, 129; professional vs. service duties in, 5, 23; and the public, 8, 13–14; public opinion on, 274n33; requirements in, 199, 206; sources of change in, 4, 9, 12, 20, 50, 52, 70, 244, 249; staffing in, 5; standard curriculum of, 267n35

College Entrance Examination Board, 134, 135, 166

College of New Jersey, Princeton, 18, 41, 44, 47, 49, 52, 56–58, 66–68, 71, 74, 84, 85, 223

College of Philadelphia. *See* College, Academy, and Charitable School of Philadelphia

College of Rhode Island, 47, 48. *See also* Brown University

colleges and universities: accessible, 4, 52, 90, 99, 103, 105–6, 110, 151–51, 204; administrators' control of, 254n12; in antebellum period, 89, 104, 258n10, 258n11; common culture as goal of, 57, 60–61, 85; costs of, 105, 108, 178, 196; enrollments in, 175–76; evangelist-founded, 32; finances of, 26; growing numbers of, 89; as hybrid institutions, 89; later twentieth century developments in, 252n10; and pedagogy, 8, 133–37, 140–41, 187–89; and privacy of religious belief, 44, 57; purpose of, 124; and religious vocations, 58. *See also* elite colleges; private colleges; public colleges; research universities; state universities

colonial New England, 24–55, 221–22; curriculum in, 25–27, 32–40; introduction of English studies during, 47–52; literacy in, 30–31; religion in, 27–32, 40–46

Columbia University, 44, 52, 66, 139. *See also* King's College; Teachers College, Columbia University

commencements, 36, 48, 71, 111

Committee of Ten, 131–34, 138, 140

The Committee on the Labor and Cost of English Teaching, 150

common schools, 87–88, 91, 100, 101

commonplace books, 36, 50

common-sense philosophy, 75–76

Communications Association of America, 147

communications movement, 21, 180–83, 228, 269n1

community colleges, 167, 175–76, 178

community literacy, 211–12, 236

community-based intellectuals, 88, 102, 123, 158–59. *See also* organic intellectuals

comparative method, 67–68

compendia, 17, 26, 35–36, 53, 65, 68, 74

composition: creative writing vs., 148, 192; denigration of, 138, 240; faculty for, 136, 143, 150–51, 185, 197, 240–41; gatekeeper role of, 130; interdisciplinary approach to, 180; in the 1960s, 192; pedagogy for, 150, 154; professionalization of, 183–84; programs in, 141–42;

composition *(cont.)*:
  research on, 188; teaching of, 143–44,
  183. *See also* rhetoric and composition;
  writing
computational literacy, 226–27
computer literacy, 195
Conference on College Composition and
  Communication (CCCC), 182–83, 244,
  271n15
Congregationalism, 28, 42, 44; *The Dangers
  of an Unconverted Ministry*, 42
Connors, Robert J., 111, 150
Constitutional Convention, 256n15
Constitutions: British, 72; U.S., 59, 72, 75,
  256n15
contact zones, 4, 215, 251n2
"content" faculty/disciplines, 10, 133, 147,
  160, 187, 235, 247
cosmopolitan tastes, 80–81, 119
covenanting tradition, 27–29
creative writing: approaches to, 191; in composition courses, 142; composition vs.,
  148, 192; at Harvard, 264n23; journalism
  vs., 10–11, 147; popularity of, 22, 191,
  231, 279n27; in women's colleges, 146
Crowley, Sharon, 114, 146, 150, 209; *Composition in the University*, 180
Culler, Jonathan, 208, 214
cultural studies, 215–16, 249
culture of the book, 6, 122, 168, 201, 215,
  220
culture wars, 7, 193
curriculum: class and, 261n29; of College
  of Philadelphia, 61–64, 254n4; in colonial New England, 25–27, 32–40; experience curriculum, 165–66; high school,
  131–34; in late nineteenth century,
  138–40; in middle colonies, 60–67; in
  1980s, 205–6; in Revolutionary America, 18; scribal approach in, 33, 35–36;
  standard college English, 267n35
Curriculum Commission, 166

Dartmouth College, 41, 44, 47, 54, 106,
  188–90, 222
Dartmouth Conference, 20–21, 247
Davidson, Cathy N., 95
Davies, Samuel, 43, 56–57, 68
Day, Henry, 114; *Elements of the Art of
  Rhetoric*, 260n21
De Man, Paul, 200, 208
De Quincy, Thomas, 118
declamations, 33, 36
Declaration of Independence, 59, 74, 75,
  256n15, 256n16
Dedham, Massachusetts, 27, 29–30

deductive reasoning, 17, 25, 26, 33, 37, 47.
  See also logic
democracy, 28–29, 115, 159, 172, 178–79,
  190, 236. *See also* civic engagement,
  teaching literature as means to;
  republicanism
Demosthenes, 63
departments of English. *See* English
  departments
Derrida, Jacques, 200
Descartes, René, 38, 40
Dewey, John, 1, 61, 97, 134, 156, 159–62,
  181, 225; *Art as Experience*, 11, 160–61;
  Democracy and Education, 159; *Experi-
  ence and Education*, 11, 159, 165, 171;
  "Science and Education," 160
Dial (magazine), 102, 138
Dickinson, John, "Letters from a Farmer in
  Pennsylvania," 83
dime-store novels, 89, 95
disputations, 33, 36, 47
Dissenters, 39, 43, 48, 50, 68, 72
Dixon, John, 189–91, 193; *Growth through
  English*, 189–90
document literacy, 195, 226
Dodsley, Robert, 254n4
Douglas, Wallace, 115, 182
Dugard, William, *Rhetorices Elementa*, 38
Duncan, William, *Elements of Logic*, 63,
  256n16

Eagleton, Terry, 15, 207–8
economics, 196–97
education: in colonial New England, 30;
  common culture as goal of, 57, 60–61,
  85; mandatory public, 26; New Lights
  and, 43; print culture and, 99–100;
  and privacy of religious belief, 44; republican, 72–76, 91–92, 97–103; state-
  mandated, 90; of women, 18–19, 97–99,
  257n4; of working people, 99, 123, 159.
  See also colleges and universities;
  curriculum
Educational Testing Service, 276n9
educationalists, 103, 130, 154, 174, 225
Edwards, Jonathan, 31, 40, 46
EFL. *See* English as a foreign language
Ehrenreich, Barbara, 174, 269n2
Ehrenreich, John, 174, 269n2
Eliot, Charles W., 131, 134
elite colleges: in antebellum period, 90;
  character of, 54; distancing of, from
  public education, 103; exclusiveness of,
  103, 105–6, 264n18. *See also* private
  colleges/universities; research
  universities

elocution, 260n20
elocutionary manuals, 100
eloquence, 87
Emerson, Ralph Waldo, 17, 89, 96, 98, 102, 115–16
Emig, Janet, *Composing Processes of Twelfth Graders*, 208
English A program, 263n12
English as a foreign language (EFL), 181, 182, 270n8. *See also* English for Speakers of Other Languages
English departments: broadly based, 23; crisis involving, 202; curricula in, 205–6, 232, 273n29; requirements in, 206
English education: in antebellum period, 91; as area of college English studies, 2; and articulation, 133; in golden age of the profession, 184–93; history of, 12; ignoring of, 128; literary studies vs., 15. *See also* teaching
English for Speakers of Other Languages (ESOL), 11, 235, 270n8
English Journal, 135, 136, 152, 153, 191
English majors, 137–38, 174, 186, 193, 197–200, 213–15, 228–37, 269n1, 280n28
English Only movement, 85, 177, 235
English Round Table, 135
English school, 61–64
Ennals, Thomas, 24–25
entrance exams, 125–26, 130–32, 135–36, 166, 179
ESOL. *See* English for Speakers of Other Languages
essays: educational use of, 17, 145; expository, 145; as expressive vehicles, 81; in periodicals, 80–82; student societies and, 70; taste discussed in, 80. *See also* English as a foreign language
ethnography, 15, 216, 233, 236, 278n17
evangelists, 32, 41–43
experience curriculum, 165–66, 225, 268n41
experimental method, 63, 64, 67, 92
expertise, 5, 21, 92, 127, 262n4. *See also* professions and professionalism
exposition, 144–45
extension courses, 109, 175
extracurriculum, 122, 224

faculty. *See* teachers
Farnaby, Thomas, *Index Rhetoricus*, 38
Febvre, Lucien, *L'Apparition du livre*, 201
federal funding, 178–79, 186–87, 196, 252n10
Federalist, 223

Federation of the Graduate Clubs, 279n25
Fiedler, Leslie, "On Remembering Freshman Comp," 184–85
Fiering, Norman, 37, 38
Fish, Stanley, 7, 123, 161, 201; *Is There a Text in this Class?*, 201
Fitch, John, 113, 259n18
Flower, Linda, 211
Foerster, Norman, 10, 270n9
Fordyce, David, 59, 63, 254n1; *Elements of Moral Philosophy*, 255n12
forensic debates, 16, 18, 25–26, 46–51
formalism, 129, 132, 149, 164, 177, 193, 229
Foucault, Michel, 229
Foxfire (magazine), 246
Franklin, Benjamin, 18–19, 41–42, 56–57, 61–63, 78–80, 83–85, 221, 251n7, 256n17; *Autobiography*, 79; *Idea of an English School*, 61
Franklin, James, 256n17
Freedom's Journal, 94
Freire, Paulo, 158, 227
Fries, Charles, 150, 263n11
Fuller, Margaret, *Woman in the Nineteenth Century*, 102
Fulton, Maurice Garland, *Expository Writing*, 144
funding. *See* federal funding

Gallagher, Chris W., 247
gateway courses, 130, 140, 234
Gateway English, 187
Gee, James Paul, 251n1
Geertz, Clifford, 229
general education, 126–27, 164, 169, 177–84, 199, 207, 269n5
General Education in a Free Society, 178
General Magazine and Historical Chronicle, for all the British Plantations in America, 78
The Gentleman Instructed, 50
Genung, John, 141, 145; *The Study of Rhetoric in College*, 145
Gerard, Alexander, 256n16
Gerber, John, 203
Gere, Anne Ruggles, 13, 122, 224
Godey's Lady's Book (magazine), 94, 155
Godzich, Wlad, 209
Goggin, Maureen, 183–84
Goldblatt, Eli, 245
Gonzalez, Roseann, 235
Goodheart, Eugene, *Does Literary Studies Have a Future*, 279n20
Goodrich, Chauncey, 92; *Select British Eloquence*, 113

government: and control of colleges, 54; higher education expenditures of, 178–79, 186–87, 196, 252n10

graduate programs, 9, 144, 153, 177, 204, 205, 208–9, 239, 241–42, 273n26

graduate students, 17, 143, 238, 239, 277n14, 279n25. *See also* teaching assistants

Graff, Gerald, 12, 87, 104, 110, 121, 122, 126, 132, 138, 139, 142, 167, 177, 178, 228, 248, 252n8; *Clueless in Academe*, 8; *Professing Literature*, 2, 7, 163, 164, 198

Graff, Harvey, 47

grammar (subject), 149

grammar schools, 30, 49

grammars (books), 94, 100

Grammatical Institute of the English Language, 92

Gramsci, Antonio, 76, 173–74, 216, 226

Great Awakening, 25, 32, 40–47

Greeley, Horace, 94, 96, 102

Guillory, John, 209, 211, 239

Habermas, Jurgen, 77

Hairston, Maxine, 208

Hall, G. Stanley, 134

Hall, Stuart, 14, 216, 272n18

Halloran, S. Michael, 260n22

Hamilton, Alexander, 59, 73

Harper's Monthly Magazine, 95, 132

Harris, Joseph, 21; "After Dartmouth," 190

Hart, James Morgan: *German Universities*, 261n1; "The College Course in English Literature, How It May Be Improved," 134–35

Hartman, Geoffrey, "Structuralism," 189

Hartman, Gertrude, *Creative Expression*, 147

Harvard College, 16, 17, 25–26, 33–35, 37–38, 44, 47–52, 70, 90, 102, 105–7, 109–10, 115, 131, 141–43, 156, 264n23

Harvard Report (1897), 125, 138

Hatfield, Walter W., 268n41; *An Experience Curriculum in English*, 166

Hayakawa, S. I., 185

Henry, George H., "Is English on the Way Out?," 168

Herman, Peter C., *Day Late, Dollar Short*, 279n20

high schools: academies developing into, 98, 121; curriculum in, 96, 131–34, 166, 168, 169, 191; enrollments in, 261n2; as pinnacle of school systems, 99. *See also* academies; secondary schools

Higher Education for American Democracy (Presidential Commission), 178

Hirsch, E. D., *Cultural Literacy*, 201

Hofstadter, Richard, 31–32, 103–4, 258n11

Hoggart, Richard, 272n18; *Uses of Literacy*, 215

Hollingsworth, Alan, "Beyond Survival," 202

Home, Henry, *Elements of Criticism*, 48

Hopkins, Edwin, *Report of the Committee on the Labor and Cost of the Teaching of English*, 136

Horner, Bruce, 278n17

Hosic, James, *English Problems*, 135

Howell, Wilbur Samuel, 18, 63, 69, 256n16

Huber, Bettina, 205–6, 232–33

humanism and the humanities: civic, 18, 48, 73–74; Gramscian concept of, 173–74; and literary studies, 7, 126; and the public, 10, 153, 178; research in, 127; social sciences and, 160–61, 169–72; status of, 196; vocationalism spurned by, 174–75

Hume, David, 18, 75

Hunt, Theodore, 116; "The Place of English in the College Curriculum," 134

Hutcheson, Francis, 39, 58, 63, 72–74, 255n12; *A Short Introduction to Moral Philosophy*, 74

Hyman, Stanley Edgar, 169–70, 267n36

Hymes, Dell H., 182

Idler (magazine), 81

Illinois State University, 248

immigrants, 60, 61, 85, 254n3

Indiana University, 248

inductive epistemology, 17–18

inductive reasoning, 26, 38–39

inequalities: economic, 196; social, 179

information literacy, 195, 226

intellectuals: community-based, 88, 102, 123, 158–59; critical, 211; organic, 173–74; technocratic, 211; traditional, 173–74

interactive technologies, 10, 23, 193, 231, 233, 249

interdisciplinary approaches, 2, 165–71, 180

Internet: and interactive technologies, 23; use of, for literature purposes, 22

Iowa State University, 181

itinerant preachers, 41–42. *See also* evangelists

Jackson, Andrew, 91

Jackson, Brian, 232, 276n7

James, William, 147, 181; "The PhD Octopus," 152; "The Social Value of the College-Bred," 145

Jamieson, Alexander, *A Grammar of Rhetoric and Polite Literature*, 114
Jardine, George, 107
Jefferson, Thomas, 59, 73–76, 107, 255n13, 256n16
Jewett, Ida A., 154
Johnson, Samuel, 33, 35, 39–40, 42, 52, 53, 65–67, 253n4, 255n9; *Elementa Philosophica*, 65
Jordan, Mary August, 157–58
journalism studies: creative writing vs., 10–11, 147; in English studies, 142, 145, 146; exit from English departments of, 6, 129, 146–47; majors in, 232; women in, 265n24
Journeyman Mechanics Advocate, 94
junior faculty, 126, 143
junior high schools, 147
Junto Club, 79

Kames, Henry Home, Lord, 118
Kates, Susan, 13, 157–59
Kaulfers, Walter Vincent, *English for Social Living*, 169
Keckerman, Bartholomew, 37
Keeler, Harriet, 111
Kefauver, Grayson, *English for Social Living*, 169
Kent, George E., "Self-Conscious Writers and Black Tradition," 216
Kernan, Alvin, 275n1
Kerr, Clark, 252n1, 252n10, 269n3, 269n4; *The Uses of the University*, 175
Kilpatrick, William, *Project Method*, 268n41
Kimme Hea, Amy C., 251n4
King's College, 47, 52, 57–58, 60, 64–66. *See also* Columbia University
Kingsley, James, 259n14
Kinnersley, Ebenezer, 63–64, 222–23
Kittredge, George, 132
Kitzhaber, Albert Raymond, 20, 188–90, 193; *Themes, Theories, and Therapy*, 188; "What is English?," 189
Korzbski, Alfred, 185

labor colleges, 159
laboratory approach, 136, 145, 147, 157
laborers. *See* working people
Lafayette College, 116, 140
Lamy, Bernard, *The Art of Speaking*, 48
Land Grant College Act, 261n29. *See also* Morrill Act
land grant colleges and universities, 123, 133, 204
Langer, Suzanne, 181

language studies: in antebellum period, 91; as area of college English studies, 2; as autonomous, 148–50; lack of attention to, 232; and the public, 11; scientific approach in, 101. *See also* linguistics
language(s): ancient, 33–34, 49, 96, 105–6, 109, 122–23, 255n9; changes in, 4; conventions of, 11; national, 92; policies on, 235; popular vs. academic, 96; as rule-governed system, 91–92, 100. *See also* English Only movement
Lanham, Richard, 7, 217, 220
Latin, 33–34, 49, 65, 106, 253n5
Laurence, David, 206, 214, 239
Law, William, 256n16
lecturers, 143, 272n42. *See also* non-tenured faculty
Lee, Richard Henry, 73
Legrand, Antoine, *Entire Body of Philosophy*, 35
Leonard, Sterling, 263n11; "How English Teachers Correct Papers," 150
Levine, Lawrence, 11, 89
liberal arts: in antebellum period, 103–12; professionalism vs., 103, 106, 122–23
libraries: of antebellum colleges, 259n17; colonial college, 34; of student societies, 70, 259n17
life adjustment models, 181, 190
Lincoln, Abraham, 96
linguistic communications movement, 181–82
Linguistic Society of America, 148
linguistics, 2, 139, 148–50, 181–82, 277n12. *See also* language studies; structural linguistics
linguistics majors, 232
literacy: of African Americans, 96; changes in, 4, 15, 21–22, 226–27; in colonial New England, 30–31; crisis involving, 220, 228–37; critical junctures in history of, 221–28; definitions of, 195; diversification and stratification of, 89; ethnographic study of, 15; expansion of, 96; and literacies, 195, 201, 226–27, 244; in the 1970s, 193–203; orality in relation to, 42; professional isolation of, 143–51; Puritans and, 30; religion and, 30–31; schooling and, 99, 118–19; as social construction, 15; technology and, 6; traditional means of acquiring, 97; of women, 99. *See also* books; reading habits
literacy campaigns, 96, 201, 225, 230, 244

literacy studies: brief history of, 15–23; and class, 158; college English studies as, 2–3, 5–6; concept of, 2–3; critical junctures in history of, 221–28; pragmatic approaches to, 244–50; professionalization of, 124–72; uses and value of, 5–6, 23, 247–50
literary criticism, 19, 161–67
literary societies, 50, 70–71, 79–80, 98, 102, 110, 259n17
literary studies: in antebellum period, 91, 112–20; as area of college English studies, 2; autonomy of, 139–40, 161–67, 219; crisis in, 193–203, 228–37; English education vs., 15; middle-class professionalism and, 158; in the 1970s, 193–203; reduction of English studies to, 23; social context for, 218–19; technology and, 218; textbooks for, 260n24. See also literature
literate, the: and literature, 15–16; the public in relation to, 40–42, 78–80, 90–96, 145
literature: autonomy of, 139; belles lettres and, 114, 118–19, 251n5, 256n19; broad conception of, 87, 89; changes in, 15; in colonial New England, 25; didactic purpose of, 95; eloquence and, 87; on entrance exams, 131–32; in high school curriculum, 132; the literate and, 15–16; masterpieces of, 132, 195; and morality, 139, 140; national, 119; popular reading of, 21–23; popular vs. polite, 89; as social construction, 15; studied first in student societies, 70; writing vs., 137, 231. See also literary studies
Livingston, William, 53
Lloyd-Jones, Richard, Research in Written Composition, 188
Locke, John, 18, 40, 73, 74; Essay Concerning Human Understanding, 34–35
Lockridge, Kenneth, 27, 29–30, 60, 222; Literacy in Colonial New England, 252n2
Log College Colleges, 43
logic, 25, 32, 33, 35–38, 49, 63. See also deductive reasoning; syllogistic reasoning
London Gazette (newspaper), 256n17
London Magazine, 78, 80
Longaker, Mark, 57, 84; Rhetoric and the Republic, 62
Longfellow, Henry Wadsworth, 142; Kavanagh, 119
Longinus, On the Sublime, 64, 68
Louisiana State University, 214
Lounsbury, Thomas R., 144, 158; History of the English Language, 148

Lowell, James Russell, 119, 142
lyceums, 89, 97–98

Madison, James, 18, 59, 66, 73, 75, 223, 256n14, 256n15
magazine fiction, 95
magazines, 78, 94, 115
Mailloux, Steven, 276n6
majors. See English majors
Manly, John Matthews, The Writing of English, 170
Mann, Horace, 61, 96, 97, 98, 99, 103
March, Francis, 140; Method of Philological Study of the English Language, 116–18
Marckwardt, Albert Henry, 191, 271n14
Marischal College, Aberdeen, 63, 254n1, 256n16
market forces, 21, 54–55, 103–9, 152, 179, 193–94, 204–5, 218, 220, 234
Martin, Henri-Jean, L'Apparition du livre, 201
Mason, Priscilla, 19
Massachusetts, education in, 26, 30, 49, 96
Massachusetts School Law (1647), 26
masterpieces of literature, 132, 195
Mather, Cotton, 36, 37
Matthews, Brander, 132, 148; "Americanisms," 144
Matthews, P. H., Grammatical Theory in the United States, 148
Matthews, Victoria Earle, "The Value of Race Literature," 158
Mayers, Tim, 234, 279n20; (Re)Writing Craft, 10
Mayo, Elizabeth, Lessons on Common Things, 101–2
McClure's Magazine, 145
McCrimmon, James, 183
McGrath, Earl James, 180–81
McGuffey, William Holmes, 257n6
McGuffey Eclectic Readers, 94, 100, 252n9
McKeon, Richard, 227, 271n11; "The Uses of Rhetoric in a Technological Age," 210–11
McLachlan, James, 110
Mead, George Herbert, 181
media/mass media: in curriculum, 212; impact of, 166, 215, 218, 228; opposition to, 189, 203, 226; origins of, 19
medieval philology, 140
meritocratic values, 179
Merriam brothers, 92
metareading, 227
metatextuality, 227

middle class: professionalism of, 159; professionalization of, 13, 105; right to education of, 190; scientific approach and, 101; taste of, 119

middle colonies, 56–86; colleges in, 56–59; curricula in, 60–67; demographics of, 60, 254n3; diversity of, 85; moral philosophy instruction in, 72–76; oratorical literature and the new learning, 67–72; professionalism of, 105, 158; reading public in, 76–83

Miheusuah, Devon A., *Cultivating the Rosebuds*, 155–56

Mill, J. S., 138

Miller, Howard, 41

Miller, J. Hillis, 189, 207–8, 215–16; "The Function of Rhetorical Study at the Present Time," 207; "My Fifty Years in the Profession," 215

Miller, Perry, 253n3

Miller, Richard, 9, 240; "Fault Lines in the Contact Zone," 8

Miller, Susan, 115, 128, 150, 247; *Rescuing the Subject*, 9; *Textual Carnivals*, 9

Miller, Thomas P.: *The Formation of College English*, 18, 76, 95, 173, 249, 275n3; "Managing to Make a Difference," 240

minorities: in college English studies, 13; and dual cultural identities, 223; enrollments of, 185–86; and magazines, 94; as teachers, 155. *See also* African Americans

Mirel, Jeffrey E., 134, 165

Modern Language Association (MLA), 19–20, 22, 134–37, 143, 160, 166, 168, 186, 197, 203, 225–26, 263n16, 271n14, 274n32, 280n29; Central Division, 152; Commission on Trends in Education, 168–69, 171; Committee on Professional Employment, 238–39; Pedagogy Committee, 152

Moffett, James, 190, 191

moral philosophy: in College of Philadelphia, 63; in colonial curriculum, 58–59; in colonial New England, 38–40; and religion, 39–40; and republican ideology, 72–76; in Revolutionary curriculum, 18

morality, literature and, 139, 140

Morrill, Justin, 261n29

Morrill Act, 123, 261n29. *See also* Second Morrill Act

Morris, Charles, 181; *Signs, Language, and Behavior*, 180

Morton, Charles, 38–39

Mount Holyoke Seminary, 98, 146, 155, 257n4

Muller, Herbert, 190

multiculturalism, 195

Murray, Donald, 191

Murray, Lindley, *Grammar*, 100

mutual education groups, 98. *See also* extracurriculum; literary societies

Myers, D. G., 10, 146–48, 234

A Nation at Risk, 194, 230

National Adult Literacy Survey, 195

National Assessment of Adult Literacy, 226, 244

National Commission on Writing, 230, 276n9

National Council of Teachers of English (NCTE), 19–20, 135–37, 143, 149, 152–53, 160, 166, 168, 182, 186, 225–26, 271n13, 271n14, 279n25; Committee on Grammar Terminology, 149; Committee on the Preparation of College Teachers of English, 152; *The National Interest and the Teaching of English*, 186–87; Public Speaking Section, 147

National Defense Education Act, 187

National Developmental Project on Rhetoric, 210

National Education Association, 131, 135, 166

National Endowment for the Arts (NEA), 22

National Endowment for the Humanities (NEH), 210

National Writing Project, 187, 234–35

NCTE. *See* National Council of Teachers of English

NEA. *See* National Endowment for the Arts

The Neglected "R" (National Commission on Writing), 230

Nelson, Cary, 239–40, 243, 278n19; *Will Teach for Food*, 239

neoclassical style, 52, 58, 64, 65, 96

New Criticism, 130, 139, 161–67, 170, 171, 177–80, 219, 225, 228, 229, 268n45

New England Courant (newspaper), 256n17

New England Primer, 30

New England's First Fruits, 25, 33, 37

A New History of English and American Literature with Henry T. Tuckerman's Sketch of American Literature, 119–20

New Humanists, 144

new learning, 18, 26, 37–39, 67–68

New Light evangelicals, 42–43, 47, 57, 85

New Literacy Studies, 15, 201, 219
New York Sun (newspaper), 94
New York Tribune (newspaper), 94, 102
New-England Weekly Journal (newspaper), 256n17
Newman, Samuel, 114; *A Practical System of Rhetoric*, 260n21
newspapers, 77–78, 94. *See also* penny papers; periodical press
Newsweek (magazine), 194
Newton, Isaac, 18, 38, 40
non-tenured faculty, 204, 207, 238, 277n14
normal schools, 99, 103, 121, 123, 127–28, 153–54
North, Stephen, 188
North American Review (magazine), 94, 115
North Central Association, 133
North Central Association of Colleges and Secondary Schools, 137
Northeast Oklahoma State University, 155
Northeastern State Normal School, 155
novels, 93. *See also* dime-store novels

Oberlin Collegiate Institute, 110–11
Ogden, C. K., *The Meaning of Meaning*, 180
Ohio Farmer (magazine), 94
Ohio State Universities, 204
Ohmann, Richard, 179, 246, 258n10
Old Light clerics, 42–43
orality: Great Awakening and, 40–47; and the interpretation of literature, 16; literacy in relation to, 42. *See also* scribal literacy
oratory: popular vs. academic language in, 96; reading as performance, 100. *See also* rhetoric
organic intellectuals, 173–74. *See also* community-based intellectuals

Paine, Thomas, 115; *Common Sense*, 75, 83
paraprofessionals, 5, 126, 142, 194, 226, 245
Parker, William Riley, 64
Parks, Steven, 245
part-time faculty, 122, 220, 238, 239, 243
Pattee, Fred Lewis, 162
pauper scholars, 105
Payne, William Morton, 138–40; *American Literary Criticism*, 19, 138; *English in American Universities*, 19, 116, 138, 161
Peabody, Elizabeth Palmer, *Record of a School*, 102
pedagogy: for African Americans, 102; alternatives in, 158–61; colleges and, 8, 133–37, 140–41, 187–89; enrollment

growth as influence on, 125; in rhetoric and composition, 101–2; for underprepared students, 106; for working people, 102
Peirce, Charles Sanders, 181
Pell Grant, 196
Pennsylvania Chronicle (newspaper), 83
Pennsylvania Gazette (newspaper), 78
penny papers, 89, 90, 91, 115
periodical press: and college English studies, 27; diversification of viewpoints in, 27, 45; essays in, 17; expansion of, 77, 83; formation of reading public through, 77–86; literacy spread by, 11; literary criticism in, 19; politics and, 83; religion and, 40, 45; rhetoric influenced by, 16. *See also* magazines; newspapers; penny papers; print and print culture
personal growth, 190
PhD degrees, 152, 197, 241
PhDs–Ten Years Later, 241
Phelps, Louise Wetherbee, 278n17
Phelps, William Lyon, 143–44, 152
Phi Beta Kappa Society, 70, 115
Philadelphia Central School, 102
philology, 33, 65, 126, 140, 148
PMLA (journal), 20, 116, 134–35, 154
Pocock, J. G. A., 75
political economy: of higher education, 27, 103–12, 122, 177–78; moral philosophy and, 39, 84; of professionalization, 240–41
politics: language policies, 235; and popular idioms, 95–96; the press and, 83; representation in, 82; rhetoric and, 24–25, 48, 69–70. *See also* democracy; republicanism
popular culture: polite vs., 89; political oratory and, 95–96; reading habits and, 93
Postman, Neil, 193
postwar period, 177–84
Pratt, Mary Louise, 4, 13, 215, 220, 236, 251n2
preaching, teaching in relation to, 154–55
Preamble to the United States Constitution, 71–72
Preceptor (self-instruction manual), 63, 254n4, 255n12
Preparing a Nation's Teachers, 248
Presbyterians, 43, 44, 66, 110
Price, Richard, 72
Priestley, Joseph, 72
Princeton University, 163, 256n15. *See also* College of New Jersey, Princeton

print and print culture: and education, 99–100; industry devoted to, 94–95; influence of, on regularization of usage, 69, 255n11; proliferation of, 95

private colleges/universities: character of, 54; public vs., 54–55, 204–5. *See also* elite colleges

professions and professionalism: in antebellum period, 103–12; civic, 88; college English studies and, 3, 5, 23, 129; college enrollment and, 105; conservatism of, 127; cosmopolitan character of, 226; downloading of work/responsibilities in, 126–27, 137, 194, 197, 226; golden age of, 184–93; hierarchies in, 126–27, 130, 151, 176, 203, 208–9, 225, 238, 248; liberal arts vs., 103, 106, 122–23; literacy studies and, 124–72; marginalized intellectuals and, 159; market criteria applied to, 21; middle class and, 105, 158, 159; organizing in, 136; political economy of, 240–41; Progressivism vs., 160; reproductive systems of, 126–27; resistance of academics to, 12–13; social context of, 184; teaching and, 88, 97–98, 103; in United States, 224; women instructors, 262n5. *See also* deprofessionalization; expertise

professorships of English, 18, 52, 57, 60–67, 83, 87, 251n7

Progressive Educational Association, 147, 166, 171, 225

Progressivism: alternative possibilities of, 129–30, 155, 158–61, 165–66; and coalition building, 159–60; and collaboration, 159–60, 166–67, 235; criticisms of, 194, 225, 262n8, 272n23; and curriculum, 190; and high school education, 133–34; Mann and, 97; NCTE and, 136; and pedagogy, 157; professionalism vs., 160; science and expressiveness fused in, 180–81; and the social sciences, 169–72; and writing, 10–11, 147, 182

Project English, 187–90, 192, 196, 217

Prokosch, Eduard, "Treason within the Castle," 168

public, the: college English studies and, 8, 13–14; defining, 45–46; humanities and, 10, 153, 178; language studies and, 11; the literate in relation to, 40–42, 78–80, 90–96, 145; and the periodical press, 76–86; reading habits of, 76–83, 93, 230–31; writing for, 129. *See also* reading public

public colleges/universities: influences on administration of, 50; private vs., 54–55, 204–5. *See also* state universities

public education, mandatory, 26. *See also* education

Publick Occurrences Both Forreign and Domestick, 77

Puritans, 28–30

Quackenbos, G. P., *Advanced Course of Composition and Rhetoric*, 260n21

quantitative literacy, 195

Quincy, John, 109, 122

Quintilian, Marcus Fabius, 63; *Institutes*, 48, 68

Radcliffe College, 156

Ramus, Peter, 24, 37, 48

Ransom, John Crowe, "Criticism, Inc.," 161–63

reader-response theory, 191, 200–201, 236, 267n40

readers (books), 90, 100, 261n27

reading: instruction and guidance of the public in, 91, 95, 162; as performance, 100; purposes of, 89, 93; revolution in, 91. *See also* reading habits

Reading at Risk (National Education Association), 22, 230–31, 276n10, 279n27

reading habits: in colonial New England, 26, 31; contemporary, 21–23; of the public, 76–83, 93, 230–31. *See also* books; reading

Reading on the Rise (NEA), 22

reading public: and consumption of literature, 119; formation of, 77–86; growth of, 93–94

recitations, 72, 100

Reed, Henry, *Lectures on English Literature*, 117–18

Reid, Thomas, 75

religion: church membership, 28; colonial colleges and, 58; colonial curriculum and, 25–27; in colonial New England, 27–32, 40–46; declining authority of, in colonial New England, 26–27, 32, 41–42, 46; literacy and, 30–31; moral philosophy and, 39–40; privacy of, in colleges, 44, 57; publication of works on, 254n2. *See also* scribal literacy

Rensselaer Polytechnic Institute, 106

Report of the Committee on Composition and Rhetoric (Harvard, 1897), 125. *See also* Harvard Report (1897)

of, 245–47; value of, 88; writing and, 9,
    128, 138, 142, 147, 182, 199. *See also*
    utilitarian concerns; vocationalism
Shaughnessy, Mina, 247
Shaw, Thomas B., 261n25; *Outlines of Eng-
    lish Literature*, 117, 119
Shoer, Lowell, *Research in Written Composi-
    tion*, 188
Shor, Ira, 177
Shugrue, Michael, "The English Profession
    in the 1970s," 203
Simmons, Sue Carter, "Radcliffe Responses
    to Harvard Rhetoric," 156
Siskin, Clifford, 252n11
slavery, 74, 96
Smith, Adam, 39, 73, 78, 119, 223, 251n7;
    *An Inquiry into the Nature and Causes of
    the Wealth of Nations*, 73
Smith, William, 56–57, 61–64, 67–68, 81,
    84–86, 223, 254n1, 256n16, 256n18; *A
    Brief View of the Conduct of Pennsylva-
    nia*, 85
Snow, C. P., 211
social diversification, 17, 25–27, 29–30, 40,
    46, 61
social mobility, 105, 179
social sciences: constitution of, 268n43;
    humanities and, 160–61, 169–72
Society for Promoting English, 85
Society for the Propagation of the Gospel
    in Foreign Parts, 85
sociolinguistics, 11
Socratic method, 68
specialization: professional standing depen-
    dent on, 5, 10; service duties contrasted
    with areas of, 5
Spectator (magazine), 50, 63, 70, 77–81,
    223, 256n17
Spectator Club, 50, 80
speech, exit from English departments of,
    6, 146–47
Speech Association, 182
Spellmeyer, Kurt, 246
Sputnik, 176, 187
Squire, James R., 191, 270n8
Stamp Act, 77, 82
Stanford University, 139, 141, 264n18
state universities, 107, 123, 138–39, 154,
    259n16
Steinberg, Erwin, 187, 211, 212; "Applied
    Humanities," 212; *English Education
    Today*, 192
Steinmann, Martin, *The New Rhetoric*, 192
Stevens, Edward, 99–100
Stevenson, John, 80
Stiles, Ezra, 49, 58

Street, Brian, 251n1
structural linguistics, 180, 189, 192
structuralism, 189, 192
students: access of, 195–96, 272n24,
    275n39 (*see also* colleges and universi-
    ties: accessible); in antebellum period,
    89, 97–99, 102, 105–6; attitudes of, 197;
    curricular changes originating with, 70;
    literary societies of, 50, 70–71, 110,
    259n17; normal school, 127–28; under-
    prepared, 139, 179–80, 239; women as,
    266n33; writing of, 113
Sturtevant, Julian, 259n14
syllogistic reasoning, 17, 26, 33, 37, 47. *See
    also* deductive reasoning; logic

Tappan, Henry, 259n16
taste, 17, 50, 59, 69–70, 78–81, 84–85, 95,
    114, 119
Tate, Allen, 162–63; "The Present Func-
    tion of Criticism," 162
Tatler (magazine), 81
teacher education, 10, 97, 103, 247–48
Teacher Education Project, 280n29
teacher institutes, 87, 98
teacher manuals, 133
teacher preparation, 5, 103, 133, 152–55,
    187, 199, 207, 248, 270n10
teachers: adjunct, 207, 239, 243, 245; Afri-
    can Americans as, 88; for common
    schools, 87–88; composition, 136; gradu-
    ate students as, 143, 238, 239, 277n14,
    279n25; lecturers, 143, 272n42; minori-
    ties as, 155; non-tenured, 204, 207, 238,
    277n14; organizing of, 239–43, 279n25;
    paraprofessionals, 5, 126, 142, 194, 226,
    245; part-time, 122, 220, 238, 239, 243;
    research faculty, 20, 126, 243; salaries of,
    264n21; status of, 97, 127–28, 142, 226,
    237, 241 (*see also* teaching: denigration
    of); teaching assistants, 5, 126, 150, 239,
    274n36, 279n25; temporary, 143, 174,
    220; tenure-track and tenured, 207, 220,
    233, 240, 278n14; unionization of, 204;
    women as, 10, 88, 99, 121–22, 155, 157;
    working conditions of, 135–36, 141, 150,
    193; working people as, 88, 155. *See also*
    teacher preparation
Teachers College, Columbia University,
    147, 181, 182, 187
teachers colleges, 154
Teachers for a Democratic Culture, 245
teaching: as classless profession, 90, 97;
    denigration of, 143–44, 151, 153, 175, 200,
    211, 226, 241 (*see also* teachers: status
    of); preaching in relation to, 154–55;

Ward, John: *Lectures on Oratory*, 51, 113, 253n9; *System of Oratory*, 48
Warren, Robert Penn, *Understanding Poetry*, 165, 171, 179, 268n45
Watkins, Evan, *Work Time*, 8, 246, 275n2
Watts, Isaac, 48, 67, 72
Wayland, Francis, 104, 108–10, 122; *Thoughts on the Present Collegiate System*, 108
Weaver, Richard, 183
Webster, Noah, 11, 92–93, 256n18, 257n2
Weeks, Ruth Mary, *A Correlated Curriculum*, 166
Wellek, Rene, 163
Wellesley College, 138
Wells, Ida, 266n34
Wendell, Barrett, 140, 147, 156
Whately, Richard, 114
Wheatley, Phillis, 253n6
Whitefield, George, 40–41, 44, 58, 253n6
Wigglesworth, Edward, 44
Wigglesworth, Michael, 24
Wilcox, Thomas, 273n29; *Anatomy of College English*, 198–99; National Survey of Undergraduate Programs in English, 273n28
Willard, Emma, 98
William and Mary College, 47, 70, 256n16
Williams, Fannie Barrier, "The Intellectual Progress of Colored Women," 155
Williams, Jeffrey, *The Institution of Literature*, 279n20
Williams, Raymond, 272n18; *The Long Revolution*, 215
Wills, Garry, 73, 74, 75, 255n13; *Explaining America*, 59; *Inventing America*, 59
Wilson, Elizabeth, 169, 172
Wilson, James, 64, 255n6
Winfrey, Oprah, 277n10
Wingspread Conference on Major Issues, 274n32
Winthrop, John, 28, 50
Witherspoon, John, 18, 49, 52, 57, 58, 66–67, 69–70, 74–75, 84, 119, 223, 255n11,

256n14, 256n15, 275n4; *Address to the Inhabitants of Jamaica*, 66
women: in college English studies, 13; education of, 18–19, 97–99, 257n4; as English majors, 200; in journalism, 265n24; literacy of, 99; at Oberlin, 111; in professions, 262n5; and republican motherhood, 19, 90, 97, 102; and rhetoric, 111; as students, 266n33; as teachers, 10, 88, 99, 121–22, 143, 155, 157
women's academies, 98, 257n4
women's colleges, 146, 155–56, 158
working people: education of, 99, 123, 159; and magazines, 94; pedagogies aimed at, 102; as teachers, 88, 155
Workplace (journal), 279n26
Wozniak, John M., 118–19
writing: current status of, 232; denigration of, 175, 246; educational use of, 125, 128, 130–31; expressionist approach to, 191; interdisciplinary approaches to, 180; literature vs., 137, 231; majors or minors in, 146, 277n13; role of, in college English studies, 9–11; teaching of, 101–2, 143–48, 180, 193. *See also* composition; creative writing; rhetoric and composition
Wyoming Resolution (1986), 278n18

Yale College, 34–35, 44, 47–48, 51–52, 54, 58, 90, 96, 103, 106, 109, 143–44, 254n11
Yale Corporation, 106
Yale Report (1828), 106, 108–9, 122, 174, 225
Yale Review (magazine), 94
Yale University, 243
Young, Art, 205
Young, Richard, 211
Young Ladies Academy, 18, 58
The Young Man's Magazine, 78
The Young Misses Magazine, 78
Young Students Library, 35

Zboray, Ronald J., 11, 94, 98